THE *Quotable* LEWIS

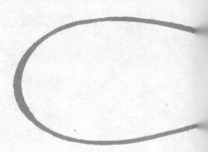

WAYNE MARTINDALE

THE

Quotable

LEWIS

and JERRY ROOT, *Editors*

Tyndale House Publishers, Inc.
WHEATON, ILLINOIS

This book is dedicated
with love and affection
to our wives:

Nita Martindale
Claudia Root

CONTENTS

PREFACE

For students, speakers, writers, and anyone who desires to contemplate great thought on a particular topic, this anthology can be put to use in several ways. You can use it for:

1. *Reference.* Who has not at times wished to reclaim the whole of a quote only partially remembered, forgetting even the book in which it appeared? Here's help.

2. *Access.* Several excerpts on a given topic are often gathered into one place, and the index points to related ideas.

3. *Illustration.* These excerpts help bring speeches, sermons, lectures, and papers to life. An author as quotable as Lewis is a godsend to communicators of every kind.

4. *Understanding.* There is enough substance in these excerpts to deepen thinking on a wide range of topics.

5. *Perspective.* A sense of the vast panorama of Lewis's remarkable mind emerges from even a brief survey of these selections.

6. *Browsing.* This Lewis anthology can fill reflective moments with pleasure and instruction—nourishment for the mind, spirit, and imagination.

Several other anthologies of Lewis are in print, and their purposes vary from devotional readings to collections of quotes on specified topics. This anthology is unique for two reasons. First, *comprehen-*

siveness. It draws on all of Lewis's published work (except uncollected letters and book reviews), something never before attempted. We have tried to represent the full range of Lewis's thought—not just the popular or catchy phrase but the representative treatment, whenever excerptible, across the entire, varied range of his work. We have read every published book, including collections of sermons, short stories, juvenilia, articles, addresses, poems, and letters—some sixty books—to insure comprehensive coverage (see the bibliographies).

Second, *organization and indexing.* The table of contents lists the topics that are included, arranged alphabetically. Many excerpts are so rich and suggestive that they could logically be categorized under a half-dozen topics. For space considerations, however, an excerpt is printed only once. Consult the index for additional quotations on a related topic and for any passage on the fringes of memory that you are trying to track down. Of necessity we made many judgment calls, not only for topic selection but for what to quote and how much. If one of your favorite Lewis quotes is nowhere to be found, we apologize in advance.

Whenever a topic includes multiple excerpts, we arranged the excerpts in chronological order. This may allow you to discover some development in Lewis's thought—how an idea in bud early on opens into full flower in his later work. For example, before Lewis became a Christian he appears to have been somewhat anti-Semitic. After his conversion he developed sympathies for the Jews and was appreciative of their literature. Ultimately he married Joy Davidman Gresham, who was of Jewish heritage. (We have not attempted to hide anything; some excerpts reveal Lewis's idiosyncrasies and ideas at odds with our own belief and practice.)

You can also discover from multiple excerpts within a topic how Lewis works out a thought from genre to genre. He expressed most of his central ideas in nonfiction, fiction, letters, and sometimes poems. We were impressed anew with how mature and settled Lewis's ideas were at an early date. The soaring imagination that created Narnia and Perelandra is anchored in a unifying concept of who God is, who we are as his fallen creatures, the destiny of humankind, the need for redemption and perfection in Christ. Entry after entry reveals and amplifies this core through a range of applications. Regardless of the genre, his conservative and biblical center always holds.

A FEW TECHNICAL DETAILS

Here are the main criteria we used for selecting excerpts. A quotation should:

1. Contain an important idea that can be stated fully in a brief compass (keeping in view the first-time reader of a given Lewis work)

2. Be notable for its clarity, compression, profundity, wit, or vividness (not all are memorable, but most are in their own way remarkable)

3. Be helpful in establishing the reach of Lewis's thought

4. Have interest because, given who he was, Lewis said it (especially true of excerpts about himself and his work)

The source of every quote is referenced. Lewis's books have been published in many editions, and for any given book there is no standard or definitive edition. We have referenced the edition most commonly available. If our page numbers don't match your copy, check the bibliography to determine which edition we used. Whenever practical, excerpts are cited with their chapter and paragraph numbers. This will help you locate a quotation in editions with different pagination. In Lewis's fiction, where dialogue is in abundance, to cite the paragraph is not practical.

Establishing a date for the chronological arrangement was a bit complicated, but here was our method: *Letters* carry the date on which they were written. *Books* and *essays* carry the date of first publication (exceptions are noted). *Addresses* carry the date of presentation, when known. *Poems* carry the date of composition or first publication, if known, but you should be aware that many of Lewis's poems were not published until after his death when Walter Hooper gathered them into a volume in 1964. Since the 1964 date could be misleading, poems whose date of composition is uncertain are flagged with the phrase "1st pub. 1964." Essays, addresses, and poems are referenced from the collected edition.

Two of the books excerpted need special comment. *Spenser's Images of Life* was written by Alastair Fowler (or "edited," as the title page has it) from Lewis's lecture notes on Spenser. Since, as Fowler says in the preface, "most of the ideas and some of the words in this book are from C. S. Lewis's Cambridge lectures," we thought it should be represented. *Letters: C. S. Lewis/Don Giovanni Calabria,* is quoted here in the English translation by Martin Moynihan. The original letters are in Latin, since that is the only language that Lewis and his Italian correspondent had in common.

The abbreviations in Lewis's letters have been retained: cd. (could), shd. (should), wd. (would), wh. (which), yr. (your), and occasionally MS (manuscript), sc. (such), and Xtianity (Christianity). Lewis's British spelling (including the omission of the period after titles such as Dr and Mr) has also been retained. In the case of published letters, the misspellings and occasional inadvertent ungrammatical word forms are kept intact. Elsewhere we have silently corrected obvious typographical errors. We have used the American convention of placing commas and periods inside quotation marks. Excerpts that begin in the middle of a sentence begin with a capital and no ellipsis, and except in the rare cases in which an excerpt concludes with a sentence fragment, excerpts do not end with an ellipsis.

WELCOME TO THE FEAST!

Having specified the uniqueness and usefulness of this book, we hasten to add that we are keenly aware of the limitations inherent in any anthology. What is lost? From Lewis's prose we lose his profoundly clear and logical chain of reasoning: his ability to probe behind assumptions, to argue from evidence to a reasoned conclusion. We lose the elegance of ideas consorting together in a great dance of harmonious thought. We lose the considerable force of words that begin to resonate in harmony with other words in a developing passage as Lewis so carefully crafts the whole, whose first sentence has the last in view.

And if our loss from the prose is great, it is greater from the fiction. It would be impossible in a few sentences or a paragraph to capture the passage from *The Great Divorce* where the angel kills the red lizard of lust that rides on the shoulder of one of the "ghosts" from hell. Attempting to capture the flow of Eustace's "undragoning" in *The Voyage of the Dawn Treader* presents similar difficulties. The memorable conclusion of "The Shoddy Lands" loses its punch when removed from its context. And who, having read *The Lion, the Witch and the Wardrobe,* is not profoundly moved by the phrase, "Aslan is on the move," or Susan's baffled and wishful cry after Aslan's death and the great noise that followed: "Is it more magic?" Aslan's response, full of irony and poignancy, "Yes! . . . It is more magic." Yet how cold such phrases would be to those who have never read this most delightful and moving of books. Fiction depends so much on context, on the accretion of acts and words that constitute our feeling for the characters, their conflicts, and their defeats and conquests. While the fiction is indeed represented in this volume, devotees of Lewis's imaginative work will be disappointed as we are at how little from the volumes of his shimmering fictional worlds is included here. As often happens even with the prose, some lines that seemed so profound when read in context fall flat when reread days later as mere excerpts. Those we omitted.

Anthologies, then, are certainly not substitutes for an author's original works in their entirety; they leave so much out. Although many memorable and enlightening quotes may have been selected, they could never capture the sublime dignity of the whole. Lewis himself had a word to say on this business of excerpting a text when once engaged in such a task: "The only use of selections is to deter those readers who will never appreciate the original, and thus to save them from wasting their time on it, and to send all the others on to the original as quickly as possible."[1] Reference to an anthology is not a substitute but an introduction, the appetizer that leads to the real feast.

This work has been a labor of love: a task worth doing in its own right. The journey through the Lewis canon has been for us a theological and liberal education of the first order. We hope for more readers of the complete works as a result of these excerpts. Our best wish for this book is that readers might exalt, not Lewis, but the God whose truth he explores and whose plans for the present creation and for human destiny satisfied Lewis's rational mind, fed his capacious imagination, and filled his deepest longings.

ACKNOWLEDGMENTS

We express our gratitude to Mrs. Jessie Root, who put on computer disk a great quantity of the manuscript and assisted in the proofing. We

---

1. "Edmund Spenser, 1552–99," in *Studies in Medieval and Renaissance Literature* (Cambridge: Cambridge University Press, 1966), 141.

also acknowledge our gratitude to Dr. Wendell Hawley of Tyndale House Publishers for his encouragement of the project and to his able staff, especially Ken Petersen, who handled the computer needs, and Dan Elliott, who from his rich resources of energy and intelligence lavished every possible service as editor. No one could ask for a better team.

For his unfailing encouragement and for his extensive knowledge of Lewis and Lewis materials so willingly shared, we also owe a great debt of gratitude to Dr. Lyle Dorsett, director of The Marion E. Wade Center at Wheaton College, Wheaton, Illinois, and to his associates, Marjorie Mead—especially for her expertise on the photographs—and Virginia Kolb. We thank Diane Turner for her patience and expertise in providing valuable secretarial help.

We gratefully acknowledge Bob and Claire Knapp for their encouragement and assistance. We also thank our families for their sacrifices while the manuscript was being prepared. And, finally, we acknowledge the forbearance of Dr. Martindale's students at Wheaton College and Rev. Root's congregation at College Church in Wheaton for tolerating an unending stream of references to Lewis in lectures and sermons!

INTRODUCTION

A book that is number one on the *New York Times* Best-seller List for several weeks may be all but forgotten a decade later. Popularity in a moment of history does not guarantee that a book will endure beyond its own time. C. S. Lewis once observed that, like fashions, the more up-to-date a book is, the sooner it is out of date. An era committed to information gathering (where newest is best) and keeping abreast of the trends is an era committed to obsolescence. We throw off what was important one moment because it is dated the next, and like a ship plowing through the sea, we leave a great wake behind us.

In light of this, more than idle curiosity leads us to question which books or authors will survive beyond their own time. We sense that our destiny and the contribution of our generation to coming generations is very much at issue. A quick survey of the Encyclopedia Britannica's great books of the Western world reveals that an average of approximately three authors per century have been included in that august collection. This being so, what authors from this century will be read in the next? Of course, we can no more than guess; only time will tell. If votes are going to be cast, however, the name C. S. Lewis ought at least to be on the ballot. The influence of his pen can hardly be overestimated. One observer noted that Lewis "is read with enormous affection and loyalty by a wide and diversified audience today. . . . In fact, more of his books are sold today than those of any other Christian writer in history."[1] Indeed, with over sixty of his books in print, Lewis has for many in this century become the dominant

1. Peter Kreeft, "Lewis and the Two Roads to God," *The Washington Times*, in *The World & I* (February 1987), 354.

exponent and champion of thoughtful Christianity.

Lewis wrote on a wide variety of subjects in many literary forms. How can this vast array of work be characterized, and what accounts for its popularity? J. A. W. Bennett, a former student of Lewis's at Oxford who later replaced him as professor of Medieval and Renaissance literature at Magdalene College, Cambridge, observed a remarkable unity within Lewis's work:

The whole man was in all his judgements and activities, and a discriminating zest for life, for "common life," informs every page he wrote. "Grete Clerke" as he was, he was never wilfully esoteric: Quotations and allusions rose unbidden to the surface of his full and fertile mind, but whether they are to Tristram Shandy or James Thurber they elucidate, not decorate. His works are all of a piece: a book in one genre will correct, illumine or amplify what is latent in another.[2]

This unity within Lewis's writings grows from two sources: first, from an honest commitment to truth, and second, from his Christian faith. C. S. Lewis's life was an echo of the great Socratic maxim that "the unexamined life is not worth living." Truth was to be pursued, and it was relevant to life. Lewis believed that life and thought were to conform to the plumb line of truth. Truth was not to be bent to fit either convenience or cultural and personal norms. Lewis wrote that "In coming to understand anything we must reject the facts as they are for us in favor of the facts as they are." Without this standard, one loses perspective, as if to believe that the railroad tracks actually narrowed the farther they were away.[3] Lewis knew that breaking out of provincialism and the subjective dungeon of a perspective centered on self is critical to objectivity. Thought and life are amendable; reality is nonnegotiable. Lewis commented that one should "never ask of anything 'Is it real?,' for everything is real. The proper question is 'A real what?' e.g., a real snake or real *delirium tremens?*"[4] Truth is discovered when thought conforms to reality. Honesty is critical, as Lewis wrote in his autobiography, *Surprised by Joy*:

2. "The Humane Medievalist: An Inaugural Address," in Douglas Gilbert and Clyde S. Kilby, *C. S. Lewis: Images of His World* (Grand Rapids, Mich.: Eerdmans, 1973), 26-27.
3. *An Experiment in Criticism* (Cambridge: Cambridge University Press, 1965), 137-138.
4. *Letters to Malcolm: Chiefly on Prayer* (New York: Harcourt Brace Jovanovich, 1964), 80.

What I like about experience is that it is such an honest thing. You may take any number of wrong turnings; but keep your eyes open and you will not be allowed to go very far before the warning signs appear. You may have deceived yourself, but experience is not trying to deceive you. The universe rings true wherever you fairly test it.[5]

This honest commitment to truth is a unifying factor in Lewis's writings.

Lewis's Christian faith is the other fundamental source of unity in his work. Unlike many who believe that the cardinal sin against objectivity is to have a point of view, Lewis was unashamed of his Christian frame of reference. From the time of his conversion, it was the integrating force behind his thought, life, and writing. He wrote, "I believe in Christianity as I believe the sun is risen not only because I see it but because by it I see everything else."[6] This was the bedrock upon which Lewis's work was built.

Christianity was not for Lewis a suitcase into which he crammed the facts of life, cutting here and snipping there until it all fit neatly into the preconceived package. On the contrary, the conclusions of Christianity were precisely what Lewis had hoped were not true. Writing in his autobiography of his reluctant conversion, he described himself as the "prodigal who is brought kicking, struggling, resentful, and darting his eyes in every direction for a chance of escape."[7] Lewis didn't find God; God found him. He continues:

The words *compelle intrare*, compel them to come in, have been so abused by wicked men that we shudder at them; but, properly understood, they plumb the depth of the Divine mercy. The hardness of God is kinder than the softness of men, and His compulsion is our liberation.[8]

With humility, Lewis recognized and submitted himself to the Reality at the core of the universe. The unifying Christian presuppositions that meet us in Lewis are reflective of what G. K. Chesterton wrote in the

5. (New York: Harcourt Brace Jovanovich, 1955), 177.
6. "Is Theology Poetry?" in *The Weight of Glory* (revised and expanded edition, New York: Macmillan, 1980), p. 92.
7. *Surprised by Joy*, 229.
8. Ibid.

first chapter of *Orthodoxy*, which he titled, "In defense of everything else":

I have attempted in a vague and personal way . . . to state the philosophy in which I have come to believe. I will not call it my philosophy; for I did not make it. God and humanity made it; and it made me.[9]

Furthermore, Lewis was not reserved about either the influence Christianity had upon him or the influence he hoped his Christianity would have on others. "Most of my books are evangelistic," Lewis stated clearly when challenged on his apologetic writing,[10] so there is no doubt about what Lewis is up to. But his thought must not be dismissed because he embraced Christianity and urges us to embrace it as well. To cry, "Dogmatic!" is not a refutation. We should rather question, "Is this the right point of view?" Lewis must be challenged on grounds of reason, not of emotion.

Lewis once complained:

Man is becoming as narrowly "practical" as the irrational animals. In lecturing to popular audiences I have repeatedly found it almost impossible to make them understand that I recommended Christianity because I thought its affirmations to be objectively *true*. They are simply not interested in the question of truth or falsehood. They only want to know if it will be comforting, or "inspiring," or socially useful.[11]

Refreshingly, in reading Lewis one never feels him to be dogmatic, narrow-minded, doctrinaire, polemical. He is not grinding an axe; he is, pre-eminently, out to do us good. He sees the spiritual need of his fellow human beings, rightly assesses the general blindness to the dangers (both temporal and eternal) that lie in wait, and writes and lectures for all he's worth to secure for others the blessings of salvation and the fullness of life in Christ. For this he uncomplainingly endured the snubs of his colleagues, who thought writing for the public to be beneath a scholar's professional dignity. What St. Paul said of himself

9. (Garden City, N.Y.: Doubleday, 1959).
10. *God in the Dock*, "Rejoinder to Dr. Pittenger," 181.
11. "Modern Man and His Categories of Thought," in *Present Concerns: Essays by C. S. Lewis* (New York: Harcourt Brace Jovanovich, 1986), 65.

could be applied to Lewis: "Though I am free from all men, I have made myself a servant to all, that I might win some" (1 Corinthians 9:19). His work not only rings of truth but peals forth charity. We sense in every book, article, and letter an author who genuinely and deeply cares for us—enough to tell us the unadulterated truth. Even if it hurts, he knows that it will ultimately heal.

The Christian religion . . . does not begin in comfort; it begins in . . . dismay. . . . In religion, as in war and everything else, comfort is the one thing you cannot get by looking for it. If you look for truth, you may find comfort in the end: If you look for comfort you will not get either comfort or truth—only soft soap and wishful thinking to begin with and, in the end, despair.[12]

As anyone who reads his books or browses in this anthology will readily see, though Lewis writes on a broad variety of subjects—from newspapers and nuclear war to heaven and hell—the unifying threads are honest commitment to truth and Christian faith on the one hand, and charity toward his reader on the other.

12. C. S. Lewis, *Mere Christianity* (New York: Macmillan, 1952), 39.

1 **Absolute Values** *The Abolition of Man,* chap. 1, para. 11, p. 29.	[The Tao is] the doctrine of objective value, the belief that certain attitudes are really true, and others really false, to the kind of thing the universe is and the kind of things we are.
2 **Absolute Values** *The Abolition of Man,* chap. 2, para. 11, p. 53.	If nothing is self-evident, nothing can be proved. Similarly, if nothing is obligatory for its own sake, nothing is obligatory at all.
3 **Absolute Values** *The Abolition of Man,* chap. 2, para. 14, pp. 56–57.	This thing which I have called for convenience the *Tao,* and which others may call Natural Law or Traditional Morality, . . . is not one among a series of possible systems of value. It is the sole source of all value judgements. If it is rejected, all value is rejected. If any value is retained, it is retained. The effort to refute it and raise a new system of value in its place is self-contradictory. There never has been, and never will be, a radically new judgement of value in the history of the world. What purport to be new systems or (as they now call them) "ideologies," all consist of fragments from the *Tao* itself,

arbitrarily wrenched from their context in the whole and then swollen to madness in their isolation, yet still owing to the *Tao* and to it alone such validity as they possess. . . . The rebellion of new ideologies against the *Tao* is a rebellion of the branches against the tree: if the rebels could succeed they would find that they had destroyed themselves. The human mind has no more power of inventing a new value than of imagining a new primary colour, or, indeed, of creating a new sun and a new sky for it to move in.

4
Absolute Values

The Abolition of Man,
chap. 3, para. 5–10,
pp. 72–80.

Human nature will be the last part of Nature to surrender to Man. The battle will then be won. . . . But who, precisely, will have won it?

For the power of Man to make himself what he pleases means, as we have seen, the power of some men to make other men what *they* please. . . . Hitherto the plans of educationalists have achieved very little of what they attempted and indeed, when we read them—how Plato would have every infant "a bastard nursed in a bureau," and Elyot would have the boy see no men before the age of seven and, after that, no women, and how Locke wants children to have leaky shoes and no turn for poetry—we may well thank the beneficent obstinacy of real mothers, real nurses, and (above all) real children for preserving the human race in such sanity as it still possesses. But the man-moulders of the new age will be armed with the powers of an omnicompetent state and an irresistible scientific technique: we shall get at last a race of conditioners who really can cut out all posterity in what shape they please. . . .

The Conditioners, then, are to choose what

kind of artificial *Tao* they will, for their own good reasons, produce in the Human race. . . .

It is not that they are bad men. They are not men at all. Stepping outside the *Tao,* they have stepped into the void. Nor are their subjects necessarily unhappy men. They are not men at all: they are artefacts. Man's final conquest has proved to be the abolition of Man.

When all that says "it is good" has been debunked, what says "I want" remains. . . . The Conditioners, therefore, must come to be motivated simply by their own pleasure. . . . My point is that those who stand outside all judgements of value cannot have any ground for preferring one of their own impulses to another except the emotional strength of that impulse. . . .

At the moment, then, of Man's victory over Nature, we find the whole human race subjected to some individual men, and those individuals subjected to that in themselves which is purely "natural"—to their irrational impulses. Nature, untrammelled by values, rules the Conditioners and, through them, all humanity. Man's conquest of Nature turns out, in the moment of its consummation, to be Nature's conquest of Man.

5
Absolute Values
The Abolition of Man, chap. 3, para. 13, pp. 84–85.

Either we are rational spirit obliged for ever to obey the absolute values of the *Tao,* or else we are mere nature to be kneaded and cut into new shapes for the pleasures of masters who must, by hypothesis, have no motive but their own "natural" impulses. Only the *Tao* provides a common human law of action which can overarch rulers and ruled alike. A dogmatic belief in objective value is necessary to the very

---

idea of a rule which is not tyranny or an obedience which is not slavery.

6
Addison, Joseph

Selected Literary Essays, "Addison" (1945), para. 3, pp. 155–156.

[The] contrast between Addison and the Tories [Pope and Swift] comes out with special clarity in their treatment of enemies. For the Tories . . . all who have, in whatever fashion, incurred their ill will are knaves, scarecrows, whores, bugs, toads, bedlamites, yahoos; Addison himself a smooth Mephistopheles. It is good fun, but it is certainly not good sense; we laugh, and disbelieve. Now mark Addison's procedure. . . . With the help of Steele, he invents Sir Roger de Coverley. The measure of his success is that we can now think of Sir Roger for a long time without remembering his Toryism; when we do remember it, it is only as a lovable whimsy. . . . The enemy, far from being vilified, is being turned into a dear old man. The thought that he could ever be dangerous has been erased from our minds; but so also the thought that anything he said could ever be taken seriously. We all love Sir Roger; but of course we do not really attend to him as we do—well, to Sir Andrew Freeport. All through the century which Addison ushered in, England was going to attend more and more seriously to the Freeports, and the de Coverleys were to be more and more effectually silenced. The figure of the dear old squire dominates—possibly, on some views, corrupts—the national imagination to the present day. This is indeed to "make a man die sweetly." That element in English society which stood against all that Addison's party was bringing in is henceforth seen through a mist of smiling tenderness—as an archaism, a lovely absurdity. What we might have been urged to attack as a fortress we are tricked into admiring as a ruin.

7
Addison, Joseph
Selected Literary Essays, "Addison" (1945), para. 5, p. 157.

The essays [of Addison] do not invite criticism in terms of any very definite theology. They are everywhere "pious." Rational Piety, together with Polite Letters and Simplicity, is one of the hall-marks of the age which Addison was partly interpreting but partly also bringing into existence. And Rational Piety is by its very nature not very doctrinal. This is one of the many ways in which Addison is historically momentous. He ushers in that period—it is just now drawing to a close—in which it is possible to talk of "piety" or (later) "religion" almost in the abstract; in which the contrast is no longer between Christian and Pagan, the elect and the world, orthodox and heretic, but between "religious" and "irreligious." The transition cannot be quite defined: absence of doctrine would have to become itself doctrinal for that to be possible. It is a change of atmosphere, which every reader of sensibility will feel if he passes suddenly from the literature of any earlier period to that of the eighteenth century.

8
Addison, Joseph
Selected Literary Essays, "Addison" (1945), para. 8, p. 160.

The mention of Rochester suggests yet another gulf between Addison and the preceding age. We may be sure that Rochester's manners lacked the "simplicity" which the Whig essayists recommended. It is, of course, a commonplace that they addressed themselves to the reform of manners; but I sometimes wonder whether the very degree of their success does not conceal from us the greatness of the undertaking. I sometimes catch myself taking it for granted that the marks of good breeding were in all ages the same as they are today—that swagger was always vulgar, that a low voice, an unpretentious manner, a show (however superficial) of self-effacement, were always demanded. But it is almost certainly false. . . . Even to this day, when we meet foreigners (only think of some *young* Frenchmen) who have not been subjected to the Addisonian "reform," we have to "make allowances" for them. . . . That sober code of manners under which we still live today, in so far as we have any code at all, and which foreigners call hypocrisy, is in some important degree a legacy from the *Tattler* and the *Spectator*.

9
Addison, Joseph
Selected Literary Essays, "Addison" (1945), para. 17–19, pp. 166–168.

I have not attempted to assess the value of Addison's work, having wished rather to bring out its immense potency. He appears to be (as far as any individual can be) the source of a quite astonishing number of mental habits which were still prevalent when men now living were born. Almost everything which my own generation ignorantly called Victorian seems to have been expressed by Addison. . . . If he is not at present the most hated of our writers, that can only be because he is so little read. Everything the moderns detest, all that they call *smugness, complacency,* and *bourgeois ideology,* is brought together in his work and given its most perfect expression.

And certainly, if it were at all times true that the Good is the enemy of the Best, it would be hard to defend Addison. His Rational Piety, his smiling indulgence to "the fair sex," his small idealisms about trade, certainly fall short of actual Christianity, and plain justice to women, and true political wisdom. They may even be obstacles to them. . . . I believe he could defend himself. He is not attempting to write sermons or philosophy, only essays. . . . All we can justly say is that his essays are rather small beer; there is no iron in them as in Johnson; they do not stir the depths.

. . . I do not think Addison's popularity is likely to return; but something to fill the same place in life will always be needed—some tranquil middle ground of quiet sentiments and pleasing melancholies and gentle humour to come in between our restless idealisms and our equally restless dissipations. Do we not after all detect in the charge of *smugness* and *complacency* the note of envy? Addison is, above all else, comfortable. He is not on that account to be condemned. He is an admirable cure for the fidgets.

10

Adoration

The Last Battle,
chap. 15, p. 164.

It is better to see the Lion and die than to be Tisroc of the world and live and not to have seen him.

11

Adoration

Letters to Malcolm: Chiefly on Prayer, chap. 17, para. 4–8, 10–12, pp. 89–91.

Pleasures are shafts of the glory as it strikes our sensibility. . . .

But aren't there bad, unlawful pleasures? Certainly there are. But in calling them "bad pleasures" I take it we are using a kind of shorthand. We mean "pleasures snatched by unlawful acts." It is the stealing of the apple that is bad, not the sweetness. The sweetness is still a beam from the glory. That does not palliate the stealing. It makes it worse. There is sacrilege in the theft. We have abused a holy thing.

I have tried, since that moment, to make

every pleasure into a channel of adoration. I
don't mean simply by giving thanks for it. One
must of course give thanks, but I mean
something different. How shall I put it?
We can't—or I can't—hear the song of a bird
simply as a sound. Its meaning or message
("That's a bird") comes with it inevitably. . . .
This heavenly fruit is instantly redolent of the
orchard where it grew. This sweet air whispers
of the country from whence it blows. It is a
message. We know we are being touched by a
finger of that right hand at which there are
pleasures for evermore. There need be no
question of thanks or praise as a separate event,
something done afterwards. To experience the
tiny theophany is itself to adore.

Gratitude exclaims, very properly, "How good
of God to give me this." Adoration says, "What
must be the quality of that Being whose far-off
and momentary coruscations are like this!" One's
mind runs back up the sunbeam to the
sun. . . .

I don't always achieve it. One obstacle is
inattention. Another is the wrong kind of
attention. One could, if one practised, hear
simply a roar and not the roaring-of-the-wind.
In the same way, only far too easily, one can
concentrate on the pleasure as an event in one's
own nervous system—subjectify it—and ignore
the smell of Deity that hangs about it. A third
obstacle is greed. Instead of saying "This also is
Thou," one may say the fatal word Encore.
There is also conceit: the dangerous reflection
that not everyone can find God in a plain slice
of bread and butter, or that others would
condemn as simply "grey" the sky in which I am
delightedly observing such delicacies of pearl
and dove and silver.

You notice that I am drawing no distinction between sensuous and aesthetic pleasures. But why should I? The line is almost impossible to draw and what use would it be if one succeeded in drawing it?

If this is Hedonism, it is also a somewhat arduous discipline. But it is worth some labour: for in so far as it succeeds, almost every day furnishes us with, so to speak, "bearings" on the Bright Blur. It becomes brighter but less blurry.

12
Adoration
Letters to Malcolm: Chiefly on Prayer, chap. 17, para. 13, p. 91.

We—or at least I—shall not be able to adore God on the highest occasions if we have learned no habit of doing so on the lowest. At best, our faith and reason will tell us that He is adorable, but we shall not have found Him so, not have "tasted and seen." Any patch of sunlight in a wood will show you something about the sun which you could never get from reading books on astronomy. These pure and spontaneous pleasures are "patches of Godlight" in the woods of our experience.

13
Adulthood
Of Other Worlds: Essays and Stories, "On Three Ways of Writing for Children" (1952), para. 9, p. 25.

Critics who treat *adult* as a term of approval, instead of as a merely descriptive term, cannot be adult themselves. To be concerned about being grown up, to admire the grown up because it is grown up, to blush at the suspicion of being childish; these things are the marks of childhood and adolescence. And in childhood and adolescence they are, in moderation, healthy symptoms. Young things ought to want to grow. But to carry on into middle life or even into early manhood this concern about being adult is a mark of really arrested development. When I was ten, I read fairy tales in secret and would have been ashamed if I had been found doing

so. Now that I am fifty I read them openly.
When I became a man I put away childish
things, including the fear of childishness and the
desire to be very grown up.

14
Advice

Mere Christianity, bk.
IV, chap. 1, para. 6,
p. 137.

We never have followed the advice of the great
teachers. Why are we likely to begin now? Why
are we more likely to follow Christ than any of
the others? Because He is the best moral
teacher? But that makes it even less likely that
we shall follow Him. If we cannot take the
elementary lessons, is it likely we are going to
take the most advanced one? If Christianity only
means one more bit of good advice, then
Christianity is of no importance. There has been
no lack of good advice for the last four
thousand years. A bit more makes no difference.

15
Affection

The Four Loves,
chap. 3, para. 26-27,
pp. 68–69.

"We can say anything to one another." The
truth behind this is that Affection at its best can
say whatever Affection at its best wishes to say,
regardless of the rules that govern public
courtesy; for Affection at its best wishes neither
to wound nor to humiliate nor to domineer. . . .
You may tease and hoax and banter. You can
say "Shut up. I want to read." You can do
anything in the right tone and at the right
moment—the tone and moment which are not
intended to, and will not, hurt. The better the
Affection the more unerringly it knows which
these are (every love has its art of love). But the
domestic Rudesby means something quite
different when he claims liberty to say
"anything." Having a very imperfect sort of
Affection himself, or perhaps at that moment
none, he arrogates to himself the beautiful
liberties which only the fullest Affection has a

right to or knows how to manage. He then uses them spitefully in obedience to his resentments; or ruthlessly in obedience to his egoism; or at best stupidly, lacking the art. And all the time he may have a clear conscience. He knows that Affection takes liberties. He is taking liberties. Therefore (he concludes) he is being affectionate. Resent anything and he will say that the defect of love is on your side. He is hurt. He has been misunderstood.

He then sometimes avenges himself by getting on his high horse and becoming elaborately "polite." The implication is of course, "Oh! So we are not to be intimate? We are to behave like mere acquaintances? I had hoped—but no matter. Have it your own way."

16

Affection

The Four Loves, chap. 3, para. 28–29, 33, pp. 70–71, 73.

Change is a threat to Affection.

. . . Affection is the most instinctive, in that sense the most animal, of the loves; its jealousy is proportionately fierce. It snarls and bares its teeth like a dog whose food has been snatched away. . . .

"Boy, boy, these wild courses of yours will break your mother's heart." That eminently Victorian appeal may often have been true. Affection was bitterly wounded when one member of the family fell from the homely ethos into something worse—gambling, drink, keeping an opera girl. Unfortunately it is almost equally possible to break your mother's heart by rising above the homely ethos. The conservative tenacity of affection works both ways. It can be a domestic counterpart to that nationally suicidal type of education which keeps back the promising child because the idlers and dunces might be "hurt" if it were undemocratically moved into a higher class than themselves.

17
Affection

The Four Loves, chap.
3, para. 43, p. 80.

Affection is responsible for nine-tenths of whatever solid and durable happiness there is in our natural lives.

18
Affection

The Four Loves,
chap. 3, para. 45–46,
pp. 81–83.

Affection produces happiness if—and only if—there is common sense and give and take and "decency." In other words, only if something more, and other, than Affection is added. The mere feeling is not enough. . . . There is no disguising the fact that this means goodness; patience, self-denial, humility, and the continual intervention of a far higher sort of love than Affection, in itself, can ever be. That is the whole point. If we try to live by Affection alone, Affection will "go bad on us."

. . . It was of erotic love that the Roman poet said, "I love and hate," but other kinds of love admit the same mixture. They carry in them the seeds of hatred. If Affection is made the absolute sovereign of a human life the seeds will germinate. Love, having become a god, becomes a demon.

19
Aging

*The Letters of C. S.
Lewis to Arthur Greeves*
(10 December 1942),
p. 494.

I have had neuralgia to-day but am otherwise alright—except for rheumatism which has prevented me from sleeping on my right side for nearly a year now. (What a series of rediscoveries life is. All the things which one used to regard as simply the nonsense grown-ups talk have one by one come true—draughts, rheumatism, Christianity. The best one of all remains to be verified.)

20
Aging

That Hideous Strength,
chap. 1, section 3, p. 21.

Youth and age touch only the surface of our lives.

21
Aging
*The Letters of C. S.
Lewis to Arthur Greeves*
(5 January 1947),
p. 509.

Funny to think we're both elderly, isn't it? And
what a sham this business of age is. Do you
(except physically) *feel* older than when we saw
the hedge pig and played gramophone records to
one another? I don't a bit. My own pupils still
seem to me in many ways older than I. Indeed
(nice men as many of them are) I am a little
worried by the fact that so few of them seem
ever to have had youth as we had it. They have
all read all the correct, "important" books: they
seem to have no private & erratic imaginative
adventures of their own. (I suppose the
explanation is that I am the last person who is
likely to hear of such things even where they
exist. I mean, with me they're all talking
"grown-up" as hard as they can. Yet I don't
know: the modern world is so desperately
serious. They have a taste for "books of
information.")

22
Aging
*Letters to an American
Lady* (1 August 1953),
pp. 19–20.

Yes, I too think there is lots to be said for being
no longer young; and I do most heartily agree
that it is just as well to be past the age when
one expects or desires to attract the other sex.
It's natural enough in our species, as in others,
that the young birds should show off their
plumage—in the mating season. But the trouble
in the modern world is that there's a tendency
to rush all the birds on to that age as soon as
possible and then keep them there as late as
possible, thus losing all the real value of the
other parts of life in a senseless, pitiful attempt
to prolong what, after all, is neither its wisest,
its happiest, or most innocent period. I suspect
merely commercial motives are behind it all: for
it is at the showing-off age that birds of both
sexes have least sales-resistance!

23
Aging
The Silver Chair,
chap. 16, p. 212.

People [have] no particular ages in Aslan's country. Even in this world, of course, it is the stupidest children who are most childish and the stupidest grown-ups who are most grown-up.

24
Aging
Letters to an American Lady (30 September 1958), p. 78.

We must both, I'm afraid, recognise that, as we grow older, we become like old cars—more and more repairs and replacements are necessary. We must just look forward to the fine new machines (latest Resurrection model) which are waiting for us, we hope, in the Divine garage!

25
Aging
Letters to an American Lady (30 October 1958), p. 79.

As for wrinkles—pshaw! Why shouldn't we have wrinkles? Honorable insignia of long service in this warfare.

26
Aging
Letters to an American Lady (5 June 1961), pp. 98–99.

We must beware of the Past, mustn't we? I mean that any fixing of the mind on old evils beyond what is absolutely necessary for repenting our own sins and forgiving those of others is certainly useless and usually bad for us. Notice in Dante that the lost souls are entirely concerned with their past! Not so the saved. This is one of the dangers of being, like you and me, old. There's so much past, now, isn't there? And so little else. But we must try very hard not to keep on endlessly chewing the cud. We must look forward more eagerly to sloughing that old skin off forever.

27
Aging
Letters of C. S. Lewis (27 October 1963), p. 308.

Yes, autumn is really the best of the seasons; and I'm not sure that old age isn't the best part of life. But of course, like autumn, it doesn't *last*.

28
Aging: Middle Age
The Screwtape Letters,
Letter XXVIII, para. 1,
p. 132.

[Senior devil Screwtape to junior devil Wormwood:] The long, dull, monotonous years of middle-aged prosperity or middle-aged adversity are excellent campaigning weather. You see, it is so hard for these creatures to persevere. The routine of adversity, the gradual decay of youthful loves and youthful hopes, the quiet despair (hardly felt as pain) of ever overcoming the chronic temptations with which we have again and again defeated them, the drabness which we create in their lives, and the inarticulate resentment with which we teach them to respond to it—all this provides admirable opportunities of wearing out a soul by attrition. If, on the other hand, the middle years prove prosperous, our position is even stronger. Prosperity knits a man to the World. He feels that he is "finding his place in it," while really it is finding its place in him. His increasing reputation, his widening circle of acquaintances, his sense of importance, the growing pressure of absorbing and agreeable work, build up in him a sense of being really at home on Earth, which is just what we want. You will notice that the young are generally less unwilling to die than the middle-aged and the old.

29
Aging: Middle Age
The Four Loves, chap.
4, para. 32, p. 107.

The middle-aged male has great powers of passive resistance.

30
Aging: Youth
Surprised by Joy, chap.
10, para. 14, p. 160.

With the cruelty of youth I allowed myself to be irritated by traits in my father which, in other elderly men, I have since regarded as lovable foibles.

31
Agnosticism
Surprised by Joy, chap.
14, para. 21, p. 227.

Amiable agnostics will talk cheerfully about
"man's search for God." To me, as I then was,
they might as well have talked about the
mouse's search for the cat.

32
Allegory
The Pilgrim's Regress,
Preface, para. 23, p. 13.

It is the sort of thing you cannot learn from
definition: you must rather get to know it as
you get to know a smell or a taste, the
"atmosphere" of a family or a country town, or
the personality of an individual.

33
Allegory
The Pilgrim's Regress,
Preface, para. 23, p. 13.

People . . . suppose that allegory is a disguise, a
way of saying obscurely what could have been
said more clearly. But in fact all good allegory
exists not to hide but to reveal; to make the
inner world more palpable by giving it an
(imagined) concrete embodiment.

34
Allegory
The Pilgrim's Regress,
Preface, para. 23, p. 13.

When allegory is at its best, it approaches myth,
which must be grasped with the imagination,
not with the intellect.

35
Allegory
The Allegory of Love,
chap. II.I, para. 2, p. 45.

The allegorist leaves the given—his own
passions—to talk of that which is confessedly
less real, which is a fiction. The symbolist leaves
the given to find that which is more real. To put
the difference in another way, for the symbolist
it is we who are the allegory. We are the "frigid
personifications"; the heavens above us are the
"shadowy abstractions"; the world which we
mistake for reality is the flat outline of that
which elsewhere veritably is all the round of its
unimaginable dimensions.

36

Allegory

The Allegory of Love,
chap. IV.II, para. 7,
p. 166.

The function of allegory is not to hide but to reveal, and it is properly used only for that which cannot be said, or so well said, in literal speech. The inner life, and specially the life of love, religion, and spiritual adventure, has therefore always been the field of true allegory; for here there are intangibles which only allegory can fix and reticences which only allegory can overcome.

37

Allegory

The Allegory of Love,
chap. V.II, para. 3,
p. 225.

When you accepted the exodus of Israel from Egypt as a type of the soul's escape from sin, you did not on that account abolish the exodus as a historical event. . . . It is a mischievous error to suppose that in an allegory the author is "really" talking about the thing symbolized, and not at all about the thing that symbolizes; the very essence of the art is to talk about both.

38

Allegory

*Studies in Medieval and
Renaissance Literature,*
"Edmund Spenser,
1552-99" (1954),
para. 27, p. 137.

We shall understand it best (though this may seem paradoxical) by not trying too hard to understand it. Many things—such as loving, going to sleep, or behaving unaffectedly—are done worst when we try hardest to do them. Allegory is not a puzzle.

39

Allegory

Letters of C. S. Lewis
(10 December 1956),
p. 273.

Indeed, in so far as the things unseen are manifested by the things seen, one might from one point of view call the whole material universe an allegory.

40

Allegory

*Of Other Worlds: Essays
and Stories,* "On
Criticism," para. 26,
p. 58.

We ought not to proceed to allegorize any work until we have plainly set out the reasons for regarding it as an allegory at all.

41
Ambition
God in the Dock (1944),
"Answers to Questions
on Christianity," ans. 9,
pp. 55–56.

Ambition! We must be careful what we mean by it. If it means the desire to get ahead of other people—which is what I think it does mean— then it is bad. If it means simply wanting to do a thing well, then it is good. It isn't wrong for an actor to want to act his part as well as it can possibly be acted, but the wish to have his name in bigger type than the other actors is a bad one.

42
Ambition
The Letters of C. S. Lewis to Arthur Greeves (18 August 1930), para. 3, 6–8, pp. 378–381.

From the age of sixteen onwards I had one single ambition [to succeed as a writer], from which I never wavered, in the prosecution of which I spent every ounce I could, on wh. I really & deliberately staked my whole contentment: and I recognise myself as having unmistakably failed in it.

. . . The side of me which longs, not to write, for no one can stop us doing that, but to be approved as a writer, is not the side of us that is really worth much. And depend upon it, unless God has abandoned us, he will find means to cauterise that side somehow or other. If we can take the pain well and truly now and by it *forever* get over the wish to be distinguished beyond our fellows, well: if not we shall get it again in some other form. And honestly, the being cured, with all the pain, has pleasure too: one creeps home, tired and bruised, into a state of mind that is really restful, when all one's ambitions have been given up. Then one can really for the first time say "Thy Kingdom come": for in that Kingdom there will be no pre-eminences and a man must have reached the stage of not caring two straws about his own status before he can enter it.

Think how difficult that would be if one

succeeded as a writer: how bitter this necessary purgation at the age of sixty, when literary success had made your whole life and you had *then* got to begin to go through the stage of seeing it all as dust and ashes. Perhaps God has been specially kind to us in forcing us to get over it at the beginning. At all events, whether we like it or not, we have got to take the shock. As you know so well, we have got to *die*. Cry, kick, swear, we may: only like Lilith to come in the end and die far more painfully and later.

. . . I would have given almost *anything*—I shudder to think what I would have given if I had been allowed—to be a successful writer. . . . I am writing as I do simply & solely because I think the only thing for you to do is absolutely to *kill* the part of you that wants success.

43
America
English Literature in the Sixteenth Century,
Introduction, para. 23,
p. 15.

Judged in the light of later events the history of English exploration in the sixteenth century may appear to modern Americans and modern Englishmen a very *Aeneid:* but judged by the aims and wishes of its own time it was on the whole a record of failures and second bests.

44
America
English Literature in the Sixteenth Century,
Introduction, para. 24,
p. 16.

The best European minds were ashamed of Europe's exploits in America. Montaigne passionately asks why so noble a discovery could not have fallen to the Ancients who might have spread civility where we have spread only corruption.

45
America, Discovery of

English Literature in the Sixteenth Century, Introduction, para. 23, p. 15.

Columbus, a man of lofty mind, with missionary and scientific interests, had the original idea of acting on the age-old doctrine of the earth's rotundity and sailing west to find the east. Lands which no one had dreamed of barred his way. Though we all know, we often forget, that the existence of America was one of the greatest disappointments in the history of Europe. . . . The English . . . had to content themselves with colonization, which they conceived chiefly as a social sewerage system, a vent for "needy people who now trouble the commonwealth" and are "daily consumed with the gallows."

46
Angels

The Screwtape Letters, Preface, para. 12, p. viii.

[Angels] are given human form because man is the only rational creature we know. Creatures higher in the natural order than ourselves, either incorporeal or animating bodies of a sort we cannot experience, must be represented symbolically if they are to be represented at all.

47
Angels

The Screwtape Letters, Preface, para. 14–15, pp. viii–ix.

In the plastic arts these symbols have steadily degenerated. *Fra Angelico's* angels carry in their face and gesture the peace and authority of Heaven. Later come the chubby infantile nudes of *Raphael*; finally the soft, slim, girlish, and consolatory angels of nineteenth century art, shapes so feminine that they avoid being voluptuous only by their total insipidity—the frigid houris of a teatable paradise. They are a pernicious symbol. In Scripture the visitation of an angel is always alarming; it has to begin by saying "Fear not." The Victorian angel looks as if it were going to say, "There, there."

The literary symbols are more dangerous because they are not so easily recognised as symbolical. Those of *Dante* are the best. Before his angels we sink in awe.

48

Anger

*The Letters of C. S.
Lewis to Arthur Greeves*
(17 January 1931),
p. 404.

I suppose that when one hears a tale of hideous cruelty anger is quite the wrong reaction, and merely wastes the energy that ought to go in a different direction: perhaps merely dulls the conscience wh., if it were awake, would ask us "Well? What are you *doing* about it? How much of your life have you spent in really combatting this? In helping to produce social conditions in which these sort of things will not occur!?"

49

Anger

Selected Literary Essays,
"Addison" (1945), para.
4, p. 156.

Reasonableness and amiability (both cheerful "habits" of the mind) are stronger in the end than the . . . spleen. To rail is the sad privilege of the loser.

50

Anger

Till We Have Faces, part
2, chap. 1, p. 266.

My anger protected me only for a short time; anger wearies itself out and truth comes in.

51

Anger

*Letters to Malcolm:
Chiefly on Prayer,* chap.
18, para. 9, p. 97.

Anger is the fluid that love bleeds when you cut it.

52

Anger

Poems, "Five Sonnets
(1)" (1st pub. 1964),
p. 125.

Anger's the anaesthetic of the mind.

53

Anxiety

*The Letters of C. S.
Lewis to Arthur Greeves*
(18 August 1930),
p. 378.

The first thing, when one is being worried as to whether one will have to have an operation or whether one is a literary failure, is *to assume absolutely mercilessly that the worst is true,* and to ask *What Then?* If it turns out in the end

that the worst is not true, so much the better:
but for the meantime the question must be
resolutely put out of mind. Otherwise your
thoughts merely go round and round a
wearisome circle, now hopeful, now
despondent, then hopeful again—that way
madness lies. Having settled then that the worst
is true, one can proceed to consider the
situation.

54
Anxiety

The Screwtape Letters,
Letter VI, para. 1–2,
pp. 28–29.

[Senior devil Screwtape to junior devil
Wormwood:] There is nothing like suspense and
anxiety for barricading a human's mind against
the Enemy. He [God] wants men to be
concerned with what they do; our business is to
keep them thinking about what will happen to
them.

Your patient will, of course, have picked up
the notion that he must submit with patience to
the Enemy's will. What the Enemy means by
this is primarily that he should accept with
patience the tribulation which has actually been
dealt out to him—the present anxiety and
suspense. It is about this that he is to say "Thy
will be done," and for the daily task of bearing
this that the daily bread will be provided.

55
Apologetics

God in the Dock,
"Christian Apologetics"
(1945), para. 4, p. 90.

Each of us has his individual emphasis: each
holds, in addition to the Faith, many opinions
which seem to him to be consistent with it and
true and important. And so perhaps they are.
But as apologists it is not our business to
defend *them*. We are defending Christianity; not
"my religion." When we mention our personal
opinions we must always make quite clear the
difference between them and the Faith itself.

56
Apologetics
God in the Dock,
"Christian Apologetics"
(1945), para. 23, p. 101.

One of the great difficulties is to keep before the audience's mind the question of Truth. They always think you are recommending Christianity not because it is *true* but because it is *good*. And in the discussion they will at every moment try to escape from the issue "True—or False" into stuff about a good society, or morals, or the incomes of Bishops, or the Spanish Inquisition, or France, or Poland—or anything whatever. You have to keep forcing them back, and again back, to the real point. Only thus will you be able to undermine . . . their belief that a certain amount of "religion" is desirable but one mustn't carry it too far. One must keep on pointing out that Christianity is a statement which, if false, is of *no* importance, and if true, of infinite importance. The one thing it cannot be is moderately important.

57
Apologetics
God in the Dock,
"Christian Apologetics"
(1945), para. 23, p. 102.

I think we must attack wherever we meet it the nonsensical idea that mutually exclusive propositions about God can both be true.

58
Apologetics
God in the Dock, "Man
or Rabbit?" (1946),
para. 9, pp. 111–112.

Here is a door, behind which, according to some people, the secret of the universe is waiting for you. Either that's true, or it isn't. And if it isn't, then what the door really conceals is simply the greatest fraud, the most colossal "sell" on record. Isn't it obviously the job of every man (that is a man and not a rabbit) to try to find out which, and then to devote his full energies either to serving this tremendous secret or to exposing and destroying this gigantic humbug?

59
Apologetics
Letters of C. S. Lewis
(2 August 1946), p. 209.

Apologetic work is so dangerous to one's own faith. A doctrine never seems dimmer to me than when I have just successfully defended it.

60
Apologetics
*Present Concerns:
Essays by C. S. Lewis,*
"Modern Man and His
Categories of Thought"
(1946), para. 8, p. 65.

Man is becoming as narrowly "practical" as the irrational animals. In lecturing to popular audiences I have repeatedly found it almost impossible to make them understand that I recommended Christianity because I thought its affirmations to be objectively *true*. They are simply not interested in the question of truth or falsehood. They only want to know if it will be comforting, or "inspiring," or socially useful. (In English we have a peculiar difficulty here because in popular speech "believe in" has two meanings, (a) To accept as true, (b) To approve of—e.g., "I believe in free trade." Hence when an Englishman says he "believes in" or "does not believe in" Christianity, he may not be thinking about *truth* at all. Very often he is only telling us whether he approves or disapproves of the Church as a social institution.) Closely connected with this unhuman Practicality is an indifference to, and contempt of, dogma. The popular point of view is unconsciously syncretistic: it is widely believed that "all religions really mean the same thing."

61
Apologetics
Poems, "The apologist's
Evening Prayer" (1st
pub. 1964), p. 129.

From all my lame defeats and oh! much more
From all the victories that I seemed to score;
From cleverness shot forth on thy behalf
At which, while angels weep, the audience
    laugh;
From all my proofs of Thy divinity
Thou, who wouldst give no sign, deliver me.

62
Architecture
Letters of C. S. Lewis
(7 August 1921), p. 66.

We lunched at Wells after seeing the Cathedral. . . . I am no architect and not much more of an antiquarian. Strange to say it was Uncle H. with his engineering more than our father with his churchmanship that helped me to appreciate it; he taught me to look at the single endless line of the aisle, with every pillar showing at once the strain and the meeting of the strain (like a ship's framework inverted); it is certainly wonderfully satisfying to look at. The pleasure one gets is like that from rhyme—a need, and the answer of it following so quickly that they make a single sensation. So now I understand the old law in architecture, "no weight without a support, and no support without an adequate weight."

63
Art and Literature
Letters of C. S. Lewis
(16 April 1940), p. 182.

I do most thoroughly agree with what you say about Art and Literature. To my mind they can only be healthy when they are either (a) admittedly aiming at nothing but innocent recreation or (b) definitely the handmaids of religious or at least moral truth. Dante is alright and Pickwick is alright. But the great *serious irreligious* art—art for art's sake—is all balderdash; and incidentally never exists when art is really flourishing. One can say of Art as an author I recently read said of love (sexual love I mean), "It ceases to be a devil when it ceases to be a god." Isn't that well put?

64
Art Appreciation
The World's Last Night and Other Essays,
"Good Work and Good Works" (1959), para. 21, p. 80.

Many modern novels, poems, and pictures which we are brow-beaten into "appreciating," are not good work because they are not *work* at all. They are mere puddles of spilled sensibility or reflection. When an artist is in the strict sense working, he of course takes into account the existing taste, interests, and capacity of his audience. These, no less than the language, the marble, or the paint, are part of his raw material; to be used, tamed, sublimated, not ignored nor defied. Haughty indifference to them is not genius nor integrity; it is laziness and incompetence.

65

Art Appreciation

An Experiment in Criticism, chap. 3, para. 12, p. 19.

The first demand any work of any art makes upon us is surrender. Look. Listen. Receive. Get yourself out of the way. (There is no good asking first whether the work before you deserves such a surrender, for until you have surrendered you cannot possibly find out.)

66

Art, Duty of

Selected Literary Essays, "Hamlet: The Prince or the Poem" (1942), para. 21, p. 103.

To interest is the first duty of art; no other excellences will even begin to compensate for failure in this, and very serious faults will be covered by this, as by charity.

67

Art, Essence of

English Literature in the Sixteenth Century, bk. I.II.I, para. 5, p. 124.

No art lives by *nature*, only by acts of voluntary attention on the part of human individuals. When these are not made it ceases to exist.

68

Art, Function of

English Literature in the Sixteenth Century, bk. III.III.III, para. 61, . p. 529.

It may well be that the author who claims to write neither for patron nor public but for himself has done our art incalculable harm and bred up infinite charlatans by teaching us to emphasize the public's duty of "recognition" instead of the artist's duty to teach and delight.

69
Art, Function of
The World's Last Night and Other Essays, "Good Work and Good Works" (1959), para. 18–19, p. 79.

In the highest aesthetic circles one now hears nothing about the artist's duty to us. It is all about our duty to him. He owes us nothing; we owe him "recognition," even though he has never paid the slightest attention to our tastes, interests, or habits. If we don't give it to him, our name is mud. In this shop, the customer is always wrong.

But this change is surely part of our changed attitude to all work. As "giving employment" becomes more important than making things men need or like, there is a tendency to regard every trade as something that exists chiefly for the sake of those who practise it. The smith does not work in order that the warriors may fight; the warriors exist and fight in order that the smith may be kept busy. The bard does not exist in order to delight the tribe; the tribe exists in order to appreciate the bard.

70
Art, Value of
Selected Literary Essays, "Sir Walter Scott" (1956), para. 11, pp. 214–215.

It may be true, as Curtius has said, that "the modern world immeasurably overvalues art." Or it may be that the modern world is right and that all previous ages have greatly erred in making art, as they did, subordinate to life, so that artists worked to teach virtue, to adorn the city, to solemnize feasts and marriages, to please a patron, or to amuse the people. Or again, a middle view may be possible; that works of art are in reality serious, and ends in themselves, but that all is lost when the artists discover this, as Eros fled when Psyche turned the lamp upon him. But wherever the truth may lie, there are two things of which I feel certain. One is, that if we do overvalue art, then art itself will be the greatest sufferer; when second things are put first, they are corrupted. The other is that, even if we of all generations have first valued art aright, yet there will certainly be loss as well as gain. We shall lose the fine careless, prodigal artists. For, if not all art, yet some art, flows best from men who treat their work as a kind of play. I at any rate cannot conceive how the exuberance, the elbow-room, the heart-easing quality of Dickens, or Chaucer, or Cervantes, could co-exist with that self-probing literary conscience we find in Pater or Henry James. Lockhart speaks somewhere of Scott "enjoying rather than exerting his genius." We may be coming to a period when there will be no room for authors who do that. If so, I admit there may be gain; I am sure there will be losses.

71
Ascham, Roger
English Literature in the Sixteenth Century, bk. II.III, para. 9–10, pp. 279–280.

Ascham . . . is everyone's friend. He is irresistible. In his own day nearly everyone seems to have liked him. Despite his avowed Protestantism, Mary made him her Latin Secretary and he found it possible all through her reign to abide by his religion with (let us hope) no disgraceful degree of prudence. His very weaknesses—"too much given to dicing and cockfighting," says Camden—were of a genial sort, and it is plain that he was a good schoolmaster, a good husband, and a good friend. His delightful, and delighted, temperament has flowed into his writing.

His *Toxophilus* (1545) is one of the most genial and winning books that had yet appeared in English. The book is, if you will, a farrago of prejudices: but then that is its charm. Ascham is everywhere writing of what he knows and loves, and is full of reality.

72
Aslan
The Lion, the Witch and the Wardrobe, chap. 8, pp. 74–76.

"Who is Aslan?" asked Susan.

"Aslan?" said Mr. Beaver, "Why don't you know? He's the King. . . . It is he, not you, that will save Mr. Tumnus. . . ."

"Is—is he a man?" asked Lucy.

"Aslan a man!" said Mr. Beaver sternly. "Certainly not. I tell you he is the King of the wood and the son of the great Emperor-Beyond-the-Sea. Don't you know who is the King of Beasts? Aslan is a lion—*the* Lion, the great Lion."

"Ooh!" said Susan. "I'd thought he was a man. Is he—quite safe? I shall feel rather nervous about meeting a lion."

"That you will, dearie, and no mistake," said Mrs. Beaver, "if there's anyone who can appear before Aslan without their knees knocking, they're either braver than most or else just silly."

"Then he isn't safe?" said Lucy.

"Safe?" said Mr. Beaver. "Don't you hear what Mrs. Beaver tells you? Who said anything about safe? 'Course he isn't safe. But he's good. He's the King, I tell you."

"I'm longing to see him," said Peter, "even if I do feel frightened when it comes to the point."

73
Aslan
Voyage of the Dawn Treader, chap. 16, pp. 214–215.

But between them and the foot of the sky there was something so white on the green grass that even with their eagles' eyes they could hardly look at it. They came on and saw that it was a Lamb.

"Come and have breakfast," said the Lamb in its sweet milky voice. . . .

"Please Lamb," said Lucy, "is this the way to Aslan's country? "

"Not for you," said the Lamb. "For you the

door into Aslan's country is from your own world."

"What!" said Edmund. "Is there a way into Aslan's country from our world too?"

"There is a way into my country from all the worlds," said the Lamb; but as he spoke his snowy white flushed into tawny gold and his size changed and he was Aslan himself, towering above them and scattering light from his mane.

"Oh, Aslan," said Lucy. "Will you tell us how to get into your country from our world?"

"I shall be telling you all the time," said Aslan. "But I will not tell you how long or short the way will be; only that it lies across a river. But do not fear that, for I am the great Bridge Builder. And now come; I will open the door in the sky and send you to your own land."

74

Aslan

Voyage of the Dawn Treader, chap. 16. pp. 215–216.

"Please, Aslan," said Lucy. "Before we go, will you tell us when we can come back to Narnia again? Please. And oh, do, do, do make it soon."

"Dearest," said Aslan very gently, "you and your brother will never come back to Narnia."

"Oh, Aslan!" said Edmund and Lucy both together in despairing voices.

"You are too old, children," said Aslan, "and you must begin to come close to your own world now."

"It isn't Narnia, you know," sobbed Lucy. "It's you. We shan't meet you there. And how can we live never meeting you?"

"But you shall meet me, dear one," said Aslan.

"Are—are you there too, Sir?" said Edmund.

"I am," said Aslan. "But there I have another name. You must learn to know me by that name. This was the very reason why you were

brought to Narnia, that by knowing me here for
a little, you may know me better there."

75

Aslan

The Silver Chair,
chap. 2, pp. 16–17.

"Are you not thirsty?" said the Lion.
   "I'm dying of thirst," said Jill.
   "Then drink," said the Lion.
   "May I—could I—would you mind going
away while I do?" said Jill.
   The Lion answered this only by a look and a
very low growl. And as Jill gazed at its
motionless bulk, she realised that she might as
well have asked the whole mountain to move
aside for her convenience.
   The delicious rippling noise of the stream was
driving her nearly frantic.
   "Will you promise not to—do anything to
me, if I do come?" said Jill.
   "I make no promise," said the Lion.
   Jill was so thirsty now that, without noticing
it, she had come a step nearer.
   "Do you eat girls?" she said.
   "I have swallowed up girls and boys, women
and men, kings and emperors, cities and
realms," said the Lion. It didn't say this as if it
were boasting, nor as if it were sorry, nor as if it
were angry. It just said it.
   "I daren't come and drink," said Jill.
   "Then you will die of thirst," said the Lion.
   "Oh dear!" said Jill, coming another step
nearer. "I suppose I must go and look for
another stream then."
   "There is no other stream," said the Lion.

76

Aslan

The Silver Chair,
chap. 16, p. 212.

"Son of Adam," said Aslan, "Go into that
thicket and pluck the thorn that you will find
there, and bring it to me." Eustace obeyed. The
thorn was a foot long and sharp as a rapier.

"Drive it into my paw, Son of Adam," said Aslan, holding up his right fore-paw and spreading out the great pads towards Eustace.

"Must I?" said Eustace.

"Yes," said Aslan.

Then Eustace set his teeth and drove the thorn into the Lion's pad. And there came out a great drop of blood, redder than all redness that you have ever seen or imagined. And it splashed into the stream over the dead body of the King. At the same moment the doleful music stopped. And the dead King began to be changed. . . . His eyes opened, and his lips both laughed, and suddenly he leaped up and stood before them.

77
Aslan
The Magician's Nephew,
chap. 10, p. 118.

"Creatures, I give you yourselves," said the strong, happy voice of Aslan. "I give to you forever this land of Narnia. I give you the woods, the fruits, the rivers. I give you the stars and I give you myself."

78
Aslan
The Magician's Nephew,
chap. 12, pp. 141–142.

"Son of Adam," said Aslan. "Are you ready to undo the wrong that you have done to my sweet country of Narnia on the very day of its birth?"

"Well, I don't see what I can do," said Digory. "You see, the Queen ran away and—"

"I asked, are you ready," said the Lion.

"Yes," said Digory. He had had for a second some wild idea of saying "I'll try to help you if you'll promise to help about my Mother," but he realised in time that the Lion was not at all the sort of person one could try to make bargains with. But when he had said "Yes," he thought of his Mother, and he thought of the great hopes he had had, and how they were all dying away, and a lump came in his throat and tears in his eyes, and he blurted out:

"But please, please—won't you—can't you give me something that will cure Mother?" Up till then he had been looking at the Lion's great front feet and the huge claws on them; now, in his despair, he looked up at its face. What he saw surprised him as much as anything in his whole life. For the tawny face was bent down near his own and (wonder of wonders) great shining tears stood in the Lion's eyes. They were such big, bright tears compared with Digory's own that for a moment he felt as if the Lion must really be sorrier about his Mother than he was himself.

"My son, my son," said Aslan. "I know. Grief is great. Only you and I in this land know that yet. Let us be good to one another."

79

Aslan

Letters of C. S. Lewis
(29 December 1958),
para. 6, p. 283.

If Aslan represented the immaterial Deity in the same way in which Giant Despair represents Despair, he would be an allegorical figure. In reality however he is an invention giving an imaginary answer to the question, "What might Christ become like, if there really were a world like Narnia and He chose to be incarnate and die and rise again in that world as He actually has done in ours?" This is not allegory at all.

80

Atheism

Mere Christianity, bk.
II, chap. 1, pp. 45–46.

[When I was an atheist] my argument against God was that the universe seemed so cruel and unjust. But how had I got this idea of *just* and *unjust*? A man does not call a line crooked unless he has some idea of a straight line. What was I comparing this universe with when I called it unjust? If the whole show was bad and senseless from A to Z, so to speak, why did I, who was supposed to be part of the show, find

---

myself in such violent reaction against it? . . .
Thus in the very act of trying to prove that God
did not exist—in other words, that the whole of
reality was senseless—I found I was forced to
assume that one part of reality—namely my idea
of justice—was full of sense. Consequently
atheism turns out to be too simple. If the whole
universe has no meaning, we should never have
found out that it has no meaning.

81

Atheism

Surprised by Joy, chap.
7, para. 20, p. 115.

I was at this time living, like so many Atheists
or Antitheists, in a whirl of contradictions. I
maintained that God did not exist. I was also
very angry with God for not existing. I was
equally angry with Him for creating a world.

82

Atheism

Surprised by Joy, chap.
12, para. 13, p. 191.

A young man who wishes to remain a sound
Atheist cannot be too careful of his reading.
There are traps everywhere—"Bibles laid open,
millions of *surprises*," as Herbert says, "fine nets
and stratagems." God is, if I may say it, very
unscrupulous.

83

Austen, Jane

Selected Literary Essays,
"A Note on Jane
Austen" (1954),
para. 3–4, 13, pp.
177–178, 181.

All four heroines [Catherine, Marianne,
Elizabeth, Emma] painfully, though with varying
degrees of pain, discover that they have been
making mistakes both about themselves and
about the world in which they live. . . . All
realize that the cause of the deception lay
within. . . . Self-hatred or contempt . . . are
common to all. . . . Tardy and surprising self-
knowledge is presented in all four. . . . And in
all four the undeception, structurally considered,
is the very pivot or watershed of the story. In
Northanger Abbey, and *Emma,* it precipitates the
happy ending. In *Sense and Sensibility* it renders

it possible. In *Pride and Prejudice* it initiates that revaluation of Darcy, both in Elizabeth's mind and in our minds, which is completed by the visit to Pemberley. . . . They have "one plot." This is not so clearly true of *Sense and Sensibility*, but then it has really two plots . . . ; it is true about one of them. . . .

[In the other two novels, Fanny and Anne,] solitary heroines who make no mistakes have, I believe—or had while she was writing—the author's complete approbation. This is connected with the unusual pattern of *Mansfield Park* and *Persuasion*. The heroines stand almost outside, certainly a little apart from, the world which the action of the novel depicts. It is in it, not in them, that self-deception occurs. They see it, but its victims do not. They do not of course stand voluntarily apart, nor do they willingly accept the role of observers and critics. They are shut out and are compelled to observe: for what they observe, they disapprove.

84
Austen, Jane
Selected Literary Essays, "A Note on Jane Austen" (1954), para. 20–22, pp. 185–186.

Though the world of the novels has [a] serious, unyielding core, it is not a tragic world. This, no doubt, is due to the author's choice; but there are also two characteristics of her mind which are, I think, essentially untragic. The first is the nature of the core itself. It is in one way exacting, in another not. It is unexacting in so far as the duties commanded are not quixotic or heroic, and obedience to them will not be very difficult to properly brought up people in ordinary circumstances. It is exacting in so far as such obedience is rigidly demanded; neither excuses nor experiments are allowed. . . . The other untragic element in her mind is its cheerful moderation. She could almost have said with Johnson, "Nothing is too little for so little a creature as man." If she envisages few great sacrifices, she also envisages no grandiose schemes of joy. She has, or at least all her favourite characters have, a hearty relish for what would now be regarded as very modest pleasures. A ball, a dinner party, books, conversation, a drive to see a great house ten miles away, a holiday as far as Derbyshire— these, with affection (that is essential) and good manners, are happiness. She is no Utopian.

She is described by someone in Kipling's worst story as the mother of Henry James. I feel much more sure that she is the daughter of Dr Johnson: she inherits his commonsense, his morality, even much of his style.

85
Bacon, Francis

English Literature in the Sixteenth Century, Epilogue, I, para. 3, pp. 537–538.

It is a shock to turn to the *Essays.* Even the completed *Essays* of 1625 is a book whose reputation curiously outweighs any real pleasure or profit that most people have found in it, a book (as my successor admirably says) which "everyone has read but no one is ever found reading." The truth is, it is a book for adolescents. It is they who underline (as I see from the copy before me) sentences like "There is little friendshipe in the worlde, and least of all betweene equals": a man of 40 either disbelieves it or takes it for granted. No one, even if he wished, could really learn "policie" from Bacon, for cunning, even more than virtue, lives in minute particulars. What makes young readers think they are learning is Bacon's manner; the dry, apophthegmatic sentences, in appearance so unrhetorical, so little concerned to produce an effect, fall on the ear like oracles and are thus in fact a most potent rhetoric. In that sense the *Essays* are a triumph of style, even of stylistic illusion. For the same reason they are better to quote than to re-read. . . . Their connexion with Montaigne's work is quite unimportant. If Bacon took his title from Montaigne, he took nothing else. His earliest essays resemble essays by Montaigne about as much as a metallic-looking cactus raised on the edge of a desert resembles a whole country-side of forest, filled with light and shade, well stocked with game, and hard to get out of. It is only in the *Meditations* that Bacon is at all like his predecessor; and even there, of course, briefly. Nor had he any successors. The cactus remains unique; interesting, curious, striking, worth going to see once, but sterile, inedible, cold and hard to the touch.

86
Baptism
Letters of C. S. Lewis (18 March 1952), p. 239.

Don't bother at all about that question of a person being "made a Christian" by baptism. It is only the usual trouble about words being used in more than one sense. Thus we might say a man "became a soldier" the moment that he joined the army. But his instructors might say six months later "I think we have made a soldier of him." Both usages are quite definable, only one wants to know which is being used in a given sentence.

87
Beauty
The Letters of C. S. Lewis to Arthur Greeves (28 February 1917), p. 171.

[Lewis commenting on a beautiful woman]: Even to see her walk across the room is a liberal education.

88
Beauty
The Letters of C. S. Lewis to Arthur Greeves (29 May 1918), para. 3–4, pp. 216–217.

The thing in your last letter with which I most want to disagree is the remark about Beauty and nature: apparently I did not make myself clear. You say that nature is beautiful because of its shape, colour and motions, and perhaps a little because of association. Now these colours etc are sensations in my eye, produced by vibrations on the aether between me and the

tree: the real tree is something quite different—
a combination of colourless, shapeless, invisible
atoms. It follows then that neither the tree, nor
any other material object can be beautiful in
itself: I can never see them as they are, and if I
could it would give me no delight. The beauty
therefore is not in matter at all, but is
something purely spiritual, arising mysteriously
out of the relation between me & the tree: or
perhaps as I suggest in my Song, out of some
indwelling spirit behind the matter of the tree—
the Dryad in fact.

You see the conviction is gaining ground on
me that after all Spirit does exist; and that we
come in contact with the spiritual element by
means of these "thrills." I fancy that there is
Something right outside time & place, which
did not create matter, as the Christians say, but
is matter's great enemy: and that Beauty is the
call of the spirit in that something to the spirit
in us. You see how frankly I admit that my
views have changed.

89
Beauty
The Weight of Glory,
"The Weight of Glory"
(1942), para. 13,
pp. 16–17.

God has given us the Morning Star already: you
can go and enjoy the gift on many fine
mornings if you get up early enough. What
more, you may ask, do we want? Ah, but we
want so much more—something the books on
aesthetics take little notice of. But the poets and
the mythologies know all about it. We do not
want merely to *see* beauty, though, God knows,
even that is bounty enough. We want something
else which can hardly be put into words—to be
united with the beauty we see, to pass into it,
to receive it into ourselves, to bathe in it, to
become part of it. That is why we have peopled
air and earth and water with gods and

goddesses and nymphs and elves—that, though we cannot, yet these projections can, enjoy in themselves that beauty, grace, and power of which Nature is the image. That is why the poets tell us such lovely falsehoods. They talk as if the west wind could really sweep into a human soul; but it can't. They tell us the "beauty born of murmuring sound" will pass into a human face; but it won't. Or not yet. For if we take the imagery of Scripture seriously, if we believe that God will one day *give* us the Morning Star and cause us to *put on* the splendour of the sun, then we may surmise that both the ancient myths and the modern poetry, so false as history, may be very near the truth as prophecy. At present we are on the outside of the world, the wrong side of the door. We discern the freshness and purity of morning, but they do not make us fresh and pure. We cannot mingle with the splendours we see. But all the leaves of the New Testament are rustling with the rumour that it will not always be so. Some day, God willing, we shall get *in*.

90
**Beethoven,
Ludwig van**
The Letters of C. S.
Lewis to Arthur Greeves
(December? 1935),
p. 475.

How *tonic* Beethoven is, and how festal—one has the feeling of having taken part in the revelry of giants.

91
Belief
A Grief Observed,
chap. 2, para. 9, p. 25.

[Lewis was grieving the death of his wife:] You never know how much you really believe anything until its truth or falsehood becomes a matter of life and death to you. It is easy to say you believe a rope to be strong and sound as

---

long as you are merely using it to cord a box. But suppose you had to hang by that rope over a precipice. Wouldn't you then first discover how much you really trusted it? . . . Only a real risk tests the reality of a belief.

92
Belief,
Christian
Miracles, chap. 7,
para. 12, p. 51.

Christianity does not involve the belief that all things were made for man. It does involve the belief that God loves man and for his sake became man and died.

93
Belief,
Christian
Mere Christianity, bk.
II, chap. 4, para. 5,
p. 58.

We are told that Christ was killed for us, that His death has washed out our sins, and that by dying He disabled death itself. That is the formula. That is Christianity. That is what has to be believed.

94
Bereavement
A Severe Mercy, Letter
to Sheldon Vanauken
(10 February 1955),
pp. 183–184.

I am sure it is never sadness—a proper, straight natural response to loss—that does people harm, but all the other things, all the resentment, dismay, doubt and self-pity with wh. it is usually complicated. I feel (indeed I tried to say something about it in that lost letter) v. strongly what you say about the "curious consolation" that "nothing now can mar" your joint lives. I sometimes wonder whether bereavement is not, at bottom, the easiest and least perilous of the ways in wh. men lose the happiness of youthful love. For I believe it must *always* be lost in some way: every merely natural love has to be crucified before it can achieve resurrection and the happy *old* couples have come through a difficult death and re-birth. But far more have missed the re-birth.

95
Bereavement
A Severe Mercy, Letter
to Sheldon Vanauken,
6 April 1955, p. 189.

Forgive me for suggesting that the form "what
Jean would have liked" could come to have its
dangers. The real question is what she wills
now; and you may be sure her will is now one
with God's. A "sovereignty in the pluperfect
subjunctive" is often a snare. The danger is that
of confusing your love for her (gradually—as the
years pass) with your love for a period in your
own past; and of trying to preserve the past in a
way in wh. it can't be preserved. Death—
corruption—resurrection is the true rhythm: not
the pathetic, horrible practice of mummification.
Sad you must be at present. You can't develop a
false sense of a duty to cling to sadness if—and
when, for *nature* will not preserve any
psychological state forever—sadness begins to
vanish. There is great good in bearing sorrow
patiently: I don't know that there is any virtue
in sorrow just as such. It is a Christian duty, as
you know, for everyone to be as happy as he
can.

96
Bereavement
A Severe Mercy, Letter
to Sheldon Vanauken
(23 September 1960),
p. 229.

My great recent discovery is that when I mourn
Joy least I feel nearest to her. Passionate sorrow
cuts us off from the dead.

97
Bereavement
A Grief Observed, chap.
3, para. 3, 5, pp. 42–44.

[Lewis was grieving the death of his wife:] Of
course it is different when the thing happens to
oneself, not to others, and in reality, not in
imagination. Yes; but should it, for a sane man,
make quite such a difference as this? No. And it
wouldn't for a man whose faith had been real
faith and whose concern for other people's
sorrows had been real concern. The case is too
plain. If my house has collapsed at one blow,

that is because it was a house of cards. The faith which "took these things into account" was not faith but imagination. The taking them into account was not real sympathy. If I had really cared, as I thought I did, about the sorrows of the world, I should not have been so overwhelmed when my own sorrow came. . . .

And I must surely admit—H. [his wife] would have forced me to admit in a few passes—that, if my house was a house of cards, the sooner it was knocked down the better. And only suffering could do it.

98
Bereavement
A Grief Observed, chap. 3, para. 12, pp. 47–48.

What sort of a lover am I to think so much about my affliction and so much less about hers? Even the insane call, "Come back," is all for my own sake. I never even raised the question whether such a return, if it were possible, would be good for her. I want her back as an ingredient in the restoration of *my* past. Could I have wished her anything worse? Having got once through death, to come back and then, at some later date, have all her dying to do over again? They call Stephen the first martyr. Hadn't Lazarus the rawer deal?

99
Bereavement
A Grief Observed, chap. 3, para. 40, pp. 63–64.

Bereavement is not the truncation of married love but one of its regular phases—like the honeymoon. What we want is to live our marriage well and faithfully through that phase too. If it hurts (and it certainly will) we accept the pains as a necessary part of this phase.

100
Bereavement
Poems, "Joys That Sting" (1st pub. 1964), p. 108.

Oh doe not die, says Donne, *for I shall hate
All women so.* How false the sentence rings.
Women? But in a life made desolate
It is the joys once shared that have the stings.

101
Bereavement
Poems, "Five Sonnets (2)" (1st pub. 1964), p. 126.

There's a repose, a safety (even a taste
Of something like revenge?) in fixed despair
Which we're forbidden. . . .
For one bereavement makes us more bereft.
It asks for all we have, to the last shred;
Read Dante, who had known its best and
    worst—
He was bereaved and he was comforted
—No one denies it, comforted—but first
Down to the frozen centre, up the vast
Mountain of pain, from world to world, he
    passed.

102
Bible as
Literature
Selected Literary Essays, "The Literary Impact of the Authorised Version" (1950), para. 2, pp. 126–127.

There is a certain sense in which "the Bible as literature" does not exist. It is a collection of books so widely different in period, kind, language, and aesthetic value, that no common criticism can be passed on them. . . . But when we turn from the originals to any version made by one man, or at least bearing the stamp of one age, a certain appearance of unity creeps in. The Septuagint, the Vulgate, Luther's Bible, or the Authorised Version, can each perhaps be regarded as a book.

103
Bible as
Literature
Selected Literary Essays, "The Literary Impact of the Authorised Version" (1950), para. 39, p. 142.

It may be asked whether now, when only a minority of Englishmen regard the Bible as a sacred book, we may anticipate an increase of its literary influence. I think we might if it continued to be widely read. But this is not very likely. Our age has, indeed, coined the expression "the Bible as literature." It is very generally implied that those who have rejected its theological pretensions nevertheless continue to enjoy it as a treasure house of English prose. It may be so. There may be people who, not having been forced upon familiarity with it by believing parents, have yet been drawn to it by its literary charms and remained as constant readers. But I never happen to meet them. Perhaps it is because I live in the provinces. But I cannot help suspecting, if I may make an Irish bull, that those who read the Bible as literature do not read the Bible.

104
Bible as Literature

Selected Literary Essays, "The Literary Impact of the Authorised Version" (1950), para. 42, p. 144.

Inevitably we ask whether any of these [literary tastes] is likely to be favourable to a literary appreciation of the Bible. Stripped (for most readers) of its divine authority, stripped of its allegorical senses, denied a romantic welcome for its historical sense, will it none the less return on the wave of some new fashion to literary pre-eminence and be read? And of course we do not know. I offer my guess. I think it very unlikely that the Bible will return as a book unless it returns as a sacred book. . . . Unless the religious claims of the Bible are again acknowledged, its literary claims will, I think, be given only "mouth honour" and that decreasingly. For it is, through and through, a sacred book. Most of its component parts were written, and all of them were brought together, for a purely religious purpose. It contains good literature and bad literature. But even the good literature is so written that we can seldom disregard its sacred character. . . . Neither Aeschylus nor even Virgil tacitly prefaces his poetry with the formula "Thus say the gods." But in most parts of the Bible everything is implicitly or explicitly introduced with "Thus saith the Lord." It is, if you like to put it that way, not merely a sacred book but a book so remorselessly and continuously sacred that it does not invite, it excludes or repels, the merely aesthetic approach. . . . It demands incessantly to be taken on its own terms: it will not continue to give literary delight very long except to those who go to it for something quite different. I predict that it will in the future be read as it always has been read, almost exclusively by Christians.

105
Bible,
Essence of the
Letters of C. S. Lewis
(8 November 1952),
p. 247.

It is Christ Himself, not the Bible, who is the true word of God. The Bible, read in the right spirit and with the guidance of good teachers, will bring us to Him.

106
Bible:
Inspiration
Selected Literary Essays,
"The Literary Impact of
the Authorized Version"
(1950), para. 2, p. 127.

A belief in strictly verbal inspiration will indeed make all Scripture a book by a single Author. Hence Donne in his seventy-ninth sermon rather comically passes favorable judgement on the style of the Omnipotent, assuring us that "the Holy Ghost is an eloquent author, a vehement and an abundant author, but yet not luxuriant."

107
Bible:
Inspiration
Letters of C. S. Lewis
(28 May 1952), para. 2,
p. 242.

Yes, Pascal does contradict several passages in Scripture and must be wrong.

108
Bible
Interpretation
Letters of C. S. Lewis (3
August 1953), para. 1,
p. 251.

I take it as a first principle that we must not interpret any one part of Scripture so that it contradicts other parts, and specially we must not use an apostle's teaching to contradict that of Our Lord.

109
Bible
Interpretation
Letters of C. S. Lewis (8 August 1953), para. 2–3, p. 253.

The two things one must *not* do are (a) to believe on the strength of Scripture or on any other evidence that God is in any way evil (In Him is no *darkness* at all) (b) to wipe off the slate any passage which seems to show that He is. Behind the shocking passage be sure there lurks some great truth which you don't understand. If one ever *does* come to understand it, one sees that it is good and just and gracious in ways we never dreamed of. Till then it must just be left on one side.

But why are baffling passages left in at all? Oh, because God speaks not only for us little ones but for the great sages and mystics who *experience* what we can only *read about,* and to whom all the words have therefore different (richer) contents. Would not a revelation which contained nothing that you and I did not understand, be for that very reason rather suspect? To a child it would seem a contradiction to say both that his parents made him and God made him, yet we see how both can be true.

110
Bible:
Modern
Translations
Letters of C. S. Lewis (9 May 1961), p. 299.

A modern translation is for most purposes far more useful than the Authorised Version.

111
Bible
Scholars
Miracles, chap. 17, para. 1, p. 164.

[And] when you turn from the New Testament to modern scholars, remember that you go among them as a sheep among wolves. Naturalistic assumptions, beggings of the question such as that which I noted on the first page of this book, will meet you on every side—even from the pens of clergymen.

112
Bible
Translation

God in the Dock,
"Modern Translations of
the Bible" (1947),
para. 2, pp. 229–230.

The only kind of sanctity that Scripture can lose (or, at least, New Testament scripture) by being modernized is an accidental kind which it never had for its writers or its earliest readers. The New Testament in the original Greek is not a work of literary art: it is not written in a solemn, ecclesiastical language, it is written in the sort of Greek which was spoken over the Eastern Mediterranean after Greek had become an international language and therefore lost its real beauty and subtlety. In it we see Greek used by people who have no real feeling for Greek words because Greek words are not the words they spoke when they were children. It is a sort of "basic" Greek; a language without roots in the soil, a utilitarian, commercial and administrative language. Does this shock us? It ought not to, except as the Incarnation itself ought to shock us. The same divine humility which decreed that God should become a baby at a peasant-woman's breast, and later an arrested field-preacher in the hands of the Roman police, decreed also that He should be preached in a vulgar, prosaic and unliterary language. If you can stomach the one, you can stomach the other. The Incarnation is in that sense an irreverent doctrine: Christianity, in that sense, an incurably irreverent religion.

113
Bible
Translation

God in the Dock,
"Modern Translations of
the Bible" (1947),
para. 3, pp. 230–231.

The truth is that if we are to have translation at all we must have periodical re-translation. There is no such thing as translating a book into another language once and for all, for a language is a changing thing. If your son is to have clothes it is no good buying him a suit once and for all: he will grow out of it and have to be re-clothed.

114
Bible Translation

English Literature in the Sixteenth Century, bk. II.I.II, para. 5, p. 206.

[Tyndale's and More's Bible translations] are equally tendentious in the sense that each presupposes a belief. In that sense all translations of scripture are tendentious: translation, by its very nature, is a continuous implicit commentary. It can become less tendentious only by becoming less of a translation.

115
Biography

The Letters of C. S. Lewis to Arthur Greeves (4 December 1932), p. 445.

It is a very consoling fact that so many books about real lives—biographies, autobiographies, letters etc.—give one such an impression of *happiness,* in spite of the tragedies they all contain. What could be more tragic than the main outlines of Lamb's or Cowper's lives? But as soon as you open the letters of either, and see what they were writing from day to day and what a relish they got out of it, you almost begin to envy them. Perhaps the tragedies of real life contain more consolation and fun and gusto than the comedies of literature?

116
Body

The Four Loves, chap. 5, para. 19–20, pp. 142–143.

Man has held three views of his body. First there is that of those ascetic Pagans who called it the prison or the "tomb" of the soul, and of Christians like Fisher to whom it was a "sack of dung," food for worms, filthy, shameful, a source of nothing but temptation to bad men and humiliation to good ones. Then there are the Neo-Pagans (they seldom know Greek), the nudists and the sufferers from Dark Gods, to whom the body is glorious. But thirdly we have the view which St. Francis expressed by calling his body "Brother Ass." All three may be—I am not sure—defensible; but give me St. Francis for my money.

Ass is exquisitely right because no one in his

senses can either revere or hate a donkey. It is a useful, sturdy, lazy, obstinate, patient, lovable and infuriating beast; deserving now the stick and now a carrot; both pathetically and absurdly beautiful. So the body. There's no living with it till we recognise that one of its functions in our lives is to play the part of buffoon.

117
Body and Spirit
Out of the Silent Planet, chap. 15, pp. 94–95.

"Body is movement. If it is at one speed, you smell something; if at another, you hear a sound; if at another you see a sight; if at another, you neither see nor hear nor smell, nor know the body in any way."

". . . If you made it faster and faster, in the end the moving thing would be in all places at once."

". . . That is the thing at the top of all bodies—so fast that it is at rest, so truly body that it has ceased being body at all. . . . The swiftest thing that touches our senses is light. We do not truly see light, we only see slower things lit by it, so that for us light is on the edge—the last thing we know before things become too swift for us. But the body of an *eldil* [spirit] is a movement swift as light; you may say its body is made of light, but not of that which is light for the *eldil*. His "light" is a swifter movement which for us is nothing at all; and what we call light is for him a thing like water, a visible thing, a thing he can touch and bathe in—even a dark thing when not illumined by the swifter. And what we call firm things— flesh and earth—seem to him thinner, and harder to see, than our light, and more like clouds, and nearly nothing. To us the *eldil* is a thin, half-real body that can go through walls and rocks: to himself he goes through them because he is solid and firm and they are like cloud. And what is true light to him and fills the heaven, so that he will plunge into the rays of the sun to refresh himself from it, is to us the black nothing in the sky at night."

118

Books

The Letters of C. S. Lewis to Arthur Greeves (16 November 1915), p. 87.

There is something awfully nice about reading a book again, with all the half-unconscious memories it brings back.

119

Books

The Letters of C. S. Lewis to Arthur Greeves (1 February 1916), p. 88.

You really lose a lot by never reading books again.

120

Books

The Letters of C. S. Lewis to Arthur Greeves (14 March 1916), p. 94.

When one has read a book, I think there is nothing so nice as discussing it with some one else—even though it sometimes produces rather fierce arguments.

121

Books

The Letters of C. S. Lewis to Arthur Greeves (10 January 1932), p. 435.

I know well from experience that state of mind in which one wants immediate and certain pleasure from a book, for nothing—i.e. without paying the price of that slight persistence, that almost imperceptible tendency *not* to go on, which, to be honest, nearly always accompanies the reading of [a] good book. Not only accompanies by the way, but (do you agree) actually makes part of the pleasure. A *little* sense of labour is necessary to all perfect pleasures I think: just as (to my palate at least) there is no really delicious taste without a touch of astringency—the "bite" in alcoholic drinks, the resistance to the teeth in nuts or meat, the tartness of fruit, the bitterness of mint sauce. The apple must not be *too* sweet, the cheese must not be *too* mild. Still, I know the other mood, when one wants a book of sheer pleasure.

122

Books

The Letters of C. S. Lewis to Arthur Greeves (February 1932), p. 438.

To enjoy a book like that thoroughly I find I have to treat it as a sort of hobby and set about it seriously. I begin by making a map on one of the end leafs: then I put in a genealogical tree or two. Then I put a running headline at the top of each page: finally I index at the end all the passages I have for any reason underlined. I often wonder—considering how people enjoy themselves developing photos or making scrapbooks—why so few people make a hobby of their reading in this way. Many an otherwise dull book which I had to read have I enjoyed in this way, with a fine-nibbed pen in my hand: one is *making* something all the time and a book so read acquires the charm of a toy without losing that of a book.

123

Books

The Letters of C. S. Lewis to Arthur Greeves (February 1932), p. 439.

I can't imagine a man really enjoying a book and reading it only once.

124

Books

The Letters of C. S. Lewis to Arthur Greeves (17 August 1933), p. 458.

Clearly one must read every good book at least once every ten years.

125
Books
*The Letters of C. S.
Lewis to Arthur Greeves*
(December 1935),
p. 474.

[Speaking of the *Faerie Queene:*] It must be a really great book because one can read it as a boy in one way, and then re-read it in middle life and get something very different out of it— and that to my mind is one of the best tests.

126
Books
*On Stories: and Other
Essays on Literature,*
"On Stories" (1947),
para. 24, p. 16.

An unliterary man may be defined as one who reads books once only. There is hope for a man who has never read Malory or Boswell or *Tristram Shandy* or Shakespeare's *Sonnets*: but what can you do with a man who says he "has read" them, meaning he has read them once, and thinks that this settles the matter?

127
Books
*An Experiment in
Criticism,* chap. 1,
para. 4, p. 2.

The sure mark of an unliterary man is that he considers "I've read it already" to be a conclusive argument against reading a work. . . . Those who read great works, on the other hand, will read the same work ten, twenty or thirty times during the course of their life.

128
Books
*An Experiment in
Criticism,* chap. 1,
para. 7, p. 3.

Scenes and characters from books provide them [the literary] with a sort of iconography by which they interpret or sum up their own experience.

129
Books
*Letters to Malcolm:
Chiefly on Prayer,*
chap. 2, para. 11, p. 12.

The more "up to date" the book is, the sooner it will be dated.

130
**Books,
Christian**
God in the Dock,
"Christian Apologetics"
(1945), para. 9, p. 93.

We must attack the enemy's line of communication. What we want is not more little books about Christianity, but more little books by Christians on other subjects—with their Christianity *latent*.

131
Bores
Letters of C. S. Lewis
(9 September 1929),
p. 136.

Consider how many bores whose history you know well after a short acquaintance, not because familiarity has in their case replaced intimacy but because they had nothing to say and would not be silent.

132
Bourgeoisie
Studies in Words (1960),
chap. 1, para. 39, p. 21.

All my life the epithet *bourgeois* has been, in many contexts, a term of contempt, but not for the same reason. When I was a boy—a *bourgeois* boy—it was applied to my social class by the class above it; *bourgeois* meant "not aristocratic, therefore vulgar." When I was in my twenties this changed. My class was now vilified by the class below it; *bourgeois* began to mean "not proletarian, therefore parasitic, reactionary." Thus it has always been a reproach to assign a man to that class which has provided the world with nearly all its divines, poets, philosophers, scientists, musicians, painters, doctors, architects, and administrators.

133
Bourgeoisie
Poems, "The Genuine Article" (1st pub. 1964), pp. 63–64.

You do not love the Bourgeoisie. . . .
You love the Proletariat, the thin, far-away
Abstraction which resembles any workman fed
On mortal food as closely as the shiny red
Chessknight resembles stallions when they stamp
    and neigh. . . .
Who, that can love nonentities, would choose
    the labour
Of loving the quotidian face and fact, his
    neighbour?

134
Bulverism
God in the Dock,
" 'Bulverism': or, the
Foundation of 20th
Century Thought"
(1944), para. 6–7,
pp. 273–274.

The modern method [of argument] is to assume
without discussion *that* he is wrong and then
distract his attention from this (the only real issue)
by busily explaining how he became so silly. In the
course of the last fifteen years I have found this
vice so common that I have had to invent a name
for it. I call it Bulverism. . . . Bulver assures us . . .
"that refutation is no necessary part of argument.
Assume that your opponent is wrong, and then
explain his error, and the world will be at your
feet. Attempt to prove that he is wrong or (worse
still) try to find out whether he is wrong or right,
and the national dynamism of our age will thrust
you to the wall."

. . . Bulverism is a truly democratic game in the
sense that all can play it all day long, and that it
gives no unfair privilege to the small and offensive
minority who reason.

135
Bunyan, John
Selected Literary Essays,
"The Vision of John
Bunyan" (1962),
para. 2–3, 18,
pp. 146, 151.

Allegory frustrates itself the moment the author
starts doing what could equally well be done in
a straight sermon or treatise. It is a valid form
only so long as it is doing what could not be
done at all, or done so well, in any other way.

But this fault is rare in Bunyan. . . . The
greater part of it is enthralling narrative or
genuinely dramatic dialogue. Bunyan stands with
Malory and Trollope as a master of perfect
naturalness in the mimesis of ordinary
conversation. . . . In dialogue Bunyan catches
not only the cadence of the speech but the tiny
twists of thought.

136
Bunyan, John
Selected Literary Essays,
"The Vision of John
Bunyan" (1962),
para. 21–23, p. 152.

Part of the unpleasant side of *The Pilgrim's
Progress* lies in the extreme narrowness and
exclusiveness of Bunyan's religious outlook. The
faith is limited "to one small sect and all are
damned beside." But I suppose that all who

read old books have learned somehow or other
to make historical allowances for that sort of
thing. Our ancestors all wrote and thought like
that. The insolence and self-righteousness which
now flourish most noticeably in literary circles
then found their chief expression in theology,
and this is no doubt a change for the better.
And one must remember that Bunyan was a
persecuted and slandered man.

For some readers the "unpleasant side" of *The
Pilgrim's Progress* will lie not so much in its
sectarianism as in the intolerable terror which is
never far away. . . . In my opinion the book
would be immeasurably weakened as a work of
art if the flames of Hell were not always
flickering on the horizon. . . . The urgency, the
harsh woodcut energy, the continual sense of
momentousness, depend on it.

137
Bureaucracy
The Screwtape Letters,
Preface, para. 17, p. x.

I live in the Managerial Age, in a world of
"Admin." The greatest evil is not now done in
those sordid "dens of crime" that Dickens loved
to paint. It is not even in concentration camps
and labour camps. In those we see its final
result. But it is conceived and ordered (moved,
seconded, carried, and minuted) in clean,
carpeted, warmed, and well-lighted offices, by
quiet men with white collars and cut fingernails
and smooth shaven cheeks who do not need to
raise their voice.

138
Bureaucracy
*Letters to an American
Lady* (5 July 1956),
para. 1, p. 58.

As some one says "The Devil used to try to
prevent people from doing good works, but he
has now learned a trick worth two of that: he
organises 'em instead."

139
Calvin, John
English Literature in the Sixteenth Century,
Introduction, para. 60, p. 42.

[In the sixteenth century] many surrendered to, all were influenced by, the dazzling figure of Calvin. It ought to be easier for us than for the nineteenth century to understand his attraction. He was a man born to be the idol of revolutionary intellectuals; an unhesitating doctrinaire, ruthless and efficient in putting his doctrine into practice. Though bred as a lawyer, he found time before he was thirty to produce the first text of the *Institutio* (1536) and never made any serious modification of its theory. By 1537 he was already at Geneva and the citizens were being paraded before him in bodies of ten to swear to a system of doctrine. . . . The moral severity of his rule laid the foundations of the meaning which the word "puritan" has since acquired. But this severity did not mean that his theology was, in the last resort, more ascetic than that of Rome. It sprang from his refusal to allow the Roman distinction between the life of "religion" and the life of the world.

140
Calvin, John:
Institutes
English Literature in the Sixteenth Century,
Introduction, para. 61, p. 43.

In it Calvin goes on from the original Protestant experience [of conversion] to build a system, to extrapolate, to raise all the dark questions and give without flinching the dark answers. It is, however, a masterpiece of literary form; and we may suspect that those who read it with most approval were troubled by the fate of predestined vessels of wrath just about as much as young Marxists in our own age are troubled by the approaching liquidation of the *bourgeoisie*. Had the word "sentimentality" been known to them, Elizabethan Calvinists would certainly have used it of any who attacked the *Institutio* as morally repulsive.

141
Cambridge/ Oxford
Letters to an American Lady (1 November 1954), p. 35.

Did I tell you I've been made a professor at Cambridge? I take up my duties on Jan. 1st at Magdalene College, Cambridge (Eng.). Note the difference in spelling. It means rather less work for rather more pay. And I think I shall like Magdalene [Cambridge] better than Magdalen [Oxford]. It's a tiny college (a perfect cameo architecturally) and they're so old fashioned, and pious, and gentle and conservative—unlike this leftist, atheist, cynical, hard-boiled, huge Magdalen. Perhaps from being the fogey and "old woman" here I shall become the *enfant terrible* there.

142
Capital Punishment
Mere Christianity, bk. III, chap. 7, para. 10, pp. 107–108.

We may kill if necessary, but we must not hate and enjoy hating. We may punish if necessary, but we must not enjoy it. . . . Even while we kill and punish we must try to feel about the enemy as we feel about ourselves—to wish that he were not bad, to hope that he may, in this world or another, be cured: in fact, to wish his good. That is what is meant in the Bible by loving him; wishing his good, not feeling fond of him nor saying he is nice when he is not.

**143
Capital
Punishment**
God in the Dock,
"Letters" (1961), letter
12, para. 4, p. 339.

Hanging is not a more irrevocable act than any
other. You can't bring an innocent man to life:
but neither can you give him back the years which
wrongful imprisonment has eaten.

**144
Catholicism
and
Protestantism**
The Allegory of Love,
chap. VII.III, para. 3,
p. 323.

When Catholicism goes bad it becomes the world-
old, world-wide *religio* of amulets and holy places
and priestcraft: Protestantism, in its corresponding
decay, becomes a vague mist of ethical platitudes.
Catholicism is accused of being much too like all
the other religions; Protestantism of being
insufficiently like a religion at all. Hence Plato,
with his transcendent Forms, is the doctor of
Protestants; Aristotle, with his immanent Forms,
the doctor of Catholics.

**145
Cats**
*Letters to an American
Lady* (31 July 1962),
p. 105.

Yes, it *is* strange that anyone should dislike cats.
But cats themselves are the worst offenders in this
respect. They very seldom seem to like one
another.

**146
Certainty**
Christian Reflections,
para. 22, p. 111.

[Speaking of historical inquiry:] We may not be
able to get certainty, but we can get probability,
and half a loaf is better than no bread.

**147
Chapman,
George**
*English Literature in the
Sixteenth Century,* bk.
III.III.III, para. 43–44,
pp. 513–516.

In 1598 Chapman achieved the work that he was
born to do; which was not, as he imagined,
translating Homer but finishing *Hero and
Leander.* The very idea of a poem begun by one
poet and ended by another is repugnant to
modern taste, and modern taste is usually
confirmed by the event. . . . Not so the *Hero and
Leander;* for there it so happens that the very

nature of the story utilizes the differing excellences of its two narrators and gets told between them better than either could have told it alone. . . . It is certain that Marlowe could not have done the tragic "waking" very well. Hero in her first love (as he had conceived love in his two Sestiads) is half an animal, half a goddess: Hero in her grief would have to have been a woman and Marlowe's women are uninteresting. Chapman, with the powers he had acquired by 1598, would indeed have done Marlowe's part, though not so well as Marlowe did it, yet better than Marlowe could have done his. . . . Any notion that Chapman is merely the dull moralist, playing skeleton at the Marlovian feast because he cannot relish it, is utterly mistaken. He knew well how Golden the "bubble" had been.

His business, however, was to tell how it broke. . . . Except for academic purposes the two parts, Marlowe's and Chapman's, should always be read together. Between them a great story is greatly told.

148
Character, Christian

God in the Dock,
"Answers to Questions
on Christianity" (1944),
ans. 12, p. 59.

Take the case of a sour old maid, who is a Christian, but cantankerous. On the other hand, take some pleasant and popular fellow, but who has never been to Church. Who knows how much more cantankerous the old maid might be if she were *not* a Christian, and how much more likeable the nice fellow might be if he *were* a Christian? You can't judge Christianity simply by comparing the *product* in these two people; you would need to know what kind of raw material Christ was working on in both cases.

149
Character, Personal

Essays Presented to Charles Williams, "On Stories," para. 12, p. 98.

No man would find an abiding strangeness on the Moon unless he were the sort of man who could find it in his own back garden.

150
Character, Personal

The Magician's Nephew, chap. 10, p. 125.

What you see and hear depends a good deal on where you are standing: it also depends on what sort of person you are.

151
Chastity

Mere Christianity, bk. III, chap. 5, para. 2, p. 89.

Chastity is the most unpopular of the Christian virtues. There is no getting away from it: the old Christian rule is, "Either marriage, with complete faithfulness to your partner, or else total abstinence."

152
Chaucer, Geoffrey

The Allegory of Love, chap. IV.II, para. 1, p. 161.

For many historians of literature, and for all general readers, the great mass of Chaucer's work is simply a background to the *Canterbury Tales,* and the whole output of the fourteenth century is simply a background to Chaucer.

153
Chaucer, Geoffrey

The Allegory of Love, chap. IV.II, para. 26, p. 196.

It is a lesson worth learning, how Chaucer can so triumphantly celebrate the flesh without becoming either delirious like Rossetti or pornographic like Ovid.

154
Chaucer, Geoffrey

The Allegory of Love, chap. IV.II, para. 27, p. 197.

Chaucer has few rivals, and no masters.

155

Chaucer, Geoffrey

The Allegory of Love, chap. IV.II, para. 27, p. 197.

Troilus is what Chaucer meant it to be—a great poem in praise of love. Here also, despite the tragic and comic elements, Chaucer shows himself, as in the *Book of the Duchesse,* the *Parlement,* and the *Canterbury Tales,* our supreme poet of happiness.

156

Chaucer, Geoffrey: *Parlement of Foules*

The Allegory of Love, chap. IV.II, para. 13, pp. 173–174.

Chaucer, whatever we may think of him, was not a "regular fellow," *un vrai businessman,* or a rotarian. He was a scholar, a courtier, and a poet, living in a highly subtle and sophisticated civilization. It is only natural that we, who live in an industrial age, should find difficulties in reading poetry that was written for a scholastic and aristocratic age. We must proceed with caution, lest our thick, rough fingers tear the delicate threads that we are trying to disentangle.

When these confusions have been removed, every reader who loves poetry may safely be alone with the *Parlement of Foules.* No such reader will misunderstand the mingling of beauty and comedy in this supremely happy and radiant work—a hearty and realistic comedy, and a beauty without effort or afterthought, like Mozartian music.

157

Chaucer, Geoffrey: *Troilus and Cryseide*

The Allegory of Love, chap. IV.II, para. 25, p. 195.

The end of *Troilus* is the great example in our literature of pathos pure and unrelieved. All is to be endured and nothing is to be done. The species of suffering is one familiar to us all, as the sufferings of Lear and Oedipus are not. All men have waited with ever-decreasing hope, day after day, for some one or for something that does not come, and all would willingly forget the experience.

158
Child Rearing
The Four Loves, chap. 3, para. 38, p. 76.

The maternal instinct . . . is a Gift-love, but one that needs to give; therefore needs to be needed. But the proper aim of giving is to put the recipient in a state where he no longer needs our gift. We feed children in order that they may soon be able to feed themselves; we teach them in order that they may soon not need our teaching. Thus a heavy task is laid upon this Gift-love. It must work towards its own abdication. We must aim at making ourselves superfluous. The hour when we can say "They need me no longer" should be our reward. But the instinct, simply in its own nature, has no power to fulfil this law. The instinct desires the good of its object, but not simply; only the good it can itself give. A much higher love—a love which desires the good of the object as such, from whatever source that good comes—must step in and help or tame the instinct before it can make the abdication.

159
Childhood
Surprised by Joy, chap. 1, para. 8, p. 10.

I am a product of long corridors, empty sunlit rooms, upstairs indoor silences, attics explored in solitude, distant noises of gurgling cisterns and pipes, and the noise of wind under the tiles. Also, of endless books. My father bought all the books he read and never got rid of any of them. There were books in the study, books in the drawing room, books in the cloakroom, books (two deep) in the great bookcase on the landing, books in a bedroom, books piled as high as my shoulder in the cistern attic, books of all kinds reflecting every transient stage of my parents' interest, books readable and unreadable, books suitable for a child and books most emphatically not. Nothing was forbidden me. In the seemingly endless rainy afternoons I took volume after volume from the shelves. I had always the same certainty of finding a book that was new to me as a man who walks into a field has of finding a new blade of grass.

160
Children
The Letters of C. S. Lewis to Arthur Greeves (December 1935), p. 476.

I theoretically hold that one ought to like children, but am shy with them in practice.

161
Children
The Abolition of Man, chap. 1, para. 11, p. 29.

I myself do not enjoy the society of small children: . . . I recognize this as a defect in myself.

162
Children's Literature
Of Other Worlds: Essays and Stories, "On Stories" (1947), para. 19, p. 15.

No book is really worth reading at the age of ten which is not equally (and often far more) worth reading at the age of fifty—except, of course, books of information. The only imaginative works we ought to grow out of are those which it would have been better not to have read at all.

163
Children's Literature
Of Other Worlds: Essays and Stories, "On Three Ways of Writing for Children" (1952), para. 7, p. 24.

I am almost inclined to set it up as a canon that a children's story which is enjoyed only by children is a bad children's story. The good ones last. A waltz which you can like only when you are waltzing is a bad waltz.

164
Children's Literature
Of Other Worlds: Essays and Stories, "Sometimes Fairy Stories May Say Best What's to Be Said" (1956), para. 12, p. 38.

It certainly is my opinion that a book worth reading only in childhood is not worth reading even then.

165
China

Letters: C. S. Lewis/Don Giovanni Calabria (7 January 1953), para. 1-2, p. 75.

There has come to hand that copy of *Friend* *(Oct.)* which contains your article on that Chinese disaster. I used myself to entertain many hopes for that nation, since the missionaries have served there for many years not unsuccessfully: now it is clear, as you write, that all is on the ebb. Many have reported to me too, in letters on this subject, many atrocities, nor was this misery absent from our thoughts and prayers.

But it did not happen, however, without sins on our part: for that justice and that care for the poor which (most mendaciously) the Communists advertise, we in reality ought to have brought about ages ago. But far from it: we Westerners preached Christ with our lips, with our actions we brought the slavery of Mammon. We are more guilty than the infidels: for to those that know the will of God and do it not, the greater the punishment. [Ed. note: Lewis later learned that he was mistaken about the authorship of the article.]

166
Chivalry

Present Concerns: Essays by C. S. Lewis, "The Necessity of Chivalry" (1940), para. 10, p. 16.

In short, there is still life in the tradition which the Middle Ages inaugurated. But the maintenance of that life depends, in part, on knowing that the knightly character is art not nature—something that needs to be achieved, not something that can be relied upon to happen. And this knowledge is specially necessary as we grow more democratic. In previous centuries the vestiges of chivalry were kept alive by a specialized class, from whom they spread to other classes partly by imitation and partly by coercion. Now, it seems, the people must either be chivalrous on its own resources, or else choose between the two remaining alternatives of brutality and softness. This is, indeed, part of the general problem of a classless society, which is too seldom mentioned. Will its *ethos* be a synthesis of what was best in all the classes, or a mere "pool" with the sediment of all and the virtues of none?

167
Choice
Perelandra, chap. 11, p. 150.

No sooner had he discovered that he would certainly try to kill the Un-man to-morrow than the doing of it appeared to him a smaller matter than he had supposed. He could hardly remember why he had accused himself of megalomania when the idea first occurred to him. It was true that if he left it undone, Maleldil [God] Himself would do some greater thing instead. In that sense, he stood for Maleldil: but no more than Eve would have stood for Him by simply not eating the apple, or than any man stands for Him in doing any good action. As there was no comparison in person, so there was none in suffering—or only such comparison as may be between a man who burns his finger putting out a spark and a fireman who loses his life in fighting a conflagration because that spark was not put out. He asked no longer "Why me?" It might as well be he as another. It might as well be any other choice as this. The fierce light which he had seen resting on this moment of decision rested in reality on all.

168
Christlikeness
Mere Christianity, bk. IV, chap. 8, para. 1, p. 166.

"Putting on Christ" . . . is not one among many jobs a Christian has to do; and it is not a sort of special exercise for the top class. It is the whole of Christianity. Christianity offers nothing else at all.

169
Christian Living
Mere Christianity, bk. II, chap. 5, para. 4, p. 64.

A live body is not one that never gets hurt, but one that can to some extent repair itself. In the same way a Christian is not a man who never goes wrong, but a man who is enabled to repent and pick himself up and begin over again after

---

each stumble—because the Christ-life is inside him, repairing him all the time, enabling him to repeat (in some degree) the kind of voluntary death which Christ Himself carried out.

170
Christian Living
Mere Christianity, bk. IV, chap. 4, para. 10, p. 153.

Now the whole offer which Christianity makes is this: that we can, if we let God have His way, come to share in the life of Christ. If we do, we shall then be sharing a life which was begotten, not made, which always has existed and always will exist. Christ is the Son of God. If we share in this kind of life we also shall be sons of God. We shall love the Father as He does and the Holy Ghost will arise in us. He came to this world and became a man in order to spread to other men the kind of life He has—by what I call "good infection." Every Christian is to become a little Christ. The whole purpose of becoming a Christian is simply nothing else.

171
Christian Perspective
Christian Reflections, "Christianity and Literature" (1939), chap. 1, para. 15, p. 10.

The Christian knows from the outset that the salvation of a single soul is more important than the production or preservation of all the epics and tragedies in the world.

172
Christian Year, The
Letters to an American Lady (15 April 1956), p. 54.

The complexity—the close texture—of all the great events in the Christian year impresses me more and more. Each is a window opening on the total mystery.

173
Christianity And

The Screwtape Letters,
Letter XXV, para. 1,
pp. 115–116.

[Senior devil Screwtape to junior devil Wormwood:] The real trouble about the set your patient is living in is that it is *merely* Christian. They all have individual interests, of course, but the bond remains mere Christianity. What we want, if men become Christians at all, is to keep them in the state of mind I call "Christianity And." You know—Christianity and the Crisis, Christianity and the New Psychology, Christianity and the New Order, Christianity and Faith Healing, Christianity and Psychical Research, Christianity and Vegetarianism, Christianity and Spelling Reform. If they must be Christians, let them at least be Christians with a difference. Substitute for the faith itself some Fashion with a Christian colouring. Work on their horror of the Same Old Thing.

174
Christianity and Comfort

Mere Christianity, bk. I,
chap. 5, para. 6, p. 39.

The Christian religion . . . does not begin in comfort; it begins in . . . dismay. . . . In religion, as in war and everything else, comfort is the one thing you cannot get by looking for it. If you look for truth, you may find comfort in the end: If you look for comfort you will not get either comfort or truth—only soft soap and wishful thinking to begin with and, in the end, despair.

175
Christianity and Controversy

God in the Dock, "On
the Reading of Old
Books" (1944), para. 3,
pp. 201–202.

The only safety is to have a standard of plain, central Christianity ("mere Christianity" as Baxter called it) which puts the controversies of the moment in their proper perspective. Such a standard can be acquired only from the old books. It is a good rule, after reading a new book, never to allow yourself another new one till you have read an old one in between. If that is too much for you, you should at least read one old one to every three new ones.

176
Christianity and Culture

Christian Reflections,
"Christianity and
Culture" (1940), para. 33,
p. 23.

Culture is a storehouse of the best (sub-Christian) values. These values are in themselves of the soul, not the spirit. But God created the soul. Its values may be expected, therefore, to contain some reflection or antepast of the spiritual values. They will save no man. They resemble the regenerate life only as affection resembles charity, or honour resembles virtue, or the moon the sun. But though "like is not the same," it is better than unlike. Imitation may pass into initiation. For some it is a good beginning. For others it is not; culture is not everyone's road into Jerusalem, and for some it is a road out.

177
Christianity and Its Detractors

The World's Last Night and Other Essays, "On Obstinacy in Belief"
(1955), para. 7, p. 18.

There is not one case against religion, but many. Some say, like Capaneus in Statius, that it is a projection of our primitive fears, *primus in orbe deos fecit timor:* others, with Euhemerus, that it is all a "plant" put up by wicked kings, priests, or capitalists; others, with Tylor, that it comes from dreams about the dead: others, with Frazer, that it is a by-product of agriculture; others, like Freud, that it is a complex; the moderns that it is a category mistake. I will never believe that an error against which so many and various defensive weapons have been found necessary was, from the outset, wholly lacking in plausibility. All this "post haste and rummage in the land" obviously implies a respectable enemy.

178
Christianity and Life-style

God in the Dock, "Man or Rabbit?" (1946), para. 2, p. 109.

If Christianity should happen to be true, then it is quite impossible that those who know this truth and those who don't should be equally well equipped for leading a good life. Knowledge of the facts must make a difference to one's actions.

179
Christianity and Literature

Surprised by Joy,
chap. 14, para. 3–5,
pp. 213–215.

All the books were beginning to turn against me. Indeed, I must have been as blind as a bat not to have seen, long before, the ludicrous contradiction between my theory of life and my actual experiences as a reader. George MacDonald had done more to me than any other writer; of course it was a pity he had that bee in his bonnet about Christianity. He was good *in spite of it.* Chesterton had more sense than all the other moderns put together; bating, of course, his Christianity. Johnson was one of the few authors whom I felt I could trust utterly; curiously enough, he had the same kink. Spenser and Milton by a strange coincidence had it too. Even among ancient authors the same paradox was to be found. The most religious (Plato, Aeschylus, Virgil) were clearly those on whom I could really feed. On the other hand, those writers who did not suffer from religion and with whom in theory my sympathy ought to have been complete—Shaw and Wells and Mill and Gibbon and Voltaire—all seemed a little thin; what as boys we called "tinny." It wasn't that I didn't like them. They were all (especially Gibbon) entertaining; but hardly more. There seemed to be no depth in them. They were too simple. The roughness and density of life did not appear in their books.

. . . The only non-Christians who seemed to me really to know anything were the Romantics; and a good many of them were dangerously tinged with something like religion, even at times with Christianity. The upshot of it all could nearly be expressed in a perversion of Roland's great line in the *Chanson—*

Christians are wrong, but all the rest are bores. The natural step would have been to inquire a little more closely whether the Christians were, after all, wrong.

180
Christianity and Social Good

The Screwtape Letters,
Letter XXIII,
pp. 108–109.

[God] will not be used as a convenience. Men or nations who think they can revive the Faith in order to make a good society might just as well think they can use the stairs of Heaven as a short cut to the nearest chemist's shop.

181
Christianity and Social Good

God in the Dock, "The Decline of Religion" (1946), para. 7, p. 220.

The decline of "religion" is no doubt a bad thing for the "World." By it all the things that made England a fairly happy country are, I suppose, endangered: the comparative purity of her public life, the comparative humanity of her police, and the possibility of some mutual respect and kindness between political opponents. But I am not clear that it makes conversions to Christianity rarer or more difficult: rather the reverse. It makes the choice more unescapable. When the Round Table is broken every man must follow either Galahad or Mordred: middle things are gone.

182
Christianity and Social Good

God in the Dock, "Some Thoughts" (1948), para. 2, p. 91.

[One looking at] Christian activities which are, in a sense, directed toward this present world . . . would find that this religion had, as a mere matter of historical fact, been the agent which preserved such secular civilisation as survived the fall of the Roman Empire; that to it Europe owes the salvation, in those perilous ages, of civilised agriculture, architecture, laws, and literacy itself. He would find that this same religion has always been healing the sick and caring for the poor; that it has, more than any other, blessed marriage; and that arts and philosophy tend to flourish in its neighbourhood.

183
Christianity and the Ancient World
The Allegory of Love,
chap. I.I, para. 8, p. 8.

That Christianity in a very general sense, by its insistence on compassion and on the sanctity of the human body, had a tendency to soften or abash the more extreme brutalities and flippancies of the ancient world in all departments of human life, and therefore also in sexual matters, may be taken as obvious.

184
Christianity and the Human Condition
Mere Christianity, bk. I, chap. 5, para. 4, p. 39.

When you have realised that our position is nearly desperate you will begin to understand what the Christians are talking about. They offer an explanation of how we got into our present state of both hating goodness and loving it. They offer an explanation of how God can be this impersonal mind at the back of the Moral Law and yet also a Person. They tell you how the demands of the law, which you and I cannot meet, have been met on our behalf, how God Himself becomes a man to save man from the disapproval of God.

185
Christianity and the Intellect
Mere Christianity, bk. III, chap. 2, para. 4, p. 75.

He [St. Paul] told us to be not only "as harmless as doves," but also "as wise as serpents." He [Christ] wants a child's heart, but a grown-up's head.

186
Christianity and Truth
God in the Dock, "Man or Rabbit?" (1946), para. 1, pp. 108–109.

Christianity is not a patent medicine. Christianity claims to give an account of *facts*—to tell you what the real universe is like. Its account of the universe may be true, or it may not, and once the question is really before you, then your natural inquisitiveness must make you want to know the answer. If Christianity is untrue, then no honest man will want to believe it, however helpful it might be: if it is true, every honest man will want to believe it, even if it gives him no help at all.

187
Christianity, Essence of
God in the Dock, "The Founding of the Oxford Socratic Club" (1942–1943), para. 5, p. 128.

Christianity is not merely what a man does with his solitude. It is not even what God does with His solitude. It tells of God descending into the coarse publicity of history and there enacting what can—and must—be talked about.

188
Christianity, Essence of
The Weight of Glory, "Is Theology Poetry?" (1944), para. 24, p. 92.

I believe in Christianity as I believe that the Sun has risen, not only because I see it, but because by it I see everything else.

189
Christianity, Essence of
God in the Dock, "Christian Apologetics" (1945), para. 23, p. 99.

Do not attempt to water Christianity down. There must be no pretence that you can have it with the Supernatural left out. So far as I can see Christianity is precisely the one religion from which the miraculous cannot be separated. You must frankly argue for supernaturalism from the very outset.

190
Christianity, Essence of
God in the Dock, "The Grand Miracle" (1945), para. 1, p. 80.

The Christian story is precisely the story of one grand miracle, the Christian assertion being that what is beyond all space and time, what is uncreated, eternal, came into nature, into human nature, descended into His own universe, and rose again, bringing nature up with Him. It is precisely one great miracle. If you take that away there is nothing specifically Christian left.

191
Christianity, Essence of
God in the Dock, "The Grand Miracle" (1945), para. 10, pp. 86–87.

[Christianity] is something telling me—well, what? Telling me that I must never, like the Stoics, say that death does not matter. Nothing is less Christian than that. Death which made Life Himself shed tears at the grave of Lazarus, and shed tears of blood in Gethsemane. This is an appalling horror; a stinking indignity. (You remember Thomas Browne's splendid remark: "I am not so much afraid of death, as ashamed of it.") And yet, somehow or other, infinitely good. Christianity does not simply affirm or simply deny the horror of death; it tells me something quite new about it. Again, it does not, like Nietzsche, simply confirm my desire to be stronger, or cleverer than other people. On the other hand, it does not allow me to say, "Oh, Lord, won't there be a day when everyone will be as good as everyone else?" In the same way, about vicariousness. It will not, in any way, allow me to be an exploiter, to act as a parasite on other people; yet it will not allow me any dream of living on my own. It will teach me to accept with glad humility the enormous sacrifice that others make for me, as well as to make sacrifices for others.

192
Christianity, Essence of
Mere Christianity, bk. I, chap. 5, para. 3–4, pp. 38–39.

If the universe is not governed by an absolute goodness, then all our efforts are in the long run hopeless. But if it is, then we are making ourselves enemies to that goodness every day, and are not in the least likely to do any better tomorrow, and so our case is hopeless again.

. . . Christianity tells people to repent and promises them forgiveness. It therefore has nothing (as far as I know) to say to people who do not know that they need any forgiveness. It is after you have realised that there is a real Moral Law, and a Power behind the law, and that you have broken that law and put yourself wrong with that Power—it is after all this, and not a moment sooner, that Christianity begins to talk. When you are sick, you will listen to the doctor.

193
**Christianity,
Essence of**
Mere Christianity, bk. II,
chap. 2, para. 3–5,
p. 47.

When you try to explain the Christian doctrine as it is really held by an instructed adult, they then complain that you are making their heads turn round and that it is all too complicated and that if there really were a God they are sure He would have made "religion" simple, . . . as if "religion" were something God invented, and not His statement to us of certain quite unalterable facts about His own nature.

Besides being complicated, reality, in my experience, is usually odd. It is not neat, not obvious, not what you expect. . . .

Reality, in fact, is usually something you could not have guessed. That is one of the reasons I believe Christianity.

194
**Christianity,
Essence of**
Mere Christianity, bk. II,
chap. 4, para. 3, p. 57.

The central Christian belief is that Christ's death has somehow put us right with God and given us a fresh start.

195
**Christianity:
Evidences**
A Severe Mercy, letter to
Sheldon Vanauken (23
December 1950),
p. 92.

I do not think there is a *demonstrative* proof (like Euclid) of Christianity, nor of the existence of matter, nor of the good will & honesty of my best & oldest friends. I think all three are (except perhaps the second) far more probable than the alternatives. The case for Xtianity in general is well given by Chesterton; and I tried to do something in my *Broadcast Talks.* As to *why* God doesn't make it demonstratively clear: are we sure that He is even interested in the kind of Theism which wd. be a compelled logical assent to a conclusive argument? Are *we* interested in it in personal matters? I demand from my friend a trust in my good faith which is *certain* without demonstrative proof. It wouldn't be confidence at all if he waited for rigorous proof. Hang it all, the very fairy-tales embody the truth. Othello believed in Desdemona's innocence when it was proved: but that was too late. Lear believed in Cordelia's love when it was proved: but that was too late. "His praise is lost who stays till all commend." The magnanimity, the generosity wh. will trust on a reasonable probability, is required of us. But supposing one believed and was wrong after all? Why, then you wd. have paid the universe a compliment it doesn't deserve. Your error wd. even so be more interesting & important than the reality. And yet how cd. that be? How cd. an idiotic universe have produced creatures whose mere dreams are so much stronger, better, subtler than itself?

196
Christianity: Evidences

The World's Last Night and Other Essays, "Religion and Rocketry" (1958), para. 27–29, p. 92.

We have been warned that *all but* conclusive evidence against Christianity, evidence that would deceive (if it were possible) the very elect, will appear with Antichrist.

And after that there will be wholly conclusive evidence on the other side.

But not, I fancy, till then on either side.

197
Christianity: Intellectual Honesty in Exploring

God in the Dock, "Man or Rabbit?" (1946?), para. 6–8, pp. 110–111.

The question before each of us is not "Can *someone* lead a good life without Christianity?" The question is, "Can *I*?" We all know there have been good men who were not Christians; men like Socrates and Confucius who had never heard of it, or men like J. S. Mill who quite honestly couldn't believe it. Supposing Christianity to be true, these men were in a state of honest ignorance or honest error. . . . But the man who asks me, "Can't I lead a good life without believing in Christianity?" is clearly not in the same position. If he hadn't heard of Christianity he would not be asking this question. If, having heard of it, and having seriously considered it, he had decided that it was untrue, then once more he would not be asking the question. The man who asks this question has heard of Christianity and is by no means certain that it may not be true. He is really asking, "Need I bother about it?" Mayn't I just evade the issue, just let sleeping dogs lie, and get on with being "good?" Aren't good intentions enough to keep me safe and blameless without knocking at that dreadful door and making sure whether there is, or isn't someone inside?'

. . . He is deliberately trying not to know whether Christianity is true or false, because he foresees endless trouble if it should turn out to be true. He is like the man who deliberately "forgets" to look at the notice board because, if he did, he might find his name down for some unpleasant duty. He is like the man who won't look at his bank account because he's afraid of what he might find there. He is like the man who won't go to the doctor when he first feels a mysterious pain, because he is afraid of what the doctor may tell him.

The man who remains an unbeliever for such reasons is not in a state of honest error. He is in a state of dishonest error, and that dishonestly will spread through all his thoughts and actions: a certain shiftiness, a vague worry in the background, a blunting of his whole mental edge, will result. He has lost his intellectual virginity. Honest rejection of Christ, however mistaken, will be forgiven and healed—"Whosoever shall speak a word against the Son of man, it shall be forgiven him" [Footnote: Luke xii.10]. But to *evade* the Son of Man, to look the other way, to pretend you haven't noticed, to become suddenly absorbed in something on the other side of the street, to leave the receiver off the telephone because it might be He who was ringing up, to leave unopened certain letters in a strange handwriting because they might be from Him— this is a different matter. You may not be certain yet whether you ought to be a Christian; but you do know you ought to be a Man, not an ostrich, hiding its head in the sand.

198

Christianity, Popular

Mere Christianity, bk. IV, chap. 1, para. 6–7, p. 137.

Is not the popular idea of Christianity simply this: that Jesus Christ was a great moral teacher and that if only we took his advice we might be able to establish a better social order and avoid another war? Now, mind you, that is quite true. But it tells you much less than the whole truth about Christianity and it has no practical importance at all.

. . . There has been no lack of advice for the last four thousand years. A bit more makes no difference.

199

Christmas

Letters to an American Lady (27 November 1953), p. 50.

I feel exactly as you do about the horrid commercial racket they have made out of Christmas. I send no cards and give no presents except to children.

200

Christmas

Letters to an American Lady (29 December 1958), p. 80.

Just a hurried line . . . to tell a story which puts the contrast between *our* feast of the Nativity and all this ghastly "Xmas" racket at its lowest. My brother heard a woman on a 'bus say, as the 'bus passed a church with a Crib outside it, "Oh Lor'! They bring religion into everything. Look— they're dragging it even into Christmas now!"

201
Christmas

Letters to an American Lady (22 December 1959), p. 88.

Let us . . . make a compact that, if we are both alive next year, whenever we write to one another it shall *not* be at Christmas time. That period is becoming a sort of nightmare to me—it means endless quill-driving!

202
Church Attendance

God in the Dock, "Answers to Questions on Christianity" (1944), ans. 16, pp. 61–62.

When I first became a Christian, about fourteen years ago, I thought that I could do it on my own, by retiring to my rooms and reading theology, and I wouldn't go to the churches and Gospel Halls; . . . I disliked very much their hymns, which I considered to be fifth-rate poems set to sixth-rate music. But as I went on I saw the great merit of it. I came up against different people of quite different outlooks and different education, and then gradually my conceit just began peeling off. I realized that the hymns (which were just sixth-rate music) were, nevertheless, being sung with devotion and benefit by an old saint in elastic-side boots in the opposite pew, and then you realize that you aren't fit to clean those boots. It gets you out of your solitary conceit.

203
Church Attendance

Letters of C. S. Lewis (7 December 1950), p. 224.

The New Testament does not envisage solitary religion; some kind of regular assembly for worship and instruction is everywhere taken for granted in the Epistles. So we must be regular practising members of the Church. Of course we differ in temperament. Some (like you—and me) find it more natural to approach God in solitude; but we must go to Church as well. For the Church is not a human society of people united by their natural affinities but the Body of Christ, in which all members, however different, (and He rejoices in their differences and by no means wishes to iron them out) must share the common life, complementing and helping one another precisely by their differences.

204

Church: Body of Christ

Mere Christianity, bk. IV, chap. 7, para. 7–8, p. 163.

He [Jesus] works on us in all sorts of ways: . . . through Nature, through our own bodies, through books, sometimes through experiences which seem (at the time) *anti*-Christian. . . . But above all, He works on us through each other.

Men are mirrors, or "carriers" of Christ to other men. Sometimes unconscious carriers.

205

Church: Diversity

Letters to Malcolm: Chiefly on Prayer, chap. 2, para. 3, p. 10.

It takes all sorts to make a world; or a church. This may be even truer of a church. If grace perfects nature it must expand all our natures into the full richness of the diversity which God intended when He made them, and Heaven will display far more variety than Hell. "One fold" doesn't mean "one pool." Cultivated roses and daffodils are no more alike than wild roses and daffodils.

206

Church: Divisions

Letters: C. S. Lewis/Don Giovanni Calabria (25 November 1947), para. 3, pp. 37, 39.

That the whole cause of schism lies in sin I do not hold to be certain. I grant that no schism is without sin but the one proposition does not necessarily follow the other. From your side Tetzel, from ours Henry VIII, were lost men: and, if you like, Pope Leo from your side and from ours Luther (although for my own part I would pass on both a lighter sentence). But what would I think of your Thomas More or of our William Tyndale? All the writings of the one and all the writings of the other I have lately read right through. Both of them seem to me most saintly men and to have loved God with their whole heart: I am not worthy to undo the shoes of either of them. Nevertheless they disagree and (what racks and astounds me) their disagreement seems to me to spring not from their vices nor from their ignorance but rather from their virtues and the depths of their faith, so that the more they were at their best the more they were at variance. I believe the judgement of God on their dissension is more profoundly hidden than it appears to you to be: for His judgements are indeed an abyss.

207

Church: Divisions

Letters: C. S. Lewis/Don Giovanni Calabria (25 November 1947), para. 5, pp. 39.

Disputations do more to aggravate schism than to heal it: united action, prayer, fortitude and (should God so will) united deaths for Christ—*these* will make us one.

208

Church: Divisions

Mere Christianity, Preface, para. 2, p. 6.

Our divisions should never be discussed except in the presence of those who have already come to believe that there is one God and that Jesus Christ is His only Son.

209

Church: Divisions

Letters: C. S. Lewis/Don Giovanni Calabria (10 August 1953), para. 1-3, p. 83.

Tomorrow I am crossing over (if God so have pleased) to Ireland: my birthplace and dearest refuge so far as charm of landscape goes, and temperate climate, although most dreadful because of the strife, hatred and often civil war between dissenting faiths.

There indeed both yours and ours [Catholic and Protestant] "know not by what Spirit they are led." They take lack of charity for zeal and mutual ignorance for orthodoxy.

I think almost all the crimes which Christians have perpetrated against each other arise from this, that religion is confused with politics. For, above all other spheres of human life, the Devil claims politics for his own, as almost the citadel of his power. Let us, however, with mutual prayers pray with all our power for that charity which "covers a multitude of sins."

210

**Church:
Endurance**

The Weight of Glory,
"Membership" (1945),
para. 16, p. 116.

The Church will outlive the universe; in it the individual person will outlive the universe. Everything that is joined to the immortal Head will share His immortality.

211

**Church:
Function**

Mere Christianity, bk. IV,
chap. 7, para. 8, p. 163.

Usually it is those who know Him that bring Him to others. That is why the Church, the whole body of Christians showing Him to one another, is so important.

212

**Church:
Function**

Mere Christianity, bk. IV,
chap. 8, para. 10,
pp. 169–170.

It is so easy to think that the Church has a lot of different objects—education, building, missions, holding services. . . . The Church exists for nothing else but to draw men into Christ, to make them little Christs. If they are not doing that, all the cathedrals, clergy, missions, sermons, even the Bible itself, are simply a waste of time. God became Man for no other purpose. It is even doubtful, you know, whether the whole universe was created for any other purpose.

213

**Church
History**

The Four Loves, chap. 2,
para. 43, p. 49.

[A] sort of love . . . can also be felt for bodies that claim more than a natural affection: for a Church or (alas) a party in a Church, or for a religious order. This terrible subject would require a book to itself. Here it will be enough to say that the Heavenly Society is also an earthly society. Our (merely natural) patriotism towards the latter can very easily borrow the transcendent claims of the former and use them to justify the most abominable actions. If ever the book which I am not going to write is written it must be the full confession by Christendom of Christendom's specific contribution to the sum of human cruelty and treachery. Large areas of "the World" will not hear us till we have publicly disowned much of our past. Why should they? We have shouted the name of Christ and enacted the service of Moloch.

214
Church Music

Christian Reflections,
"On Church Music"
(1949), para. 9–10,
pp. 96–97.

There are two musical situations on which I think we can be confident that a blessing rests. One is where a priest or an organist, himself a man of trained and delicate taste, humbly and charitably sacrifices his own (aesthetically right) desires and gives the people humbler and coarser fare than he would wish, in a belief (even, as it may be, the erroneous belief) that he can thus bring them to God. The other is where the stupid and unmusical layman humbly and patiently, and above all silently, listens to music which he cannot, or cannot fully, appreciate, in the belief that it somehow glorifies God, and that if it does not edify him this must be his own defect. Neither such a High Brow nor such a Low Brow can be far out of the way. To both, Church Music will have been a means of grace: not the music they have liked, but the music they have disliked. They have both offered, sacrificed, their taste in the fullest sense. But where the opposite situation arises, where the musician is filled with the pride of skill or the virus of emulation and looks with contempt on the unappreciative congregation, or where the unmusical, complacently entrenched in their own ignorance and conservatism, look with the restless and resentful hostility of an inferiority complex on all who would try to improve their taste—there, we may be sure, all that both offer is unblessed and the spirit that moves them is not the Holy Ghost.

These highly general reflections will not, I fear, be of much practical use to any priest or organist in devising a working compromise for a particular church. The most they can hope to do is to suggest that the problem is never a merely musical one. Where both the choir and the congregation are spiritually on the right road no insurmountable difficulties will occur. Discrepancies of taste and capacity will, indeed, provide matter for mutual charity and humility.

215
Church: Unity
God in the Dock,
"Answers to Questions on Christianity" (1944), ans. 14, p. 60.

The time is always ripe for re-union. Divisions between Christians are a sin and a scandal, and Christians ought at all times to be making contributions toward re-union, if it is only by their prayers.

216
Church: Unity
Mere Christianity,
Preface, para. 9, p. 9.

It is at her centre, where her truest children dwell, that each communion is really closest to every other in spirit, if not in doctrine. And this suggests at the centre of each there is something, or a Someone, who against all divergences of belief, all differences of temperament, all memories of mutual persecution, speaks with the same voice.

217
Church: Unity
Mere Christianity, bk. III, chap. 3, para. 4, p. 80.

Christianity is the total plan for the human machine. We have all departed from that total plan in different ways, and each of us wants to make out that his own modification of the original plan is the plan itself. You will find this again and again about anything that is really Christian: every one is attracted by bits of it and wants to pick out those bits and leave the rest. That is why we do not get much further: and that is why people who are fighting for quite opposite things can both say they are fighting for Christianity.

218
Church of England
Christian Reflections, "Modern Theology and Biblical Criticism" (1959), para. 36, p. 166.

Once the layman was anxious to hide the fact that he believed so much less than the Vicar: he now tends to hide the fact that he believes so much more. Missionary to the priests of one's own church is an embarrassing role; though I have a horrid feeling that if such mission work is not soon undertaken the future history of the Church of England is likely to be short.

219
Circumstances
The Allegory of Love, chap. II.III, para. 1. p. 56.

Conditions . . . are not causes.

220
Civilization
Rehabilitations, "Our English Syllabus" (1st pub. 1939), para. 2, pp. 82–83.

One of the most dangerous errors instilled into us by nineteenth-century progressive optimism is the idea that civilization is automatically bound to increase and spread. The lesson of history is the opposite; civilization is a rarity, attained with difficulty and easily lost. The normal state of humanity is barbarism, just as the normal surface of our planet is salt water. Land looms large in our imagination of the planet and civilization in our history books, only because sea and savagery are, to us, less interesting. And if you press to know what I mean by civilization, I reply "Humanity," by which I do not mean kindness so much as the realization of the human idea.

Human life means to me the life of beings for whom the leisured activities of thought, art, literature, conversation are the end, and the preservation and propagation of life merely the means. That is why education seems to me so important: it actualizes that potentiality for leisure, if you like for amateurishness, which is man's prerogative. You have noticed, I hope, that man is the only amateur animal; all the others are professionals. They have no leisure and do not desire it. When the cow has finished eating she chews the cud; when she has finished chewing she sleeps; when she has finished sleeping she eats again. She is a machine for turning grass into calves and milk—in other words, for producing more cows. The lion cannot stop hunting, nor the beaver building dams, nor the bee making honey. When God made the beasts dumb He saved the world from infinite boredom, for if they could speak they would all of them, all day, talk nothing but shop.

221

Civilization

The Abolition of Man,
Intro. to Appendix,
p. 96.

It is by no means certain that there has ever (in the sense required) been more than one civilization in all history. It is at least arguable that every civilization we find has been derived from another civilization and, in the last resort, from a single centre—"carried" like an infectious disease or like the Apostolical succession.

222

Clergy

Mere Christianity, bk. III,
chap. 3, para. 3, p. 79.

The clergy are those particular people within the whole Church who have been specially trained and set aside to look after what concerns us as creatures who are going to live for ever.

223
Cliques

The Screwtape Letters,
Letter VII, pp. 33–34.

[Senior devil Screwtape to junior devil Wormwood:] Some ages are lukewarm and complacent, and then it is our business to soothe them yet faster asleep. Other ages, of which the present is one, are unbalanced and prone to faction, and it is our business to inflame them. Any small coterie, bound together by some interest which other men dislike or ignore, tends to develop inside itself a hothouse mutual admiration, and towards the outer world, a great deal of pride and hatred which is entertained without shame because the "Cause" is its sponsor and it is thought to be impersonal. Even when the little group exists originally for the Enemy's own purposes, this remains true. We want the Church to be small not only that fewer men may know the Enemy but also that those who do may acquire the uneasy intensity and the defensive self-righteousness of a secret society or a clique.

224
Colet, John

English Literature in the Sixteenth Century, bk. II.I.I, para. 2–4, pp. 158–160.

Colet is, in fact, a declamatory moralist. By calling him declamatory I do not at all mean that he is insincere, but that his methods are those of the declamation; repetition, hyperbole, and a liberal use of emotional adjectives. The morality he wishes to enforce is harsh and ascetic. . . . The truth is that Colet is a Platonist at heart and has really little interest in the temporal and mutable world below the moon. . . . A cloistered perfectionist, who happens to be also a rhetorician, often says, not exactly more than he means, but more than he understands. He leaves out the reservations: he has really no idea of the crudely literal applications which will be made. . . .

Colet has two other characters besides that of the moralist; he has an important place in the history of Biblical studies and he is the most virulent of the humanists. In the first capacity he is one of those who helped to banish the old allegorical methods of interpretation, at least as regards the New Testament, and made some attempt to see the Pauline epistles in their real historical setting. . . . In his capacity of humanist we see Colet at his worst. . . . The spirit of the classical writers was to be avoided like the plague and their form to be imposed as an indispensable law. When Colet founded St. Paul's School this extraordinary position was embodied in its statutes. The boys were to be guarded from every word that did not occur in Virgil or Cicero, and equally from every idea that did. As an inevitable result, their fare was to be Lactantious, Prudentius, Sedulius, Mantuan, and Erasmus. No more deadly and irrational scheme could have been propounded—deadly, because it cuts the boys off from nearly all the best literature that existed in Latin, and irrational because it puts an arbitrary value on certain formal elements dissociated from the spirit which begot them and for whose sake they existed.

225
Comedy
Selected Literary Essays,
"A Note on Jane Austen" (1954), para. 19, p. 185.

[Speaking of Jane Austen:] The hard core of morality and even of religion seems to me to be just what makes good comedy possible. . . . Where there is no norm, nothing can be ridiculous, except for a brief moment of unbalanced provincialism in which we may laugh at the merely unfamiliar. Unless there is something about which the author is never ironical, there can be no true irony in the work.

226
Commitment

Poems, "Pindar Sang"
(1949), para. 3, p. 16.

"But we are tethered to Hope that will promise
    anything without blushing,
And the flowing water of foreknowledge is far
    away beyond our reach.
Therefore neither ashore nor in the hollow ships
    will any praise
Be given to an act on which the doer does not
    stake his life."

227
Common People

Spirits in Bondage, "In
Praise of Solid People,"
part II, poem XXIV,
pp. 62–63.

Thank God that there are solid folk . . .
Who feel the things that all men feel
And think in well-worn grooves of thought
Whose honest spirits never reel
Before man's mystery, overwrought.
Yet not unfaithful nor unkind
With work-day virtues surely staid
Theirs is the sane and humble mind
And dull affections undismayed.
O happy people! I have seen
No verse yet written in your praise
And, truth to tell, the time has been
I would have scorned your easy ways.
But now thro' weariness and strife
I learn your worthiness indeed
The world is better for such life
As stout, suburban people lead.

228
Common People

*Present Concerns: Essays
by C. S. Lewis,* "Private.
Bates" (1944), para. 9,
p. 49.

We must get rid of our arrogant assumption that it
is the masses who can be led by the nose. As far
as I can make out, the shoe is on the other foot.
The only people who are really the dupes of their
favourite newspapers are the *intelligentsia.* It is
they who read leading articles: the poor read the
sporting news, which is mostly true.

229
Communism
Letters of C. S. Lewis
(17 January 1940), p.
176.

Fascism and Communism, like all other evils, are
potent because of the good they contain or
imitate. . . . And of course their occasion is the
failure of those who left humanity starved of that
particular good. This does not for me alter the
conviction that they are very bad indeed. One of
the things we must guard against is the
penetration of both into Christianity—availing
themselves of that very truth you have suggested
and I have admitted. Mark my words: you will
presently see both a Leftist and a Rightist pseudo-
theology developing—the abomination will stand
where it ought not.

230
Companionship
That Hideous Strength,
chap. 7, Section 2,
p. 148.

Those who are enjoying something, or suffering
something together, are companions. Those who
enjoy or suffer one another, are not.

231
Comparisons
A Severe Mercy, Letter to
Sheldon Vanauken (14
December 1950),
pp. 89–90.

I don't agree with your picture of the history of
religion—Christ, Buddha, Mohammed and others
elaborating an original simplicity. I believe
Buddhism to be a simplification of Hinduism and
Islam to be a simplification of Xtianity. Clear,
lucid, transparent, simple religion (Tao *plus* a
shadowy, ethical god in the background) is a late
development, usually arising among highly
educated people in great cities. What you really
start with is ritual, myth, and mystery, the death
& return of Balder or Osiris, the dances, the
initiations, the sacrifices, the divine kings. Over
against that are the Philosophers, Aristotle or
Confucius, hardly religious at all. The only two
systems in which the mysteries and the
philosophies come together are Hinduism &

Xtianity: there you get both Metaphysics and Cult (continuous with the primeval cults). That is why my first step was to be sure that one or other of these had the answer. For the reality can't be one that appeals *either* only to savages *or* only to high brows. Real things aren't like that (e.g. *matter* is the first most obvious thing you meet—milk, chocolates, apples, and also the object of quantum physics). There is no question of just a crowd of disconnected religions. The choice is between (a.) The materialist world picture: wh. I *can't* believe. (b.) The real archaic primitive religions: wh. are not moral enough. (c.) The (claimed) fulfilment of these in Hinduism. (d.) The claimed fulfilment of these in Xtianity. But the weakness of Hinduism is that it *doesn't* really join the two strands. Unredeemably savage religion goes on in the village; the hermit philosophises in the forest: and neither really interferes with the other. It is only Xtianity wh. compels a high brow like me to partake in a ritual blood feast, and also compels a central African convert to attempt an enlightened universal code of ethics.

Have you tried Chesterton's *The Everlasting Man?* the best popular apologetic I know.

Meanwhile, the attempt to practice the *Tao* is certainly the right line. Have you read the *Analects* of Confucius? He ends up by saying "This is the Tao. I do not know if any one has ever kept it." That's significant: one can really go direct from there to the *Epistle to the Romans.*

232
Conscience
A Preface to "Paradise Lost," chap. 2, para. 4, p. 11.

Disobedience to conscience makes conscience blind. . . . The moral blindness consequent on being a bad man must therefore fall on every one who is not a good man.

233
Conscience
Letters to an American Lady (21 March 1955), p. 40.

We were talking about cats and dogs the other day and decided that both have consciences but the dog, being an honest, humble person, always has a bad one, but the cat is a Pharisee and always has a good one. When he sits and stares you out of countenance he is thanking God that he is not as these dogs, or these humans, or even as these other cats!

234
Contentment
The Letters of C. S. Lewis to Arthur Greeves (31 January 1917), para. 8, p. 161.

Nobody who gets enough food and clothing in a world where most are hungry and cold has any business to talk about "misery."

235
Contentment
Out of the Silent Planet, chap. 12, p. 74.

Every day in a life fills the whole life with expectation and memory.

236
Contentment
Letters: C. S. Lewis/Don Giovanni Calabria (13 January 1948), para. 1, p. 41.

Recently (although the outward condition of my life has not changed for the better) it has pleased God to pour into my soul great tranquillity—I may even say gaiety. I give thanks not without apprehension as one who keeps firmly in mind that salutary observation in *The Imitation of Christ* "remember in Grace what you would be without Grace." Would that we had attained to everlasting constancy with no shadow of turning!

237
Contentment
Poems, "Pindar Sang" (1949), para. 5, p. 17.

Of unattainable longings sour is the fruit.

238
Conversion
See also eternal life, redemption, salvation.

The Letters of C. S. Lewis to Arthur Greeves (22 December 1929), para. 3, pp. 319–320.

I should like to know, too, in general, what you think of all the darker side of religion as we find it in old books. Formerly I regarded it as mere devil worship based on horrible superstitions. Now that I have found, and am still finding more and more, the element of truth in the old beliefs, I feel I cannot dismiss even their dreadful side so cavalierly. There must be something in it: only what?

239
Conversion
Letters of C. S. Lewis (1930?), para. 1, p. 141.

Terrible things are happening to me. The "Spirit" or "Real I" is showing an alarming tendency to become much more personal and is taking the offensive, and behaving just like God. You'd better come on Monday at the latest or I may have entered a monastery.

240
Conversion
The Letters of C. S. Lewis to Arthur Greeves (29 October 1930), para. 5, p. 395.

I have started going to morning Chapel at 8, wh. means going to bed earlier: and indeed I live such vigorous days that I am usually glad to go. My moral history of late has been deplorable. More and more clearly one sees how much of one's philosophy & religion is mere talk: the boldest hope is that concealed somewhere within it there is some seed however small of the real thing.

241
Conversion
The Letters of C. S. Lewis to Arthur Greeves (10 January 1931), para. 6, p. 401.

He [Lewis's brother Warren] and I even went together to Church twice: and—will you believe it—he said to me in conversation that he was beginning to think the religious view of things was after all true. Mind you (like me, at first) he didn't *want* it to be, nor like it: but his intellect is beginning to revolt from the semi-scientific assumptions we all grew up in, and the other explanation of the world seems to him daily more probable. Of course I have not had and probably never shall have any *real* talks on the heart of the subject with him. But it is delightful to feel the whole lot of us gradually beginning to move in that direction. It has done me good to be with him: because while his idea of the good is much lower than mine, he is in so many ways better than I am. I keep on crawling up to the heights & slipping back to the depths: he seems to do neither.

242

Conversion

The Letters of C. S. Lewis to Arthur Greeves (1 October 1931), para. 4, p. 425.

I have just passed on from believing in God to definitely believing in Christ—in Christianity. I will try to explain this another time. My long night talk with Dyson and Tolkien had a good deal to do with it.

243

Conversion

The Letters of C. S. Lewis to Arthur Greeves (18 October 1931), para. 3–6, pp. 426–428.

[Ed. note: Lewis converted to theism, belief in God, in 1929 and to Christianity in 1931.] About Christianity: . . . What has been holding me back (at any rate for the last year or so) has not been so much a difficulty in believing as a difficulty in knowing what the doctrine *meant*: you can't believe a thing while you are ignorant *what* the thing is. My puzzle was the whole doctrine of Redemption: in what sense the life and death of Christ "saved" or "opened salvation to" the world. I could see how miraculous salvation might be necessary: one could see from ordinary experience how sin (e.g. the case of a drunkard) could get a man to such a point that he was bound to reach Hell (i.e. complete degradation and misery) in this life unless something quite beyond mere natural help or effort stepped in. And I could well imagine a whole world being in the same state and similarly in need of miracle. What I couldn't see was how the life and death of Someone Else (whoever he was) 2000 years ago could help us here and now—except in so far as his *example*

helped us. And the example business, tho' true
and important, is not Christianity: right in the
centre of Christianity, in the Gospels and St Paul,
you keep on getting something quite different and
very mysterious expressed in those phrases I have
so often ridiculed ("propitiation"—"sacrifice"—
"the blood of the Lamb")—expressions wh. I cd.
only interpret in senses that seemed to me either
silly or shocking.

Now what Dyson and Tolkien showed me was
this: that if I met the idea of sacrifice in a Pagan
story I didn't mind it at all: again, that if I met the
idea of a god sacrificing himself to himself . . . I
liked it very much and was mysteriously moved by
it: again, that the idea of the dying and reviving
god (Balder, Adonis, Bacchus) similarly moved me
provided I met it anywhere *except* in the Gospels.
The reason was that in Pagan stories I was
prepared to feel the myth as profound and
suggestive of meanings beyond my grasp even tho'
I could not say in cold prose "what it meant."

Now the story of Christ is simply a true myth:
a myth working on us in the same way as the
others, but with this tremendous difference that *it
really happened*: and one must be content to
accept it in the same way, remembering that it is
God's myth where the others are men's myths: i.e.
the Pagan stories are God expressing Himself
through the minds of poets, using such images as
He found there, while Christianity is God
expressing Himself through what we call "real
things." Therefore it is *true,* not in the sense of
being a "description" of God (that no finite mind
could take in) but in the sense of being the way
in which God chooses to (or can) appear to our
faculties. The "doctrines" we get *out of* the true
myth are of course *less* true: they are translations
into our *concepts* and *ideas* of that wh. God has

CONVERSION   *Martindale & Root*
already expressed in a language more adequate,
namely the actual incarnation, crucifixion, and
resurrection. Does this amount to a belief in
Christianity? At any rate I am now certain (a)
That this Christian story is to be approached, in a
sense, as I approach the other myths. (b) That it is
the most important and full of meaning. I am also
nearly certain that it really happened.

244
Conversion
*The Letters of C. S.
Lewis to Arthur Greeves*
(8 November 1931),
para. 5, p. 430.

I, like you, am worried by the fact that the
spontaneous appeal of the Christian story is so
much less to me than that of Paganism. Both the
things you suggest (unfavourable associations from
early up-bringing and the corruption of one's
nature) probably are causes: but I have a sort of
feeling that *the* cause must be elsewhere, and I
have not yet discovered it. I think the thrill of the
Pagan stories and of romance may be due to the
fact that they are mere beginnings—the first, faint
whisper of the wind from beyond the world—
while Christianity is the thing itself: and no thing,
when you have really started on it, can have for
you then and there just the same thrill as the first
hint. For example, the experience of being married
and bringing up a family, cannot have the old
bittersweet of first falling in love. But it is futile
(and, I think, wicked) to go on trying to get the
old thrill again: you must go forward and not
backward. Any *real* advance will in its turn be
ushered in by a new thrill, different from the old:
doomed in its turn to disappear and to become in
its turn a temptation to retrogression. Delight is a
bell that rings as you set your foot on the first
step of a new flight of stairs leading upwards.
Once you have started climbing you will notice
only the hard work: it is when you have reached

122

the landing and catch sight of the new stair that you may expect the bell again. This is only an idea, and may be all rot: but it seems to fit in pretty well with the general law (thrills also must die to live) of autumn & spring, sleep and waking, death and resurrection, and "Whosoever loseth his life, shall save it." On the other hand, it may be simply part of our probation—one needs the sweetness to *start* one on the spiritual life but, once started, one must learn to obey God for his own sake, not for the pleasure.

245
Conversion
Letters of C. S. Lewis (21 December 1941), para. 3, p. 197.

Dyson and Tolkien were the immediate human causes of my conversion. Is any pleasure on earth as great as a circle of Christian friends by a good fire?

246
Conversion
The Screwtape Letters, Letter XXIII, para. 3, p. 108.

The earliest converts were converted by a single historical fact (the Resurrection) and a single historical doctrine (the Redemption) operating on a sense of sin which they already had . . . against the old, platitudinous, universal moral law.

247
Conversion
God in the Dock, "The Decline of Religion" (1946), para. 9, p. 221.

Conversion requires an alteration of the will, and an alteration which, in the last resort, does not occur without the intervention of the supernatural.

248
Conversion
Taliessin Through Logres, . . . Arthurian Torso, "Williams and the Arthuriad" (1948), chap. V, para. 11, p. 347.

All conversion involves death and re-birth; but sometimes the one, sometimes the other, of these elements is more noticeably present to the consciousness of the patient.

249

Conversion

Letters of C. S. Lewis
(5 March 1951), para. 2,
p. 227.

I think that all Christians have found that he
[Satan] is v. active near the altar or on the eve of
conversion; worldly anxieties, physical discomforts,
lascivious fancies, doubt, are often poured in at
such junctures. . . . But the Grace is not frustrated.

250

Conversion

Mere Christianity, bk. IV,
chap. 10, para. 9, p. 179.

It costs God nothing, so far as we know, to create
nice things: but to convert rebellious wills cost
Him crucifixion.

251

Conversion

Surprised by Joy, chap. 4,
para. 8, pp. 62–63.

[Ed. note: Lewis reflects on his view of
Christianity as a yet unconverted young man:]
This ludicrous burden of false duties in prayer
provided, of course, an unconscious motive for
wishing to shuffle off the Christian faith; but
about the same time, or a little later, conscious
causes of doubt arose. One came from reading the
classics. Here, especially in Virgil, one was
presented with a mass of religious ideas; and all
teachers and editors took it for granted from the
outset that these religious ideas were sheer illusion.
Not one ever attempted to show in what sense
Christianity fulfilled Paganism or Paganism
prefigured Christianity. The accepted position
seemed to be that religions were normally a mere
farrago of nonsense, though our own, by a
fortunate exception, was exactly true. The other
religions were not even explained, in the earlier
Christian fashion, as the work of devils. That I
might, conceivably, have been brought to believe.
But the impression I got was that religion in
general, though utterly false, was a natural
growth, a kind of endemic nonsense into which
humanity tended to blunder. In the midst of a
thousand such religions stood our own, the
thousand and first, labeled True. But on what
grounds could I believe in this exception? It

obviously was in some general sense the same kind of thing as all the rest. Why was it so differently treated? Need I, at any rate continue to treat it differently? I was very anxious not to.

252

Conversion

Surprised by Joy,
chap. 14, para. 23,
pp. 228–229.

In the Trinity Term of 1929 I gave in, and admitted that God was God, and knelt and prayed; perhaps, that night, the most dejected and reluctant convert in all England. I did not then see what is now the most shining and obvious thing; the Divine humility which will accept a convert even on such terms. The Prodigal Son at least walked home on his own feet. But who can duly adore that Love which will open the high gates to a prodigal who is brought in kicking, struggling, resentful, and darting his eyes in every direction for a chance of escape? The words *compelle intrare,* compel them to come in, have been so abused by wicked men that we shudder at them; but, properly understood, they plumb the depth of the Divine mercy. The hardness of God is kinder than the softness of men, and His compulsion is our liberation.

253

Conversion

Surprised by Joy,
chap. 15, para. 5, p. 233.

For many healthy extroverts self-examination first begins with conversion. For me it was almost the other way round. Self-examination did of course continue. But it was (I suppose, for I cannot quite remember) at stated intervals, and for a practical purpose; a duty, a discipline, an uncomfortable thing, no longer a hobby or a habit. To believe and to pray were the beginning of extroversion. I had been, as they say, "taken out of myself."

254

Conversion

Surprised by Joy,
chap. 15, para. 8, p. 237.

As I drew near the conclusion, I felt a resistance almost as strong as my previous resistance to Theism. As strong, but shorter-lived, for I understood it better. Every step I had taken, from the Absolute to "Spirit" and from "Spirit" to "God," had been a step toward the more concrete, the more imminent, the more compulsive. At each step one had less chance "to call one's soul one's own." To accept the Incarnation was a further step in the same direction. It brings God nearer, or near in a new way. And this, I found, was something I had not wanted. But to recognize the ground for my evasion was of course to recognize both its shame and its futility. I know very well when, but hardly how, the final step was taken. I was driven to Whipsnade one sunny morning. When we set out I did not believe that Jesus Christ is the Son of God, and when we reached the zoo I did. Yet I had not exactly spent the journey in thought. Nor in great emotion. "Emotional" is perhaps the last word we can apply to some of the most important events. It was more like when a man, after long sleep, still lying motionless in bed, becomes aware that he is now awake. And it was, like that moment on top of the bus, ambiguous. Freedom, or necessity? Or do they differ at their maximum? At that maximum a man is what he does; there is nothing of him left over or outside the act.

255

Conversion, Excitement at

Letters of C. S. Lewis (15 May 1952), p. 241.

[Responding to news of conversion:] All our prayers are being answered, and I thank God for it. The only (possibly, not necessarily) unfavourable symptom is that you are just a trifle too excited. It is quite right that you should feel that "something terrific" has happened to you. . . . Accept these sensations with thankfulness as birthday cards from God, but remember that they are only greetings, not the real gift. I mean that it is not the sensations that are the real thing. The real thing is the gift of the Holy Spirit which can't usually be—perhaps not ever—experienced as a sensation or emotion. The sensations are merely the response of your nervous system. Don't depend on them. Otherwise when they go and you are once more emotionally flat (as you certainly will be quite soon), you might think that the real thing had gone too. But it won't. It will be there when you can't feel it. May even be most operative when you can feel it least.

Don't imagine it is all "going to be an exciting adventure from now on." It won't. Excitement, of whatever sort, never lasts. This is the push to start you off on your first bicycle: you'll be left to lots of dogged pedalling later on. And no need to feel depressed about it either. It will be good for your spiritual leg muscles. So enjoy the push while it lasts, but enjoy it as a treat, not as something normal.

256
Conviction
The Problem of Pain,
chap. 4, para. 15, p. 67.

We actually are, at present, creatures whose character must be, in some respects, a horror to God, as it is, when we really see it, a horror to ourselves. This I believe to be a fact: and I notice that the holier a man is, the more fully he is aware of that fact.

257
Correspondence
The Letters of C. S.
Lewis to Arthur Greeves
(10 November 1914),
p. 60.

It is the immemorial privilege of letter-writers to commit to paper things they would not say: to write in a more grandiose manner than that in which they speak: and to enlarge upon feelings which would be passed by unnoticed in conversation.

258

Correspondence

The Letters of C. S.
Lewis to Arthur Greeves
(17 November 1914),
p. 62.

However many pages one may fill in a letter, it is only a tithe of what ten minutes conversation would cover: it is curious, too, how the thoughts that bubble up so freely when one meets a friend, seem to congeal on paper, when writing to him.

259

Correspondence

The Letters of C. S.
Lewis to Arthur Greeves
(4 July 1947), para. 2,
p. 510.

No more now: the daily letter writing without W. [Lewis's brother Warren] to help me is appalling—an hour and a half or two hours every morning before I can get to my own work.

260

Correspondence

The Letters of C. S.
Lewis to Arthur Greeves
(22 April 1951), para. 2,
p. 520.

My correspondence involves a great number of theological letters already which *can't* be neglected because they are answers to people in great need of help & often in great misery.

261

Correspondence

Letters to an American
Lady (1 January 1954),
pp. 23–24.

Christmas mails have "got me down." This season is to me mainly hard, gruelling work—write, write, write, till I wickedly say that if there were less *good will* (going through the post) there would be more *peace on earth*.

262

Correspondence

Letters to an American
Lady (29 January 1955),
p. 37.

Yes, I've been treating you (and others) badly of late, but, I think, with some excuse. First there were visitors; then the preparations for the move; then the move itself (at which moment my brother got ill so that I had all the correspondence to tackle single handed); then the settling in at Cambridge plus various delights like burst water-pipes; repeated journeys to and fro—in fact a period during which life seemed to consist entirely of journeys and letter writing—the pen has become to me what the oar is to a galley slave; then (God be praised) influenza and long half-comatose days in bed. Yesterday was my first day out. I hope to go back to work and Cambridge on Thursday next. So I was about as likely to ride in a steeplechase as to write a poem! But you have never been absent from my prayers. So try not to be hurt by my silence. And always remember that there is no time in the whole year when I am less willing to write than near Christmas, for it is then that my burden is heaviest. I suspect you have a very false idea of what my days are like!

263

Correspondence

Letters to Children (26 March 1956), para. 1, p. 60.

The funny thing is that I was far worse about writing letters when I had far fewer to write; now that I have such a lot to write I've just got to do them all at once, first thing every morning.

264

Courage

The Screwtape Letters, Letter XXIX, para. 6, pp. 137–138.

Courage is not simply *one* of the virtues, but the form of every virtue at the testing point, which means, at the point of highest reality. A chastity or honesty or mercy which yields to danger will be chaste or honest or merciful only on conditions. Pilate was merciful till it became risky.

265

Courtesy

The Allegory of Love, chap. I.I, para. 2, p. 2.

Only the courteous can love, but it is love that makes them courteous.

266

Coverdale, Myles

English Literature in the Sixteenth Century, bk. II.I.II, para. 7–8, pp. 207–209.

Tyndale's immediate successor was Myles Coverdale. . . . He claims the honour of having produced the first complete English Bible. . . . Only a part of this Bible was new. Coverdale used the Pentateuch, Jonah, and New Testament of Tyndale; the residue of the Old Testament he translated himself with help from the Vulgate, Pagninus, Luther, and the Zurich Bible. From this onward Coverdale becomes, in a sense, the official government translator, repeatedly employed on authorized revisions of his own and other men's work for the Matthew's Bible and the Great Bibles. The tendency of his revisions was influenced by the official policy of the moment. We need not accuse him of insincerity. He had not learning enough to have solid grounds of his own for choosing between the various interpreters who all lay together on his desk: ignorance, in a sense, left him free to be accommodating.

It may also be suspected that ignorance left him free to indulge aesthetic preferences, to follow this or that interpretation according as it agreed with his own, often exquisitely melodious, English style. . . . There are felicities everywhere. He is responsible for "baptized into his death," for "tender mercies," and for "lovingkindness"; "respect of persons" instead of "parcialite" was also his. Compared with great divines and scholars like Ximenes, Erasmus, Tyndale, and those who made the Geneva, the Rheims, and the Authorized, Coverdale might perhaps be regarded as a mere hack: but he is often an inspired hack.

267
Coverdale, Myles
Selected Literary Essays, "The Literary Impact of the Authorised Version" (1950), para. 14, pp. 132–133.

Coverdale was probably the one whose choice of a rendering [of the Bible] came nearest to being determined by taste. His defects as well as his qualities led to this. Of all the translators he was the least scholarly. Among men like Erasmus, Tyndale, Munster, or the Jesuits at Rheims he shows like a rowing boat among battleships. This gave him a kind of freedom. Unable to judge between rival interpretations, he may often have been guided, half consciously, to select and combine by taste. Fortunately his taste was admirable.

268

Cowper, William

Letters of C. S. Lewis (25 February 1928), p. 124.

Have you ever read the letters of the poet Cowper? He had nothing—literally nothing—to tell anyone about; private life in a sleepy country town where Evangelical distrust of "the world" denied him even such miserable society as the place would have afforded. And yet one reads a whole volume of his letters with unfailing interest. How his tooth came loose at dinner, how he made a hutch for a tame hare, what he is doing about his cucumbers—all this he makes one follow as if the fate of empires hung on it.

269

Cowper, William

Letters of C. S. Lewis (25 December 1931), p. 146.

I had set a paper the other day for School Certificate on . . . Cowper. . . . How delicious Cowper is—the letters even more than the poetry. Under every disadvantage—presented to me as raw material for a paper, and filling with a job an evening I had hoped to have free—even so he charmed me. He is the very essence of what Arthur calls "the homely," which is Arthur's favourite genre. All these cucumbers, books, parcels, tea-parties, parish affairs. It is wonderful what he makes of them.

270

Cranmer, Thomas

English Literature in the Sixteenth Century, bk. II.I.I, para. 53, p. 195.

Cranmer writes a prose with which it is difficult to find any fault, but it gives curiously little pleasure. It never drags and never hurries; it never disappoints the ear; and (*pace* John Foxe) there is hardly a single sentence that leaves us in doubt of its meaning. He could have taught More and even Tyndale some things about the art of English composition: but they can be loved and he cannot. This is partly because while avoiding their vices he lacks their virtues. He is not stodgy and verbose like More: but then he has neither humour nor pathos. He is not digressive like Tyndale, but then he lacks Tyndale's fire. The explanation is that Cranmer always writes in an official capacity. Everything he says has been threshed out in committee. We never see a thought growing: his business is to express the agreed point of view. Everyone who has tried to draw up a report knows how fatal such conditions are to good writing.

271
Creation

A Preface to "Paradise Lost," chap. 12, para. 16, p. 89.

Milton certainly rejects . . . the orthodox teaching that God made the material universe "out of nothing," i.e. not out of any pre-existing raw material. He holds it to be "an argument of supreme power and goodness that such diversified, multi-form, and inexhaustible virtue" (sc. as that of matter) "should exist and be substantially inherent in God." Spirit, according to Milton, "being the more excellent substance virtually and essentially contains within itself the inferior one." It is not easy to understand this doctrine, but we may note that it does not fall into the heresy against which the doctrine of "creation out of nothing" was intended to guard. That doctrine was directed against dualism— against the idea that God was the sole origin of things, but found Himself from the beginning faced with something other than Himself. This Milton does not believe: if he has erred he has erred by flying too far from it, and believing that God made the world "out of Himself." And this view must *in a certain sense* be accepted by all Theists: in the sense that the world was modelled on an *idea* existing in God's mind, that God *invented* matter, that (*salva reverentia*) He "thought of" matter as Dickens "thought of" Mr Pickwick. From that point of view it could be said that God "contained" matter as Shakespeare "contained" Hamlet.

272
Creation
God in the Dock, "The Laws of Nature," (1945), para. 8–9, pp. 78–79.

Either the stream of events had a beginning or it had not. If it had, then we are faced with something like creation. If it had not (a supposition, by the way, which some physicists find difficult), then we are faced with an everlasting impulse which, by its very nature, is opaque to scientific thought. Science, when it becomes perfect, will have explained the connection between each link in the chain and the link before it. But the actual existence of the chain will remain wholly unaccountable. We learn more and more about the pattern. We learn nothing about that which "feeds" real events into the pattern. If it is not God, we must at the very least call it Destiny—the immaterial, ultimate, one-way pressure which keeps the universe on the move.

The smallest event, then, if we face the fact that it occurs (instead of concentrating on the pattern into which, if it can be persuaded to occur, it must fit), leads us back to a mystery which lies outside natural science. It is certainly a possible supposition that behind this mystery some mighty Will and Life is at work.

273
Creation
Miracles, chap. 4, para. 15, p. 33.

No philosophical theory which I have yet come across is a radical improvement on the words of *Genesis,* that "in the beginning God made Heaven and Earth."

274
Creation
Miracles, chap. 16, para. 16–17, pp. 151–152.

You could almost define the future as the period in which what is now living will be dead and in which what order still remains will be diminished.

But entropy by its very character assures us that though it may be the universal rule in the Nature we know, it cannot be universal absolutely.

. . . A clock can't run down unless it has been

wound up. Humpty Dumpty can't fall off a wall which never existed. If a Nature which disintegrates order were the whole of reality, where would she find any order to disintegrate?

275
Creation
Miracles, chap. 16, para. 26, p. 158.

It is not an accident that simple-minded people, however spiritual, should blend the ideas of God and Heaven and the blue sky. It is a fact, not a fiction, that light and life-giving heat do come down from the sky to Earth. The analogy of the sky's role to begetting and of the Earth's role to bearing is sound as far as it goes. The huge dome of the sky is of all things sensuously perceived the most like infinity. And when God made space and worlds that move in space, and clothed our world with air, and gave us such eyes and such imaginations as those we have, He knew what the sky would mean to us. And since nothing in His work is accidental, if He knew, He intended. We cannot be certain that this was not indeed one of the chief purposes for which Nature was created.

276
Creation
God in the Dock, "Some Thoughts" (1948), para. 5, p. 148.

Because God created the Natural—invented it out of His love and artistry—it demands our reverence.

277
Creation
Taliessin Through Logres, . . . Arthurian Torso, "Williams and the Arthuriad" (1948), chap. II, para. 24, p. 291.

In order that we finite beings may apprehend the Emperor He translates His glory into multiple forms—into stars, woods, waters, beasts, and the bodies of men.

278
Creativity
Letters of C. S. Lewis
(20 February 1943),
p. 203.

"Creation" as applied to human authorship seems to me to be an entirely misleading term. We re-arrange elements He has provided. There is not a vestige of real creativity *de novo* in us. Try to imagine a new primary colour, a third sex, a fourth dimension, or even a monster which does not consist of bits of existing animals stuck together. Nothing happens. And that surely is why our works (as you said) never mean to others quite what we intended: because we are re-combining elements made by Him and already containing *His* meanings.

279
Criminal Justice
God in the Dock, "Is Progress Possible?"
(1958), para. 7–10,
p. 313.

On the humanitarian view all crime is patho-logical; it demands not retributive punishment but cure. This separates the criminal's treatment from the concepts of justice and desert; a "just cure" is meaningless.

On the old view public opinion might protest against a punishment (it protested against our old penal code) as excessive, more than the man "deserved"; an ethical question on which anyone might have an opinion. But a remedial treatment can be judged only by the probability of its success; a technical question on which only experts can speak. Thus the criminal ceases to be a person, a subject of rights and duties, and becomes merely an object on which society can work. And this is, in principle, how Hitler treated the Jews. They were objects; killed not for ill desert but because, on his theories, they were a disease in society. If society can mend, remake, and unmake men at its pleasure, its pleasure may, of course, be humane or homicidal. The difference is important. But, either way, rulers have become owners.

Observe how the "humane" attitude to crime

could operate. If crimes are diseases, why should diseases be treated differently from crimes? And who but the experts can define disease? One school of psychology regards my religion as a neurosis. If this neurosis ever becomes inconvenient to Government, what is to prevent my being subjected to a compulsory "cure"? It may be painful; treatments sometimes are. But it will be no use asking, "What have I done to deserve this?" The Straightener will reply: "But, my dear fellow, no one's *blaming* you. We no longer believe in retributive justice. We're healing you."

This would be no more than an extreme application of the political philosophy implicit in most modern communities. It has stolen on us unawares.

280
Criticism
Rehabilitations, "The Idea of an 'English School,'" para. 1, p. 59.

[Speaking of the Final Honour School of English at Oxford:] We are doubtless full of faults and do not shun criticism, provided such criticism is based on an understanding of our aims. You may not agree with these aims—though I hope that you will—but do not blame a man for making slow progress to the North when he is trying to get to the East.

281
Criticism
The Personal Heresy: A Controversy, chap. 5, para. 17, p. 113.

It is by art or skill that the poets contrive to utter concretely what it is that they want to say; but the thing said is not "Art"—it is something more like a remark. The skill which went to the utterance of it has all the privileges of art; it is exempt (like plumbing or boot-blacking) from moral and logical criticism, and it is best judged by fellow artists. To claim similar immunities for the thing said is a confusion. I will let the plumber tell me how culpable his predecessor was in

---

allowing my scullery to get flooded; I will not let him decide *whether* it is flooded, still less whether it ought to be.

282
Criticism
The Four Loves, chap. 4, para. 44, p. 114.

The little pockets of early Christians survived because they cared exclusively for the love of "the brethren" and stopped their ears to the opinion of the Pagan society all round them. But a circle of criminals, cranks, or perverts survives in just the same way; by becoming deaf to the opinion of the outer world, by discounting it as the chatter of outsiders who "don't understand," of the "conventional," "the bourgeois," the "Establishment," of prigs, prudes and humbugs.

283
Criticism
Of Other Worlds: Essays and Stories, "On Criticism" (1st pub. 1966), para. 3, p. 44.

Authors no doubt suffer from self-love, but it need not always be voracious to the degree that abolishes all discrimination. I think fatuous praise from a manifest fool may hurt more than any depreciation.

284
Criticism, Anthropological
Selected Literary Essays, "The Anthropological Approach" (1962), para. 29–30, p. 310.

Until our own age readers accepted this world [the imaginative world of the romance] as the romancers' "noble and joyous" invention. It was not, to be sure, wholly unrelated to the real world. It was invented by and for men who felt the real world, in its rather different way, to be also cryptic, significant, full of voices and "the mystery of all life." There has now arisen a type of reader who cannot thus accept it. The tale in itself does not seem to him to provide adequate grounds for the feelings to which he is dimly aware that he is being prompted. He therefore invents new ground for them in his own life as a reader. And he does this by building up round himself a second romance which he mistakes for reality. This second romance is a distorted version of the first one. It also is a quest story, but it is he, not Perceval or Gawain, that is on the quest. The forests are not those of Broceliande but those of anthropological theory. It is he himself who quivers at the surmise that everything he meets may be more important, and other, than it seemed. It is to him that such hermits as Frazer and Miss Weston, dwelling in the heart of the forest, explain the *significacio* of the ferlies. Prompted by them, he does not, like Perceval, omit to ask the all-important question.

And he has his reward. He gets in the end an experience qualitatively not unlike the experience the romancers meant to give. The process is very roundabout. He rejects the fiction as it was actually written. He can respond to it only indirectly, only when it is mirrored in a second fiction, which he mistakes for a reality. This is better than nothing. But it might do a good deal of harm to real literary and cultural history and even to anthropology itself if it were taken as a serious contribution to any of these disciplines.

285
Cruelty
God in the Dock,
"Vivisection" (1947),
para. 10, p. 228.

In justifying cruelty to animals we put ourselves also on the animal level. We choose the jungle and must abide by our choice.

286
Daniel,
Samuel
English Literature in the Sixteenth Century, bk. III.III.III, para. 19, pp. 491–492.

His [sonnet] sequence *Delia* . . . offers no ideas, no psychology, and of course no story: it is simply a masterpiece of phrasing and melody. To anyone who complains that it is a series of commonplaces we can only reply, "Yes, but listen." . . . In him, as in Shakespeare, the most ordinary statement turns liquid and delicious. . . . The truth is that while everything Daniel says would be commonplace in a prose abstract, nothing is commonplace as it actually occurs in the poetry. In that medium all the Petrarchan gestures become compulsive invitations to enormous sorrows and delights.

287
Daniel,
Samuel
English Literature in the Sixteenth Century, bk. III.III.III, para. 63, pp. 530–531.

Though Daniel's poetry is often uninspired, sometimes obscure, and not seldom simply bad, he has two strong claims on our respect. In the first place, he can at times achieve the same masculine and unstrained majesty which we find in Wordsworth's greater sonnets, and I believe that Wordsworth learned it from Daniel. (The two poets had much in common and Daniel would have liked *Laodamia*.) And secondly Daniel is, in the nineteenth-century sense of the words, a poet of ideas. There had of course been ideas in Chaucer, and Spenser: but I think those poets felt themselves to be simply transmitting an inherited and accepted wisdom. There are, again, plenty of ideas in Donne, but they are, in my opinion, treated merely as the tools of his peculiar rhetoric: he was not interested in their truth or falsehood. But Daniel actually thinks in verse: thinks deeply, arduously, and perhaps with some originality. This is something quite different from Dryden's power of neatly poetizing all the stock arguments for the side on which he is briefed. Dryden states: Daniel can doubt and wrestle. It is no necessary quality in a poet, and Daniel's thinking is not always poetical. But its result is that though Daniel is not one of our greatest poets, he is the most interesting man of letters whom that century produced in England.

288

Dante

The Letters of C. S. Lewis to Arthur Greeves (1930), pp. 325–326.

Aristotle's *Ethics* all morning, walk after lunch, and then Dante's *Paradiso* for the rest of the day.

The latter has really opened a new world to me. I don't know whether it is really very different from the *Inferno* (B. [Barfield] says its as different as chalk from cheese—heaven from hell, would be more appropriate!) or whether I was specially receptive, but it certainly seemed to me that I had never seen at all what Dante was like before. Unfortunately the impression is one so unlike anything else that I can hardly describe it for your benefit—a sort of mixture of intense, even crabbed, complexity in language and thought with (what seems impossible) *at the very same time* a feeling of spacious gliding movement, like a slow dance, or like flying. It is like the stars—endless mathematical subtility of orb, cycle, epicycle and ecliptic, unthinkable & unpicturable, & yet at the same time the freedom and liquidity of empty space and the triumphant certainty of movement. I should describe it as feeling more *important* than any poetry I have ever read. . . . Its blend of complexity and beauty is very like Catholic theology—wheel within wheel, but wheels of glory, and the One radiated through the Many.

289

Dante

The Allegory of Love, chap. III.V, para. 11, p. 155.

Dante remains a strong candidate for the supreme poetical honours of the world.

290

Dante

Selected Literary Essays, "Shelley, Dryden, and Mr Eliot" (1939), para. 30–31, p. 204.

Dante is eminently the poet of beatitude. He has not only no rival, but none second to him. But if we were asked to name the poet who most nearly deserved this inaccessible *proxime accessit,* I should name Shelley. Indeed, my claim for Shelley might be represented by the proposition that Shelley and Milton are, each, the half of Dante. I do not know how we could describe Dante better to one who had not read him, than by some such device as the following:

"You know the massive quality of Milton, the sense that every word is being held in place by a gigantic pressure, so that there is an architectural sublime in every verse whether the matter be sublime at the moment or not. You know also the air and fire of Shelley, the very antithesis of the Miltonic solidity, the untrammelled, reckless speed through pellucid spaces which makes us imagine while we are reading him that we have somehow left our bodies behind. If now you can imagine (but you cannot, for it must seem impossible till you see it done) a poetry which combined these two all-but incompatibles—a poetry as bright and piercing and aereal as the one, yet as weighty, as pregnant and as lapidary as the other, then you will know what Dante is like."

291
Dante
Studies in Medieval and Renaissance Literature, "Dante's Similes" (1966), para. 16. p. 76.

He is the most translatable of the poets—not, probably, that he entrusts less wealth than others to the music of the words and the *nuance* of the phrase but that he entrusts more than others to the "plain sense."

292
Dante
Studies in Medieval and Renaissance Literature, "Dante's Similes" (1966), para. 16, pp. 76–77.

I think Dante's poetry, on the whole, the greatest of all the poetry I have read: yet when it is at its highest pitch of excellence, I hardly feel that Dante has very much to do. . . . I draw the conclusion that the highest reach of the whole poetic art turns out to be a kind of abdication, and is attained when the whole image of the world the poet sees has entered so deeply into his mind that henceforth he has only to get himself out of the way, to let the seas roll and the mountains shake their leaves or the light shine and the spheres revolve, and all this will *be* poetry, not things you write poetry about. Dare I confess that after Dante even Shakespeare seems to me a little factitious? It almost sounds as if he were "just making it up." But one cannot feel that about Dante even when one has stopped reading him.

293
Dante
Studies in Medieval and Renaissance Literature, "Dante's Similes" (1966), para. 15, p. 75.

There is so much besides poetry in Dante that anyone but a fool can enjoy him in some way or other.

294
De la Mare, Walter
The Letters of C. S. Lewis to Arthur Greeves (26 June 1927), p. 297.

De la Mare's poems I have had for a long time and I read them more often than any other book. I put him above Yeats and all the other moderns, and in spite of his fantasy find him nearer than any one else to the essential truth of life.

295

de Meun, Jean

The Allegory of Love,
chap. III.V, para. 9,
p. 151.

It was the misfortune of Jean de Meun to have read and remembered everything: and nothing that he remembered could be kept out of his poem [*Roman de la Rose*].

296

de Troyes, Chretien

The Allegory of Love,
chap. I.II, para. 1, p. 23.

His *Lancelot* is the flower of the courtly tradition in France, as it was in its early maturity. . . . We must conceive him as a poet of the same type with Dryden: one of those rare men of genius who can trim their sails to every breeze of novelty without forfeiting their poetic rank. He was among the first to welcome the Arthurian stories; and to him, as much as to any single writer, we owe the colouring with which the "matter of Britain" has come down to us. . . . He stamped upon men's minds indelibly the conception of Arthur's court as the home *par excellence* of true and noble love.

297

Death

The Pilgrim's Regress, bk.
9, chap. 3, p. 167.

"Do not think that you can escape me; do not think you can call me Nothing. To you I am not Nothing; I am the being blindfolded, the losing all power of self-defence, the surrender, not because any terms are offered, but because resistance is gone: the step into the dark: the defeat of all precautions: utter helplessness turned out to utter risk: the final loss of liberty. The Landlord's Son who feared nothing, feared me."

"What am I to do?" said John.

"Which you choose," said the voice. "Jump, or be thrown. Shut your eyes or have them bandaged by force. Give in or struggle."

"I would sooner do the first, if I could."

"Then I am your servant and no more your master. The cure of death is dying. He who lays

down his liberty in that act receives it back. Go
down to Mother Kirk."

298 **Death** *Out of the Silent Planet,* chap. 20, p. 140.	"The weakest of my people does not fear death. It is the Bent One [Satan], the lord of your world, who wastes your lives and befouls them with flying from what you know will overtake you in the end. If you were subjects of Maleldil [God] you would have peace."
299 **Death** *The Problem of Pain,* chap. 8, para. 8, p. 124.	[Some say] that death ought not to be final, that there ought to be a second chance. I believe that if a million chances were likely to do good, they would be given. But a master often knows, when boys and parents do not, that it is really useless to send a boy in for a certain examination again. Finality must come sometime, and it does not require a very robust faith to believe that omniscience knows when.
300 **Death** *The Screwtape Letters,* Letter V, para. 2, pp. 26–27.	[Senior devil Screwtape to junior devil Wormwood:] How much better for us if *all* humans died in costly nursing homes amid doctors who lie, nurses who lie, friends who lie, as we have trained them, promising life to the dying, encouraging the belief that sickness excuses every indulgence, and even, if our workers know their job, withholding all suggestion of a priest lest it should betray to the sick man his true condition.
301 **Death** *Selected Literary Essays,* "Hamlet: The Prince or the Poem" (1942), para. 17, p. 100.	Any serious attention to the state of being dead, unless it is limited by some definite religious or anti-religious doctrine, must, I suppose, paralyse the will by introducing infinite uncertainties and rendering all motives inadequate. Being dead is the

unknown *x* in our sum. Unless you ignore it or else give it a value, you can get no answer.

302
Death
The Great Divorce,
chap. 11, pp. 104–105.

"Nothing, not even the best and noblest, can go on as it now is. Nothing, not even what is lowest and most bestial, will not be raised again if it submits to death. It is sown a natural body, it is raised a spiritual body. Flesh and blood cannot come to the Mountains [heaven]. Not because they are too rank, but because they are too weak. What is a Lizard compared with a stallion? Lust is a poor, weak, whimpering whispering thing compared with that richness and energy of desire which will arise when lust has been killed."

303
Death
The Letters of C. S. Lewis to Arthur Greeves
(5 January 1947), p. 509.

If only you and I (or you *or* I) doesn't go and die before we have a chance to meet! And yet, if we did no doubt there wd. be some good and loving reason for it. I am (except in bad moods) more convinced of that all the time. We shall meet and be happy together if it is good for us: otherwise not (e.g. I might after all be disappointed in a hope I sometimes cherish that you wd. find me a little less aggressive and dictatorial and arrogant than I have often been in the old days. But who knows? The first argument might shatter all these good resolutions!)

304
Death
Miracles, chap. 14,
para. 25, p. 125.

On the one hand Death is the triumph of Satan, the punishment of the Fall, and the last enemy. Christ shed tears at the grave of Lazarus and sweated blood in Gethsemane: the Life of Lives that was in Him detested this penal obscenity not less than we do, but more. On the other hand, only he who loses his life will save it. We are baptized into the death of Christ, and it is the remedy for the Fall. Death is, in fact, what some modern people call "ambivalent." It is Satan's great weapon and also God's great weapon: it is holy and unholy; our supreme disgrace and our only hope; the thing Christ came to conquer and the means by which He conquered.

305
Death
Miracles, chap. 14,
para. 31, p. 128.

Human Death is the result of sin and the triumph of Satan. But it is also the means of redemption from sin, God's medicine for Man and His weapon against Satan.

306
Death
Miracles, chap. 14,
para. 32, p. 130.

[Death] is a safety-device because, once Man has fallen, natural immortality would be the one utterly hopeless destiny for him.

307
Death
Miracles, chap. 14,
para. 32, p. 130.

Humanity must embrace death freely, submit to it with total humility, drink it to the dregs, and so convert it into that mystical death which is the secret of life. But only a Man who did not need to have been a Man at all unless He had chosen, only one who served in our sad regiment as a volunteer, yet also only one who was perfectly a Man, could perform this perfect dying; and thus (which way you put it is unimportant) either defeat death or redeem it. He tasted death on behalf of all others. He is the representative "Die-er" of the universe: and for that very reason the Resurrection and the life. Or conversely, because He truly lives, He truly dies, for that is the very pattern of reality. Because the higher can descend into the lower He who from all eternity has been incessantly plunging Himself in the blessed death of self-surrender to the Father can also most fully descend into the horrible and (for us) involuntary death of the body. Because Vicariousness is the very idiom of the reality He has created, his death can become ours.

308
Death
Essays Presented to Charles Williams, Preface, para. 19, p. xiv.

No event has so corroborated my faith in the next world as Williams did simply by dying. When the idea of death and the idea of Williams thus met in my mind, it was the idea of death that was changed.

309
Death
God in the Dock, "Some Thoughts" (1948), para. 7, pp. 149–150.

The world, knowing how all our real investments are beyond the grave, might expect us to be less concerned than other people who go in for what is called Higher Thought and tell us that "death doesn't matter"; but we "are not high-minded," and we follow One who stood and wept at the grave of Lazarus—not surely, because He was grieved that Mary and Martha wept, and sorrowed for their lack of faith (though some thus interpret) but because death, the punishment of sin, is even more horrible in His eyes than in ours. The nature which He had created as God, the nature which He had assumed as Man, lay there before Him in its ignominy; a foul smell, food for worms. Though He was to revive it a moment later, He wept at the shame; if I may here quote a writer of my own communion, "I am not so much afraid of death as ashamed of it." And that brings us again to the paradox. Of all men, we hope most of death; yet nothing will reconcile us to— well, its *unnaturalness.* We know that we were not made for it; we know how it crept into our destiny as an intruder; and we know Who has defeated it. Because Our Lord is risen we know that on one level it is an enemy already disarmed; but because we know that the natural level also is God's creation we cannot cease to fight against the death which mars it, as against all those other blemishes upon it, against pain and poverty, barbarism and ignorance. Because we love something else more than this world we love even this world better than those who know no other.

310
Death

A *Severe Mercy*, Letter to Sheldon Vanauken (8 May 1955), pp. 209–210.

One way or another the thing [romantic love] had to die. Perpetual springtime is not allowed. You were not cutting the wood of life according to the grain. There are various possible ways in wh. it cd. have died tho' both the parties went on living. You have been treated with a severe mercy. You have been brought to see (how true & how v. frequent this is!) that you were jealous of God. So from US you have been led back to US AND GOD; it remains to go on to GOD AND US. She was further on than you, and she can help you more where she now is than she could have done on earth. You must go on. That is one of the many reasons why suicide is out of the question. (Another is the absence of any ground for believing that death *by that route* wd. reunite you with her. Why should it? You might be digging an eternally unbridgeable chasm. Disobedience is not the way to get nearer to the obedient.)

311
Death

The Last Battle, chap. 16, pp. 183–184.

"There *was* a real railway accident," said Aslan softly. "Your father and mother and all of you are—as you used to call it in the Shadow-Lands— dead. The term is over: the holidays have begun. The dream is ended: this is the morning."

And as He spoke He no longer looked to them like a lion; but the things that began to happen after that were so great and beautiful that I cannot write them. And for us this is the end of all the stories, and we can most truly say that they all lived happily ever after. But for them it was only the beginning of the real story. All their life in this world and all their adventures in Narnia had only been the cover and the title page: now at last they were beginning Chapter One of the Great Story, which no one on earth has read: which goes on for ever: in which every chapter is better than the one before.

312
Death

Letters to Children
(27 April 1956), para. 3,
p. 61.

People do find it hard to keep on feeling as if you believed in the next life: but then it is just as hard to keep on feeling as if you believed you were going to be nothing after death. I know this because in the old days before I was a Christian I used to try.

313
Death

Till We Have Faces, part
2, chap. 2, p. 279.

"Die before you die. There is no chance after."

314
Death

*Letters to an American
Lady* (7 June 1959),
p. 84.

There are, aren't there, only three things we can do about death: to desire it, to fear it, or to ignore it.

315
Death

*Letters: C. S. Lewis/Don
Giovanni Calabria* (15
December 1959), para. 3,
p. 101.

[In anticipation of his wife's death, Lewis asks:] Has He not promised comfort to those who mourn?

316
Death

A Grief Observed,
chap. 1, para. 30, p. 16.

[Lewis was grieving the death of his wife:] It is hard to have patience with people who say "There is no death" or "Death doesn't matter." There is death. And whatever is matters. And whatever happens has consequences, and it and they are irrevocable and irreversible. You might as well say that birth doesn't matter. I look up at the night sky. Is anything more certain than that in all those vast times and spaces, if I were allowed to search them, I should nowhere find her face, her voice, her touch? She died. She is dead. Is the word so difficult to learn?

317
Death
A Grief Observed,
chap. 2, para. 6, p. 22.

[Lewis was grieving the death of his wife:] What pitiable cant to say, "She will live forever in my memory!" *Live*? That is exactly what she won't do. You might as well think like the old Egyptians that you can keep the dead by embalming them. Will nothing persuade us that they are gone? . . . As if I wanted to fall in love with my memory of her, an image in my own mind! It would be a sort of incest.

318
Death
*The Letters of C. S.
Lewis to Arthur Greeves*
(11 September 1963),
p. 566.

Tho' I am by no means unhappy I can't help feeling it was rather a pity I did revive in July. I mean, having been glided so painlessly up to the Gate it seems hard to have it shut in one's face and know that the whole process must some day be gone thro' again, and perhaps far less pleasantly! Poor Lazarus! But God knows best.

319
Death
Letters of C. S. Lewis
(undated), pp. 190–191.

Only He who really lived a human life (and I presume that only one did) can fully taste the horror of death.

320
**Death:
Lazarus**
*Letters to an American
Lady* (25 June 63),
para. 1, p. 119.

How awful it must have been for poor Lazarus who had actually died, got it all over, and then was brought back to go through it all, I suppose, a few years later. I think he, not St. Stephen, ought really to be celebrated as the first martyr.

321
Deception
An Experiment in Criticism, chap. 6, para. 13, p. 56.

Nothing can deceive unless it bears a plausible resemblance to reality.

322
Deception
An Experiment in Criticism, chap. 7, para. 17, pp. 67–68.

No one can deceive you unless he makes you think he is telling the truth. The un-blushingly romantic has far less power to deceive than the apparently realistic. Admitted fantasy is precisely the kind of literature which never deceives at all. Children are not deceived by fairy-tales; they are often and gravely deceived by school-stories. Adults are not deceived by science-fiction; they can be deceived by the stories in the women's magazines.

323
Decisions
The Letters of C. S. Lewis to Arthur Greeves (13 April 1954), p. 530.

For one's own peace of mind I think it is best to set a time limit for one's decisions (I mean, decisions of mere pleasure where duty & necessity don't come in).

324
Decorum
English Literature in the Sixteenth Century, Epilogue, II, para. 4, p. 540.

The rule of decorum exists to avoid clashes or shocks to organized sensibility: but it was an early discovery that an occasional defiance of the rule, resulting in a shock, can give pleasure; a pleasure rich in tragic or comic possibilities. Indeed one of the purposes for which the rule exists is that it may sometimes be broken.

325
Definitions
Studies in Words (1960), chap. 1, para. 33–34, pp. 18–19.

When we leave the dictionaries we must view all definitions with grave distrust. It is the greatest simplicity in the world to suppose that when, say, Dryden defines *wit* or Arnold defines *poetry*, we can use their definition as evidence of what the word really meant when they wrote. The fact that

they define it at all is itself a ground for
scepticism. Unless we are writing a dictionary, or a
text-book of some technical subject, we define
our words only because we are in some measure
departing from their real current sense. Otherwise
there would be no purpose in doing so.

. . . The word *wit* will illustrate this. We . . .
find old critics giving definitions of it which are
contradicted not only by other evidence but out
of the critics' own mouths. Off their guard they
can be caught using it in the very sense their
definition was contrived to exclude. A student
who should read the critical debate of the
seventeenth century on wit under the impression
that what the critics say they mean by *wit* is
always, or often, what they really mean by *wit*
would end in total bewilderment. He must
understand that such definitions are purely
tactical. They are attempts to appropriate for one
side, and to deny to the other, a potent word.
You can see the same "war of positions" going on
today. A certain type of writer begins "The
essence of poetry is" or "All vulgarity may be
defined as," and then produces a definition which
no one ever thought of since the world began,
which conforms to no one's actual usage, and
which he himself will probably have forgotten by
the end of the month.

326

Democracy

*Present Concerns: Essays
by C. S. Lewis,
"Equality" (1943),
para. 1, p. 17.*

I am a democrat because I believe in the Fall of
Man. I think most people are democrats for the
opposite reason. A great deal of democratic
enthusiasm descends from the ideas of people like
Rousseau, who believed in democracy because
they thought mankind so wise and good that
everyone deserved a share in the government. The
danger of defending democracy on those grounds
is that they're not true. . . . I find that they're not

---

true without looking further than myself. I don't deserve a share in governing a hen-roost, much less a nation. . . . The real reason for democracy is . . . Mankind is so fallen that no man can be trusted with unchecked power over his fellows. Aristotle said that some people were only fit to be slaves. I do not contradict him. But I reject slavery because I see no men fit to be masters.

327
Democracy
Present Concerns: Essays by C. S. Lewis, "Democratic Education" (1944), para. 11, p. 36.

Democracy demands that little men should not take big ones too seriously; it dies when it is full of little men who think they are big themselves.

328
Democracy
The Weight of Glory, "Membership" (1945), para. 11–12, pp. 113–114.

I believe in political equality. But there are two opposite reasons for being a democrat. You may think all men so good that they deserve a share in the government of the commonwealth, and so wise that the commonwealth needs their advice. That is, in my opinion, the false, romantic doctrine of democracy. On the other hand, you may believe fallen men to be so wicked that not one of them can be trusted with any irresponsible power over his fellows.

That I believe to be the true ground of democracy. I do not believe that God created an egalitarian world. I believe the authority of parent over child, husband over wife, learned over simple, to have been as much a part of the original plan as the authority of man over beast.

329
Democracy
Present Concerns: Essays by C. S. Lewis, "Talking About Bicycles" (1946), para. 25, p. 72.

A society which becomes democratic in *ethos* as well as in constitution is doomed. And not much loss either.

330
Democracy
Mere Christianity, bk. III,
chap. 1, para. 9, p. 73.

Immortality makes this other difference between totalitarianism and democracy. If individuals live only seventy years, then a state, or a nation, or a civilisation, which may last for a thousand years, is more important than an individual. But if Christianity is true, then the individual is not only more important but incomparably more important, for he is everlasting and the life of a state or a civilisation, compared with his, is only a moment.

331
Democracy
Christian Reflections,
"Interim Report" (1956),
para. 11, p. 98.

Democracy is all very well as a political device. It must not intrude into the spiritual, or even the aesthetic, world.

332
Democracy
The Screwtape Letters,
"Screwtape Proposes a
Toast" (1959), para. 19,
21–22, 24, pp. 161–163.

[Senior devil Screwtape in a speech at the "Annual Dinner of the Tempters' Training College for Young Devils":] *Democracy* is the word with which you must lead them by the nose. . . .

The feeling I mean is of course that which prompts a man to say *I'm as good as you.*

The first and most obvious advantage is that you thus induce him to enthrone at the centre of his life a good, solid, resounding lie. I don't mean merely that his statement is false in fact, that he is no more equal to everyone he meets in kindness, honesty, and good sense than in height or waist-measurement. I mean that he does not believe it himself. No man who says *I'm as good as you* believes it. He would not say it if he did. The St. Bernard never says it to the toy dog, nor the scholar to the dunce, nor the employable to the bum, nor the pretty woman to the plain. The claim to equality, outside the strictly political field, is made only by those who feel themselves to be in some way inferior. What it expresses is precisely the itching, smarting, writhing awareness of an inferiority which the patient refuses to accept. . . .

Now this useful phenomenon is in itself by no means new. Under the name of Envy it has been known to the humans for thousands of years. But hitherto they always regarded it as the most odious, and also the most comical, of vices. Those who were aware of feeling it felt it with shame; those who were not gave it no quarter in others. The delightful novelty of the present situation is that you can sanction it—make it respectable and even laudable—by the incantatory use of the word *democratic.*

333

Democracy

The Screwtape Letters, "Screwtape Proposes a Toast" (1959), para. 35–36, pp. 168–169.

[Senior devil Screwtape in a speech at the "Annual Dinner of the Tempters' Training College for Young Devils":] We, in Hell, would welcome the disappearance of Democracy in the strict sense of that word; the political arrangement so called. . . . What we must realise is that "democracy" in the diabolical sense (*I'm as good as you,* Being like Folks, Togetherness) is the finest instrument we could possibly have for extirpating political Democracies from the face of the earth.

For "democracy" or the "democratic spirit" (diabolical sense) leads to a nation without great men, a nation mainly of subliterates, morally flaccid from lack of discipline in youth, full of the cocksureness which flattery breeds on ignorance, and soft from lifelong pampering, and that is what Hell wishes every democratic people to be.

334

Democracy

The Screwtape Letters, "Screwtape Proposes a Toast" (1959), para. 37, p. 169.

[Senior devil Screwtape in a speech at the "Annual Dinner of the Tempters' Training College for Young Devils":] One Democracy was surprised lately when it found that Russia had got ahead of it in science. What a delicious specimen of human blindness! If the whole tendency of their society is opposed to every sort of excellence, why did they expect their scientists to excel?

335

Dependence on God

Letters to an American Lady (16 December 1955), p. 49.

I feel it almost impossible to say anything (in my comfort and security—apparent security, for real security is in Heaven and thus earth affords only imitations) which would not sound horribly false and facile. Also, you know it all better than I do. I should in your place be (I *have* in similar places *been*) far more panic-stricken and even perhaps rebellious. For it is a dreadful truth that the state of (as you say) "having to depend solely on God" is what we all dread most. And of course that just shows how very much, how almost exclusively, we have been depending on things. But trouble goes so far back in our lives and is now so deeply ingrained, we *will* not turn to him as long as He leaves us anything else to turn to. I suppose all one can say is that it was bound to come. In the hour of death and the day of judgment, what else shall we have? Perhaps when those moments come, they will feel happiest who have been forced (however unwittingly) to begin practising it here on earth. It is good of Him to *force* us; but dear me, how hard to *feel* that it is good at the time.

336

Dependence on God

Letters of C. S. Lewis (undated), para. 2, p. 220.

As you say, the thing is to rely *only* on God. The time will come when you will regard all this misery as a small price to pay for having been brought to that dependence. Meanwhile (don't I know) the trouble is that relying on God has to begin all over again every day as if nothing had yet been done.

337
Depravity
The Problem of Pain,
chap. 4, para. 4, p. 57.

A recovery of the old sense of sin is essential to Christianity. Christ takes it for granted that men are bad. Until we really feel this assumption of His to be true, though we are part of the world He came to save, we are not part of the audience to whom His words are addressed.

338
Depravity
Mere Christianity, bk. III,
chap. 11, para. 7, p. 124.

No man knows how bad he is till he has tried very hard to be good.

339
Design
Perelandra, chap. 17,
p. 218.

"All that is made seems planless to the darkened mind, because there are more plans than it looked for."

340
Despair
The Screwtape Letters,
Letter XXIX, para. 7,
p. 138.

Despair is a greater sin than any of the sins which provoke it.

341
Devils
The Screwtape Letters,
Preface (1941), para. 2,
p. 3.

There are two equal and opposite errors into which our race can fall about the devils. One is to disbelieve in their existence. The other is to believe, and to feel an excessive and unhealthy interest in them. They themselves are equally pleased by both errors, and hail a materialist or a magician with the same delight.

342
Devils
The Screwtape Letters,
Letter VII, para. 1, p. 33.

[Senior devil Screwtape to junior devil Wormwood:] "The fact that 'devils' are predominantly *comic* figures in the modern imagination will help you. If any faint suspicion of your existence begins to arise in his mind, suggest to him a picture of something in red tights, and persuade him that since he cannot believe in that (it is an old textbook method of confusing them) he therefore cannot believe in you."

343
Devils
God in the Dock,
"Answers to Questions on Christianity" (1944), ans. 9, pp. 56–57.

No reference to the Devil or devils is included in any Christian Creeds, and it is quite possible to be a Christian without believing in them. I do believe such beings exist, but that is my own affair. Supposing there to be such beings, the degree to which humans were conscious of their presence would presumably vary very much. I mean, the more a man was in the Devil's power, the less he would be aware of it, on the principle that a man is still fairly sober as long as he knows he's drunk. It is the people who are fully awake and trying hard to be good who would be most aware of the Devil. It is when you start arming against Hitler that you first realize your country is full of Nazi agents. Of course, they don't want you to believe in the Devil. If devils exist, their first aim is to give you an anaesthetic—to put you off your guard. Only if that fails, do you become aware of them.

344
Devils
That Hideous Strength,
chap. 14, Section 5, p. 317.

In fighting those who serve devils one always has this on one's side; their Masters hate them as much as they hate us.

345
Devils
The Screwtape Letters,
Preface (1960), para. 15, p. ix.

[Dante's] devils, as Ruskin rightly remarked, in their rage, spite, and obscenity, are far more like what the reality must be than anything in Milton. Milton's devils, by their grandeur and high poetry, have done great harm, and his angels owe too much to Homer and Raphael. But the really pernicious image is Goethe's *Mephistopheles*. It is Faust, not he, who really exhibits the ruthless, sleepless, unsmiling concentration upon self which is the mark of Hell. The humorous, civilised, sensible, adaptable Mephistopheles has helped to strengthen the illusion that evil is liberating.

346

Devils

The Screwtape Letters,
Preface (1960), para. 17,
p. xi.

Bad angels, like bad men, are entirely practical. They have two motives. The first is fear of punishment: for as totalitarian countries have their camps for torture, so my Hell contains deeper Hells, its "houses of correction." Their second motive is a kind of hunger. I feign that devils can, in a spiritual sense, eat one another; and us. Even in human life we have seen the passion to dominate, almost to digest, one's fellow; to make his whole intellectual and emotional life merely an extension of one's own—to hate one's hatreds and resent one's grievances and indulge one's egoism through him as well as through oneself. His own little store of passion must of course be suppressed to make room for ours. If he resists this suppression he is being very selfish.

347

Devotions

God in the Dock, "Cross-
Examination" (1963),
p. 266.

[Question, Mr. Wirt:] What is your view of the daily discipline of the Christian life—the need for taking time to be alone with God?

[Answer, Lewis:] We have our New Testament regimental orders upon the subject. I would take it for granted that everyone who becomes a Christian would undertake this practice. It is enjoined upon us by Our Lord; and since they are His commands, I believe in following them. It is always just possible that Jesus Christ meant what he said when He told us to seek the secret place and to close the door.

348
Devotions
Letters to Malcolm:
Chiefly on Prayer, chap.
21, para. 2, 4, 6–7,
10–12, 16, pp. 113–116.

The truth is, I haven't any language weak enough to depict the weakness of my spiritual life. If I weakened it enough it would cease to be language at all. As when you try to turn the gas-ring a little lower still, and it merely goes out.

. . . Prayer is irksome. An excuse to omit it is never unwelcome. When it is over, this casts a feeling of relief and holiday over the rest of the day. We are reluctant to begin. We are delighted to finish. While we are at prayer, but not while we are reading a novel or solving a cross-word puzzle, any trifle is enough to distract us. . . .

The odd thing is that this reluctance to pray is not confined to periods of dryness. When yesterday's prayers were full of comfort and exaltation, today's will still be felt as, in some degree, a burden.

. . . What can be done *for*—or what should be done *with*—a rose-tree that *dislikes* producing roses? Surely it ought to want to? . . .

The painful effort which prayer involves is no proof that we are doing something we were not created to do.

. . . I must say my prayers to-day whether I feel devout or not; but that is only as I must learn my grammar if I am ever to read the poets.

. . . I have a notion that what seem our worst prayers may really be, in God's eyes, our best. Those, I mean, which are least supported by devotional feeling and contend with the greatest disinclination. For these, perhaps, being nearly all will, come from a deeper level than feeling.

349
Didacticism
A Preface to "Paradise
Lost," Dedication, p. v.

[From the dedication to Charles Williams:] Many will understand henceforward that when the old poets made some virtue their theme they were not teaching but adoring, and that what we take for the didactic is often the enchanted.

350
Disappoint-
ment

The Screwtape Letters,
Letter II, para. 3,
pp. 13–14.

[Senior devil Screwtape to junior devil Wormwood:] "Work hard, then, on the disappointment or anti-climax which is certainly coming to the patient during his first few weeks as a churchman. The Enemy allows this disappointment to occur on the threshold of every human endeavour. It occurs when the boy who has been enchanted in the nursery by *Stories from the Odyssey* buckles down to really learning Greek. It occurs when lovers have got married and begin the real task of learning to live together. In every department of life it marks the transition from dreaming aspiration to laborious doing. The Enemy takes this risk because He has a curious fantasy of making all these disgusting little human vermin into what He calls His "free" lovers and servants—"sons" is the word He uses, with His inveterate love of degrading the whole spiritual world by unnatural liaisons with the two-legged animals. Desiring their freedom, He therefore refuses to carry them, by their mere affections and habits, to any of the goals which He sets before them: He leaves them to "do it on their own." And there lies our opportunity. But also, remember, there lies our danger. If once they get through this initial dryness successfully, they become much less dependent on emotion and therefore much harder to tempt."

351
Disappoint-
ment

The Screwtape Letters,
Letter XXX, para. 2,
p. 141.

[Senior devil Screwtape to junior devil Wormwood:] "Whatever men expect, they soon come to think they have a right to; the sense of disappointment can, with very little skill on our part, be turned into a sense of injury."

352
Discipline
A Preface to "Paradise Lost," chap. 11, para. 14, p. 81.

Discipline, while the world is yet unfallen, exists for the sake of what seems its very opposite—for freedom, almost for extravagance. The pattern deep hidden in the dance, hidden so deep that shallow spectators cannot see it, alone gives beauty to the wild, free gestures that fill it, just as the decasyllabic norm gives beauty to all the licences and variations of the poet's verse. The happy soul is, like a planet, a *wandering* star; yet in that very wandering (as astronomy teaches) invariable; she is eccentric beyond all predicting, yet equable in her eccentricity.

353
Discipline
Poems, "Five Sonnets (4)" (1st pub. 1964), p. 127.

"That long way round which Dante trod was
    meant
For mighty saints and mystics not for me,"
So Nature cries. Yet if we once assent
To Nature's voice, we shall be like the bee
That booms against the window-pane for hours
Thinking that way to reach the laden flowers.

354
Divorce
Mere Christianity, bk. III, chap. 6, para. 3, p. 96.

Churches all agree with one another about marriage a great deal more than any of them agrees with the outside world. I mean, they all regard divorce as something like cutting up a living body, as a kind of surgical operation. Some of them think the operation so violent that it cannot be done at all; others admit it as a desperate remedy in extreme cases. They are all agreed that it is more like having both your legs cut off than it is like dissolving a business partnership or even deserting a regiment. What they all disagree with is the modern view that it is a simple readjustment of partners, to be made whenever people feel they are no longer in love with one another or when either of them falls in love with someone else.

355
Doctrine
God in the Dock, "The
Founding of the Oxford
Socratic Club" (1942–
1943), para. 4, p. 128.

If I may trust my personal experience no doctrine is, for the moment, dimmer to the eye of faith than that which a man has just successfully defended.

356
Doctrine
Mere Christianity, bk. IV,
chap. 1, para. 4, p. 136.

Doctrines are not God: they are only a kind of map. But that map is based on the experience of hundreds of people who really were in touch with God.

357
Donne, John
Selected Literary Essays,
"Donne and Love
Poetry" (1938), para. 24,
p. 125.

Donne was a "good influence"—a better influence than many greater poets. It would hardly be too much to say that the final cause of Donne's poetry is the poetry of Herbert, Crashaw, and Marvell; for the very qualities which make Donne's kind of poetry unsatisfying poetic food make it a valuable ingredient.

358
Donne, John
*English Literature in the
Sixteenth Century,*
Epilogue, II, para. 17,
pp. 549.

In Donne's most serious lyrics, which I suppose to be his best, we have a poetry which is almost exactly opposite to that of Shakespeare's *Sonnets.* In Shakespeare each experience of the lover becomes a window through which we look out on immense prospects—on nature, the seasons, life and death, time and eternity. In Donne it is more like a burning-glass; angelology, natural philosophy, law, institutions are all drawn together, narrowed and focused at this one place and moment where a particular man is mocking, flattering, browbeating, laughing at, or laughing with, or adoring, a particular woman. And they all have, for Donne in the poem, no value or even existence except as they articulate and render more fully self-conscious the passion of that moment. His imagination is centripetal. . . . Each of Donne's lyrics is a world in itself; or, if you prefer, is the whole world foreshortened and transformed by, and sacrificed to, some one precise shade of passion. Each would therefore be suffocating, monstrous, if it lasted too long. But this intense concentration within the individual lyric is, of course, balanced by a great versatility of mood in the collection as a whole. When we re-read the *Songs and Sonnets* they always seem to be fewer than we had remembered. It is remarkable that in such short space so many different modes of love—frivolous, petulant, embittered, tragic, "Platonic," rapturous, or tranquil—have found such striking expression.

359
Donne, John: Love Poetry
Selected Literary Essays, "Donne and Love Poetry" (1938), para. 22, p. 123.

Donne's love poetry is parasitic. . . . Donne's love poems could not exist unless love poems of a more genial character existed first. He shows us amazing shadows cast by love upon the intellect, the passions, and the appetite; to learn of the substance which casts them we must go to other poets, more balanced, more magnanimous, and more humane. . . . In the main, his love poetry is *Hamlet* without the prince.

360
Doubt
The Letters of C. S. Lewis to Arthur Greeves (24 December 1930), para. 9, pp. 398–399.

I think the trouble with me is *lack of faith*. I have no *rational* ground for going back on the arguments that convinced me of God's existence: but the irrational deadweight of my old sceptical habits, and the spirit of this age, and the cares of the day, steal away all my lively feeling of the truth, and often when I pray I wonder if I am not posting letters to a non-existent address. Mind you I don't *think* so—the whole of my reasonable mind is convinced: but I often *feel* so. However, there is nothing to do but to peg away. One falls so often that it hardly seems worth while picking oneself up and going through the farce of starting over again as if you could ever hope to walk. Still, this seeming absurdity is the only sensible thing I do, so I must continue it.

361
Doubt
A Grief Observed,
chap. 1, para. 9, p. 5.

[Lewis was grieving the death of his wife:] Not that I am (I think) in much danger of ceasing to believe in God. The real danger is of coming to believe such dreadful things about Him. The conclusion I dread is not "So there's no God after all," but "So this is what God's really like. Deceive yourself no longer."

362
Doubt
A Grief Observed,
chap. 3, para. 4, p. 43.

[Lewis was grieving the death of his wife:] Bridge-players tell me that there must be some money on the game "or else people won't take it seriously." Apparently it's like that. Your bid—for God or no God, for a good God or the Cosmic Sadist, for eternal life or nonentity—will not be serious if nothing much is staked on it. And you will never discover how serious it was until the stakes are raised horribly high; until you find that you are playing not for counters or for sixpences but for every penny you have in the world.

363
Drayton, Michael
English Literature in the Sixteenth Century, bk. III.III.III, para. 23, pp. 496–497.

There are hints of that quality (by no means its only virtue) which sets Drayton's final sequence apart from those of all his contemporaries—that exaltation, that wildness, which, as Mrs. Tillotson says, sounds "almost as if Marlowe were writing sonnets." . . . When he speaks simply as any lover he can sometimes outsoar all the sonneteers except Shakespeare. . . . Yet again, and in quite a different vein, that of towering hyperbole, Drayton (this time with no rival at all, neither Shakespeare nor any other) sets up the seamark beyond which

---

poetry in that kind has never gone nor could go:
And Queens hereafter shall be glad to live
Upon the almes of thy superfluous prayse.

If he had never written another verse, these two would secure him that praise which is due to men who have done some one thing to perfection.

364
Drayton, Michael

English Literature in the Sixteenth Century, bk. III.III.III, para. 64, p. 531.

He was in a sense too poetical to be a sound poet. His sensibility responded almost too quickly to every kind of subject—myth, the heroic past, tragic story, and (most of all) the fruitful, sheep-dotted, river-veined, legend-haunted expanse of England. He had an unquenchable desire to write poetry about them all, and he always seemed to himself to be succeeding because he mistook the heat which they roused in him for a heat he was communicating to the reader. He himself has told us (in the *Epistle To Henry Reynolds*) how at the age of ten he hugged his "mild tutor" begging to be made into a poet, and how the good man granted his request, in typically sixteenth-century fashion, by starting him on Mantuan. In that scene we have what is essential in Drayton the man: a man with one aim, devoted for life to his art, like Milton or Pope. If the Muse regarded merit he would have been one of our greatest poets.

365
Dreams

The Letters of C. S. Lewis to Arthur Greeves (2 November 1918), p. 238.

So at last dreams come to pass and I have sat in the sanctum of a publisher discussing my own book (Notice the hideous vulgarity of success already growing in me). Yet—though it is very pleasant—you will understand me when I say that it has not the utter romance which the promise of it had a year ago. Once a dream has become a fact I suppose it loses something. This isn't affectation: we long & long for a thing and when

it comes it turns out to be just a pleasant incident,
very much like others.

366
Dreams
Narrative Poems, Dymer,
VI.24, 26 (1918),
pp. 61–62.

For broken dreams the cure is, Dream again
And deeper. . . .
"In dreams the fool is free from scorning voices.
Grey-headed whores are virgin there again.
Out of the past dream brings long-buried choices
All in a moment snaps the tenfold chain
That life took years in forging. There the stain
Of oldest sins—how do the good words go?—
Though they were scarlet, shall be white as snow."

367
Dryden, John
Selected Literary Essays,
"Shelley, Dryden, and Mr
Eliot" (1939), para. 3–4,
p. 188.

When we turn to Dryden, we must . . . admit
that we have here a great, flawed poet, in whom
the flaws, besides being characteristically
unclassical, are scarcely forgivable even by the
most romantic or revolutionary standards. . . . Of
the greatness I wish to make no question; and it is
a greatness to which the name of *genius* is
peculiarly applicable. The most abiding impression
which Dryden makes upon us is that of exuberant
power. . . . He excels in beginnings.

368
Dryden, John
Selected Literary Essays,
"Shelley, Dryden, and Mr
Eliot" (1939), para. 5–7,
10, pp. 190–193.

Is he, in fine, a man ready, for every ray of
accidental beauty that may come in his way, to
sacrifice the integrity of his work—a dabbler in
"good passages"—a man who can produce good
poetry but not good poems?" . . . [*Absalom*] is
not merely maimed, it is diseased at the heart.
Like many human invalids, it is not lacking in
charms and happy moments; but classicists like
Mr Eliot (and myself) should not accept any
amount of littered poetry as a poem. If we turn
to the *Hind and the Panther* we find the same

irredeemable defect in an aggravated form. Of course it is full of "good things"; but of the plan itself, the nerve and structure of the poem, what are we to say if not that the very design of conducting in verse a theological controversy allegorized as a beast fable suggests in the author a state of mind bordering on aesthetic insanity? . . . It is not a poem: it is simply a name which we give for convenience to a number of pieces of good description, vigorous satire, and "popular" controversy, which have all been yoked together by external violence. . . . In *Sigismonda and Guiscardo* . . . he destroys, and is content to destroy, the kind of poem he sat down to write, if only he can win in return one guffaw from the youngest and most graceless of his audience. There is in this a poetic blasphemy, an arrogant contempt for his own art, which cannot, I think, be paralleled in any other great writer.

369
Dryden, John
Selected Literary Essays,
"Shelley, Dryden, and Mr
Eliot" (1939), para. 12,
p. 194.

The man is irremediably ignorant of that world he chooses so often to write about. When he confines himself to satire, he is at home; but even here, the fatal lack of architectonic power seldom allows him to make a satisfactory poem. That is the case against Dryden.

370
**Dumas,
Alexandre**
*The Letters of C. S.
Lewis to Arthur Greeves*
(25 March 1933), p. 451.

I tried, at W's [Lewis's brother Warren's] earnest recommendation, to read the *Three Musketeers,* but not only got tired of it but also found it disgusting. All these swaggering bullies, living on the money of their mistresses—faugh! One never knows how good Scott is till one tries to read Dumas. Have you noticed how completely Dumas lacks any background? In Scott, behind the adventures of the hero, you have the whole society of the age, with all the interplay of town

and country, Puritan and Cavalier, Saxon and
Norman, or what not, and all the racy humour of
the minor characters: and behind that again you
have the eternal things—the actual countryside,
the mountains, the weather, the very *feel* of
travelling. In Dumas, if you try to look even an
inch behind the immediate intrigue, you find just
nothing at all. You are in an abstract world of
gallantry and adventure which has no *roots*—no
connection with human nature or mother earth.
When the scene shifts from Paris to London there
is no sense that you have reached a new country,
no change of atmosphere. And I don't think there
is a single passage to show that Dumas had ever
seen a cloud, a road, or a tree.

371
**Dunbar,
William**
*English Literature in the
Sixteenth Century,* bk.
I.I.I, para. 45, p. 98.

His poems are not "human documents." We
remain his audience, not his confidants, cut off
from him (as it were) by the footlights. . . . He
will in our time be more often admired than
loved; a reaction with which he would have been
quite content. But he was a very great man. When
you are in the mood for it, his poetry has a sweep
and volume of sound and an assured virility which
(while the mood lasts) makes most other poets
seem a little faint and tentative and half-hearted. If
you like half-tones and nuances you will not enjoy
Dunbar; he will deafen you.

372
Duty
*Boxen: The Imaginary
World of the Young C. S.
Lewis* (1905–1913), "The
Sailor," I.IX, p. 178.

"What is duty?"
  "Well, I suppose, work."

373
Duty
The Letters of C. S. Lewis to Arthur Greeves (3 October 1929), p. 310.

Unfortunately the morning has to be given to uninteresting work done as fast as I can manage to get through it—a process which would rob even voluntary work of its interest. How thankful you should be that you never have tasks which are not chosen by yourself. And yet I don't know. So many things have now become interesting to me because at first I had to do them whether I liked them or not, and thus one is kicked into new countries where one is afterwards at home.

374
Duty
The Letters of C. S. Lewis to Arthur Greeves (30 January 1930), p. 339.

One cannot be too careful: one must try to hold fast to one's duties (I wish I did) which are the prose of the spiritual life and not learn to depend too much on these delightful moments.

375
Duty
The Weight of Glory, "Learning in War-Time" (1939), chap. 4, para. 6, pp. 24–25.

Every duty is a religious duty, and our obligation to perform every duty is therefore absolute. Thus we may have a duty to rescue a drowning man, and perhaps, if we live on a dangerous coast, to learn life-saving so as to be ready for any drowning man when he turns up. It may be our duty to lose our own lives in saving him. But if anyone devoted himself to life-saving in the sense of giving it his total attention—so that he thought and spoke of nothing else and demanded the cessation of all other human activities until everyone had learned to swim—he would be a monomaniac. The rescue of drowning men is, then, a duty worth dying for, but not worth living for. It seems to me that all political duties (among which I include military duties) are of this kind. A man may have to die for our country: but no man must, in any exclusive sense, live for his country. He who surrenders himself without reservation to the temporal claims of a nation, or a party, or a class is rendering to Caesar that which, of all things, most emphatically belongs to God: himself.

376
Duty
Letters of C. S. Lewis
(18 July 1957), p. 276.

A *perfect* man wd. never act from sense of duty; he'd always *want* the right thing more than the wrong one. Duty is only a substitute for love (of God and of other people) like a crutch which is a substitute for a leg. Most of us need the crutch at times; but of course it is idiotic to use the crutch when our own legs (our own loves, tastes, habits, etc) can do the journey on their own.

377
Duty
Reflections on the Psalms,
chap. 9, para. 7, p. 97.

Meanwhile of course we are merely, as Donne says, tuning our instruments. The tuning up of the orchestra can be itself delightful, but only to those who can in some measure, however little, anticipate the symphony. The Jewish sacrifices, and even our own most sacred rites, as they actually occur in human experience, are, like the tuning, promise, not performance. Hence, like the tuning, they may have in them much duty and little delight; or none. But the duty exists for the delight. When we carry out our "religious duties" we are like people digging channels in a waterless land, in order that when at last the water comes, it may find them ready. I mean, for the most part. There are happy moments, even now, when a trickle creeps along the dry beds; and happy souls to whom this happens often.

378
Duty
Letters to Malcolm:
Chiefly on Prayer,
chap. 21, para. 14,
p. 116.

Duty is always conditioned by evil.

379
Dying to Self
The Weight of Glory,
"A Slip of the Tongue"
(1st pub. 1965), para. 9,
p. 130.

It is not so much of our time and so much of our attention that God demands; it is not even all our time and all our attention: it is our selves. For each of us the Baptist's words are true: "He must increase and I decrease." He will be infinitely merciful to our repeated failures; I know no promise that he will accept a deliberate compromise. For He has, in the last resort, nothing out of our territory; but we must be in the Resistance, to give us but Himself; and He can give that only in so far as our self-affirming will retires and makes room for Him in our souls. Let us make up our minds to it; there will be nothing "of our own" left over to live on; no "ordinary" life.

380
Dying to Self
The Weight of Glory,
"A Slip of the Tongue"
(1st pub. 1965), para. 10,
pp. 130–131.

He cannot bless us unless he has us. When we try to keep within us an area that is our own, we try to keep an area of death. Therefore, in love, He claims all. There's no bargaining with Him.

381
Dying to Self
The Weight of Glory,
"A Slip of the Tongue"
(1st pub. 1965), para. 11,
p. 131.

Thomas More said, "If ye make indentures with God how much ye will serve Him, ye shall find ye have signed both of them yourself." Law, in his terrible, cool voice, said, "Many will be rejected at the last day, not because they have taken no time and pains about their salvation, but because they have not taken time and pains enough"; . . . "If you have not chosen the Kingdom of God, it will make in the end no difference what you have chosen instead." Those are hard words to take. Will it really make no difference whether it was women or patriotism, cocaine or art, whisky or a seat in the Cabinet, money or science? Well, surely no difference that matters. We shall have missed the end for which we are formed and rejected the only thing that satisfies. Does it matter to a man dying in a desert, by which choice of route he missed the only well?

382
Easter
Letters: C. S. Lewis/Don Giovanni Calabria (27 March 1948), para. 8, p. 47.

[Lewis has just addressed his correspondent's concern for the troubles of the world:] Tomorrow [Easter] we shall celebrate the glorious Resurrection of Christ. I shall be remembering you in the Holy Communion. Away with tears and fears and troubles! United in wedlock with the eternal Godhead Itself, our nature ascends into the Heaven of Heaven. So it would be impious to call ourselves "miserable." On the contrary, Man is a creature whom the Angels— were they capable of envy—would envy. Let us lift up our hearts! "At some future time perhaps even these things it will be a joy to recall."

383
Economics
Letters to an American Lady (19 December 1955), p. 50.

I wish we didn't live in a world where buying and selling things (especially selling) seems to have become almost more important than either producing or using them.

384
Education
The Weight of Glory, "Learning in War-Time" (1939), para. 1–3, 5, pp. 20–21, 23–24.

A University is a society for the pursuit of learning. . . . At first sight this seems to be an odd thing to do during a great war. What is the use of beginning a task which we have so little chance of finishing? . . . Is it not like fiddling while Rome burns?

Now it seems to me that we shall not be able

to answer these questions until we have put them by the side of certain other questions which every Christian ought to have asked himself in peacetime. I spoke just now of fiddling while Rome burns. But to a Christian the true tragedy of Nero must be not that he fiddled while the city was on fire but that he fiddled on the brink of hell.

. . . Every Christian who comes to a university must at all times face a question compared with which the questions raised by the war are relatively unimportant. He must ask himself how it is right, or even psychologically possible, for creatures who are every moment advancing either to heaven or to hell, to spend any fraction of the little time allowed them in this world on such comparative trivialities as literature or art, mathematics or biology.

. . . Before I became a Christian I do not think I fully realized that one's life, after conversion, would inevitably consist in doing most of the same things one had been doing before: one hopes, in a new spirit, but still the same things. . . . If you attempted, in either case, to suspend your whole intellectual and aesthetic activity, you would only succeed in substituting a worse cultural life for a better. You are not, in fact, going to read nothing, either in the Church or in the line: if you don't read good books you will read bad ones. If you don't go on thinking rationally, you will think irrationally. If you reject aesthetic satisfactions you will fall into sensual satisfactions.

385
Education
The Weight of Glory,
"Learning in War-Time"
(1939), para. 12, p. 30.

The only people who achieve much are those who want knowledge so badly that they seek it while the conditions are still unfavourable. Favourable conditions never come.

386
Education

God in the Dock, "On the Transmission of Christianity" (1946), para. 5–7. p. 116–117.

This very obvious fact—that each generation is taught by an earlier generation—must be kept very firmly in mind. . . . The mental world also has its time-bombs—of obsolete adolescence, now middle-aged and dominating its form room. Hence the futility of many schemes for education. None can give to another what he does not possess himself. No generation can bequeath to its successor what it has not got. . . . If we are sceptical we shall teach only scepticism to our pupils, if fools only folly, if vulgar only vulgarity, if saints sanctity, if heroes heroism. . . . We shall admit that a man who knows no Greek himself cannot teach Greek to his form: but it is equally certain that a man whose mind was formed in a period of cynicism and disillusion, cannot teach hope or fortitude.

A society which is predominantly Christian will propagate Christianity through its schools: one which is not, will not. All the ministries of education in the world cannot alter this law. We have, in the long run, little either to hope or fear from government.

. . . All the teaching must still be done by concrete human individuals. The State has to use the men who exist. Nay, as long as we remain a democracy, it is men who give the State its powers. And over these men, until all freedom is extinguished, the free winds of opinion blow. Their minds are formed by influences which government cannot control. And as they come to be, so will they teach.

387
Education and Christianity

Mere Christianity, bk. III, chap. 2, para. 4, p. 75.

One of the reasons why it needs no special education to be a Christian is that Christianity is an education itself. That is why an uneducated believer like Bunyan was able to write a book that has astonished the whole world.

388
Education, Decline of

Selected Literary Essays,
"De Descriptione
Temporum" (1955),
para. 6, p. 4.

We have lived to see the second death of ancient learning. In our time something which was once the possession of all educated men has shrunk to being the technical accomplishment of a few specialists. . . . If one were looking for a man who could not read Virgil though his father could, he might be found more easily in the twentieth century than in the fifth.

389
Education, Democracy in

The Screwtape Letters,
"Screwtape Proposes a
Toast" (1959), para. 29,
32–34, pp. 164–168.

[The devil Screwtape in a speech at the "Annual Dinner of the Tempters' Training College for Young Devils":] What I want to fix your attention on is the vast overall movement towards the discrediting, and finally the elimination of every kind of human excellence—moral, cultural, social or intellectual. And is it not pretty to notice how "democracy" (in the incantatory sense) is now doing for us the work that was once done by the most ancient Dictatorships, and by the same methods?

. . . The basic principal of the new education is to be that dunces and idlers must not be made to feel inferior to intelligent and industrious pupils. That would be "undemocratic." . . . Children who are fit to proceed to a higher class may be artificially kept back, because the others would get a trauma . . . by being left behind. The bright pupil thus remains democratically fettered to his own age group throughout his school career, and a boy who would be capable of tackling Aeschylus or Dante sits listening to his coeval's attempts to spell out A CAT SAT ON A MAT.

In a word, we may reasonably hope for the virtual abolition of education when *I'm as good as you* has fully had its way. All incentives to learn and all penalties for not learning will vanish. The few who might want to learn will be prevented;

who are they to overtop their fellows? And anyway the teachers—or should I say, nurses?—will be far too busy reassuring the dunces and patting them on the back to waste any time of real teaching. We shall no longer have to plan and toil to spread imperturbable conceit and incurable ignorance among men. The little vermin themselves will do it for us.

390
Education, Function of

The Weight of Glory,
"Learning in War-Time"
(1939), para. 10–11,
pp. 28–29.

If all the world were Christian, it might not matter if all the world were uneducated. But, as it is, a cultural life will exist outside the Church whether it exists inside or not. To be ignorant and simple now—not to be able to meet enemies on their own ground—would be to throw down our weapons, and to betray our uneducated brethren who have, under God, no defence but us against the intellectual attacks of the heathen. Good philosophy must exist, if for no other reason, because bad philosophy needs to be answered. The cool intellect must work not only against cool intellect on the other side, but against the muddy heathen mysticisms which deny intellect altogether. Most of all, perhaps, we need intimate knowledge of the past. Not that the past has any magic about it, but because we cannot study the future, and yet need something to set against the present, to remind us that the basic assumptions have been quite different in different periods and that much which seems certain to the uneducated is merely temporary fashion. A man who has lived in many places is not likely to be deceived by the local errors of his native village: the scholar has lived in many times and is therefore in some degree immune from the great cataract of nonsense that pours from the press and the microphone of his own age.

The learned life then is, for some, a duty.

391

Education, Function of

The Abolition of Man, chap. 1, para. 8, p. 24.

The task of the modern educator is not to cut down jungles but to irrigate deserts. The right defence against false sentiments is to inculcate just sentiments. By starving the sensibility of our pupils we only make them easier prey to the propagandist when he comes. For famished nature will be avenged and a hard heart is no infallible protection against a soft head.

392

Education, Goal of

The Abolition of Man, chap. 1, para. 10, p. 26.

Aristotle says that the aim of education is to make the pupil like and dislike what he ought. When the age for reflective thought comes, the pupil who has been thus trained in "ordinate affections" or "just sentiments" will easily find the first principles in Ethics: but to the corrupt man they will never be visible at all and he can make no progress in that science.

393

Education, Purpose of

Rehabilitations, "Our English Syllabus" (1st pub. 1939), para. 1–2, 4–5, pp. 81–82, 84–85.

Schoolmasters in our time are fighting hard in defence of education against vocational training; universities, on the other hand, are fighting against education on behalf of learning.

Let me explain. The purpose of education has been described by Milton as that of fitting a man "to perform justly, skilfully, and magnanimously all the offices both private and public, of peace and war." Provided we do not overstress "skilfully" Aristotle would substantially agree with this, but would add the conception that it should also be a preparation for leisure, which according to him is the end of all human activity. "We wage war in order to have peace; we work in order to have leisure." Neither of them would dispute that the purpose of education is to produce the good man and the good citizen, though it must be remembered that we are not here using the word "good" in any narrowly ethical sense. The "good man" here means the man of good taste and good feeling, the interesting and interested man, and almost the happy man. . . . Vocational training, on the other hand, prepares the pupil not for leisure, but for work; it aims at making not a good man but a good banker, a good electrician, a good scavenger, or a good surgeon. You see at once that education is essentially for freemen and vocational training for slaves.

. . . If education is beaten by training, civilization dies. That is a thing very likely to happen.

. . . Now learning, considered in itself, has, on my view, no connexion at all with education. It is an activity for . . . all [who] desire to know. . . . Societies have usually held a belief . . . that knowledge is the natural food of the human mind: that those who specially pursue it are being specially human; and that their activity is good in itself besides being always honourable and sometimes useful to the whole society. Hence we come to have such associations as universities—institutions for the support and encouragement of men devoted to learning.

. . . Our colleges at Oxford were founded not in order to teach the young but in order to support masters of arts. . . . A school without pupils would cease to be school; a college without undergraduates would be as much a college as ever, would perhaps be more a college.

394
Education, Quality of
Letters to Children (29 September 1958), p. 83.

All schools, both here [in England] and in America, ought to teach far fewer subjects and teach them far better.

395

Education: Teacher/Pupil Relationship

Reflections on the Psalms, chap. 1, para. 1, pp. 1–2.

The fellow-pupil can help more than the master because he knows less. The difficulty we want him to explain is one he has recently met. The expert met it so long ago that he has forgotten. He sees the whole subject, by now, in such a different light that he cannot conceive what is really troubling the pupil; he sees a dozen other difficulties which ought to be troubling him but aren't.

396

Embarrassment

Present Concerns: Essays by C. S. Lewis, "After Priggery—What?" (1945), para. 5, p. 57.

We have lost the invaluable faculty of being shocked—a faculty which has hitherto almost distinguished the Man or Woman from the beast or the child.

397

Endurance

Letters to an American Lady (1 April 1957), pp. 64–65.

I must try not to let my own present unhappiness harden my heart against the woes of others! You too are going through a dreadful time. Ah well, it will not last forever. There will come a day for all of us when "it is finished." God help us all.

398

England, Religion in

Mere Christianity, bk. IV, chap. 1, para. 4, p. 137.

To believe in the popular religion of modern England is retrogression—like believing the earth is flat.

399

Envy

The Four Loves, chap. 4, para. 41, p. 112.

Envy always brings the truest charge, or the charge nearest to the truth, that she can think up; it hurts more.

400

Equality

A Preface to "Paradise Lost," chap. 11, para. 3, p. 74.

Justice means equality for equals, and inequality for unequals.

401
Equality
A Preface to "Paradise Lost," chap. 11, para. 5, p. 75.

The greatest statement of the Hierarchical conception in its double reference to civil and cosmic life is, perhaps, the speech of Ulysses in Shakespeare's *Troilus*. Its special importance lies in its clear statement of the alternative to Hierarchy. If you take "Degree" away "each thing meets in mere oppugnancy," "strength" will be lord, everything will "include itself in power." In other words, the modern idea that we can choose between hierarchy and equality is, for Shakespeare's Ulysses, mere moonshine. The real alternative is tyranny; if you will not have authority you will find yourself obeying brute force.

402
Equality
A Preface to "Paradise Lost," chap. 11, para. 6-7, p. 76.

It seems to me beyond doubt that Shakespeare agreed with Montaigne that "to obey is the proper office of a rational soul."

Now if once the conception of Hierarchy is fully grasped, we see that order can be destroyed in two ways: (1) By ruling or obeying natural equals, that is by Tyranny or Servility. (2) By failing to obey a natural superior or to rule a natural inferior—that is, by Rebellion or Remissness.

403
Equality
A Preface to "Paradise Lost," chap. 11, para. 10, p. 78.

Tyranny, the rule over equals as if they were inferiors, is rebellion. And equally, as Shakespeare's Ulysses saw, rebellion is tyranny.

404
Equality
Present Concerns: Essays by C. S. Lewis, "Equality" (1943), para. 2, pp. 17-18.

I do not think that equality is one of those things (like wisdom or happiness) which are good simply in themselves and for their own sakes. I think it is in the same class as medicine, which is good because we are ill, or clothes which are good

because we are no longer innocent. I don't think
the old authority in kings, priests, husbands, or
fathers, and the old obedience in subjects, laymen,
wives, and sons, was in itself a degrading or evil
thing at all. I think it was intrinsically as good and
beautiful as the nakedness of Adam and Eve. It
was rightly taken away because men became bad
and abused it. To attempt to restore it now would
be the same error as that of the Nudists. Legal
and economic equality are absolutely necessary
remedies for the Fall, and protection against
cruelty.

405
Equality

*Present Concerns: Essays
by C. S. Lewis,
"Equality" (1943),
para. 4, p. 18.*

When equality is treated not as a medicine or a
safety-gadget but as an ideal we begin to breed
that stunted and envious sort of mind which hates
all superiority.

406
Equality

*Present Concerns: Essays
by C. S. Lewis,
"Equality" (1943),
para. 6, p. 19.*

Have as much equality as you please—the more
the better—in our marriage laws: but at some
level consent to inequality, nay, delight in
inequality, is an *erotic* necessity.

407
Equality

*Present Concerns: Essays
by C. S. Lewis,
"Equality" (1943),
para. 9, p. 20.*

Every intrusion of the spirit that says "I'm as good
as you" into our personal and spiritual life is to be
resisted just as jealously as every intrusion of
bureaucracy or privilege into our politics.
Hierarchy within can alone preserve egalitarianism
without. . . . Human nature will not permanently
endure flat equality if it is extended from its
proper political field into the more real, more
concrete fields within. Let us *wear* equality; but
let us undress every night.

408
Equality
Present Concerns: Essays by C. S. Lewis, "Democratic Education" (1944), para. 6, p. 33.

The demand for equality has two sources; one of them is among the noblest, the other is the basest, of human emotions. The noble source is the desire for fair play. But the other source is the hatred of superiority.

409
Equality
Present Concerns: Essays by C. S. Lewis, "Democratic Education" (1944), para. 7–8, p. 34.

The kind of "democratic" education which is already looming ahead is bad because it endeavours to propitiate evil passions, to appease envy. There are two reasons for not attempting this. In the first place, you will not succeed. Envy is insatiable. The more you concede to it the more it will demand. No attitude of humility which you can possibly adopt will propitiate a man with an inferiority complex. In the second place, you are trying to introduce equality where equality is fatal.

Equality (outside mathematics) is a purely social conception. It applies to man as a political and economic animal. It has no place in the world of the mind. Beauty is not democratic; she reveals herself more to the few than to the many, more to the persistent and disciplined seekers than to the careless. Virtue is not democratic; she is achieved by those who pursue her more hotly than most men. Truth is not democratic; she demands special talents and special industry in those to whom she gives her favours. Political democracy is doomed if it tries to extend its demand for equality into these higher spheres. Ethical, intellectual, or aesthetic democracy is death.

410
Equality
God in the Dock, "The Grand Miracle" (1945), para. 7, p. 85.

I cannot conceive how one would get through the boredom of a world in which you never met anyone more clever, or more beautiful, or stronger than yourself. The very crowds who go after the football celebrities and film-stars know better than to desire that kind of equality!

411
Equality
That Hideous Strength,
chap. 7, section 2,
p. 148.

"Ah, equality!" said the Director. "We must talk of that some other time. Yes, we must all be guarded by equal rights from one another's greed, because we are fallen. Just as we must all wear clothes for the same reason. But the naked body should be there underneath the clothes, ripening for the day when we shall need them no longer. Equality is not the deepest thing, you know."

"I always thought that was just what it was. I thought it was in their souls that people were equal."

"You were mistaken," said he gravely. "That is the last place where they are equal. Equality before the law, equality of incomes—that is very well. Equality guards life; it doesn't make it. It is medicine, not food."

412
Equality and Christianity
*Present Concerns: Essays
by C. S. Lewis,*
"Equality" (1943),
para. 5, p. 19.

Under the necessary outer covering of legal equality, the whole hierarchal dance and harmony of our deep and joyously accepted spiritual inequalities should be alive. It is there, of course, in our life as Christians: there, as laymen, we can obey—all the more because the priest has no authority over us on the political level. It is there in our relation to parents and teachers—all the more because it is now a willed and wholly spiritual reverence. It should be there also in marriage.

413
Equality and Christianity
The Weight of Glory,
"Membership" (1945),
para. 15, pp. 115–116.

Equality is a quantitative term and therefore love often knows nothing of it. . . . Even in the life of the affections, much more in the body of Christ, we step outside that world which says "I am as good as you." . . . We become, as Chesterton said, taller when we bow; we become lowlier when we instruct.

414 **Eternal Life** See also conversion, redemption, salvation. *The Weight of Glory,* "Membership" (1945), para. 16, p. 117.	A rejection, or in Scripture's strong language, a crucifixion of the natural self is the passport to everlasting life. Nothing that has not died will be resurrected.

415 **Eternal Life** *The Weight of Glory,* "Membership" (1945), para. 16, p. 117.	As organs in the Body of Christ, as stones and pillars in the temple, we are assured of our eternal self-identity and shall live to remember the galaxies as an old tale.

416 **Eternal Life** *Mere Christianity,* bk. III, chap. 1, para. 9, p. 73.	Christianity asserts that every individual human being is going to live for ever, and this must be either true or false. Now there are a good many things which would not be worth bothering about if I were going to live only seventy years, but which I had better bother about very seriously if I am going to live for ever. Perhaps my bad temper or my jealousy are gradually getting worse—so gradually that the increase in seventy years will not be very noticeable. But it might be absolute hell in a million years: in fact, if Christianity is true, hell is the precisely correct technical term for what it would be.

417 **Eternal Life** *Mere Christianity,* bk. IV, chap. 1, para. 4, p. 136.	A vague religion—all about feeling God in nature, and so on—is so attractive. It is all thrills and no work; like watching the waves from the beach. But you will not get to Newfoundland by studying the Atlantic, and you will not get eternal life by simply feeling the presence of God in Flowers or music.

418
Eternity
A Severe Mercy, Letter to
Sheldon Vanauken (23
December 1950), p. 93.

You say the materialist universe is "ugly." I wonder how you discovered that! If you are really a product of a materialistic universe, how is it you don't feel at home there? Do fish complain of the sea for being wet? Or if they did, would that fact itself not strongly suggest that they had not always been, or wd. not always be, purely aquatic creatures? Notice how we are perpetually *surprised* at Time. ("How time flies! Fancy John being grown-up & married! I can hardly believe it!") In heaven's name, why? Unless, indeed, there is something in us which is *not* temporal.

419
Eternity
A Severe Mercy, Letter
to Sheldon Vanauken
(5 June 1955), p. 205.

I'm pretty sure eternal life doesn't mean this width-less line of moments endlessly prolonged (as if by prolongation it cd. "catch up with" that wh. it so obviously cd. never hold) but getting off that line onto its plane or even the solid.

420
Eternity
Reflections on the Psalms,
chap. 12, para. 17,
p. 138.

We are so little reconciled to time that we are even astonished at it. "How he's grown!" we exclaim, "How time flies!" as though the universal form of our experience were again and again a novelty. It is as strange as if a fish were repeatedly surprised at the wetness of water. And that would be strange indeed; unless of course the fish were destined to become, one day, a land animal.

421
Eternity
The Four Loves,
chap. 16, para. 39,
p. 188.

All that is not eternal is eternally out of date.

422
Ethics
The Abolition of Man,
chap. 2, para. 18, p. 59.

Aristotle said that only those who have been well brought up can usefully study ethics: to the corrupted man, the man who stands outside the *Tao,* the very starting point of this science is invisible.

423
Ethics
Christian Reflections,
"On Ethics" (1943?),
chap. 4, para. 22, p. 53.

Let us very clearly understand that, in a certain sense, it is no more possible to invent a new ethics than to place a new sun in the sky. Some precept from traditional morality always has to be assumed. We never start from a *tabula rasa*; if we did, we should end, ethically speaking, with a *tabula rasa.*

424
Ethics
God in the Dock,
"Letters," letter 4 (2 March 1944), para. 1, p. 329.

My reason for thinking that a mere statement of even the highest ethical principles is not enough is precisely that to know these things is not necessarily to do them, and if Christianity brought no healing to the impotent will, Christ's teaching would not help us.

425
Evangelism
Letters of C. S. Lewis (15 May 1941), pp. 193–194.

[Following a reference to his upcoming BBC radio talks on Christianity:] I've given talks to the RAF [Royal Air Force] at Abingdon already, and so far as I can judge they were a complete failure. . . . Yes, jobs one dare neither refuse or perform. One must take comfort in remembering that God used an ass to convert the prophet; perhaps if we do our poor best we shall be allowed a stall near it in the celestial stable.

426
Evangelism
God in the Dock,
"Christian Apologetics" (1945), para. 21, p. 99.

I am not sure that the ideal missionary team ought not to consist of one who argues and one who (in the fullest sense of the word) preaches. Put up your arguer first to undermine their intellectual prejudices; then let the evangelist proper launch his appeal. I have seen this done with great success.

427

Evangelism

God in the Dock, "On the Transmission of Christianity" (1946), para. 11, p. 119.

To convert one's adult neighbour and one's adolescent neighbour (just free from school) is the practical thing. . . . If you make the adults of today Christian, the children of tomorrow will receive a Christian education. What a society has, that, be sure, and nothing else, it will hand on to its young.

428

Evangelism

A Severe Mercy, Letter to Sheldon Vanauken (22 April 1953), p. 134.

My feeling about people in whose conversion I have been allowed to play a part is always mixed with awe and even fear: such as a boy might feel on first being allowed to fire a rifle. The disproportion between his puny finger on the trigger and the thunder & lightning wh. follow is alarming. And the seriousness with which the other party takes my words always raises the doubt whether I have taken them seriously enough myself. By writing the things I write, you see, one especially qualifies for being hereafter "condemned out of one's own mouth." Think of me as a fellow-patient in the same hospital who, having been admitted a little earlier, cd. give some advice.

429

Evangelism

Letters of C. S. Lewis (2 February 1955), p. 261.

It is right and inevitable that we should be much concerned about the salvation of those we love. But we must be careful not to expect or demand that their salvation shd. conform to some ready-made pattern of our own.

430

Evangelism

Letters of C. S. Lewis (2 February 1955), p. 261.

What we practise, not (save at rare intervals) what we preach, is usually our great contribution to the conversion of others.

431
Evangelism
God in the Dock,
"Rejoinder to Dr
Pittenger" (1958),
para. 16, p. 183.

When I began, Christianity came before the great mass of my unbelieving fellow-countrymen either in the highly emotional form offered by revivalists or in the unintelligible language of highly cultured clergymen. Most men were reached by neither. My task was therefore simply that of a *translator*—one turning Christian doctrine, or what he believed to be such, into the vernacular, into language that unscholarly people would attend to and could understand. For this purpose a style more guarded, more *nuance,* finelier shaded, more rich in fruitful ambiguities—in fact, a style more like Dr Pittenger's own—would have been worse than useless. It would not only have failed to enlighten the common reader's understanding; it would have aroused his suspicion. He would have thought, poor soul, that I was facing both ways, sitting on the fence, offering at one moment what I withdrew the next, and generally trying to trick him. I may have made theological errors. My manner may have been defective. Others may do better hereafter. I am ready, if I am young enough, to learn. Dr Pittenger would be a more helpful critic if he advised a cure as well as asserting many diseases. How does he himself do such work? What methods, and with what success, does he employ when he is trying to convert the great mass of storekeepers, lawyers, realtors, morticians, policemen and artisans who surround him in his own city?

One thing at least is sure. If the real theologians had tackled this laborious work of translation about a hundred years ago, when they began to lose touch with the people (for whom Christ died), there would have been no place for me.

432
Evangelism
Christian Reflections,
"Modern Theology and
Biblical Criticism" (1959),
para. 1, p. 152.

[Lewis addressing theology students:] Woe to you if you do not evangelize.

433
Evangelism
God in the Dock, "Cross-
Examination" (1963),
para. 30, p. 262.

As Christians we are tempted to make unnecessary concessions to those outside the Faith. We give in too much. Now, I don't mean that we should run the risk of making a nuisance of ourselves by witnessing at improper times, but there comes a time when we must show that we disagree. We must show our Christian colours, if we are to be true to Jesus Christ. We cannot remain silent or concede everything away.

434
Evangelism
God in the Dock, "Cross-
Examination" (1963),
p. 265.

In a civilization like ours, I feel that everyone has to come to terms with the claims of Jesus Christ upon his life, or else be guilty of inattention or of evading the question.

435
Evil in Society
That Hideous Strength,
chap. 13, Section 5,
p. 293.

"If all the West part of the world is apostate, might it not be lawful, in our great need, to look farther . . . beyond Christendom? Should we not find some even among the heathen who are not wholly corrupt? There were tales in my day of some such: men who knew not the articles of our most holy Faith, but who worshipped God as they could and acknowledged the Law of Nature. Sir, I believe it would be lawful to seek help even there. Beyond Byzantium . . ."

Ransom shook his head. "You do not understand," he said. "The poison was brewed in these West lands but it has spat itself everywhere by now. . . . You might go East so far that the East became West and you returned to Britain across the great Ocean, but even so you would not have come out anywhere into the light. The shadow of one dark wing is over all Tellus."

436
Evil Men
Reflections on the Psalms, chap. 3, para. 20, p. 32.

If the Divine call does not make us better, it will make us very much worse. Of all bad men religious bad men are the worst. Of all created beings the wickedest is one who originally stood in the immediate presence of God.

437
Evil, Motivation of
Mere Christianity, bk. II, chap. 2, para. 9–10, pp. 49–50.

Wickedness, when you examine it, turns out to be the pursuit of some good in the wrong way. You can be good for the mere sake of goodness: you cannot be bad for the mere sake of badness. You can do a kind action when you are not feeling kind and when it gives you no pleasure, simply because kindness is right; but no one ever did a cruel action simply because cruelty is wrong—only because cruelty was pleasant or useful to him. In other words badness cannot succeed even in being bad in the same way in which goodness is good. Goodness is, so to speak, itself: badness is only spoiled goodness. . . . Evil is a parasite, not an original thing.

438
Evolution
Letters of C. S. Lewis (30 March 1927), p. 113.

We live in the most absurd age. I met a girl the other day who had been teaching in an infant school (boys and girls up to the age of six) where these infants are taught the theory of evolution. Or rather the Headmistress's version of it. Simple people like ourselves had an idea that Darwin said that life developed from simple organisms up to the higher plants and animals, finally to the monkey group, and from the monkey group to man. The infants seem to be taught however that "in the beginning was the Ape," from whom all other life developed, including such dainties as the Brontosaurus and the Iguanadon. Whether the plants were supposed to be descendants of the apes I didn't gather. And then people talk about the credulity of the Middle Ages! Apropos of this, can you tell me who said, "Before you begin these studies, I should warn you that you need much more *faith* in science than in theology." It was Huxley or Clifford or one of the nineteenth century scientists I think. Another good remark I read long ago in one of E. Nesbitt's fairy tales— "Grown ups know that children can believe almost anything; that's why they tell you that the earth is round and smooth like an orange when you can see perfectly well for yourself that it's flat and lumpy."

439
Evolution
Perelandra, chap. 13, p. 164.

In vain did Ransom try to remember that he had been in "space" and found it Heaven, tingling with a fulness of life for which infinity itself was not one cubic inch too large. All that seemed like a dream. That opposite mode of thought which he had called in mockery The Empirical Bogey, came surging into his mind—the great myth of our century with its gases and galaxies, its light years and evolutions, its nightmare perspectives of simple arithmetic in which everything that can possibly hold significance for the mind becomes the mere by-product of essential disorder.

440
Evolution
The Weight of Glory, "Is Theology Poetry?" (1944), para. 22, p. 89.

The Bergsonian critique of orthodox Darwinism is not easy to answer. More disquieting still is Professor D. M. S. Watson's defence. "Evolution itself," he wrote, "is accepted by zoologists not because it has been observed to occur or . . . can be proved by logically coherent evidence to be true, but because the only alternative, special creation, is clearly incredible." Has it come to that? Does the whole vast structure of modern naturalism depend not on positive evidence but simply on an *a priori* metaphysical prejudice? Was it devised not to get in facts but to keep out God?

441

Evolution

The Weight of Glory,
"Is Theology Poetry?"
(1944), para. 22,
pp. 90–91.

We should distinguish Evolution in this strict sense from what may be called the universal evolutionism of modern thought. By universal evolutionism I mean the belief that the very formula of universal process is from imperfect to perfect, from small beginnings to great endings, from the rudimentary to the elaborate: the belief which makes people find it natural to think that morality springs from savage taboos, adult sentiment from infantile sexual maladjustments, thought from instinct, mind from matter, organic from inorganic, cosmos from chaos. This is perhaps the deepest habit of mind in the contemporary world. It seems to me immensely unplausible, because it makes the general course of nature so very unlike those parts of nature we can observe. You remember the old puzzle as to whether the owl came from the egg or the egg from the owl. The modern acquiescence or universal evolutionism is a kind of optical illusion, produced by attending exclusively to the owl's emergence from the egg. We are taught from childhood to notice how the perfect oak grows from the acorn and to forget that the acorn itself was dropped by a perfect oak. We are reminded constantly that the adult human being was an embryo, never that the life of the embryo came from two adult human beings. We love to notice that the express engine of to-day is the descendant of the "Rocket"; we do not equally remember that the "Rocket" springs not from some even more rudimentary engine, but from something much more perfect and complicated than itself—namely, a man of genius. The obviousness or naturalness which most people seem to find in the idea of emergent evolution thus seems to be a pure hallucination.

442
Evolution
Christian Reflections,
"The Funeral of a Great
Myth" (1945?), chap. 7,
para. 23, p. 93.

It appeals to every part of me except my reason.
. . . I believe it no longer.

443
Evolution
God in the Dock, "Two
Lectures" (1945),
para. 10, p. 211.

An egg which came from no bird is no more "natural" than a bird which had existed from all eternity. And since the egg-bird-egg sequence leads us to no plausible beginning, is it not reasonable to look for the real origin somewhere outside sequence altogether? You have to go outside the sequence of engines, into the world of men, to find the real originator of the rocket. Is it not equally reasonable to look outside Nature for the real Originator of the natural order?

444
Evolution
*English Literature in the
Sixteenth Century,* bk.
I.I.I, para. 68, p. 113.

[This is] a truth which the incurably evolutionary or developmental character of modern thought is always urging us to forget. What is vital and healthy does not necessarily survive. Higher organisms are often conquered by lower ones. Arts as well as men are subject to accident and violent death.

445
Evolution
Poems, "Evolutionary
Hymn" (1957),
pp. 55–56.

Lead us, Evolution, lead us
        Up the future's endless stair:
Chop us, change us, prod us, weed us.
        For stagnation is despair:

Groping, guessing, yet progressing
        Lead us nobody knows where. . . .

Ask not if it's god or devil
        Brethren, lest your words imply
Static norms of good and evil
        (As in Plato) throned on high;
Such scholastic, inelastic
        Abstract yardsticks we deny.

Far too long have sages vainly
        Glossed great Nature's simple text;
He who runs can read it plainly
        "Goodness=what comes next."
By evolving, Life is solving
        All the questions we perplexed.

On then! Value means survival-
        Value. If our progeny
Spreads and spawns and licks each rival
        That will prove its deity
(Far from pleasant, by our present
        Standards, though it well may be).

446

Exaggeration

Letters to Children (20
April 1959), p. 87.

I think you are exaggerating a bit at the end.
Everything I need is in my soul? The Heck it is!
Or if so, it must contain a great many virtues and
a great deal of wisdom which neither I nor anyone
else could ever find there. Very little of what I
need is at present in my soul. I mean, even things
of the soul's own sort, like humility or
truthfulness. And it certainly does not in any
obvious sense contain a number of other things
which I need at the moment; e.g. a stamp for this
letter. Never exaggerate. Never say more than you
really mean.

447
Excerpts
Studies in Medieval and Renaissance Literature, "Edmund Spenser, 1552–99" (1954), para. 32, p. 141.

The only use of selections is to deter those readers who will never appreciate the original, and thus to save them from wasting their time on it, and to send all the others on to the original as quickly as possible.

448
Excerpts
Letters of C. S. Lewis (20 January 1959), p. 284.

I think an anthology of extracts from a living writer would make both him and the collector look rather ridiculous and I'm sure publishers would not agree to the plan. I am sorry to reply so ungraciously to a proposal which does me so much honour. But I'm convinced it would not do.

449
Expectations of Others
Letters to an American Lady (24 February 1961), pp. 96–97.

"Blessed are they that expect little for they shall not be disappointed.". . . Probably the safe rule will be "When in doubt what to do or say, do or say nothing." I feel this very much with my stepsons. I so easily *meddle* and *gas*: when all the time what will really influence them, for good or ill, is not anything I do or say but what I *am*. And this unfortunately one can't know and can't much alter, though God can. Two rules from Wm. Law must be always before our minds.

1. "There can be no surer proof of a confirmed pride than a belief that one is sufficiently humble."

2. "I earnestly beseech all who conceive they have suffered an affront to believe that it is very much less than they suppose."

450
Expectations, Realistic
God in the Dock, Part III, "The Sermon and the Lunch" (1945), para. 5–9, pp. 284–286.

If Christian teachers wish to recall Christian people to domesticity—and I, for one, believe that people must be recalled to it—the first necessity is to stop telling lies about home life and to substitute realistic teaching. Perhaps the fundamental principles would be something like this.

1. Since the Fall no organization or way of life
whatever has a natural tendency to go right. . . .
The family, like the nation, can be offered to God,
can be converted and redeemed, and will then
become the channel of particular blessings and
graces. But, like everything else that is human, it
needs redemption. Unredeemed, it will produce
only particular temptations, corruptions, and
miseries. Charity begins at home: so does un-
charity.

2. By the conversion or sanctification of family
life we must be careful to mean something more
than the preservation of "love" in the sense of
natural affection. Love (in that sense) is not
enough. Affection, as distinct from charity, is not
a cause of lasting happiness. Left to its natural
bent affection becomes in the end greedy,
naggingly solicitous, jealous, exacting, timorous. It
suffers agony when its object is absent—but is not
repaid by any long enjoyment when the object is
present. . . . The greed to be loved is a fearful
thing. . . .

3. We must realize the yawning pitfall in that
very characteristic of home life which is so often
glibly paraded as its principal attraction. "It is
there that we appear as we really are: it is there
that we can fling aside the disguises and be
ourselves.". . . In fact, he [such a person] values
home as the place where he can "be himself" in
the sense of trampling on all the restraints which
civilized humanity has found indispensable for
tolerable social intercourse. And this, I think is
very common. What chiefly distinguishes domestic
from public conversation is surely very often
simply its downright rudeness. What distinguishes
domestic behavior is often its selfishness, sloven-
liness, incivility—even brutality. . . .

4. How, then, *are* people to behave at home? If

a man can't be comfortable and unguarded, can't take his ease and "be himself" in his own house, where can he? That is, I confess, the trouble. The answer is an alarming one. There is *nowhere* this side of heaven where one can safely lay the reins on the horse's neck. It will never be lawful simply to "be ourselves" until "ourselves" have become sons of God. . . .

Must we not abandon sentimental eulogies and begin to give practical advise on the high, hard, lovely, and adventurous art of really creating the Christian family?

451
Experience
God in the Dock,
"Miracles" (1942),
para. 1, pp. 25–26.

Experience by itself proves nothing. If a man doubts whether he is dreaming or waking, no experiment can solve his doubt, since every experiment may itself be part of the dream. Experience proves this, or that, or nothing, according to the preconceptions we bring to it.

452
Experience
Surprised by Joy,
chap. 11, para. 15,
p. 177.

What I like about experience is that it is such an honest thing. You may take any number of wrong turnings; but keep your eyes open and you will not be allowed to go very far before the warning signs appear. You may have deceived yourself, but experience is not trying to deceive you. The universe rings true wherever you fairly test it.

453
Extremes
The Screwtape Letters,
Letter VII, para. 2, 4,
pp. 33, 35.

[Senior devil Screwtape to junior devil Wormwood:] "I had not forgotten my promise to consider whether we should make the patient an extreme patriot or an extreme pacifist. All extremes except extreme devotion to the Enemy [God] are to be encouraged. . . .

"Whichever he adopts, your main task will be the same. Let him begin by treating the Patriotism or the Pacifism as a part of his religion. Then let him, under the influence of partisan spirit, come to regard it as the most important part. Then quietly and gradually nurse him on to the stage at which the religion becomes merely part of the "Cause," in which Christianity is valued chiefly because of the excellent arguments it can produce in favour of the British war effort or of pacifism. The attitude which you want to guard against is that in which temporal affairs are treated primarily as material for obedience. Once you have made the World an end, and faith a means, you have almost won your man, and it makes very little difference what kind of worldly end he is pursuing. Provided that meetings, pamphlets, policies, movements, causes, and crusades matter more to him than prayers and sacraments and charity, he is ours—and the more "religious" (on those terms), the more securely ours. I could show you a pretty cageful down here."

454
Fairy Tales
The Letters of C. S.
Lewis to Arthur Greeves
(7 August 1918), p. 228.

In my present mood few things have pleased me more than Macdonald's "The Goblin and the Princess," which I borrowed from Maureen Moore. This child has a well stocked library of fairy tales which form her continual reading—an excellent taste at her age, I think, which will lead her in later life to romance and poetry and not to the twaddling novels that make up the diet of most educated women apparently.

455
Fairy Tales
Of Other Worlds: Essays
and Stories, "On Three
Ways of Writing for
Children" (1952),
para. 10, p. 26.

I now enjoy the fairy tales better than I did in childhood: being now able to put more in, of course, I get more out.

456
Fairy Tales
Of Other Worlds: Essays
and Stories, "On Three
Ways of Writing for
Children" (1952),
para. 14–17, pp. 28–30.

About once every hundred years some wiseacre gets up and tries to banish the fairy tale. Perhaps I had better say a few words in its defence, as reading for children.

It is accused of giving children a false impression of the world they live in. But I think no literature that children could read gives them less of a false impression. I think what profess to

be realistic stories for children are far more likely
to deceive them. I never expected the real world
to be like the fairy tales. I think that I did expect
school to be like the school stories. The fantasies
did not deceive me: the school stories did. All
stories in which children have adventures and
successes which are possible, in the sense that
they do not break the laws of nature, but almost
infinitely improbable, are in more danger than the
fairy tales of raising false expectations.

. . . Do fairy tales teach children to retreat into
a world of wish-fulfilment—"fantasy" in the
technical psychological sense of the word—instead
of facing the problems of the real world? Now it
is here that the problem becomes subtle. Let us
again lay the fairy tale side by side with the school
story or any other story which is labelled a "Boy's
Book" or a "Girl's Book," as distinct from a
"Children's Book." There is no doubt that both
arouse, and imaginatively satisfy, wishes. We long
to go through the looking glass, to reach fairy
land. We also long to be the immensely popular
and successful schoolboy or schoolgirl, or the
lucky boy or girl who discovers the spy's plot or
rides the horse that none of the cowboys can
manage. But the two longings are very different.
The second, especially when directed on
something so close as school life, is ravenous and
deadly serious. Its fulfilment on the level of
imagination is in very truth compensatory: we run
to it from the disappointments and humiliations of
the real world: it sends us back to the real world
undivinely discontented. For it is all flattery to the
ego. The pleasure consists in picturing oneself the
object of admiration. The other longing, that for
fairy land, is very different. In a sense a child does
not long for fairy land as a boy longs to be the
hero of the first eleven. Does anyone suppose that

he really and prosaically longs for all the dangers and discomforts of a fairy tale?—really wants dragons in contemporary England? It is not so. It would be much truer to say that fairy land arouses a longing for he knows not what. It stirs and troubles him (to his life-long enrichment) with the dim sense of something beyond his reach and, far from dulling or emptying the actual world, gives it a new dimension of depth. He does not despise real woods because he has read of enchanted woods: the reading makes all real woods a little enchanted. This is a special kind of longing. The boy reading the school story of the type I have in mind desires success and is unhappy (once the book is over) because he can't get it: the boy reading the fairy tale desires and is happy in the very fact of desiring. For his mind has not been concentrated on himself, as it often is in the more realistic story.

. . . This distinction holds for adult reading too. The dangerous fantasy is always superficially realistic. The real victim of wishful reverie does not batten on the *Odyssey, The Tempest,* or *The Worm Ouroboros*: he (or she) prefers stories about millionaires, irresistible beauties, posh hotels, palm beaches and bedroom scenes—things that really might happen, that ought to happen, that would have happened if the reader had had a fair chance. For, as I say, there are two kinds of longing. The one is . . . a spiritual exercise, and the other is a disease.

457
Fairy Tales
Of Other Worlds: Essays and Stories, "On Three Ways of Writing for Children" (1952), para. 14–17, pp. 28–30.

I rejected any approach which begins with the question "What do modern children like?" I might be asked, "Do you equally reject the approach which begins with the question 'What do modern children need?'—in other words, with the moral or didactic approach?" I think the answer is Yes.

Not because I don't like stories to have a moral: certainly not because I think children dislike a moral. Rather because I feel sure that the question "What do modern children need?" will not lead you to a good moral. If we ask that question we are assuming too superior an attitude. It would be better to ask "What moral do I need?" for I think we can be sure that what does not concern us deeply will not deeply interest our readers, whatever their age. But it is better not to ask the question at all. Let the pictures tell you their own moral. For the moral inherent in them will rise from whatever spiritual roots you have succeeded in striking during the whole course of your life.

458
Fairy Tales
Letters to an American Lady (22 June 1953), p. 17.

You and I who still enjoy fairy tales have less reason to wish actual childhood back. We have kept its pleasures and added some grown-up ones as well.

459
Fairy Tales
Surprised by Joy, chap. 3, para. 13, pp. 54–55.

Curiously enough it is at this time [age 12], not in earlier childhood, that I chiefly remember delighting in fairy tales. I fell deeply under the spell of Dwarfs—the old bright-hooded, snowy-bearded dwarfs we had in those days before Arthur Rackham sublimed, or Walt Disney vulgarized, the earthmen. I visualized them so intensely that I came to the very frontiers of hallucination; once, walking in the garden, I was for a second not quite sure that a little man had not run past me into the shrubbery. I was faintly alarmed, but it was not like my night fears. A fear that guarded the road to Faerie was one I could face. No one is a coward at all points.

460
Faith
Christian Reflections,
"Religion: Reality or
Substitute?" (1941),
chap. 3, para. 10, p. 42.

The American in the old story defined Faith as "the power of believing what we know to be untrue." Now I define Faith as the power of continuing to believe what we once honestly thought to be true until cogent reasons for honestly changing our minds are brought before us.

461
Faith
Christian Reflections,
"Religion: Reality or
Substitute?" (1941),
para. 11, pp. 42–43.

There are things, say in learning to swim or to climb, which look dangerous and aren't. Your instructor tells you it's safe. You have good reason from past experience to trust him. Perhaps you can even see for yourself, by your own reason, that it is safe. But the crucial question is, will you be able to go on believing this when you actually see the cliff edge below you or actually feel yourself unsupported in the water? You will have no *rational* grounds for disbelieving. It is your senses and your imagination that are going to attack belief. Here, as in the New Testament, the conflict is not between faith and reason but between faith and sight. We can face things which we *know* to be dangerous if they don't look or sound too dangerous; our real trouble is often with things we *know* to be safe but which look dreadful. Our faith in Christ wavers not so much when real arguments come against it as when it *looks* improbable—when the whole world takes on the desolate *look* which really tells us much more about the state of our passions and even our digestion than about reality.

462
Faith
Christian Reflections,
"Religion: Reality or
Substitute?" (1941),
para. 12, p. 43.

If we wish to be rational, not now and then, but constantly, we must pray for the gift of Faith, for the power to go on believing not in the teeth of reason but in the teeth of lust and terror and jealousy and boredom and indifference that which reason, authority, or experience, or all three, have once delivered to us for truth.

463
Faith
Perelandra, chap. 2, p. 27.

"If you mean, Does my reason accept the view that he will (accidents apart) deliver me safe on the surface of Perelandra?—the answer is Yes," said Ransom. "If you mean, Do my nerves and my imagination respond to this view?—I'm afraid the answer is No. One can believe in anaesthetics and yet feel in a panic when they actually put the mask over your face. I think I feel as a man who believes in the future life feels when he is taken out to face a firing party. Perhaps it's good practice."

464
Faith
Letters of C. S. Lewis (18 March 1952), p. 239.

The Bible itself gives us one short prayer which is suitable for all who are struggling with the beliefs and doctrines. It is: Lord I believe, help Thou my unbelief.

Would something of this sort be any good? "Almighty God, who art the father of lights and who hast promised by thy dear Son that all who do thy will shall know thy doctrine: give me grace so to live that by daily obedience I daily increase in faith and in the understanding of thy Holy Word, through Jesus Christ our Lord. Amen."

465
Faith
Mere Christianity, bk. III, chap. 11, para. 5, pp. 123–124.

Faith, in the sense in which I am here using the word, is the art of holding on to things your reason has once accepted, in spite of your changing moods. For moods will change, whatever view your reason takes. I know that by experience. Now that I am a Christian I do have moods in which the whole thing looks very improbable: but when I was an atheist I had moods in which Christianity looked terribly

probable. This rebellion of your moods against
your real self is going to come anyway. That is
why Faith is such a necessary virtue: unless you
teach your moods "where they get off," you can
never be either a sound Christian or even a sound
atheist, but just a creature dithering to and fro,
with its beliefs really dependent on the weather
and the state of its digestion.

466
Faith
Mere Christianity, bk. III,
chap. 12, para. 5–6,
p. 128.

[Salvation] is the change from being confident
about our own efforts to the state in which we
despair of doing anything for ourselves and leave it
to God.

I know the words "leave it to God" can be
misunderstood, but they must stay for the
moment. The sense in which a Christian leaves it
to God is that he puts all his trust in Christ: trusts
that Christ will somehow share with him the
perfect human obedience which He carried out
from His birth to His crucifixion: that Christ will
make the man more like Himself and, in a sense,
make good his deficiencies. In Christian language,
He will share His "sonship" with us, will make us,
like Himself, "Sons of God."

467
Faith
Mere Christianity, bk. IV,
chap. 7, para. 9, p. 163.

Never, never pin your whole faith on any human
being: not if he is the best and wisest in the
whole world. There are lots of nice things you
can do with sand; but do not try building a house
on it.

468
Faith
*The World's Last Night
and Other Essays,* "On
Obstinacy in Belief"
(1955), para. 7,
pp. 17–18.

It is not the purpose of this essay to weigh the
evidence, of whatever kind, on which Christians
base their belief. To do that would be to write a
full-dress *apologia*. All that I need do here is to
point out that, at the very worst, this evidence
cannot be so weak as to warrant the view that all

whom it convinces are indifferent to evidence. The history of thought seems to make this quite plain. We know, in fact, that believers are not cut off from unbelievers by any portentous inferiority of intelligence or any perverse refusal to think. Many of them have been people of powerful minds. Many of them have been scientists. We may suppose them to have been mistaken, but we must suppose that their error was at least plausible.

469
Faith

The World's Last Night and Other Essays, "On Obstinacy in Belief" (1955), para. 11–12, pp. 23–24.

The Christians seem to praise an adherence to the original belief which holds out against any evidence whatever. I must now try to show why such praise is in fact a logical conclusion from the original belief itself.

This can be done best by thinking for a moment of situations in which the thing is reversed. In Christianity such faith is demanded of us; but there are situations in which we demand it of others. There are times when we can do all that a fellow creature needs if only he will trust us. In getting a dog out of a trap, in extracting a thorn from a child's finger, in teaching a boy to swim or rescuing one who can't, in getting a frightened beginner over a nasty place on a mountain, the one fatal obstacle may be their distrust. We are asking them to trust us in the teeth of their senses, their imagination, and their intelligence. We ask them to believe that what is painful will relieve their pain and what looks dangerous is their only safety. We ask them to accept apparent impossibilities: that moving the paw farther back into the trap is the way to get it out—that hurting the finger very much more will stop the finger hurting—that water which is obviously permeable will resist and support the body—that holding onto the only support within reach is not the way to avoid sinking—that to go higher and onto a more exposed ledge is the way not to fall. To support all these *incredibilia* we can rely only on the other party's confidence in us—a confidence certainly not based on demonstration, admittedly shot through with emotion, and perhaps, if we are strangers, resting on nothing but such assurance as the look of our face and the tone of our voice can supply, or even, for the dog, on our smell. Sometimes, because of their unbelief, we can do no mighty works. But if we succeed, we do so because they have maintained their faith in us against apparently contrary evidence. No one blames us for demanding such faith. No one blames them for giving it. No one says afterwards what an unintelligent dog or child or boy that must have been to trust us.

470

Faith

The World's Last Night and Other Essays, "On Obstinacy in Belief" (1955), para. 13, p. 25.

We trust not because "a God" exists, but because *this* God exists.

471

Faith

The World's Last Night and Other Essays, "On Obstinacy in Belief" (1955), para. 18, pp. 29–30.

Our opponents, then, have a perfect right to dispute with us about the grounds of our original assent. But they must not accuse us of sheer insanity if, after the assent has been given, our adherence to it is no longer proportioned to every fluctuation of the apparent evidence. They cannot of course be expected to know on what assurance feeds, and how it revives and is always rising from its ashes. . . . That is knowledge we cannot communicate. But they can see how the assent, of necessity, moves us from the logic of speculative

---

thought into what might perhaps be called the logic of personal relations. What would, up till then, have been variations simply of opinion become variations of conduct by a person to a Person. *Credere Deum esse* turns into *Credere in Deum*. And *Deum* here is this God, the increasingly knowable Lord.

472
Faith and Works
God in the Dock,
"Answers to Questions on Christianity" (1944), ans. 8, p. 55.

The controversy about faith and works is one that has gone on for a very long time, and it is a highly technical matter. I personally rely on the paradoxical text: "Work out your own salvation . . . for it is God that worketh in you." It looks as if in one sense we do nothing, and in another case we do a damned lot. "Work out your own salvation with fear and trembling," but you must have it in you before you can work it out.

473
Fall, The
The Allegory of Love,
chap. I.I, para. 13, p. 15.

[Our] pleasure would have been greater if we had remained in Paradise. The real trouble about fallen man is not the strength of his pleasures but the weakness of his reason: unfallen man could have enjoyed any degree of pleasure without losing sight, for a moment, of the First Good.

474
Fall, The
The Problem of Pain,
chap. 5, para. 5, pp. 75–76.

From the moment a creature becomes aware of God as God and of itself as self, the terrible alternative of choosing God or self for the centre is opened to it. This sin is committed daily by young children and ignorant peasants as well as by sophisticated persons, by solitaries no less than by those who live in society: it is the fall in every individual life, and in each day of each individual life, the basic sin behind all particular sins: at this very moment you and I are either committing it, or about to commit it, or repenting it. We try,

when we wake, to lay the new day at God's feet;
before we have finished shaving, it becomes *our*
day and God's share in it is felt as a tribute which
we must pay out of "our own" pocket, a
deduction from the time which ought, we feel, to
be "our own." . . . Thus all day long, and all the
days of our life, we are sliding, slipping, falling
away—as if God were, to our present consciousness, a smooth inclined plane on which there is
no resting. And indeed we are now of such
a nature that we must slip off, and the sin, because it is unavoidable, may be venial. But God
cannot have made us so. The gravitation away
from God, "the journey homeward to habitual
self," must, we think, be a product of the Fall.

475
Fall, The
The Problem of Pain,
chap. 5, para. 6, p. 78.

[Before the Fall] however rich and varied man's
experience of his fellows (or fellow) in charity and
friendship and sexual love, or of the beasts, or of
the surrounding world then first recognised as
beautiful and awful, God came first in his love
and in his thought, and that without painful
effort.

476
Fall, The
The Problem of Pain,
chap. 5, para. 8, p. 80.

They [human beings] wanted, as we say, to "call
their souls their own." But that means to live a lie,
for our souls are not, in fact, our own. They
wanted some corner in the universe of which they
could say to God, "This is our business, not
yours." But there is no such corner.

477
Fall, The
The Problem of Pain,
chap. 5, para. 10, p. 83.

It [the human spirit] had turned from God and
become its own idol, so that though it could still
turn back to God, it could do so only by painful
effort, and its inclination was self-ward. Hence
pride and ambition, the desire to be lovely in its

own eyes and to depress and humiliate all rivals, envy, and restless search for more, and still more, security, were now the attitudes that came easiest to it. . . . A new species, never made by God, had sinned itself into existence.

478
Fall, The
A Preface to "Paradise Lost," chap. 10, para. 13. pp. 70–71.

The Fall is simply and solely Disobedience—doing what you have been told not to do: and it results from Pride—from being too big for your boots, forgetting your place, thinking that you are God.

479
Fall, The
Perelandra, chap. 11, pp. 143–144.

Long since on Mars, and more strongly since he came to Perelandra, Ransom had been perceiving that the triple distinction of truth from myth and of both from fact was purely terrestrial—was part and parcel of that unhappy division between soul and body which resulted from the Fall. Even on earth the sacraments existed as a permanent reminder that the division was neither wholesome nor final. The Incarnation had been the beginning of its disappearance. In Perelandra it would have no meaning at all. Whatever happened here would be of such a nature that earth-men would call it mythological. All this he had thought before. Now he knew it. The Presence in the darkness, never before so formidable, was putting these truths into his hands like terrible jewels.

480
Fall, The
Miracles, chap. 14, para. 27, p. 126.

Human Death, according to the Christians, is a result of human sin; Man, as originally created, was immune from it: Man when redeemed, and recalled to a new life (which will in some undefined sense, be a bodily life) in the midst of a more organic and more fully obedient Nature, will be immune from it again. This doctrine is of course simply nonsense if a man is nothing but a

Natural organism. But if he were, then, as we have seen, all thoughts would be equally nonsensical, for all would have irrational causes. Man must therefore be a composite being—a natural organism tenanted by, or in a state of *symbiosis* with, a supernatural spirit. The Christian doctrine, startling as it must seem to those who have not fully cleared their minds of Naturalism, states that the relations which we now observe between that spirit and that organism, are abnormal or pathological ones. At present spirit can retain its foothold against the incessant counterattacks of Nature (both physiological and psychological) only by perpetual vigilance, and physiological Nature always defeats it in the end. Sooner or later it becomes unable to resist the disintegrating processes at work in the body and death ensues. A little later the Natural organism (for it does not long enjoy its triumph) is similarly conquered by merely physical Nature and returns to the inorganic. But, on the Christian view, this was not always so. The spirit was once not a garrison, maintaining its post with difficulty in a hostile Nature, but was fully "at home" with its organism, like a king in his own country or a rider on his own horse. . . . Where spirit's power over the organism was complete and unresisted, death would never occur.

481
Fall, The
The World's Last Night and Other Essays, "Religion and Rocketry" (1958), para. 19, p. 89.

[On extra-terrestrials in space exploration:] It is interesting to wonder how things would go if they met an unfallen race. At first, to be sure, they'd have a grand time jeering at, duping, and exploiting its innocence; but I doubt if our half-animal cunning would long be a match for godlike wisdom, selfless valour, and perfect unanimity.

482
Fall, The
Letters to an American Lady (8 November 1962), p. 110.

We are *all* fallen creatures and *all* very hard to live with.

483
Fall, The
Poems, "Eden's Courtesy" (1st pub. 1964), p. 98.

When a creature's dread, or mine, has built
A wall between, I think I feel the pains
That Adam earned and do confess my guilt.
　　For till I tame sly fox and timorous hare
And lording lion in my self, no peace
Can be without; but after, I shall dare
Uncage the shadowy zoo and war will cease;
　　Because the brutes within, I do not doubt
Are archetypal of the brutes without.

484
Fame
English Literature in the Sixteenth Century, bk. III.II.II, para. 16, p. 426.

Even posthumous fame depends largely on accident.

485
Family
Letters of C. S. Lewis (20 June 1918), p. 43.

[Lewis wrote this letter to his father in Ireland (his mother died when he was small). Lewis was in a London hospital recovering from wounds received during World War I. His father never came to visit him:] Wherever I am I know that you will come and see me. You know I have some difficulty in talking of the greatest things; it is the fault of our generation and of the English schools. But at least you will believe that I was never before so eager to cling to every bit of our old home life and to see you. I know I have often been far from what I should be in my relation to you, and have undervalued an affection and generosity which an experience of "other people's parents" has shown me in a new light. But, please God, I shall do

better in the future. Come and see me, I am
homesick, that is the long and the short of it.

486
**Family
Manners**
The Four Loves,
chap. 3, para. 23, p. 66.

We hear a great deal about the rudeness of the
rising generation. I am an oldster myself and
might be expected to take the oldsters' side, but
in fact I have been far more impressed by the bad
manners of parents to children than by those of
children to parents. Who has not been the
embarrassed guest at family meals where the
father or mother treated their grown-up offspring
with an incivility which, offered to any other
young people, would simply have terminated the
acquaintance? Dogmatic assertions of matters
which the children understand and their elders
don't, ruthless interruptions, flat contradictions,
ridicule of things the young take seriously—
sometimes of their religion—insulting references to
their friends, all provide an easy answer to the
question "Why are they always out? Why do they
like every house better than their home?" Who
does not prefer civility to barbarism?

487
Fantasy
*Studies in Medieval and
Renaissance Literature,*
"Edmund Spenser,
1552–99" (1954),
para. 25, p. 136.

Some published fantasies of my own have had
foisted on them (often by the kindliest critics) so
many admirable allegorical meanings that I never
dreamed of as to throw me into doubt whether it
is possible for the wit of man to devise anything
in which the wit of some other man cannot find,
and plausibly find, an allegory.

488
Fasting
*Letters to an American
Lady* (7 March 1962),
pp. 104–105.

Perhaps if we had done more voluntary fasting
before God would not now have put us on these
darn diets! Well, the theologians say that an
imposed mortification can have all the merit of a
voluntary one if it is taken in the right spirit.

489
Fatherhood
George MacDonald:
An Anthology, Preface,
para. 2, p. 10.

[Writing of George Macdonald:] An almost
perfect relationship with his father was the earthly
root of all his wisdom. From his own father, he
said, he first learned that Fatherhood must be at
the core of the universe. He was thus prepared in
an unusual way to teach that religion in which the
relation of Father and Son is of all relations the
most central.

490
Fear
The Screwtape Letters,
Letter XXIX, para. 8,
p. 139.

The *act* of cowardice is all that matters; the
emotion of fear is, in itself, no sin.

491
Feelings
The World's Last Night
and Other Essays, "The
World's Last Night"
(1952), para. 30, p. 109.

Feelings come and go, and when they come a
good use can be made of them: they cannot be
our regular spiritual diet.

492
Firsthand
Knowledge
God in the Dock, "On
the Reading of Old
Books" (1944), para. 1,
p. 200.

I have found as a tutor in English Literature that
if the average student wants to find out something
about Platonism, the very last thing he thinks of
doing is to take a translation of Plato off the
library shelf and read the *Symposium.* He would
rather read some dreary modern book ten times
as long, all about "isms" and influences and only
once in twelve pages telling him what Plato
actually said. The error is rather an amiable one,
for it springs from humility. The student is half
afraid to meet one of the great philosophers face
to face. He feels himself inadequate and thinks he
will not understand him. But if he only knew, the
great man, just because of his greatness, is much
more intelligible than his modern commentator.

The simplest student will be able to understand, if not all, yet a very great deal of what Plato said; but hardly anyone can understand some modern books of Platonism. It has always therefore been one of my main endeavours as a teacher to persuade the young that first-hand knowledge is not only more worth acquiring than second-hand knowledge, but is usually much easier and more delightful to acquire.

493
Forgetfulness
Letters to an American Lady (24 November 1960), para. 1, pp. 93–94.

About forgetting things. Dr. Johnson said "If, on leaving the company, a young man cannot remember where he has left his ha', it is nothing. But when an old man forgets, everyone says, Ah, his memory is going." So with ourselves. We have *always* been forgetting things: but now, when we do so, we attribute it to our age. Why, it was years ago that, on finishing my work before lunch, I stopped myself only just in time from putting my cigarette-end into my spectacle case and throwing my spectacles into the fire!

494
Forgiveness
God in the Dock, "Dangers of National Repentance" (1940), para. 3, p. 191.

We must forgive all our enemies or be damned.

495
Forgiveness
The Problem of Pain, chap. 8, para. 6, p. 122.

The demand that God should forgive such a man [one bent on evil] while he remains what he is, is based on a confusion between condoning and forgiving. To condone an evil is simply to ignore it, to treat it as if it were good. But forgiveness needs to be accepted as well as offered if it is to be complete: and a man who admits no guilt can accept no forgiveness.

496
Forgiveness
The Weight of Glory,
"On Forgiveness" (1947),
para. 3–4, pp. 122–123.

If you had a perfect excuse you would not need forgiveness: if the whole of your action needs forgiveness then there was no excuse for it. But the trouble is that what we call "asking God's forgiveness" very often really consists in asking God to accept our excuses. What leads us into this mistake is the fact that there usually is some amount of excuse, some "extenuating circumstances." We are so very anxious to point these out to God (and to ourselves) that we are apt to forget the really important thing; that is, the bit left over, the bit which the excuses don't cover, the bit which is inexcusable but not, thank God, unforgivable.

. . . What we have got to take to him is the inexcusable bit, the sin. We are only wasting time by talking about all the parts which can (we think) be excused. When you go to a doctor you show him the bit of you that is wrong—say, a broken arm. It would be a mere waste of time to keep on explaining that your legs and eyes and throat are all right. You may be mistaken in thinking so; and anyway, if they are really all right, the doctor will know that.

497
Forgiveness
The Weight of Glory,
"On Forgiveness" (1947),
para. 6, pp. 124–125.

The difference between this situation [forgiving my neighbor] and the one in which you are asking God's forgiveness is this. In our own case we accept them easily enough. As regards my own sins it is a safe bet (though not a certainty) that the excuses are not really so good as I think: as regards other men's sins against me it is a safe bet (though not a certainty) that the excuses are better than I think. One must therefore begin by attending carefully to everything which may show that the other man was not so much to blame as we thought. But even if he is absolutely fully to blame we still have to forgive him; and even if ninety-nine per cent of his apparent guilt can be explained away by really good excuses, the problem of forgiveness begins with the one per cent of guilt which is left over. To be a Christian means to forgive the inexcusable, because God has forgiven the inexcusable in you.

498
Forgiveness
The Weight of Glory,
"On Forgiveness" (1947),
para. 7, p. 125.

To forgive the incessant provocations of daily life—to keep on forgiving the bossy mother-in-law, the bullying husband, the nagging wife, the selfish daughter, the deceitful son—how can we do it? Only, I think, by remembering where we stand, by meaning our words when we say in our prayers each night "Forgive us our trespasses as we forgive those that trespass against us." We are offered forgiveness on no other terms. To refuse it is to refuse God's mercy for ourselves. There is no hint of exceptions and God means what he says.

499
Forgiveness
Letters of C. S. Lewis
(19 April 1951), p. 230.

I think that if God forgives us we must forgive ourselves. Otherwise it is almost like setting up ourselves as a higher tribunal than Him.

500
Forgiveness
Letters: C. S. Lewis/Don Giovanni Calabria
(26 December 1951),
para. 2–5, p. 67.

During the past year a great joy has befallen me. Difficult though it is, I shall try to explain this in words.

It is astonishing that sometimes we believe that we believe what, really, in our heart, we do not believe.

For a long time I believed that I believed in the forgiveness of sins. But suddenly (on St Mark's Day) this truth appeared in my mind in so clear a light that I perceived that never before (and that after many confessions and absolutions) had I believed it with my whole heart.

So great is the difference between mere affirmation by the intellect and that faith, fixed in the very marrow and as it were palpable, which the Apostle wrote was *substance*.

501

Forgiveness

Mere Christianity,
chap. 5, para. 12,
pp. 93–94.

We may, indeed, be sure that perfect chastity—like perfect charity—will not be attained by any merely human efforts. You must ask for God's help. Even when you have done so, it may seem to you for a long time that no help, or less help than you need, is being given. Never mind. After each failure, ask forgiveness, pick yourself up, and try again. Very often what God first helps us towards is not the virtue itself but just this power of always trying again. For however important chastity (or courage, or truthfulness, or any other virtue) may be, this process trains us in habits of the soul which are more important still. It cures our illusions about ourselves and teaches us to depend on God. We learn, on the one hand, that we cannot trust ourselves even in our best moments, and, on the other, that we need not despair even in our worst, for our failures are forgiven. The only fatal thing is to sit down content with anything less than perfection.

502

Forgiveness

Mere Christianity, bk. III,
chap. 7, para. 6, p. 106.

Christianity does not want us to reduce by one atom the hatred we feel for cruelty and treachery. We ought to hate them. Not one word of what we have said about them needs to be unsaid. But it does want us to hate them in the same way in which we hate things in ourselves: being sorry the man should have done such things, and hoping, if it is anyway possible, that somehow, sometime, somewhere, he can be cured and made human again.

503
Forgiveness

Reflections on the Psalms,
chap. 3, para. 10, pp.
24–25.

There is no use in talking as if forgiveness were easy. We all know the old joke, "You've given up smoking once; I've given it up a dozen times." In the same way I could say of a certain man, "Have I forgiven him for what he did that day? I've forgiven him more times than I can count." For we find that the work of forgiveness has to be done over and over again.

504
Free Will

Poems, "Nearly They
Stood" (1933),
pp. 102–103.

Nearly they stood who fall.
Themselves, when they look back
See always in the track
One torturing spot where all
By a possible quick swerve
Of will yet unenslaved—
By the infinitesimal twitching of a nerve—
Might have been saved.

Nearly they fell who stand.
These with cold after-fear
Look back and note how near
They grazed the Siren's land
Wondering to think that fate
By threads so spidery-fine
The choice of ways so small, the event so great
Should thus entwine.

Therefore I sometimes fear
Lest oldest fears prove true
Lest, when no bugle blew
My mort, when skies looked clear
I may have stepped one hair's
Breadth past the hair-breadth bourn
Which, being once crossed forever unawares
Forbids return.

505
Free Will
The Problem of Pain,
chap. 5, para. 1, p. 69.

Man is now a horror to God and to himself and a creature ill-adapted to the universe not because God made him so but because he has made himself so by the abuse of his free will.

506
Free Will
The Problem of Pain,
chap. 7, p. 135.

Evil comes from the abuse of free will.

507
Free Will
The Screwtape Letters,
Letter VI, para. 5, p. 31.

[Senior devil Screwtape to junior devil Wormwood:] "Think of your man as a series of concentric circles, his will being the innermost, his intellect coming next, and finally his fantasy. You can hardly hope, at once, to exclude from all the circles everything that smells of the Enemy: but you must keep on shoving all the virtues outward till they are finally located in the circle of fantasy, and all the desirable qualities inward into the Will. It is only in so far as they reach the will and are there embodied in habits that the virtues are really fatal to us."

508
Free Will
Perelandra, chap. 11,
pp. 140–142.

The Enemy was using Third Degree methods. It seemed to Ransom that, but for a miracle, the Lady's resistance was bound to be worn away in the end. Why did no miracle come? Or rather, why no miracle on the right side? For the presence of the Enemy was in itself a kind of Miracle. Had Hell a prerogative to work wonders? Why did Heaven work none? Not for the first time he found himself questioning Divine Justice. He could not understand why Maleldil [God] should remain absent when the Enemy was there in person. . . . "Where is Maleldil's representative?"

The answer which came back to him, quick as a fencer's or a tennis player's *riposte,* out of the

silence and the darkness, almost took his breath
away. It seemed Blasphemous. "Anyway, what can
I do?" babbled the voluble self. "I've done all I
can. I've talked till I'm sick of it. It's no good, I
tell you." He tried to persuade himself that he,
Ransom, could not possibly be Maleldil's
representative as the Un-man, was the representative of Hell. The suggestion was, he argued,
itself diabolical—a temptation to fatuous pride, to
megalomania. He was horrified when the darkness
simply flung back this argument in his face,
almost impatiently. And then—he wondered how
it had escaped him till now—he was forced to
perceive that his own coming to Perelandra was
at least as much of a marvel as the Enemy's.
That miracle on the right side, which he had
demanded, had in fact occurred. He himself was
the miracle.

. . . His journey to Perelandra was not a moral
exercise, nor a sham fight. If the issue lay in
Maleldil's hands, Ransom and the Lady *were* those
hands. The fate of a world really depended on
how they behaved in the next few hours. The
thing was irreducibly, nakedly real. They could, if
they chose, decline to save the innocence of this
new race, and if they declined its innocence
would not be saved. It rested with no other
creature in all time or all space.

509
Free Will
Perelandra, chap. 11,
p. 142.

Thus, and not otherwise, the world was made.
Either something or nothing must depend on
individual choices. And if something, who could
set bounds to it? A stone may determine the
course of a river. He was that stone at this
horrible moment which had become the centre of
the whole universe. The eldila of all worlds, the
sinless organisms of everlasting light, were silent in

Deep Heaven to see what Elwin Ransom of
Cambridge would do.

510
Free Will
Perelandra, chap. 11,
pp. 148–149.

"My name also is Ransom," said the Voice.
It was some time before the purport of this
saying dawned upon him. He whom the other
worlds call Maleldil, was the world's ransom, his
own ransom, well he knew. But to what purpose
was it said now? Before the answer came to him
he felt its insufferable approach and held out his
arms before him as if he could keep it from
forcing open the door of his mind. But it came.
So *that* was the real issue. If he now failed, this
world also would hereafter be redeemed. If he
were not the ransom, Another would be. Yet
nothing was ever repeated. Not a second
crucifixion: perhaps—who knows—not even a
second Incarnation . . . some act of even more
appalling love, some glory of yet deeper humility.
For he had seen already how the pattern grows
and how from each world it sprouts into the next
through some other dimension. The small external
evil which Satan had done in Malacandra was
only as a line: the deeper evil he had done in
Earth was as a square: if Venus fell, her evil
would be a cube—her Redemption beyond
conceiving. Yet redeemed she would be. He had
long known that great issues hung on his choice;
but as he now realised the true width of the
frightful freedom that was being put into his
hands—a width to which all merely spatial infinity
seemed narrow—he felt like a man brought out
under naked heaven, on the edge of a precipice,
into the teeth of a wind that came howling from
the Pole. He had pictured himself, till now,
standing before the Lord, like Peter. But it was

worse. He sat before Him like Pilate. It lay with
him to save or to spill. His hands had been
reddened, as all men's hands have been, in the
slaying before the foundation of the world; now, if
he chose, he could dip them again in the same
blood. "Mercy," he groaned; and then, "Lord, why
me?" But there was no answer.

The thing still seemed impossible. . . . And
then, without any apparent movement of the will,
as objective and unemotional as the reading on a
dial, there had arisen before him, with perfect
certitude, the knowledge "about this time
tomorrow you will have done the impossible. . . ."
The future act stood there, fixed and unaltered as
if he had already performed it. It was a mere
irrelevant detail that it happened to occupy the
position we call future instead of that which we
call past. The whole struggle was over, and yet
there seemed to have been no moment of victory.
You might say, if you liked, that the power of
choice had been simply set aside and an inflexible
destiny substituted for it. On the other hand, you
might say that he had delivered from the rhetoric
of his passions and had emerged into unassailable
freedom. Ransom could not, for the life of him,
see any difference between these two statements.
Predestination and freedom were apparently
identical. He could no longer see any meaning in
the many arguments he had heard on this subject.

511
Free Will
The Great Divorce,
chap. 13, pp. 124–125.

"Ye can know nothing of the end of all things.
. . ."

"Because they are too terrible, Sir?"

"No. Because all answers deceive. If ye put the
question from within Time and are asking about
possibilities, the answer is certain. The choice of

ways is always before you. Neither is closed. Any man may choose eternal death. Those who choose it will have it. But if ye are trying to leap on into eternity, if ye are trying to see the final state of all things as it *will* be (for so ye must speak) when there are no more possibilities left but only the Real, then ye ask what cannot be answered to mortal ears. Time is the very lens through which ye see—small and clear, as men see through the wrong end of a telescope—something that would otherwise be too big for ye to see at all. That thing is Freedom: the gift whereby ye most resemble your Maker and are yourselves parts of eternal reality. But ye can see it only through the lens of Time, in a little clear picture, through the inverted telescope. . . . For every attempt to see the shape of eternity except through the lens of Time destroys your knowledge of Freedom. Witness the doctrine of Predestination which shows (truly enough) that eternal reality is not waiting for a future in which to be real; but at the price of removing Freedom which is the deeper truth of the two. And wouldn't Universalism do the same? Ye *cannot* know eternal reality by a definition. Time itself, and all acts and events that fill Time, are the definition, and it must be lived."

512
Free Will
Miracles, chap. 14,
para. 20, pp. 121–122.

The sin, both of men and of angels, was rendered possible by the fact that God gave them free will; thus surrendering a portion of His omnipotence (it is again a deathlike or descending movement) because He saw that from a world of free creatures, even though they fell, He could work out (and this is the re-ascent) a deeper happiness and a fuller splendour than any world of automata would admit.

513
Free Will
Of Other Worlds: Essays and Stories, "On Stories" (1947), para. 20, p. 15.

Free will is the *modus operandi* of destiny.

514
Free Will
God in the Dock, "The Trouble with 'X' . . ." (1948), para. 5, pp. 152–153.

God has made it a rule for Himself that He won't alter people's character by force. He can and will alter them—but only if the people will let Him. . . . He would rather have a world of free beings, with all its risks, than a world of people who did right like machines because they couldn't do anything else. The more we succeed in imagining what a world of perfect automatic beings would be like, the more, I think, we shall see His wisdom.

515
Free Will
Mere Christianity, bk.II, chap. 3, pp. 52–53.

God created things which had free will. That means creatures which can go either wrong or right. Some people think they can imagine a creature which was free but had no possibility of going wrong; I cannot. If a thing is free to be good it is also free to be bad. And free will is what has made evil possible. Why, then, did God give them free will? Because free will, though it makes evil possible, is also the only thing that makes possible any love or goodness or joy worth having. A world of automata—of creatures that worked like machines—would hardly be worth creating. The happiness which God designs for His higher creatures is the happiness of being freely, voluntarily united to Him and to each other in an ecstasy of love and delight compared with which the most rapturous love between a man and a woman on this earth is mere milk and water. And for that they must be free.
    . . . If God thinks this state of war in the

universe a price worth paying for free will—that
is, for making a live world in which creatures can
do real good or harm and something of real
importance can happen, instead of a toy world
which only moves when He pulls the strings—
then we may take it it is worth paying.

516

Free Will

Mere Christianity, bk. IV,
chap. 3, para. 11,
pp. 148–149.

God is outside and above the Time-line. In that
case, what we call "tomorrow" is visible to Him
in just the same way as what we call "today." All
the days are "Now" for Him. He does not
remember you doing things yesterday; He simply
sees you doing them, because, though you have
lost yesterday, He has not. He does not "foresee"
you doing things tomorrow; He simply sees you
doing them: because, though tomorrow is not yet
there for you, it is for Him. You never suppose
that your actions at this moment were any less
free because God knows what you are doing.

517

Free Will

Poems, "Legion" (1955),
p. 119.

Lord, hear my voice, my present voice I mean
Not that which may be speaking an hour hence
(For I am Legion) in an opposite sense,
And not by show of hands decide between
The multiple factions which my state has seen
Or will see. Condescend to the pretence
That what speaks now is I; in its defence
Dissolve my parliament and intervene.

Thou wilt not, though we asked it, quite recall
Free will once given. Yet to this moment's choice
Give unfair weight. Hold me to this. Oh strain
A point—use legal fictions; for if all
My quarrelling selves must bear an equal voice,
Farewell, thou hast created me in vain.

518
Free Will
Selected Literary Essays,
"The Vision of John
Bunyan" (1962), para. 24,
p. 153.

Most, I fancy, have discovered that to be born is
to be exposed to delights and miseries greater
than imagination could have anticipated; that the
choice of ways at any cross-road may be more
important than we think; and that short cuts may
lead to very nasty places.

519
Freudian Criticism
Selected Literary Essays,
"Psycho-Analysis and
Literary Criticism"
(1942), para. 17, p. 293.

If it is true that all our enjoyment of the images,
without remainder, can be explained in terms of
infantile sexuality, then, I confess, our literary
judgements are in ruins. But I do not believe it is
true.

520
Freudian Criticism
Selected Literary Essays,
"Psycho-Analysis and
Literary Criticism"
(1942), para. 19–20,
pp. 294–295.

I am sometimes tempted to wonder whether
Freudianism is not a great school of prudery and
hypocrisy. . . . Does not Freud underrate the
extent to which nothing, in private, is really
shocking so long as it belongs to ourselves? . . .
The feeling with which we reject the psycho-
analytic theory of poetry is not one of shock. It is
not even a vague disquietude or an unspecified
reluctance. It is a quite definite feeling of
anticlimax, of frustration. . . .

   In general, of course, the fact that a supposed
discovery is disappointing does not tend to prove
that it is false: but in this question I think it does,
for desires and fulfilments and disappointments
are what we are discussing. If we are disappointed
at finding only sex where we looked for
something more, then surely the something more
had a value for us? If we are conscious of loss in
exchanging the garden for the female body, then
clearly the garden added something more than
concealment, something positive, to our pleasure.
Let us grant that the body was, in fact, concealed
behind the garden: yet since the removal of the

garden lowers the value of the experience, it follows that the body gained some of its potency by association with the garden. We have not merely removed a veil, we have removed ornaments. Confronted with what is supposed to be the original (the female body) we still prefer the translation—from which any critic must conclude that the translation had merits of its own. Or perhaps "prefer" is the wrong word. We really want both. Poetry is not a substitute for sexual satisfaction, nor sexual satisfaction for poetry. But if so, poetical pleasure is not sexual pleasure *simply* in disguise. It is, at worst, sexual pleasure *plus* something else, and we really want the something else for its own sake.

521
Freudian Criticism
Mere Christianity, bk. III, chap. 4, para. 3–4, p. 84.

The philosophy of Freud . . . is in direct contradiction to Christianity: and also in direct contradiction to the other great psychologist, Jung. . . . But psychoanalysis itself, apart from all the philosophical additions that Freud and others have made to it, is not in the least contradictory to Christianity. . . .

When a man makes a moral choice two things are involved. One is the act of choosing. The other is the various feelings [either normal or abnormal]. . . . What psychoanalysis undertakes to do is to remove the abnormal feelings, that is, to give the man better raw material for his acts of choice: Morality is concerned with the acts of choice themselves.

522
Friendship
The Letters of C. S. Lewis to Arthur Greeves (29 December 1935), p. 477.

Friendship is the greatest of worldly goods. Certainly to me it is the chief happiness of life. If I had to give a piece of advice to a young man about a place to live, I think I shd. say, "sacrifice almost everything to live where you can be near your friends." I know I am v. fortunate in that respect.

523
Friendship
Letters of C. S. Lewis (21 December 1941), para. 3, p. 197.

Is any pleasure on earth as great as a circle of Christian friends by a fire?

524
Friendship
Selected Literary Essays, "Hamlet: The Prince or the Poem" (1942), para. 15, p. 99.

The next best thing to being wise oneself is to live in a circle of those who are.

525
Friendship
Present Concerns: Essays by C. S. Lewis, "Equality" (1943), para. 7, pp. 19–20.

The error here has been to assimilate all forms of affection to that special form we call friendship. It indeed does imply equality. But it is quite different from the various loves within the same household. Friends are not primarily absorbed in each other. It is when we are doing things together that friendship springs up—painting, sailing ships, praying, philosophizing, fighting shoulder to shoulder. Friends look in the same direction. Lovers look at each other: that is, in opposite directions.

526
Friendship
The Weight of Glory, "Membership" (1945), para. 2, pp. 106–107.

When I first went to Oxford the typical undergraduate society consisted of a dozen men, who knew one another intimately, hearing a paper by one of their own number in a small sitting-room and hammering out their problem till one or two in the morning. Before the war the typical undergraduate society had come to be a mixed audience of one or two hundred students assembled in a public hall to hear a lecture from some visiting celebrity. Even on those rare occasions when a modern undergraduate is not attending some such society he is seldom engaged in those solitary walks, or walks with a single companion, which built the minds of the previous generations. He lives in a crowd; caucus has replaced friendship.

527
Friendship
The Four Loves,
chap. 4, para. 1, 3,
pp. 87, 89.

To the Ancients, Friendship seemed the happiest and most fully human of all loves; the crown of life and the school of virtue. The modern world, in comparison, ignores it. . . . Affection and Eros [romantic love] were too obviously connected with our nerves, too obviously shared with the brutes. You could feel these tugging at your guts and fluttering in your diaphragm. But in Friendship—in that luminous, tranquil, rational world of relationships freely chosen—you got away from all that. This alone, of all the loves, seemed to raise you to the level of gods or angels.

528
Friendship
The Four Loves,
chap. 4, para. 9,
pp. 92-93.

In each of my friends there is something that only some other friend can fully bring out. By myself I am not large enough to call the whole man into activity; I want other lights than my own to show all his facets. Now that Charles is dead, I shall never again see Ronald's reaction to a specifically Caroline joke. Far from having more of Ronald, having him "to myself" now that Charles is away, I have less of Ronald. Hence true friendship is the least jealous of loves. Two friends delight to be joined by a third, and three by a fourth, if only the newcomer is qualified to become a real friend. . . . In this, Friendship exhibits a glorious "nearness by resemblance" to Heaven itself where the very multitude of the blessed (which no man can number) increases the fruition which each has of God. For every soul, seeing Him in her own way, doubtless communicates that unique vision to all the rest.

529
Friendship
The Four Loves,
chap. 4, para. 16, 18,
pp. 96–97.

Friendship arises out of mere Companionship
when two or more of the companions discover
that they have in common some insight or interest
or even taste which the others do not share and
which, till that moment, each believed to be his
own unique treasure (or burden). The typical
expression of opening Friendship would be
something like, "What? You too? I thought I was
the only one." . . . In this kind of love, as
Emerson said, *Do you love me?* means *Do you see
the same truth?*—Or at least, "Do you *care about*
the same truth?" The man who agrees with us
that some question, little regarded by others, is of
great importance can be our Friend. He need not
agree with us about the answer.

530
Friendship
The Four Loves,
chap. 4, para. 19–21,
pp. 98–99.

We picture lovers face to face but Friends side by
side; their eyes look ahead.

That is why those pathetic people who simply
"want friends" can never make any. The very
condition of having Friends is that we should
want something else besides Friends. Where the
truthful answer to the question *Do you see the
same truth?* would be "I see nothing and I don't
care about the truth; I only want a Friend," no
Friendship can arise—though Affection of course
may. There would be nothing for the Friendship
to be *about*; and Friendship must be about
something, even if it were only an enthusiasm for
dominoes or white mice. Those who have nothing
can share nothing; those who are going nowhere
can have no fellow-travellers.

When the two people who thus discover that
they are on the same secret road are of different
sexes, the friendship which arises between them
will very easily pass—may pass in the first half-
hour—into erotic love. Indeed, unless they are

physically repulsive to each other or unless one or both already loves elsewhere, it is almost certain to do so sooner or later. And conversely, erotic love may lead to Friendship between the lovers. But this, so far from obliterating the distinction between the two loves, puts it in a clearer light. If one who was first, in the deep and full sense, your Friend, is then gradually or suddenly revealed as also your lover you will certainly not want to share the Beloved's erotic love with any third. But you will have no jealousy at all about sharing the Friendship. Nothing so enriches an erotic love as the discovery that the Beloved can deeply, truly and spontaneously enter into Friendship with the Friends you already had: to feel that not only are we two united by erotic love but we three or four or five are all travellers on the same quest, have all a common vision.

531
Friendship
The Four Loves,
chap. 4, para. 27–28,
p. 103.

In a circle of true Friends each man is simply what he is: stands for nothing but himself. No one cares twopence about any one else's family, profession, class, income, race, or previous history. . . . That is the kingliness of Friendship. We meet like sovereign princes of independent states, abroad, on neutral ground, freed from our contexts. This love (essentially) ignores not only our physical bodies but that whole embodiment which consists of our family, job, past and connections. . . .

Hence (if you will not misunderstand me) the exquisite arbitrariness and irresponsibility of this love. I have no duty to be anyone's Friend and no man in the world has a duty to be mine. No claims, no shadow of necessity. Friendship is unnecessary, like philosophy, like art, like the universe itself (for God did not need to create). It has no survival value; rather it is one of those things which give value to survival.

532
Friendship
The Four Loves,
chap. 4, para. 29, p. 104.

The common quest or vision which unites Friends does not absorb them in such a way that they remain ignorant or oblivious of one another. On the contrary it is the very medium in which their mutual love and knowledge exist. One knows nobody so well as one's "fellow." Every step of the common journey tests his metal [sic]; and the tests are tests we fully understand because we are undergoing them ourselves. Hence, as he rings true time after time, our reliance, our respect and our admiration blossom into an Appreciative Love of a singularly robust and well-informed kind. If, at the outset, we had attended more to him and less to the thing our Friendship is "about," we should not have come to know or love him so well. You will not find the warrior, the poet, the philosopher or the Christian by staring in his eyes as if he were your mistress: better fight beside him, read with him, argue with him, pray with him.

533
Friendship
The Four Loves,
chap. 4, para. 38, p. 111.

Friendship is something that raised us almost above humanity. This love, free from instinct, free from all duties but those which love has freely assumed, almost wholly free from jealousy, and free without qualification from the need to be needed, is eminently spiritual. It is the sort of love one can imagine between angels.

534
Friendship
The Four Loves,
chap. 4, para. 47, p. 116.

People who bore one another should meet seldom; people who interest one another, often.

535
Friendship
The Four Loves,
chap. 4, para. 59, p. 124.

Friendship, then, like the other natural loves, is unable to save itself. In reality, because it is spiritual and therefore faces a subtler enemy, it must, even more whole-heartedly than they, invoke the divine protection if it hopes to remain sweet. For consider how narrow its true path is. It must not become what the people call a "mutual admiration society"; yet if it is not full of mutual admiration, of appreciative love, it is not Friendship at all.

536
Friendship
The Four Loves,
chap. 4, para. 61,
pp. 126–127.

For a Christian, there are, strictly speaking, no chances. A secret Master of the Ceremonies has been at work. Christ, who said to the disciples "Ye have not chosen me, but I have chosen you," can truly say to every group of Christian friends "You have not chosen one another but I have chosen you for one another." The Friendship is not a reward for our discrimination and good taste in finding one another out. It is the instrument by which God reveals to each the beauties of all the others. They are no greater than the beauties of a thousand other men; by Friendship God opens our eyes to them. They are, like all beauties, derived from Him, and then, in a good Friendship, increased by Him through the Friendship itself, so that it is His instrument for creating as well as for revealing. At this feast it is He who has spread the board and it is He who has chosen the guests. It is He, we may dare to hope, who sometimes does, and always should, preside. Let us not reckon without our Host.

537
Friendship, Dangers of
The Four Loves,
chap. 4, para. 43, p. 113.

Friendship . . . is born at the moment when one man says to another "What! You too? I thought that no one but myself. . . ." But the common taste or vision or point of view which is thus discovered need not always be a nice one. From such a moment art, or philosophy, or an advance in religion or morals might well take their rise; but why not also torture, cannibalism, or human sacrifice? Surely most of us have experienced the ambivalent nature of such moments in our own youth? It was wonderful when we first met someone who cared for our favourite poet. What we had hardly understood before now took clear shape. What we had been half ashamed of we now freely acknowledged. But it was no less delightful when we first met someone who shared with us a secret evil. This too became far more palpable and explicit; of this too, we ceased to be ashamed. Even now, at whatever age, we all know the perilous charm of a shared hatred or grievance. (It is difficult not to hail as a Friend the only other man in College who really sees the faults of the Sub-Warden.)

538
Friendship, Dangers of
The Four Loves,
chap. 4, para. 45–46,
48–49, pp. 114–117.

Every real Friendship is a sort of secession, even a rebellion. It may be a rebellion of serious thinkers against accepted clap-trap or of faddists against accepted good sense; of real artists against popular ugliness or of charlatans against civilised taste; of good men against the badness of society or of bad men against its goodness. . . . The dangers are perfectly real. Friendship (as the ancients saw) can be a school of virtue; but also (as they did not see) a school of vice. It is ambivalent. It makes good men better and bad men worse. . . .

The danger is that this partial indifference or deafness to outside opinion, justified and necessary though it is, may lead to a wholesale indifference or deafness. . . . Like an aristocracy, it can create around it a vacuum across which no voice will carry.

539
Friendship, Dangers of

The Four Loves,
chap. 4, para. 55, 57,
pp. 122–124.

We can thus detect the pride of Friendship—whether Olympian, Titanic, or merely vulgar—in many circles of Friends. It would be rash to assume that our own is safe from its danger; for of course it is in our own that we should be slowest to recognise it. The danger of such pride is indeed almost inseparable from Friendly love. Friendship must exclude. From the innocent and necessary act of excluding to the spirit of exclusiveness is an easy step; and thence to the degrading pleasure of exclusiveness. . . . The common vision which first brought us together may fade quite away. We shall be a coterie that exists for the sake of being a coterie; a little self-elected (and therefore absurd) aristocracy, basking in the moonshine of our collective self-approval. . . . Pride [is] the danger to which Friendships are naturally liable. Just because this is the most spiritual of loves the danger which besets it is spiritual too.

540
Fun

Letters to Children
(18 July 1957), p. 72.

You are quite right if you mean that giving up fun for no reason except that you think it's "good" to give it up, is all nonsense.

541
Futility

Christian Reflections, "De Futilitate" (given at Oxford during WW II), chap. 5, para. 6, p. 60.

A machine or plan is futile when it does not serve the purpose for which it was devised. In calling the universe futile, therefore, we are really applying to it a means-and-end pattern of thought: treating it as if it were a thing manufactured and manufactured for some purpose. In calling it futile we are only expressing our naive surprise at the discovery that basic reality does not possess the characteristics of a human artefact—a thing made by men to serve the purposes of men—and the demand that it should may be regarded as preposterous: it is rather like complaining that a tree is futile because the branches don't happen to come just where we want them for climbing it— or even a stone because it doesn't happen to be edible.

542
Future
God in the Dock, "Cross-Examination" (1963), para. 55, p. 266.

The great thing is to be found at one's post as a child of God, living each day as though it were our last, but planning as though our world might last a hundred years.

543

Gambling

God in the Dock,
"Answers to Questions
on Christianity" (1944),
ans. 13, pp. 59–60.

Gambling ought never to be an important part of a man's life. If it is a way in which large sums of money are transferred from person to person without doing any good (e.g., producing employment, goodwill, etc.) then it is a bad thing.
If it is carried out on a small scale, I am not sure that it is bad. I don't know much about it, because it is about the only vice to which I have no temptation at all, and I think it is a risk to talk about things which are not in my own make-up, because I don't understand them. If anyone comes to me asking to play bridge for money, I just say: "How much do you hope to win? Take it and go away."

544

**Gascoigne,
George**

*English Literature in the
Sixteenth Century,* bk.
II.II, para. 68,
pp. 269–270.

George Gascoigne (1539?–77) . . . does not belong completely to the Drab Age. In him at last we find what we have vainly sought among his contemporaries, a transitional poet—one in whom we see Golden quality coming to birth. . . . It is on his shorter pieces that Gascoigne's fame as a poet depends. He writes poulter's, fourteeners, songs, sonnets, decasyllabic stanzas, and couplets. What sets him at times above the Drab poets and brings him to the verge of the Golden quality is his grace and melody. He is only a minor poet. He

---

has neither enough invention for narrative nor enough passion for lyric. If he had followed, instead of anticipating (however faintly) the Golden poets, he would be nothing. As things are, he is like the first streak of dawn.

545
Gender
Perelandra, chap. 16, p. 200.

Everyone must sometimes have wondered why in nearly all tongues certain inanimate objects are masculine and others feminine. What is masculine about a mountain or feminine about certain trees? Ransom has cured me of believing that this is a purely morphological phenomenon, depending on the form of the word. Still less is gender an imaginative extension of sex. Our ancestors did not make mountains masculine because they projected male characteristics into them. The real process is the reverse. Gender is a reality, and a more fundamental reality than sex. Sex is, in fact, merely the adaptation to organic life of a fundamental polarity which divides all created beings. Female sex is simply one of the things that have feminine gender; there are many others, and Masculine and Feminine meet us on planes of reality where male and female would be simply meaningless. Masculine is not attenuated male, nor feminine attenuated female. On the contrary, the male and female of organic creatures are rather faint and blurred reflections of masculine and feminine. Their reproductive functions, their differences in strength and size, partly exhibit, but partly also confuse and misrepresent, the real polarity.

546
Giving
Perelandra, chap. 17, p. 210.

"The best fruits are plucked for each by some hand that is not his own."

547
Giving
Christian Reflections,
"On Church Music"
(1949), para. 12, p. 99.

All our offerings, whether of music or martyrdom, are like the intrinsically worthless present of a child, which a father values indeed, but values only for the intention.

548
Giving
Mere Christianity, bk. III,
chap. 3, para. 7,
pp. 81–82.

Charity—giving to the poor—is an essential part of Christian morality. . . . I do not believe one can settle how much we ought to give. I am afraid the only safe rule is to give more than we can spare. In other words, if our expenditure on comforts, luxuries, amusements, etc., is up to the standard common among those with the same income as our own, we are probably giving away too little. If our charities do not at all pinch or hamper us, I should say they are too small. There ought to be things we should like to do and cannot do because our charitable expenditure excludes them.

549
Giving
*English Literature in the
Sixteenth Century,*
Introduction, para. 53,
p. 35.

The limit of giving is to be the limit of our ability to give.

550
Giving
The Four Loves,
chap. 3, para. 38, p. 76.

The proper aim of giving is to put the recipient in a state where he no longer needs our gift.

551
Giving
*Letters to an American
Lady* (26 October 1962),
p. 108.

Another thing that annoys me is when people say "Why did you give that man money? He'll probably go and drink it." My reply is "But if I'd kept [it] *I* should probably have drunk it."

552
Giving
Letters to an American Lady (26 October 1962), p. 108.

It will not bother me in the hour of death to reflect that I have been "had for a sucker" by any number of impostors; but it would be a torment to know that one had refused even one person in need.

553
Glory
The Weight of Glory, "The Weight of Glory" (1942), para. 15, pp. 18-19.

It may be possible for each to think too much of his own potential glory hereafter; it is hardly possible for him to think too often or too deeply about that of his neighbour. The load, or weight, or burden of my neighbour's glory should be laid on my back, a load so heavy that only humility can carry it, and the backs of the proud will be broken. It is a serious thing to live in a society of possible gods and goddesses, to remember that the dullest and most uninteresting person you can talk to may one day be a creature which, if you saw it now, you would be strongly tempted to worship, or else a horror and a corruption such as you now meet, if at all, only in a nightmare. All day long we are, in some degree, helping each other to one or other of these destinations. It is in the light of these overwhelming possibilities, it is with the awe and the circumspection proper to them, that we should conduct all our dealings with one another, all friendships, all loves, all play, all politics. There are no *ordinary* people. You have never met a mere mortal. Nations, cultures, arts, civilisations—these are mortal, and their life is to ours as the life of a gnat. But it is immortals whom we joke with, work with, marry, snub, and exploit—immortal horrors or everlasting splendours.

554
God:
Approaching
Him
A Grief Observed,
chap. IV, para. 21, p. 79.

He can't be used as a road. If you're approaching Him not as the goal but as a road, not as the end but as a means, you're not really approaching Him at all. That's what was really wrong with all those popular pictures of happy reunions "on the further shore"; not the simple-minded and very earthly images, but the fact that they make an End of what we can get only as a by-product of the true End.

555
God:
Completeness
Perelandra, chap. 17,
p. 217.

"He has no need at all of anything that is made. An eldil [angel] is not more needful to Him than a grain of the Dust: a peopled world no more needful than a world that is empty: but all needless alike, and what all add to Him is nothing. We also have no need of anything that is made. Love me, my brothers, for I am infinitely superfluous, and your love shall be like His, born neither of your need nor of my deserving, but a plain bounty. Blessed be He!"

556
God: Creator
Miracles, chap. 11,
para. 11, p. 88.

[God] is so brim-full of existence that He can give existence away, can cause things to be, and to be really other than Himself, can make it untrue to say that He is everything.

557
God: Creator
Letters to Malcolm:
Chiefly on Prayer,
chap. 5, para. 12, p. 27.

It would be rash to say that there is any prayer which God *never* grants. But the strongest candidate is the prayer we might express in the single word *encore*. And how should the Infinite repeat Himself? All space and time are too little for Him to utter Himself in them *once*.

558
God: Eternity
Christian Reflections,
"The Poison of
Subjectivism: (1943),
para. 21, p. 80.

It might be permissible to lay down two negations: that God neither obeys nor creates the moral law. The good is uncreated; it never could have been otherwise; it has in it no shadow of contingency; it lies, as Plato said, on the other side of existence.

559
God: Eternity
Miracles, chap. 11,
para. 12, p. 88.

It is clear that there never was a time when nothing existed; otherwise nothing would exist now.

560
God: Eternity
Mere Christianity, bk. IV,
chap. 3, para. 7,
p. 147.

God is not hurried along in the Time-stream of this universe any more than an author is hurried along in the imaginary time of his own novel. He has infinite attention to spare for each one of us. He does not have to deal with us in the mass. You are as much alone with Him as if you were the only being He had ever created. When Christ died, He died for you individually just as much as if you had been the only man in the world.

561
God: Gender Imagery for
God in the Dock,
"Priestesses in the
Church?" (1948),
para. 8–9, p. 237.

Common sense, disregarding the discomfort, or even the horror, which the idea of turning all our theological language into the feminine gender arouses in most Christians, will ask "Why not? Since God is in fact not a biological being and has no sex, what can it matter whether we say *He* or *She, Father* or *Mother, Son* or *Daughter?*"

But Christians think that God Himself has taught us how to speak of Him. To say that it does not matter is to say either that all the masculine imagery is not inspired, is merely human in origin, or else that, though inspired, it is quite arbitrary and unessential. And this is surely intolerable: or, if tolerable, it is an argument not in favour of Christian priestesses but against Christianity.

562
**God:
Glorifying
Him**
Reflections on the Psalms,
chap. 9, para. 6,
pp. 96–97.

The Scotch catechism says that man's chief end is "to glorify God and enjoy Him forever." But we shall then know that these are the same thing. Fully to enjoy is to glorify. In commanding us to glorify Him, God is inviting us to enjoy Him.

563
God: Glory
Christian Reflections,
"Christianity and
Literature" (1939),
para. 15, p. 10.

We can play, as we can eat, to the glory of God.

564
God: Glory
God in the Dock,
"Miracles" (1942),
para. 9, p. 32.

The filth that our poor, muddled, sincere, resentful enemies fling at the Holy One, either does not stick, or, sticking, turns into glory.

565
**God:
Goodness**
The Problem of Pain,
chap. 3, para. 17, p. 50.

God has no needs. Human love, as Plato teaches us, is the child of Poverty—of want or lack; it is caused by a real or supposed good in its beloved which the lover needs and desires. But God's love, far from being caused by goodness in the object, causes all the goodness which the object has, loving it first into existence and then into real, though derivative, loveability. God is Goodness. He can give good, but cannot need or get it. In that sense all His love is, as it were, bottomlessly selfless by very definition; it has everything to give and nothing to receive.

566
**God:
Goodness**
The Problem of Pain,
chap. 4, p. 58.

When we merely *say* that we are bad, the "wrath" of God seems a barbarous doctrine; as soon as we *perceive* our badness, it appears inevitable, a mere corollary from God's goodness.

567

God:
Goodness

Christian Reflections,
"The Poison of
Subjectivism" (1943),
para. 21, p. 80.

God is not merely good, but goodness; goodness is not merely divine, but God.

568

God:
Goodness

Perelandra, chap. 7,
p. 93.

"Didn't we agree that God is a spirit? Don't you worship Him because He is pure spirit?"

"Good heavens, no! We worship Him because He is wise and good. There's nothing specially fine about simply being a spirit. The Devil is a spirit."

569

God:
Goodness

The Great Divorce,
chap. 11, pp. 97–98.

"There is but one good; that is God. Everything else is good when it looks to Him and bad when it turns from Him. And the higher and mightier it is in the natural order, the more demoniac [sic] it will be if it rebels. It's not out of bad mice or bad fleas you make demons, but out of bad archangels. The false religion of lust is baser than the false religion of mother-love or patriotism or art: but lust is less likely to be made into a religion."

570

God:
Goodness

A Grief Observed,
chap. 3, para. 17,
pp. 49–50.

The terrible thing is that a perfectly good God is in this matter hardly less formidable than a Cosmic Sadist. The more we believe that God hurts only to heal, the less we can believe that there is any use in begging for tenderness. A cruel man might be bribed—might grow tired of his vile sport—might have a temporary fit of mercy, as alcoholics have fits of sobriety. But suppose that what you are up against is a surgeon whose intentions are wholly good. The kinder and more conscientious he is, the more inexorably he will go on cutting. If he yielded to your entreaties, if he stopped before the operation was complete, all the pain up to that point would have been useless. But is it credible that such extremities of torture should be necessary for us? Well, take your choice. The tortures occur. If they are unnecessary, then there is no God or a bad one. If there is a good God, then these tortures are necessary. For no even moderately good Being could possibly inflict or permit them if they weren't.

571

God: Holiness

The Problem of Pain,
chap. 4, para. 5, p. 58.

A God who did not regard this [our own worst sins] with unappeasable distaste would not be a good being. We cannot even wish for such a God—it is like wishing that every nose in the universe were abolished, that smell of hay or roses or the sea should never again delight any creature, because our own breath happens to stink.

572

God: Image of

Prince Caspian,
chap. 15, pp. 211–212.

"Do you mark all this well, King Caspian?"

"I do indeed, Sir," said Caspian. "I was wishing that I came of a more honourable lineage."

"You come of the Lord Adam and the Lady Eve," said Aslan. "And that is both honour enough to erect the head of the poorest beggar, and shame enough to bow the shoulders of the greatest emperor in earth. Be content." Caspian bowed.

573

God: Indescribability

Letters to Malcolm: Chiefly on Prayer,
chap. 16, para. 1, p. 83.

"Bright blur" is not a very good description. In fact you can't have a good description of anything so vague. If the description became good it would become false.

574
God: Infinity
God in the Dock,
"Dogma and the
Universe" (1943),
para. 17, p. 47.

Do not let us deceive ourselves. No possible complexity which we can give to our picture of the universe can hide us from God: there is no copse, no forest, no jungle thick enough to provide cover.

575
God: Infinity
Perelandra, chap. 17,
p. 218.

"Yet this seeming also is the end and final cause for which He spreads out Time so long and Heaven so deep; lest if we never met the dark, and the road that leads nowhither, and the question to which no answer is imaginable, we should have in our minds no likeness of the Abyss of the Father, into which if a creature drop down his thoughts for ever he shall hear no echo return to him. Blessed, blessed, blessed be He!"

576
God: Infinity
Miracles, chap. 11,
para. 18, p. 93.

We may find a violence in some of the traditional imagery which tends to obscure the changelessness of God, the peace, which nearly all who approach Him have reported—the "still, small voice." . . . The stillness in which the mystics approach Him is intent and alert—at the opposite pole from sleep or reverie. They are becoming like Him. Silences in the physical world occur in empty places: but the ultimate Peace is silent through very density of life. Saying is swallowed up in being. There is no movement because His action (which is Himself) is timeless. You might, if you wished, call it movement at an infinite speed, which is the same thing as rest, but reached by a different—perhaps a less misleading—way of approach.

577
God: Infinity
The Four Loves,
chap. 6, para. 20,
pp. 174–175.

The humblest of us, in a state of Grace, can have some "knowledge-by-acquaintance" (*con-naitre*), some "tasting," of Love Himself; but man even at his highest sanctity and intelligence has no direct "knowledge about" (*savoir*) the ultimate Being—

only analogies. We cannot see light, though by light we can see things. Statements about God are extrapolations from the knowledge of other things which the divine illumination enables us to know.

578
God:
Language
about
Letters to Malcolm:
Chiefly on Prayer,
chap. 4, para. 9, p. 21.

Never, here or anywhere else, let us think that while anthropomorphic images are a concession to our weakness, the abstractions [metaphysical and theological] are the literal truth. Both are equally concessions; each singly misleading, and the two together mutually corrective.

579
God: Lewis's
Childhood
Conception
Surprised by Joy,
chap. 1, para. 22, p. 21.

[Lewis recalls his thinking about God at the time of his mother's illness and death:] The belief into which I had hypnotized myself was itself too irreligious for its failure to cause any religious revolution. I had approached God, or my idea of God, without love, without awe, even without fear. He was, in my mental picture of this miracle [resurrecting his mother], to appear neither as Savior nor as Judge, but merely as a magician; and when He had done what was required of Him I supposed He would simply—well, go away. It never crossed my mind that the tremendous contact which I solicited should have any consequences beyond restoring the *status quo*. I imagine that a "faith" of this kind is often generated in children and that its disappointment is of no religious importance.

580
God: Love
The Weight of Glory,
"Membership" (1945),
para. 14, p. 115.

The infinite value of each human soul is not a Christian doctrine. God did not die for man because of some value He perceived in him. The value of each human soul considered simply in itself, out of relation to God, is zero. As St. Paul writes, to have died for valuable men would have

---

been not divine but merely heroic; but God died for sinners. He loved us not because we were lovable, but because He is Love.

581
God: Love
Miracles, chap. 11, para. 17, pp. 92–93.

[A] mistake is easily made because we (correctly) deny that God has passions; and with us a love that is not passionate means a love that is something less. But the reason why God has no passions is that passions imply passivity and intermission. The passion of love is something that happens to us, as "getting wet" happens to a body: and God is exempt from that "passion" in the same way that water is exempt from "getting wet." He cannot be affected with love, because He *is* love. To imagine that love as something less torrential or less sharp than our own temporary and derivative "passions" is a most disastrous fantasy.

582
God: Modern Attitude
God in the Dock, "God in the Dock" (1948), para. 7, p. 244.

The ancient man approached God (or even the gods) as the accused person approaches his judge. For the modern man the roles are reversed. He is the judge: God is in the dock. He is quite a kindly judge: if God should have a reasonable defence for being the god who permits war, poverty and disease, he is ready to listen to it. The trial may even end in God's acquittal. But the important thing is that Man is on the Bench and God in the Dock.

583
God: Omnipresence
A Preface to "Paradise Lost," chap. 12, para. 15, p. 88.

Thomas Aquinas, in defining the mode of God's omnipresence, distinguishes three different meanings of the words "to be in a place" (or "in place"). A *body* is in a place in such a way as to be bounded by it, i.e. it occupies a place *circumscriptive*. An angel is in a place not *circumscriptive,* for it is not bounded by it, but *definitive,* because it is in that one place and *not* in any other. But God is in a place neither *circumscriptive* nor *definitive,* because he is everywhere (*Sum. Theol.* Ia. Q. LII, Art. 2).

584
God:
Omnipresence
Perelandra, chap. 17,
pp. 214–215.

"They who add years to years in lumpish aggregation, or miles to miles and galaxies to galaxies, shall not come near His greatness. The day of the fields of Arbol [the Sun] will fade and the days of Deep Heaven itself are numbered. Not thus is He great. He dwells (all of Him dwells) within the seed of the smallest flower and is not cramped: Deep Heaven is inside Him who is inside the seed and does not distend Him. Blessed be He!"

585
God:
Omnipresence
Letters to Malcolm:
Chiefly on Prayer,
chap. 14, para. 11, p. 75.

We may ignore, but we can nowhere evade, the presence of God. The world is crowded with Him. He walks everywhere *incognito.* And the *incognito* is not always hard to penetrate. The real labour is to remember, to attend. In fact, to come awake. Still more, to remain awake.

586
God:
Our Need for
The Four Loves,
chap. 1, para. 7,
pp. 13–14.

Our whole being by its very nature is one vast need; incomplete, preparatory, empty yet cluttered, crying out for Him who can untie things that are now knotted together and tie up things that are still dangling loose.

587
God:
Personalness
Miracles, chap. 11,
para. 2, p. 81.

God . . . has purposes and performs particular actions, . . . does one thing and not another, [is] a concrete, choosing, commanding, prohibiting God with a determinate character.

588

God: Personalness

The World's Last Night and Other Essays, "On Obstinacy in Belief" (1955), para. 14, p. 26.

To believe that God—at least this God—exists is to believe that you as a person now stand in the presence of God as a Person. What would, a moment before, have been variations in opinion, now become variations in your personal attitude to a Person. You are no longer faced with an argument which demands your assent, but with a Person who demands your confidence.

589

God: Personalness

Letters to Malcolm: Chiefly on Prayer, chap. 18, para. 6–7, p. 96.

You suggest that what is traditionally regarded as our experience of God's anger would be more helpfully regarded as what inevitably happens to us if we behave inappropriately towards a reality of immense power. As you say, "The live wire doesn't feel angry with us, but if we blunder against it we get a shock."

My dear Malcolm, what do you suppose you have gained by substituting the image of a live wire for that of angered majesty? You have shut us all up in despair; for the angry can forgive, and electricity can't.

590

God: Providence

A Severe Mercy, Letter to Sheldon Vanauken (6 April 1955), pp. 188–189.

Once we have accepted an omniscient & providential God, the distinction we used to draw between the significant and the fortuitous must either break down or be restated in some v. much subtler form. If an event coming about in the ordinary course of nature becomes to me the occasion of hope and faith and love or increased efforts after virtue, do we suppose that this result was unforeseen by, or is indifferent to, God? Obviously not. What we should have called its fortuitous effects must have been present to Him for all eternity. And indeed, we can't suppose God saying (as a human artist might) "That effect, though it has turned out rather well, was, I must admit, no part of my original design." Then the total act of creation, including *our own* creation (wh. is going on all the time) meets us, doesn't it? in every event at every moment: the act of a Person dealing with persons and knowing what He does.

591
God: Reality
Miracles, chap. 11,
para. 15, p. 91.

God is basic Fact or Actuality, the source of all other facthood. At all costs therefore He must not be thought of as a featureless generality. If He exists at all, He is the most concrete thing there is, the most individual, "organised and minutely articulated." He is unspeakable not by being indefinite but by being too definite for the unavoidable vagueness of language.

592
God: Reality
Miracles, chap. 11,
para. 16, pp. 91–92.

It is just the recognition of God's positive and concrete reality which the religious imagery preserves. The crudest Old Testament picture of Jahweh thundering and lightning out of dense smoke, making mountains skip like rams, threatening, promising, pleading, even changing His mind, transmits that sense of *living* Deity which evaporates in abstract thought. . . . Perhaps we may rightly reject much of the Old Testament imagery. But we must be clear why we are doing so: not because the images are too strong but because they are too weak. The ultimate spiritual reality is not vaguer, more inert, more transparent than the images, but more positive, more dynamic, more opaque.

593
God: Reality
Miracles, chap. 11,
para. 19, p. 94.

It is always shocking to meet life where we thought we were alone. "Look out!" we cry, "it's *alive*." And therefore this is the very point at which so many draw back—I would have done so myself if I could—and proceed no further with

Christianity. An "impersonal God"—well and good. A subjective God of beauty, truth and goodness, inside our own heads—better still. A formless life-force surging through us, a vast power which we can tap—best of all. But God Himself, alive, pulling at the other end of the cord, perhaps approaching at an infinite speed, the hunter, king, husband—that is quite another matter. There comes a moment when the children who have been playing at burglars hush suddenly: was that a *real* footstep in the hall? There comes a moment when people who have been dabbling in religion ("Man's search for God!") suddenly draw back. Supposing we really found Him? We never meant it to come to *that!* Worse still, supposing He had found us?

594

God: Reality

Christian Reflections,
"The Seeing Eye" (1963),
para. 10–11, 14–16,
pp. 167–168.

Looking for God—or Heaven—by exploring space is like reading or seeing all Shakespeare's plays in the hope that you will find Shakespeare as one of the characters or Stratford as one of the places. Shakespeare is in one sense present at every moment in every play. But he is never present in the same way as Falstaff or Lady Macbeth. . . .

If there were an idiot who thought plays existed on their own, without an author (not to mention actors, producer, manager, stagehands and what not), our belief in Shakespeare would not be much affected by his saying, quite truly, that he had studied all the plays and never found Shakespeare in them. . . .

My point is that, if God does exist, He is related to the universe more as an author is related to a play than as one object in the universe is related to another.

If God created the universe, He created space-

---

time, which is to the universe as the metre is to a poem or the key is to music. To look for Him as one item within the framework which He Himself invented is nonsensical.

If God—such a God as any adult religion believes in—exists, mere movement in space will never bring you any nearer to Him or any farther from Him than you are at this very moment. You can neither reach Him nor avoid Him by travelling to Alpha Centauri or even to other galaxies. A fish is no more, and no less, in the sea after it has swum a thousand miles than it was when it set out.

595
God: Self-Existence
Miracles, chap. 11,
para. 9–10, p. 87.

If anything is to exist at all, then the Original Thing must be, not a principle nor a generality, much less an "ideal" or a "value," but an utterly concrete fact.

. . . We must beware, as Professor Whitehead says, of paying God ill-judged "metaphysical compliments." We say that God is "infinite." In the sense that His knowledge and power extend not to some things but to all, this is true. But if by using the word "infinite" we encourage ourselves to think of Him as a formless "everything" about whom nothing in particular and everything in general is true, then it would be better to drop that word altogether. Let us dare to say that God is a particular Thing. Once He was the only Thing: but He is creative, He made other things to be. He is not those other things. He is not "universal being": if He were there would be no creatures, for a generality can make nothing. He is "absolute being"—or rather *the* Absolute Being—in the sense that He alone exists in His own right.

596
God:
Sovereignty
The Pilgrim's Regress, bk.
8, chap. 6, p. 148.

Beating my wings, all ways, within your cage
I flutter, but not out.

597
God:
Sovereignty
The Weight of Glory,
"Learning in War-Time"
(1939), para. 7, p. 25.

[Religion] must occupy the whole of life. There is
no question of a compromise between the claims
of God and the claims of culture, or politics, or
anything else. God's claim is infinite and
inexorable. You can refuse it: or you can begin to
try to grant it. There is no middle way. Yet in
spite of this it is clear that Christianity does not
exclude any of the ordinary human activities. St.
Paul tells people to get on with their jobs.

598
God:
Sovereignty
Christian Reflections,
"Christianity and
Culture" (1940), Section
III, para. 11, p. 33.

Our leisure, even our play, is a matter of serious
concern. There is no neutral ground in the
universe: every square inch, every split second, is
claimed by God and counterclaimed by Satan.

599
God:
Sovereignty
The Problem of Pain,
chap. 2, para. 16, p. 35.

The freedom of God consists in the fact that no
cause other than Himself produces His acts and
no external obstacle impedes them—that His own
goodness is the root from which they all grow
and His own omnipotence the air in which they
all flower.

600
God:
Sovereignty
The Problem of Pain,
chap. 3, para. 17, p. 49.

God can no more be in competition with a
creature than Shakespeare can be in competition
with Viola.

601
God:
Sovereignty
Miracles, chap. 11,
para. 19, p. 93.

Men are reluctant to pass over from the notion of an abstract and negative deity to the living God. I do not wonder. Here lies the deepest tap-root of Pantheism and of the objection to traditional imagery. It was hated not, at bottom, because it pictured Him as man but because it pictured Him as king, or even as warrior. The Pantheist's God does nothing, demands nothing. He is there if you wish for Him, like a book on a shelf. He will not pursue you. There is no danger that at any time heaven and earth should flee away at His glance.

602
God:
Sovereignty
Miracles, chap. 14,
para. 23, p. 124.

Where a God who is totally purposive and totally foreseeing acts upon a Nature which is totally interlocked, there can be no accidents or loose ends, nothing whatever of which we can safely use the word *merely.* Nothing is "merely a by-product" of anything else.

603
God:
Sovereignty
Mere Christianity, bk. IV,
chap. 2, para. 13,
p. 144.

When you come to knowing God, the initiative lies on His side. If He does not show Himself, nothing you can do will enable you to find Him. And, in fact, He shows much more of Himself to some people than to others—not because He has favourites, but because it is impossible for Him to show Himself to a man whose whole mind and character are in the wrong condition. Just as sunlight, though it has no favourites, cannot be reflected in a dusty mirror as clearly as a clean one.

604
God:
Sovereignty
Surprised by Joy,
chap. 15, para. 3,
pp. 231–232.

God was to be obeyed simply because he was God. Long since, through the gods of Asgard, and later through the notion of the Absolute, He had taught me how a thing can be revered not for what it can do to us but for what it is in itself. That is why, though it was a terror, it was no surprise to learn that God is to be obeyed because of what He is in Himself. If you ask why we should obey God, in the last resort the answer is, "I am." To know God is to know that our obedience is due to Him. In His nature His sovereignty *de jure* is revealed.

605
God:
Sovereignty
The Four Loves,
chap. 3, para. 13, p. 61.

The rivalry between all natural loves and the love of God is something a Christian dare not forget. God is the great Rival, the ultimate object of human jealousy.

606
God:
Sovereignty
The Four Loves,
chap. 6, para. 21, p. 175.

In God there is no hunger that needs to be filled, only plenteousness that desires to give. The doctrine that God was under no necessity to create is not a piece of dry scholastic speculation. It is essential. Without it we can hardly avoid the conception of what I can only call a "managerial" God; a Being whose function or nature is to "run" the universe, who stands to it as a head-master to a school or a hotelier to a hotel. But to be sovereign of the universe is no great matter to God. In Himself; at home in "the land of the Trinity," he is Sovereign of a far greater realm.

607
God:
Timelessness
Mere Christianity, bk. IV,
chap. 3, para. 5,
p. 146.

Almost certainly God is not in Time. His life does not consist of moments following one another. If a million people are praying to Him at ten-thirty tonight, He need not listen to them all in that one little snippet which we call ten-thirty. Ten-thirty—and every other moment from the beginning of the world—is always the Present for Him.

608
God: Transcendence/ Immanence
Letters to Malcolm: Chiefly on Prayer, chap. 14, para. 6–8, p. 74.

Therefore of each creature we can say, "This also is Thou: neither is this Thou."

Simple faith leaps to this with astonishing ease. I once talked to a continental pastor who had seen Hitler, and had, by all human standards, good cause to hate him. "What did he look like?" I asked. "Like all men," he replied. "That is, like Christ."

One is always fighting on at least two fronts. When one is among Pantheists one must emphasise the distinctness, and relative independence, of the creatures. Among Deists—or perhaps in Woolwich, if the laity there really think God is to be sought in the sky—one must emphasise the divine presence in my neighbour, my dog, my cabbage-patch.

609
God's Will
The Problem of Pain, chap. 6, p. 100.

God's will is determined by His wisdom which always perceives, and His goodness which always embraces, the intrinsically good.

610
God's Will
Perelandra, chap. 9, p. 116.

To walk out of His will is to walk into nowhere.

611
God's Will
Prince Caspian, chap. 10, pp. 137–138.

"Please, Aslan! Am I not to know?"

"To know what *would* have happened, child?" said Aslan. "No, Nobody is ever told that."

"Oh dear," said Lucy.

"But anyone can find out what *will* happen," said Aslan. "If you go back to the others now, and wake them up; and tell them you have seen me again; and that you must all get up at once and follow me—what will happen? There is only one way of finding out. . . ."

"But they won't believe me!" said Lucy.

"It doesn't matter," said Aslan.

"Oh dear, oh dear," said Lucy. "And I was so pleased at finding you again. And I thought you'd let me stay. And I thought you'd come roaring in and frighten all the enemies away—like last time. And now everything is going to be horrid."

"It is hard for you, little one," said Aslan. "But things never happen the same way twice. It has been hard for us all in Narnia before now."

Lucy buried her head in his mane to hide from his face. But there must have been magic in his mane. She could feel lion-strength going into her. Quite suddenly she sat up.

"I'm sorry, Aslan," she said. "I'm ready now."

612
God's Will
Letters of C. S. Lewis (20 June 1952), para. 2, p. 243.

I don't doubt that the Holy Spirit guides your decisions from within when you make them with the intention of pleasing God. The error wd. be to think that He speaks *only* within, whereas in reality He speaks also through Scripture, the Church, Christian friends, books etc.

613
Gods, Greek
Miracles, chap. 2, para. 9, p. 8.

The gods of Greece were not really supernatural in the strict sense which I am giving to the word. They were products of the total system of things and included within it.

614
Good and Evil
The Letters of C. S. Lewis to Arthur Greeves (12 September 1933), p. 463.

[I] deny another remark of yours—where you say "no good without evil." This on my view is absolutely untrue: but the opposite "no evil without good" is absolutely true.

615
**Good and
Evil**

*The Letters of C. S.
Lewis to Arthur Greeves*
(12 September 1933),
p. 465.

I think one may be quite rid of the old haunting suspicion—which raises its head in every temptation—that there is something *else* than God—some other country . . . into which He forbids us to trespass—some kind of delight wh. He "doesn't appreciate" or just chooses to forbid, but which wd. be real delight if only we were allowed to get it. The thing *just isn't there.* Whatever we desire is either what God is trying to give us as quickly as He can, or else a false picture of what He is trying to give us—a false picture or else a false picture wh. would not attract us for a moment if we saw the real thing. Therefore God does really in a sense contain evil—i.e. contains what is the real motive power behind all our evil desires. He knows what we want, even in our vilest acts: He is longing to give it to us. He is not looking on from the outside at some new "taste" or "separate desire of our own." Only because he has laid up *real* goods for us to desire are we able to go wrong by snatching at them in greedy, misdirected ways. The truth is that evil is not a real *thing* at all, like God. It is simply good *spoiled.* That is why I say there can be good without evil, but no evil without good. You know what the biologists mean by a parasite—an animal that lives on another animal. Evil is a parasite. It is there only because good is there for it to spoil and confuse.

616
**Good and
Evil**

Christian Reflections,
"Christianity and
Culture" (1940), Section
III, para. 5, p. 29.

Many preferences which seem to the ignorant to be simply "matter of taste" are visible to the trained critic as choices between good and evil, or truth and error.

617
**Good and
Evil**
God in the Dock, "Evil
and God" (1941),
para. 5, p. 23.

A sound theory of value demands . . . that good
should be original and evil a mere perversion; that
good should be the tree and evil the ivy; that
good should be able to see all round evil (as when
sane men understand lunacy) while evil cannot
retaliate in kind; that good should be able to exist
on its own while evil requires the good on which
it is parasitic in order to continue its parasitic
existence.

618
**Good and
Evil**
*A Preface to "Paradise
Lost,"* chap. 10,
para. 2–5, pp. 66–67.

[Commenting on St. Augustine's theological
influence on Milton:]
    1. God created all things without exception
good, and because they are good, "No *Nature*
(i.e., no positive reality) is bad and the word Bad
denotes merely privation of good." . . .
    2. What we call bad things are good things
perverted. . . . This perversion arises when a
conscious creature becomes more interested in
itself than in God, . . . and wishes to exist "on its
own." . . . This is the sin of Pride. . . .
    3. From [Augustine's] doctrine of good and evil
it follows (a) That good can exist without evil, . . .
but not evil without good. . . . (b) That good and
bad angels have the same Nature, happy when it
adheres to God and miserable when it adheres to
itself. . . .
    4. Though God has made all creatures good He
foreknows that some will voluntarily make
themselves bad . . . and also foreknows the good
use which He will then make of their badness. . . .
For as He shows His benevolence in creating
good Natures, He shows His justice in *exploiting*
evil wills. . . . Whoever tries to rebel against God
produces the result opposite to his intention.

619

Good and Evil

The Screwtape Letters,
Letter XXIX, para. 2,
pp. 135–136.

To be greatly and effectively wicked a man needs some virtue. What would Attila have been without his courage, or Shylock without self-denial as regards the flesh?

620

Good and Evil

Perelandra, chap. 9,
p. 111.

As there is one Face above all worlds merely to see which is irrevocable joy, so at the bottom of all worlds that face is waiting whose sight alone is the misery from which none who beholds it can recover. And though there seemed to be, and indeed were, a thousand roads by which a man could walk through the world, there was not a single one which did not lead sooner or later either to the Beatific or the Miserific Vision.

621

Good and Evil

The Great Divorce,
chap. 9, pp. 67–68.

"Ye cannot in your present state understand eternity. . . . But ye can get some likeness of it if ye say that both good and evil, when they are full grown, become retrospective. Not only this valley but all this earthly past will have been Heaven to those who are saved. Not only the twilight in that town, but all their life on earth too, will then be seen by the damned to have been Hell. That is what mortals misunderstand. They say of some temporal suffering, 'No future bliss can make up for it,' not knowing that Heaven, once attained, will work backwards and turn even that agony into a glory. And of some sinful pleasure they say 'Let me but have *this* and I'll take the consequences': little dreaming how damnation will spread back and back into their past and contaminate the pleasure of the sin. Both processes begin even before death. The good man's past begins to change so that his forgiven sins and remembered sorrows take on the quality of Heaven: the bad man's past already conforms to his badness and is filled only with dreariness. And that is why, at the end of all things, when the sun rises here and the twilight turns to blackness down there, the Blessed will say, 'We have never lived anywhere except in Heaven,' and the Lost, 'We were always in Hell.' And both will speak truly."

622
Good and Evil

Mere Christianity, bk. III, chap. 4, para. 10, p. 87.

The right direction leads not only to peace but to knowledge. When a man is getting better, he understands more and more clearly the evil that is still left in him. When a man is getting worse, he understands his own badness less and less. A moderately bad man knows he is not very good: a thoroughly bad man thinks he is all right. This is common sense, really. You understand sleep when you are awake, not while you are sleeping. . . . You can understand the nature of drunkenness when you are sober, not when you are drunk. Good people know about both good and evil: bad people do not know about either.

623
Good and Evil

Mere Christianity, bk. III, chap. 9, para. 8, p. 117.

Good and evil both increase at compound interest. That is why the little decisions you and I make every day are of such infinite importance.

624
Good and Evil

Surprised by Joy, chap. 5, para. 9, p. 77.

Divine punishments are also mercies, and particular good is worked out of particular evil.

625
Good and Evil
The Four Loves,
chap. 5, para. 21,
pp. 144–145.

When natural things look most divine, the demoniac[sic] is just round the corner.

626
Good Life
God in the Dock, "Man or Rabbit?" (1946), para. 11, pp. 112–113.

"When that which is perfect is come, then that which is in part shall be done away." The idea of reaching "a good life" without Christ is based on a double error. Firstly, we cannot do it; and secondly, in setting up "a good life" as our final goal, we have missed the very point of our existence. Morality is a mountain which we cannot climb by our own efforts; and if we could we should only perish in the ice and unbreathable air of the summit, lacking those wings with which the rest of the journey has to be accomplished. For it is *from* there that the real ascent begins. The ropes and axes are "done away" and the rest is a matter of flying.

627
Good Works
Mere Christianity, bk. II, chap. 5, para. 5, p. 64.

The Christian is in a different position from other people who are trying to be good. They hope, by being good, to please God if there is one; or—if they think there is not—at least they hope to deserve approval from good men. But the Christian thinks any good he does comes from the Christ-life inside him. He does not think God will love us because we are good, but that God will make us good because He loves us.

628
Good Works
Mere Christianity, bk. III, chap. 12, para. 7, p. 129.

Christians have often disputed as to whether what leads the Christian home is good actions or Faith in Christ. . . . It does seem to me like asking which blade in a pair of scissors is most necessary. A serious moral effort is the only thing that will bring you to the point where you throw up the sponge. Faith in Christ is the only thing to save you from despair at that point: and out of the Faith in Him good actions must inevitably come.

629

Good Works

Mere Christianity, bk. III, chap. 12, para. 8, p. 130.

The Bible really seems to clinch the matter when it puts the two things [faith and works] together into one amazing sentence. The first half is, "Work out your own salvation with fear and trembling"—which looks as if everything depended on us and our good actions: but the second half goes on, "For it is God who worketh in you"—which looks as if God did everything and we nothing. I am afraid that is the sort of thing we come up against in Christianity. I am puzzled, but I am not surprised. You see, we are now trying to understand, and to separate in water-tight compartments, what exactly God does and what man does when God and man are working together.

630

Good Works

Reflections on the Psalms, chap. 11, para. 3, p. 110.

No good work is done anywhere without aid from the Father of Lights.

631

Goodness

A Preface to "Paradise Lost," chap. 13, para. 7, p. 101.

We do not really know what it feels like to be a man much better than ourselves. His whole inner landscape is one we have never seen, and when we guess it we blunder. It is in their "good" characters that novelists make, unawares, the most shocking self-revelations. Heaven understands Hell and Hell does not understand Heaven, and all of us, in our measure, share the Satanic, or at least the Napoleonic, blindness. To project ourselves into a wicked character, we have only to stop doing something, and something that we are already tired of doing; to project ourselves into a good one we have to do what we cannot and become what we are not.

632
Goodness
Taliessin Through Logres, . . . Arthurian Torso, "Williams and the Arthuriad" (1948), chap. V, para. 47, p. 368.

Good is hard to preserve: but it is also terribly hard to eradicate completely. As Professor Powicke says, "In all ages there have been civilized persons." As Williams said to me in Addison's Walk, talking of the invasion of Norway, "And yet, even there, at this moment, people are falling in love."

633
Government
Mere Christianity, bk. IV, chap. 8, para. 10, p. 169.

It is easy to think the State has a lot of different objects—military, political, economic, and what not. But in a way things are much simpler than that. The State exists simply to promote and to protect the ordinary happiness of human beings in this life. A husband and wife chatting over a fire, a couple of friends having a game of darts in a pub, a man reading a book in his own room or digging in his own garden—that is what the State is there for. And unless they are helping to increase and prolong and protect such moments, all the laws, parliaments, armies, courts, police, economics, etc., are simply a waste of time.

634
Government
God in the Dock, "Is Progress Possible?" (1958), para. 16, p. 315.

I believe in God, but I detest theocracy. For every Government consists of mere men and is, strictly viewed, a makeshift; if it adds to its commands "Thus saith the Lord," it lies, and lies dangerously.

635

Grace

*Taliessin Through Logres,
. . . Arthurian Torso,*
"Williams and the
Arthuriad" (1948),
chap. IV, para. 36,
p. 340.

God gives His gifts where He finds the vessel
empty enough to receive them.

636

Grace

Letters of C. S. Lewis
(17 July 1953), p. 250.

If and when a horror turns up you will then be
given Grace to help you. I don't think one is
usually given it in advance. "Give us our daily
bread" (not an annuity for life) applies to spiritual
gifts too; the little *daily* support for the *daily* trial.
Life has to be taken day by day and hour by
hour.

637

Grace

*Letters to an American
Lady* (31 March 1958),
p. 73.

St. Augustine says "God gives where He finds
empty hands." A man whose hands are full of
parcels can't receive a gift.

638

**Grammar,
Rules of**

*Letters to an American
Lady* (24 November
1960), p. 9.

[Regarding] a sentence ending with a preposition.
The silly "rule" against it was invented by Dryden.
I think he disliked it only because you can't do it
in either French or Latin which he thought more
"polite" languages than English.

639

Greatness

Reflections on the Psalms,
chap. 3, para. 17,
p. 28.

It seems that there is a general rule in the moral
universe which may be formulated "The higher,
the more in danger." The "average sensual man"
who is sometimes unfaithful to his wife,
sometimes tipsy, always a little selfish, now and
then (within the law) a trifle sharp in his deals, is
certainly, by ordinary standards, a "lower" type
than the man whose soul is filled with some great

Cause, to which he will subordinate his appetites, his fortune, and even his safety. But it is out of the second man that something really fiendish can be made; an Inquisitor, a Member of the Committee of Public Safety. It is great men, potential saints, not little men, who become merciless fanatics. Those who are readiest to die for a cause may easily become those who are readiest to kill for it.

640
Greed
Voyage of the Dawn Treader, chap. 6, p. 75.

He had turned into a dragon while he was asleep. Sleeping on a dragon's hoard with greedy, dragonish thoughts in his heart, he had become a dragon himself.

641
Grief
Letters of C. S. Lewis (20 May 1945), p. 206.

I also have become much acquainted with grief now through the death of my great friend Charles Williams, my friend of friends, the comforter of all our little set, the most angelic man. The odd thing is that his death has made my faith stronger than it was a week ago. And I find that all that talk about "feeling that he is closer to us than before" isn't just talk. It's just what it does feel like—I can't put it into words. One seems at moments to be living in a new world. Lots, lots of pain, but not a particle of depression or resentment.

642
Grief
Letters of C. S. Lewis (27 March 1951), p. 230.

I have just got your letters of the 22nd containing the sad news of your father's death. But, dear lady, I hope you and your mother are not really trying to pretend it didn't happen. It does happen, happens to all of us, and I have no patience with the high-minded people who make out that it "doesn't matter." It matters a great deal, and very solemnly.

643
Grief
Surprised by Joy,
chap. 1, para. 20, p. 18.

Children suffer not (I think) less than their elders, but differently.

644
Grief
Surprised by Joy,
chap. 1, para. 21,
pp. 19–20.

Grief in childhood is complicated with many other miseries. I was taken into the bedroom where my mother lay dead; as they said, "to see her," in reality, as I at once knew, "to see it." There was nothing that a grown-up would call disfigurement—except for that total disfigurement which is death itself. Grief was overwhelmed in terror. To this day I do not know what they mean when they call dead bodies beautiful. The ugliest man alive is an angel of beauty compared with the loveliest of the dead.

645
Grief
A Grief Observed,
chap. I, para. 7–8,
pp. 4–5; chap. III, para.
25–26, pp. 53–54.

[Lewis was grieving the death of his wife:] Meanwhile, where is God? This is one of the most disquieting symptoms. When you are happy, so happy that you have no sense of needing Him, so happy that you are tempted to feel His claims upon you as an interruption, if you remember yourself and turn to Him with gratitude and praise, you will be—or so it feels—welcomed with open arms. But go to Him when your need is desperate, when all other help is vain, and what do you find? A door slammed in your face, and a sound of bolting and double bolting on the inside. After that, silence. You may as well turn away. The longer you wait, the more emphatic the silence will become. There are no lights in the windows. It might be an empty house. Was it ever inhabited? It seemed so once. And that seeming was as strong as this. What can this mean? Why is He so present a commander in our time of prosperity and so very absent a help in time of trouble?

I tried to put some of these thoughts to C. this afternoon. He reminded me that the same thing seems to have happened to Christ: "Why hast thou forsaken me?" I know. Does that make it easier to understand?

. . . I have gradually been coming to feel that the door is no longer shut and bolted. Was it my own frantic need that slammed it in my face? The time when there is nothing at all in your soul except a cry for help may be just the time when God can't give it: you are like the drowning man who can't be helped because he clutches and grabs. Perhaps your own reiterated cries deafen you to the voice you hoped to hear.

On the other hand, "Knock and it shall be opened." But does knocking mean hammering and kicking the door like a maniac? And there's also "To him that hath shall be given." After all, you must have a capacity to receive, or even omnipotence can't give. Perhaps your own passion temporarily destroys the capacity.

646
Grief

A Grief Observed,
chap. II, para. 31,
pp. 38–39; chap. III,
para. 28, p. 55.

Grief still feels like fear. Perhaps, more strictly, like suspense. Or like waiting; just hanging about waiting for something to happen. It gives life a permanently provisional feeling. It doesn't seem worth starting anything. I can't settle down. I yawn, I fidget, I smoke too much. Up till this I always had too little time. Now there is nothing but time. Almost pure time, empty successiveness.

. . .

I think I am beginning to understand why grief feels like suspense. It comes from the frustration of so many impulses that had become habitual. Thought after thought, feeling after feeling, action after action, had H. for their object. Now their target is gone. I keep on through habit fitting an arrow to the string; then I remember and have to lay the bow down. So many roads lead thought to H. I set out on one of them. But now there's an impassable frontier-post across it. So many roads once; now so many *culs de sac*.

647
Grief
A Grief Observed,
chap. III, para. 45, p. 67.

In grief nothing "stays put." One keeps on emerging from a phase, but it always recurs. Round and round. Everything repeats. Am I going in circles, or dare I hope I am on a spiral?

648
Grief
A Grief Observed,
chap. IV, para. 6,
pp. 72–73.

The notes [about grieving] have been about myself, and about H., and about God. In that order. The order and the proportions exactly what they ought not to have been. And I see that I have nowhere fallen into that mode of thinking about either which we call praising them. Yet that would have been best for me. Praise is the mode of love which always has some element of joy in it. Praise in due order; of Him as the giver, of her as the gift. Don't we in praise somehow enjoy what we praise, however far we are from it? I must do more of this.

649
Growth
Selected Literary Essays,
"Hamlet: The Prince or
the Poem" (1942),
para. 23, p. 105.

Mere change is not growth. Growth is the synthesis of change and continuity, and where there is no continuity there is no growth.

650
Growth
*Of Other Worlds: Essays
and Stories,* "On Three
Ways of Writing for
Children" (1952),
para. 10, pp. 25–26.

They accuse us of arrested development because we have not lost a taste we had in childhood. But surely arrested development consists not in refusing to lose old things but in failing to add new things? I now like hock, which I am sure I should not have liked as a child. But I still like lemon-squash. I call this growth or development because I have been enriched: where I formerly had only one pleasure, I now have two. But if I had to lose the taste for lemon-squash before I acquired the taste for hock, that would not be growth but simple change. I now enjoy Tolstoy and Jane Austen and Trollope as well as fairy tales and I call that growth: if I had had to lose the fairy tales in order to acquire the novelists, I would not say that I had grown but only that I had changed. A tree grows because it adds rings: a train doesn't grow by leaving one station behind and puffing on to the next.

651
Guests
The Letters of C. S. Lewis to Arthur Greeves (December 1935), p. 474.

Minto [Mrs. Moore] told you about our present bother. The guests are still here, and will be, so far as I can see, until the end of January. Oh Arthur, what a snag it is that the people who are *pitiable* are not necessarily *likeable*. Molly Askins is emphatically one of those people of whom old Foord-Kelsie said "We must learn to love those whom we can't like." She's what you would call an encroaching person—do you know the type of small, dark woman with big gentle eyes and soft voice, who just gently and softly and even pathetically gets her own way in everything and really treats the house as a hotel? However, the thing's a duty and there's an end of it: tho', by the bye, as W. [Lewis's brother Warren] and I were saying the other day, the New Testament tells us to *visit* the widows, not to let them visit us!

652
Guests
The Letters of C. S. Lewis to Arthur Greeves (23 June 1949), pp. 512–513.

Thanks for asking me to the cottage but I think the relation of guest & host prevents friends from getting the most out of one another. The one feels responsible & the other feels grateful and the old *camaraderie* is lost. So make it the Inn please.

653
Guilt
Letters to an American Lady (21 July 1958), p. 77.

(1.) Remember what St. John says: "If our *heart* condemn us, God is stronger than our heart." The *feeling* of being, or not being, forgiven and loved, is not what matters. One must come down to brass tacks. If there is a particular sin on your conscience, repent and confess it. If there isn't, tell the despondent devil not to be silly. You can't help *hearing* his voice (the odious inner radio) but you must treat it merely like a buzzing in your ears or any other irrational nuisance. (2.) Remember the story in the *Imitation,* how the Christ on the crucifix suddenly spoke to the monk who was so anxious about his salvation and said "If you knew that all was well, what would you, to-day, do, or stop doing?" When you have found the answer, do it or stop doing it. You see, one must always get back to the practical and definite. What the devil loves is that vague cloud of unspecified guilt feeling or unspecified virtue by which he lures us into despair or presumption. "Details, please?" is the answer. (3.) The sense of dereliction cannot be a bad symptom for Our Lord Himself experienced it in its depth—"Why hast thou forsaken me?"

654

Happiness
God in the Dock,
"Answers to Questions
on Christianity" (1944),
ans. 5, p. 52.

If you think of this world as a place intended simply for our happiness, you find it quite intolerable: think of it as a place of training and correction and it's not so bad.

Imagine a set of people all living in the same building. Half of them think it is a hotel, the other half think it is a prison. Those who think it a hotel might regard it as quite intolerable, and those who thought it was a prison might decide that it was really surprisingly comfortable. So that what seems the ugly doctrine is one that comforts and strengthens you in the end. The people who try to hold an optimistic view of this world would become pessimists: the people who hold a pretty stern view of it become optimistic.

655

Happiness
Mere Christianity, bk. II,
chap. 3, para. 7,
p. 54.

God designed the human machine to run on Himself. He Himself is the fuel our spirits were designed to burn, or the food our spirits were designed to feed on. There is no other. That is why it is just no good asking God to make us happy in our own way without bothering about religion. God cannot give us a happiness and peace apart from Himself, because it is not there. There is no such thing.

656
Happiness
God in the Dock, "We
Have No 'Right to
Happiness' " (1963),
para. 5–6, p. 318.

A "right to happiness" . . . sounds to me as odd as a right to good luck. For I believe—whatever one school of moralists may say—that we depend for a very great deal of our happiness or misery on circumstances outside all human control. A right to happiness doesn't, for me, make much more sense than a right to be six feet tall, or to have a millionaire for your father, or to get good weather whenever you want to have a picnic.

657
Happiness and Christianity
God in the Dock,
"Answers to Questions
on Christianity" (1944),
ans. 11, pp. 58–59.

Which of the religions of the world gives to its followers the greatest happiness? While it lasts, the religion of worshipping oneself is the best.

. . . As you perhaps know, I haven't always been a Christian. I didn't go to religion to make me happy. I always knew a bottle of Port would do that. If you want a religion to make you feel really comfortable, I certainly don't recommend Christianity. I am certain there must be a patent American article on the market which will suit you far better, but I can't give any advice on it.

658
Hatred
The Screwtape Letters,
Letter XXIX, para. 4,
p. 136.

[Senior devil Screwtape to junior devil Wormwood:] Hatred is best combined with Fear. Cowardice, alone of all the vices, is purely painful—horrible to anticipate, horrible to feel, horrible to remember; Hatred has its pleasures. It is therefore often the *compensation* by which a frightened man reimburses himself for the miseries of Fear. The more he fears, the more he will hate.

659
Hatred
Narrative Poems, Preface
to *Dymer* (1950), para. 5,
p. 5.

"The heresies that men leave are hated most" and lovers' quarrels can be the bitterest of all.

660
Health
Mere Christianity, bk. III,
chap. 10, para. 1,
pp. 118–119.

Health is a great blessing, but the moment you make health one of your main, direct objects you start becoming a crank and imagining there is something wrong with you. You are only likely to get health provided you want other things more— food, games, work, fun, open air.

661
Heaven
Letters of C. S. Lewis (18 December 1939), para. 1,
p. 173.

I quite agree about Johnson. If one had not experienced it, it wd. be hard to understand how a dead man out of a book can be almost a member of one's family circle—still harder to realize, even now, that you and I have a chance of some day really meeting him.

662
Heaven
The Problem of Pain,
chap. 4, para. 9, p. 61.

It may be that salvation consists not in the cancelling of these eternal moments [in which our sins are forever before God] but the perfected humility that bears the shame forever, rejoicing in the occasion which it furnished to God's compassion and glad that it should be common knowledge to the universe. . . . The joys of Heaven are, for most of us in our present condition, "an acquired taste"—and certain ways of life may render the taste impossible of acquisition. Perhaps the lost are those who dare not go to such a *public* place.

663
Heaven
The Problem of Pain,
chap. 10, para. 3,
pp. 147–148.

Your soul has a curious shape because it is a hollow made to fit a particular swelling in the infinite contours of the divine substance, or a key to unlock one of the doors in the house with many mansions. For it is not humanity in the abstract that is to be saved, but you—you, the individual reader. . . . Blessed and fortunate creature, your eyes shall behold Him and not another's. All that you are, sins apart, is destined,

if you will let God have His good way, to utter
satisfaction. . . . Your place in heaven will seem to
be made for you and you alone, because you were
made for it.

664

Heaven

*The Letters of C. S.
Lewis to Arthur Greeves*
(22 February 1944),
para. 1, p. 501.

Heaven enters wherever Xt [Christ] enters, even in
this life.

665

Heaven

The Great Divorce,
Preface, para. 2, p. 6.

If we insist on keeping Hell (or even earth) we
shall not see Heaven: if we accept Heaven we
shall not be able to retain even the smallest and
most intimate souvenirs of Hell.

666

Heaven

The Great Divorce,
Preface, para. 3, p. 7.

Earth, I think, will not be found by anyone to be
in the end a very distinct place. I think earth, if
chosen instead of Heaven, will turn out to have
been, all along, only a region in Hell: and earth, if
put second to Heaven, to have been from the
beginning a part of Heaven itself.

667

Heaven

Miracles, chap. 16,
para. 27, p. 159.

Let us confess that probably every Christian now
alive finds a difficulty in reconciling the two things
he has been told about "heaven"—that it is on the
one hand, a life in Christ, a vision of God, a
ceaseless adoration, and that it is, on the other
hand, a bodily life. When we seem nearest to the
vision of God in this life, the body seems almost
an irrelevance. And if we try to conceive our
eternal life as one in a body (any kind of body)
we tend to find that some vague dream of
Platonic paradises and gardens of the Hesperides
has substituted itself for that mystical approach
which we feel (and I think rightly) to be more

important. But if that discrepancy were final then it would follow—which is absurd—that God was originally mistaken when He introduced our spirits into the Natural order at all. We must conclude that the discrepancy itself is precisely one of the disorders which the New Creation comes to heal. . . . Spirit and Nature have quarrelled in us; that is our disease.

668

Heaven

Miracles, chap. 16, para. 28, pp. 159–160.

The letter and spirit of scripture, and of all Christianity, forbid us to suppose that life in the New Creation will be a sexual life; and this reduces our imagination to the withering alternative either of bodies which are hardly recognisable as human bodies at all or else of a perpetual fast. As regards the fast, I think our present outlook might be like that of a small boy who, on being told that the sexual act was the highest bodily pleasure should immediately ask whether you ate chocolates at the same time. On receiving the answer "No," he might regard absence of chocolates as the chief characteristic of sexuality. In vain would you tell him that the reason why lovers in their carnal raptures don't bother about chocolates is that they have something better to think of. The boy knows chocolate: he does not know the positive thing that excludes it. We are in the same position. We know the sexual life; we do not know, except in glimpses, the other thing which, in Heaven, will leave no room for it. Hence where fulness awaits us we anticipate fasting. In denying that sexual life, as we now understand it, makes any part of the final beatitude, it is not of course necessary to suppose that the distinction of sexes will disappear. What is no longer needed for biological purposes may be expected to survive for splendour. Sexuality is the instrument both of virginity and of conjugal virtue; neither men nor women will be asked to throw away weapons they have used victoriously. It is the beaten and the fugitives who throw away their swords. The conquerors sheathe theirs and retain them. "Transsexual" would be a better word than "sexless" for the heavenly life.

669

Heaven

Miracles, chap. 16, para. 29, p. 161.

When Nature and Spirit are fully harmonised— when Spirit rides Nature so perfectly that the two together make rather a *Centaur* than a mounted knight . . . there will be no room to get the finest razor-blade of thought in between Spirit and Nature. Every state of affairs in the New Nature will be the perfect expression of a spiritual state and every spiritual state the perfect informing of, and bloom upon, a state of affairs; one with it as the perfume with a flower or the "spirit" of great poetry with its form.

670

Heaven

Mere Christianity, bk. III, chap. 2, para. 12, pp. 77–78.

The point is not that God will refuse you admission to His eternal world if you have not got certain qualities of character: the point is that if people have not got at least the beginnings of those qualities inside them, then no possible external conditions could make a "Heaven" for them.

671

Heaven

Mere Christianity, bk. III, chap. 10, para. 6, pp. 120–121.

There is no need to be worried by facetious people who try to make the Christian hope of "Heaven" ridiculous by saying they do not want "to spend eternity playing harps." The answer to such people is that if they cannot understand books written for grown-ups, they should not talk about them. All the scriptural imagery (harps, crowns, gold, etc.) is, of course, a merely symbolical attempt to express the inexpressible. . . . People who take these symbols literally might as well think that when Christ told us to be like doves, He meant that we were to lay eggs.

672
Heaven
The Four Loves, chap. 6, para. 43, p. 190.

We find thus by experience that there is no good applying to Heaven for earthly comfort. Heaven can give heavenly comfort; no other kind. And earth cannot give earthly comfort either. There is no earthly comfort in the long run.

673
Heaven
Poems, "Five Sonnets" (4), (1st pub. 1964), pp. 126–127.

Pitch your demands heaven-high and they'll be
　　met.
Ask for the Morning Star and take (thrown in)
Your earthly love.

674
Heaven: Longing for
The Problem of Pain, chap. 10, para. 1, p. 145.

We are afraid that heaven is a bribe, and that if we make it our goal we shall no longer be disinterested. It is not so. Heaven offers nothing that a mercenary soul can desire. It is safe to tell the pure in heart that they shall see God, for only the pure in heart want to.

675
Heaven: Longing for
The Screwtape Letters, Letter XXVIII, para. 2–3, pp. 132–134.

[Senior devil Screwtape to junior devil Wormwood:] "The truth is that the Enemy, having oddly destined these mere animals to life in His own eternal world, has guarded them pretty effectively from the danger of feeling at home anywhere else. That is why we must often wish long life to our patients; seventy years is not a day too much for the difficult task of unravelling their souls from Heaven and building up a firm attachment to the Earth. While they are young we find them always shooting off at a tangent. Even if we contrive to keep them ignorant of explicit religion, the incalculable winds of fantasy and music and poetry—the mere face of a girl, the song of a bird, or the sight of a horizon—are always blowing our whole structure away. They *will* not apply themselves steadily to worldly advancement, prudent connections, and the policy of safety first. So inveterate is their appetite for Heaven, that our best method, at this stage, of attaching them to Earth is to make them believe that Earth can be turned into Heaven at some future date by politics or eugenics or "science" or psychology or what not. Real worldliness is a work of time. . . .

"How valuable time is to us may be gauged by the fact that the Enemy allows us so little of it. The majority of the human race dies in infancy; of the survivors, a good many die in youth. It is obvious that to Him human birth is important chiefly as the qualification for human death, and death solely as the gate to that other kind of life. We are allowed to work only on a selected minority of the race, for what humans call a "normal life" is the exception. Apparently He wants some—but only a very few—of the human animals with which He is peopling Heaven to have had the experience of resisting us through an earthly life of sixty or seventy years. Well, there is our opportunity. The smaller it is, the better we must use it."

676
Heaven:
Longing for
Mere Christianity, bk. III,
chap. 10, para. 2,
p. 119.

Most of us find it very difficult to want "Heaven" at all—except in so far as "Heaven" means meeting again our friends who have died. One reason for this difficulty is that we have not been trained: our whole education tends to fix our minds on this world. Another reason is that when the real want for Heaven is present in us, we do not recognise it. Most people, if they had really learned to look into their own hearts, would know that they do want, and want acutely, something that cannot be had in this world. There are all sorts of things in this world that offer to give it to you, but they never quite keep their promise.

677
Heaven: Longing for
Mere Christianity, bk. III, chap. 10, para. 5, p. 120.

If I find in myself a desire which no experience in this world can satisfy, the most probable explanation is that I was made for another world.

678
Heaven: Longing for
Letters to Children (29 May 1954), para. 2, p. 45.

Anyone in our world who devotes his whole life to seeking heaven will be like R[eepicheep, in *The Voyage of the "Dawn Treader"*].

679
Heaven: Ultimate Reality
The Great Divorce, chap. 9, pp. 68–69.

"Then those people are right who say that Heaven and Hell are only states of mind?"

"Hush," said he sternly. "Do not blaspheme. Hell is a state of mind—ye never said a truer word. And every state of mind, left to itself, every shutting up of the creature within the dungeon of its own mind—is, in the end, Hell. But Heaven is not a state of mind. Heaven is reality itself. All that is fully real is Heavenly. For all that can be shaken will be shaken and only the unshakable remains."

680

Heaven: Ultimate Reality

Miracles, chap. 16, para. 22, p. 155.

Most certainly, beyond all worlds, unconditioned and unimaginable, transcending discursive thought, there yawns for ever the ultimate Fact, the fountain of all other facthood, the burning and undimensioned depth of the Divine Life. Most certainly also, to be united with that Life in the eternal Sonship of Christ is, strictly speaking, the only thing worth a moment's consideration. And in so far as *that* is what you mean by *Heaven*, Christ's divine nature never left it, and therefore never returned to it: and His human nature ascended thither not at the moment of the Ascension but at every moment. . . . I allow and insist that the Eternal Word, the Second Person of the Trinity, can never be, nor have been, confined to any place at all: it is rather in Him that all places exist.

681

Heaven: Ultimate Reality

Miracles, chap. 16, para. 31, pp. 162–163.

I suspect that our conception of Heaven as *merely* a state of mind is not unconnected with the fact that the specifically Christian virtue of Hope has in our time grown so languid.

682

Hell: Escape

A Preface to "Paradise Lost," chap. 14, para. 2, pp. 104–105.

For human beings there is often an escape from this Hell, but there is never more than one—the way of humiliation, repentance, and (where possible) restitution.

683

Hell: God's Mercy

Poems, "Divine Justice" (1st pub. 1933), p. 98.

God in His mercy made
The fixed pains of Hell.

684
Hell:
Judgment
The Problem of Pain,
chap. 8, para. 13,
p. 128.

In all discussions of hell we should keep steadily before our eyes the possible damnation, not of our enemies nor our friends . . . but of ourselves.

685
Hell:
Judgment
The Great Divorce,
chap. 13, p. 120.

"What some people say on earth ·is that the final loss of one soul gives the lie to all the joy of those who are saved. . . ."

"That sounds very merciful: but see what lurks behind it. . . ."

"The demand of the loveless and the self-imprisoned that they should be allowed to blackmail the universe: that till they consent to be happy (on their own terms) no one else shall taste joy: that theirs should be the final power; that Hell should be able to *veto* Heaven."

686
Hell:
Judgment and
Mercy
Letters of C. S. Lewis
(31 January 1952),
para. 2, p. 238.

On the heathen, see Tim. IV.10. Also in Matt. XXV.31–46 the people don't sound as if they were believers. Also the doctrine of Christ's descending into Hell (i.e. Hades, the land of the dead; not Gehenna the land of the lost) and preaching to the dead; and that would be outside time and would include those who died long after Him as well as those who died before He was·born as Man. I don't think we know the details; we must just stick to the view that (a) all justice and mercy will be done, (b) but nevertheless it is our duty to do all we can to convert unbelievers.

687
Hell: Mental Torment

The Letters of C. S. Lewis to Arthur Greeves (13 May 1946), para. 5, p. 508.

About Hell. All I have ever said is that the N.T. [New Testament] plainly implies the possibility of some being finally left in "the outer darkness." Whether this means (horror of horror) being left to a purely *mental* existence, left with nothing at all but one's own envy, prurience, resentment, loneliness & self conceit, or whether there is still some sort of environment, something you cd. call a world or a reality, I wd. never pretend to know. But I wouldn't put the question in the form "do I believe in an *actual* Hell." One's own mind is actual enough. If it doesn't seem fully actual *now* that is because you can always escape from it a bit into the physical world—look out of the window, smoke a cigarette, go to sleep. But when there is nothing for you *but* your own mind (no body to go to sleep, no books or landscape, nor sounds, no drugs) it will be as actual as—as—well, as a coffin is actual to a man buried alive.

688
Hell: Self-Centeredness

The Problem of Pain, chap. 8, para. 7, pp. 122–123.

Though Our Lord often speaks of Hell as a sentence inflicted by a tribunal, He also says elsewhere that the judgement consists in the very fact that men prefer darkness to light, and that not He, but His "word," judges men. We are therefore at liberty—since the two conceptions, in the long run, mean the same thing—to think of this bad man's perdition not as a sentence imposed on him but as the mere fact of being what he is. The characteristic of lost souls is "their rejection of everything that is not simply themselves."

689
Hell: Self-Centeredness
Perelandra, chap. 14, p. 173.

There was, no doubt, a confusion of persons in damnation: what Pantheists falsely hoped of Heaven bad men really received in Hell. They were melted down into their Master, as a lead soldier slips down and loses his shape in the ladle held over the gas ring.

690
Hell: Self-Centeredness
The Great Divorce, chap. 13, pp. 123–124.

"A damned soul is nearly nothing: it is shrunk, shut up in itself. Good beats upon the damned incessantly as sound waves beat on the ears of the deaf, but they cannot receive it. Their fists are clenched, their teeth are clenched, their eyes fast shut. First they will not, in the end they cannot, open their hands for gifts, or their mouths for food, or their eyes to see."

"Then no one can ever reach them?"

"Only the Greatest of all can make Himself small enough to enter Hell. For the higher a thing is, the lower it can descend—a man can sympathise with a horse but a horse cannot sympathise with a rat. Only One has descended into Hell."

"And will He ever do so again?"

"It was not once long ago that He did it. Time does not work that way when once ye have left the Earth. All moments that have been or shall be were, or are, present in the moment of His descending. There is no spirit in prison to Whom He did not preach."

691
Hell: Self-Centeredness
The Screwtape Letters, Preface (1960), para. 16, p. ix.

We must picture Hell as a state where everyone is perpetually concerned about his own dignity and advancement, where everyone has a grievance, and where everyone lives the deadly serious passions of envy, self-importance, and resentment.

692
Hell: Self-Centeredness

The Screwtape Letters,
Preface (1960), para. 17,
p. x.

Hell is something like the bureaucracy of a police state or the offices of a thoroughly nasty business concern.

693
Hell: Self-Centeredness

The Screwtape Letters,
Preface (1960), para. 18,
pp. x–xi.

[Hell is] an official society held together entirely by fear and greed. On the surface, manners are normally suave. Rudeness to one's superiors would obviously be suicidal; rudeness to one's equals might put them on their guard before you were ready to spring your mine. For of course "Dog eat dog" is the principle of the whole organisation. Everyone wishes everyone else's discrediting, demotion, and ruin; everyone is an expert in the confidential report, the pretended alliance, the stab in the back. Over all this their good manners, their expressions of grave respect, their "tributes" to one another's invaluable services form a thin crust. Every now and then it gets punctured, and the scalding lava of their hatred spurts out.

694
Hell: Self-Chosen

*The Dark Tower &
Other Stories,* "The Dark
Tower" (1938, first pub.
1977), chap. 3, p. 49.

"A man can't be *taken* to hell, or *sent* to hell: you can only get there on your own steam."

695
Hell: Self-Chosen

The Problem of Pain,
chap. 8, para. 11,
p. 127.

I willingly believe that the damned are, in one sense, successful, rebels to the end; that the doors of hell are locked on the *inside*.

696

Hell: Self-Chosen

A Preface to "Paradise Lost," chap. 14, para. 2, p. 105.

[On the unrepentant devils:] That door out of Hell is firmly locked, by the devils themselves, on the inside; whether it is also locked on the outside need not, therefore, be considered.

697

Hell: Self-Chosen

The Great Divorce, chap. 9, pp. 69–70.

"How *can* they choose it [hell]?"

"Milton was right," said my Teacher. "The choice of every lost soul can be expressed in the words 'Better to reign in Hell than serve in Heaven.' There is always something they insist on keeping, even at the price of misery. There is always something they prefer to joy—that is, to reality. We see it easily enough in a spoiled child that would sooner miss its play and its supper than say it was sorry and be friends."

698

Hell: Self-Chosen

The Great Divorce, chap. 9, pp. 72–73.

"There are only two kinds of people in the end: those who say to God, 'Thy will be done,' and those to whom God says, in the end, '*Thy* will be done.' All that are in Hell, choose it. Without that self-choice there could be no Hell. No soul that seriously and constantly desires joy will ever miss it. Those who seek find. To those who knock it is opened."

699

Hell: Self-Chosen

The Great Divorce, chap. 9, p. 75.

"The whole difficulty of understanding Hell is that the thing to be understood is so nearly Nothing. But ye'll have had experiences . . . it begins with a grumbling mood, and yourself still distinct from it: perhaps criticising it. And yourself, in a dark hour, may will that mood, embrace it. Ye can repent and come out of it again. But there may come a day when you can do that no longer. Then there will be no *you* left to criticise the mood, nor even to enjoy it, but just the grumble itself going on forever like a machine."

700
**Hell:
Self-Chosen**
God in the Dock, " 'The
Trouble with "X" . . . ' "
(1948), para. 10, p. 155.

It's not a question of God "sending" us to Hell. In
each of us there is something growing up which
will of itself *be Hell* unless it is nipped in the bud.
The matter is serious: let us put ourselves in His
hands at once—this very day, this hour.

701
**Hell:
Separation
from God**
The Problem of Pain,
chap. 8, para. 12,
p. 128.

In the long run the answer to all those who
object to the doctrine of hell is itself a question:
"What are you asking God to do?" To wipe out
their past sins and, at all costs, to give them a
fresh start, smoothing every difficulty and offering
every miraculous help? But He has done so, on
Calvary. To forgive them? They will not be
forgiven. To leave them alone? Alas, I am afraid
that is what He does.

702
**Hell:
Separation
from God**
Surprised by Joy, chap.
15, para. 4, p. 232.

While it is true to say that God's own nature is
the real sanction of His commands, yet to
understand this must, in the end, lead us to the
conclusion that union with that Nature is bliss and
separation from it horror. Thus Heaven and Hell
come in. But it may well be that to think much
of either except in this context of thought, to
hypostatize them as if they had a substantial
meaning apart from the presence or absence of
God, corrupts the doctrine of both and corrupts
us while we so think of them.

703
**Hell:
Separation
from Heaven**
The Problem of Pain,
chap. 10, para. 4,
p. 148.

We can understand Hell in its aspect of privation.
All your life an unattainable ecstasy has hovered
just beyond the grasp of your consciousness. The
day is coming when you will wake to find,
beyond all hope, that you have attained it, or else,
that it was within your reach and you have lost it
forever.

704
**Hell:
Separation
from
Humanity**
The Problem of Pain,
chap. 8, para. 9,
pp. 125–126.

To enter heaven is to become more human than you ever succeeded in being in earth; to enter hell is to be banished from humanity. What is cast (or casts itself) into hell is not a man: it is "remains." To be a complete man means to have the passions obedient to the will and the will offered to God: to *have been* a man—to be an ex-man or "damned ghost"—would presumably mean to consist of a will utterly centered in its self and passions utterly uncontrolled by the will.

705
**Hell:
Separation
from
Humanity**
The Problem of Pain,
chap. 8, para. 10,
p. 127.

We know much more about heaven than hell, for heaven is the home of humanity and therefore contains all that is implied in a glorified human life: but hell was not made for men. It is in no sense *parallel* to heaven: it is "the darkness outside," the outer rim where being fades away into nonentity.

706
**Hell:
Unfulfilled
Potential**
The Great Divorce, chap.
13, pp. 122–123.

"Do you mean then that Hell—all that infinite empty town—is down in some little crack like this?"

"Yes. All Hell is smaller than one pebble of your earthly world: but it is smaller than one atom of *this* world, the Real World [Heaven]. Look at yon butterfly. If it swallowed all Hell, Hell would not be big enough to do it any harm or to have any taste."

"It seems big enough when you're in it, Sir."

"And yet all loneliness, angers, hatreds, envies and itchings that it contains, if rolled into one single experience and put into the scale against the least moment of the joy that is felt by the least in Heaven, would have no weight that could be registered at all. Bad cannot succeed even in being bad as truly as good is good. If all Hell's miseries together entered the consciousness of yon wee yellow bird on the bough there, they would be swallowed up without trace, as if one drop of ink had been dropped into that Great Ocean to which your terrestrial Pacific itself is only a molecule."

707
Hero Worship
The Personal Heresy: A Controversy, chap. 3, para. 22, pp. 67–68.

There is a reaction at present going on against the excessive love of pet animals. We have been taught to despise the rich, barren woman who loves her lap dog too much and her neighbor too little. It may be that when once the true impulse is inhibited, a dead poet is a nobler substitute than a live Peke, but this is by no means obvious. You can do something for the Peke, and it can make some response to you. It is at least sentient; but most poetolaters hold that a dead man has no consciousness, and few indeed suppose that he has any which we are likely to modify. Unless you hold beliefs which enable you to obey the colophons of the old books by praying for the authors' souls, there is nothing that you can do for a dead poet: and certainly he will do nothing for you. He did all he could for you while he lived: nothing more will ever come. I do not say that a personal emotion towards the author will not sometimes arise spontaneously while we read; but if it does we should let it pass swiftly over the mind like a ripple that leaves no trace. If we retain it we are cosseting with substitutes an emotion whose true object is our neighbour. Hence it is not surprising that those who most amuse themselves with personality after this ghostly fashion often show little respect for it in their parents, their servants, or their wives.

708
Hero Worship
*The Personal Heresy: A
Controversy,* chap. 5,
para. 3, pp. 98–99.

You can use a poet, not as a poet, but as a saint
or hero; and if your poet happens to have been a
saintly or heroic man as well as a poet you may
even be acting wisely. If there lives any man so
destitute of all traditions human and divine and so
unfortunate in his acquaintance that he can find
no better example among the living or the dead
than Shelley or Baudelaire, I no more blame him
for following them than we blame a castaway on
an island for making shift to use a pen-knife as a
saw. But my pity will not induce me to say that
pen-knives are made for sawing.

709
Heywood, John
*English Literature in the
Sixteenth Century,* bk.
I.II.I, para. 38,
pp. 146–147.

Though Heywood the poet cannot be
recommended, what we know of the man
deserves respect, and he made on his death-bed
(then long an exile for his religion) a better joke
than he ever put in a book. His kindly old
confessor (*bonus quidam sacerdos*) answered,
when he deplored his sins, that the flesh is frail,
carnem esse fragilem, and again and again *carnem
esse fragilem,* till at last "Marry, Father," said the
old man, "it will go hard but you shall prove that
God should a made me a fish" (*Deum arguere
videris quod me non fecerit piscem*). That is
Heywood's best title to fame.

710
Hierarchy
*A Preface to "Paradise
Lost,"* chap. 11, para. 2,
pp. 73–74.

The Hierarchical conception . . . Everything
except God has some natural superior; everything
except unformed matter has some natural inferior.
The goodness, happiness, and dignity of every
being consists in obeying its natural superior and
ruling its natural inferiors. When it fails in either
part of this twofold task we have disease or
monstrosity in the scheme of things until the
peccant being is either destroyed or corrected.

One or the other it will certainly be; for by stepping out of its place in the system (whether it step up like a rebellious angel or down like an uxorious husband) it has made the very nature of things its enemy. It cannot succeed.

711
Hierarchy
That Hideous Strength,
chap. 13, section 5,
p. 292.

"This Saxon king of yours who sits at Windsor, now. Is there no help in him?"
    "He has no power in this matter."
    "Then is he not weak enough to be overthrown?"
    "I have no wish to overthrow him. He is the king. He was crowned and anointed by the Archbishop. In the order of Logres I may be Pendragon, but in the order of Britain I am the King's man."

712
Hierarchy
Letters of C. S. Lewis (4
April 1949), para. 3,
p. 217.

Henry 7th had some mastiffs hanged for fighting a lion: said they were rebelling against their natural sovereign. That's the stuff. Also, had his own hawk decapitated for fighting an eagle.

713
Historians
Letters of C. S. Lewis (12
December 1927), para. 1,
p. 123.

I am almost coming to the conclusion that all histories are bad. Whenever one turns from the historian to the writings of the people he deals with, there is always such a difference.

714
Historians
God in the Dock,
" 'Horrid Red Things' "
(1944), para. 3, p. 69.

A historian who has based his work on the misreading of a document may afterwards (when his mistake has been exposed) exercise great ingenuity in showing that his account of a certain battle can still be reconciled with what the document records. But the point is that none of these ingenious explanations would ever have come into existence if he had read his documents

---

correctly at the outset. They are therefore really a waste of labour; it would be manlier of him to admit his mistake and begin all over again.

715
History Books
*The Dark Tower &
Other Stories,* "The Dark
Tower" (1938?, 1st pub.
1977), chap. 3, p. 17.

The most important events in every age never reach the history books.

716
**History,
Christian
View of**
The Discarded Image,
chap. 7, section H, para.
1–2, p. 174.

To the Greeks, we are told, the historical process was a meaningless flux or cyclic reiteration. Significance was to be sought not in the world of becoming but in that of being, not in history but in metaphysics, mathematics, and theology. Hence Greek historians wrote of such past action—the Persian or the Peloponesian War, or the lives of great men—as have a unity in themselves, and were seldom curious to trace from its beginnings the development of a people or a state. History, in a word, was not for them a story with a plot. The Hebrews, on the other hand, saw their whole past as a revelation of the purposes of Jahweh. Christianity, going on from there, makes world-history in its entirety a single, transcendentally significant, story with a well-defined plot pivoted on Creation, Fall, Redemption, and Judgement.

On this view the *differentia* of Christian historiography ought to be what I call Historicism; the belief that by studying the past we can learn not only historical but meta-historical or transcendental truth.

**717
History,
Christian
View of**
The Discarded Image,
chap. 7, section H, para.
5, p. 176.

No doubt all history in the last resort must be held by Christians to be a story with a divine plot.

**718
History,
Function of**
Selected Literary Essays,
"De Descriptione
Temporum" (1955),
para. 21, p. 12.

To study the past does indeed liberate us from the present, from the idols of our own market-place. But I think it liberates us from the past too. I think no class of men are less enslaved to the past than historians.

**719
History,
Importance of**
The Weight of Glory,
"Learning in War-Time,"
(1939), para. 10,
pp. 28–29.

We need intimate knowledge of the past. Not that the past has any magic about it, but because we cannot study the future, and yet need something to set against the present, to remind us that the basic assumptions have been quite different in different periods and that much which seems certain to the uneducated is merely temporary fashion. A man who has lived in many places is not likely to be deceived by the local errors of his native village: the scholar has lived in many times and is therefore in some degree immune from the great cataract of nonsense that pours from the press and the microphone of his own age.

**720
History,
Periods of**
Selected Literary Essays,
"De Descriptione
Temporum" (1955),
para. 3, p. 2.

All lines of demarcation between what we call "periods" should be subject to constant revision. Would that we could dispense with them altogether! As a great Cambridge historian has said: "Unlike dates, periods are not facts."

721
**History,
Philosophy of**
Selected Literary Essays,
"De Descriptione
Temporum" (1955),
para. 4, pp. 3–4.

About everything that could be called "the philosophy of history" I am a desperate sceptic. I know nothing of the future, not even whether there will be any future. I don't know whether past history has been necessary or contingent. I don't know whether the human tragicomedy is now in Act I or Act V; whether our present disorders are those of infancy or of old age. I am merely considering how we should arrange or schematise those facts—ludicrously few in comparison with the totality—which survive to us (often by accident) from the past. I am less like a botanist in a forest than a woman arranging a few cut flowers for the drawing-room. So, in some degree, are the greatest historians. We can't get into the real forest of the past; that is part of what the word *past* means.

722
**History,
Scientific**
Selected Literary Essays,
"De Descriptione
Temporum" (1955),
para. 11–12, p. 7.

The sciences long remained like a lion-cub whose gambols delighted its master in private; it had not yet tasted man's blood. All through the eighteenth century the tone of the common mind remained ethical, rhetorical, juristic, rather than scientific. . . . Science was not the business of Man because Man had not yet become the business of science. It dealt chiefly with the inanimate; and it threw off few technological by-products. When Watt makes his engine, when Darwin starts monkeying with the ancestry of Man, and Freud with his soul, and the economists with all that is his, then indeed the lion will have got out of its cage. Its liberated presence in our midst will become one of the most important factors in everyone's daily life. But not yet; not in the seventeenth century.

It is by these steps that I have come to regard as the greatest of all divisions in the history of the West that which divides the present from, say, the age of Jane Austen and Scott.

723
History, Skeptics of

God in the Dock, "Christian Apologetics" (1945), para. 13, pp. 94–95.

I find that the uneducated Englishman is an almost total sceptic about History. I had expected he would disbelieve the Gospels because they contain miracles: but he really disbelieves them because they deal with things that happened 2000 years ago. . . . In his mind the Present occupies almost the whole field of vision. Beyond it, isolated from it, and quite unimportant, is something called "The Old Days"—a small, comic jungle in which highwaymen, Queen Elizabeth, knights-in-armour etc. wander about. Then (strangest of all) beyond The Old Days comes a picture of "Primitive Man." He is "Science," not "history," and is therefore felt to be much more real than The Old Days. In other words, the Pre-historic is much more believed in than the Historic.

724
History, Skeptics of

God in the Dock, "God in the Dock" (1948), para. 3, p. 241.

The educated man habitually, almost without noticing it, sees the present as something that grows out of a long perspective of centuries. In the minds of my R.A.F. hearers this perspective simply did not exist. It seemed to me that they did not really believe that we have any reliable knowledge of historic man. But this was often curiously combined with a conviction that we knew a great deal about Pre-Historic Man: doubtless because Pre-Historic Man is labelled "Science" (which is reliable) whereas Napoleon or Julius Caesar is labelled as "History" (which is not).

725
Holiness

A Severe Mercy, Letter to Sheldon Vanauken (5 June 1955), chap. IX, para. 25, p. 206.

"Seek ye first the Kingdom . . . and all these other things shall be added unto you." Infinite comfort in the second part; inexorable demand in the first. Hopeless if it were to be done by your own endeavours at some particular moment. But "God must do it." Your part is what you are already doing: "Take me—no conditions." After that, through the daily duty, through the increasing effort after holiness—well, like the seed growing secretly . . .

726
Holy Spirit
Mere Christianity, bk. IV, chap. 4, para. 6, p. 152.

The union between the Father and Son is such a live concrete thing that this union itself is also a Person. I know that among human beings, when they get together in a family, or a club, or a trade union, people talk about the "spirit" of that family, or club, or trade union. They talk about its "spirit" because the individual members, when they are together, do really develop particular ways of talking and behaving which they would not have if they were apart. It is as if a sort of communal personality came into existence. Of course, it is not a real person: it is only rather like a person. But that is just one of the differences between God and us. What grows out of the joint life of the Father and Son is a real Person, is in fact the Third of the three Persons who are God.

This third Person is called . . . the Holy Ghost or the "spirit" of God.

727
Home
Letters of C. S. Lewis (16 March 1955), para. 2, p. 262

As Dr. Johnson said, "To be happy at home is the end of all human endeavour." (1st to be happy to prepare for being happy in our own real home hereafter; 2nd in the meantime to be happy in our houses).

728
Homesickness
Letters of C. S. Lewis to Arthur Greeves (30 March 1915), para. 2, pp. 67–68.

[Ed. note: Though Lewis writes here of going home to Ireland, it is a precursor to all he would write about Sehnsucht and Heaven and Joy.] These last few days! Every little nuisance, every stale or tiresome bit of work, every feeling of that estrangement which I never quite get over in another country, serves as a delightful reminder of how different it will all be soon. Already one's mind dwells upon the sights and sounds and smells of home. . . .

729
Homo-
sexuality

A Severe Mercy, Letter to Sheldon Vanauken (14 May 1954), chap. 6, pp. 147–148.

First, to map out the boundaries within which all discussion must go on, I take it for certain that the *physical* satisfaction of homosexual desires is sin. This leaves the homo. no worse off than any normal person who is, for whatever reason, prevented from marrying. Second, our speculations on the cause of the abnormality are not what matters and we must be content with ignorance. The disciples were not told *why* (in terms of efficient cause) the man was born blind (Jn. IX 1–3): only the final cause, that the works of God shd. be made manifest in him. This suggests that in homosexuality, as in every other tribulation, those works can be made manifest: i.e. that every disability conceals a vocation, if only we can find it, wh. will "turn the necessity to glorious gain." Of course, the first step must be to accept any privations wh., if so disabled, we can't lawfully get. The homo. has to accept sexual abstinence just as the poor man has to forego otherwise lawful pleasures because he wd. be unjust to his wife and children if he took them. That is merely a negative condition. What shd. the positive life of the homo. be? I wish I had a letter wh. a pious male homo., now dead, once wrote me—but of course it was the sort of letter one takes care to destroy. He believed that his necessity *could* be turned to spiritual gain: that there were certain kinds of sympathy and understanding, a certain social role which mere *men* and mere *women* cd. not give. But it is all horribly vague—too long ago. Perhaps any homo. who humbly accepts his cross and puts himself under Divine guidance will, however, be shown the way. I am sure that any attempt to evade it (e.g. by mock- or quasi-marriage with a member of one's own sex *even* if this does not lead to any carnal act) is the wrong way. . . . All I have really said is that, like all other tribulations, it must be offered to God and His guidance how to use it must be sought.

730
Hooker, Richard
English Literature in the Sixteenth Century, bk. III.II.III, para. 49–50, pp. 459–460, 462.

Every system offers us a model of the universe; Hooker's model has unsurpassed grace and majesty. . . . Few model universes are more filled—one might say, more drenched—with Deity than his. . . . God is unspeakably transcendent; but also unspeakably immanent. It is this conviction which enables Hooker, with no anxiety, to resist any inaccurate claim that is made for revelation against reason, Grace against Nature, the spiritual against the secular. We must not honour even heavenly things with compliments that are not quite true: "though it seem an honour, it is an injury" (II. vii. 7). All good things, reason as well as revelation, nature as well as Grace, the commonwealth as well as the Church, are equally though diversely, "of God." . . . All kinds of knowledge, all good arts, sciences, and disciplines come from the Father of lights and are "as so many sparkles resembling the bright fountain from which they rise" (II.ii.I). . . . The style is, for its purpose, perhaps the most perfect in English.

731
Hope
Mere Christianity, bk. III, chap. 10, para. 1, p. 118.

Hope . . . means . . . a continual looking forward to the eternal world. . . . It does not mean that we are to leave the present world as it is. If you read history you will find that the Christians who did most for the present world were just those who thought most of the next. . . . It is since Christians have largely ceased to think of the other world that they have become so ineffective in this. Aim at Heaven and you will get earth "thrown in": aim at earth and you will get neither.

732
Horizon
The Four Loves, chap. 4, para. 33, p. 108.

The horizon ceases to be the horizon when you get there.

733
Houseman, A. E.
The Letters of C. S. Lewis to Arthur Greeves (6 October 1929), para. 1, p. 312.

I also glanced through A. E. Houseman's *Shropshire Lad* for the hundredth time. What a terrible little book it is—perfect and deadly, the beauty of the gorgon.

734
Human Desires
The Problem of Pain, chap. 3, para. 18, p. 52.

The place for which He designs them [human beings] in His scheme of things is the place they are made for. When they reach it their nature is fulfilled and their happiness attained: a broken bone in the universe has been set, the anguish is over. When we want to be something other than the thing God wants us to be, we must be wanting what, in fact, will not make us happy. Those Divine demands which sound to our natural ears most like those of a despot and least like those of a lover, in fact marshall us where we should want to go if we knew what we wanted.

735
Human Destiny
The Problem of Pain, chap. 3, para. 19, pp. 53–54.

God gives what He has, not what He has not: He gives the happiness that there is, not the happiness that is not. To be God—to be like God and to share His goodness in creaturely response—to be miserable—these are the only three alternatives. If we will not learn to eat the only food that the universe grows—the only food that any possible universe ever can grow—then we must starve.

736
Human Destiny
The Problem of Pain, chap. 6, para. 3, pp. 90–91.

Now the proper good of a creature is to surrender itself to its Creator—to enact intellectually, volitionally, and emotionally, that relationship which is given in the mere fact of its being a creature. When it does so, it is good and happy. Lest we should think this a hardship, this kind of good begins on a level far above the creatures, for God Himself, as Son, from all eternity renders back to God as Father by filial obedience the being which the Father by paternal love eternally generates in the Son. This is the pattern which man was made to imitate—which Paradisal man did imitate—and wherever the will conferred by the Creator is thus perfectly offered back in delighted and delighting obedience by the creature, there, most undoubtedly, is Heaven, and there the Holy Ghost proceeds. In the world as we now know it, the problem is how to recover this self-surrender.

737
Human Destiny
The Problem of Pain, chap. 7, para. 6, p. 115.

The Christian doctrine of suffering explains, I believe, a very curious fact about the world we live in. The settled happiness and security which we all desire, God withholds from us by the very nature of the world: but joy, pleasure, and merriment He has scattered broadcast. We are never safe, but we have plenty of fun, and some ecstasy. It is not hard to see why. The security we crave would teach us to rest our hearts in this world and oppose an obstacle to our return to God: a few moments of happy love, a landscape, a symphony, a merry meeting with our friends, a bathe or a football match, have no such tendency. Our Father refreshes us on the journey with some pleasant inns, but will not encourage us to mistake them for home.

738
Human Destiny
The Problem of Pain,
chap. 10, para. 3,
p. 147.

He [God] makes each soul unique. If He had no use for all these differences, I do not see why He should have created more souls than one. Be sure that the ins and outs of your individuality are no mystery to Him; and one day they will no longer be a mystery to you.

739
Human Destiny
The Problem of Pain,
chap. 10, para. 7,
p. 150.

Each of the redeemed shall forever know and praise some one aspect of the divine beauty better than any other creature can. Why else were individuals created, but that God, loving all infinitely, should love each differently?

740
Human Destiny
The Screwtape Letters,
"Screwtape Proposes a
Toast," para. 14, p. 158.

He [God] did not create the humans—He did not become one of them and die among them by torture—in order to produce candidates for Limbo, "failed" humans. He wanted to make Saints; gods; things like Himself.

741
Human Destiny
The Great Divorce,
Preface, para. 1,
pp. 5–6.

We are not living in a world where all roads are radii of a circle and where all, if followed long enough, will therefore draw gradually nearer and finally meet at the centre: rather in a world where every road, after a few miles, forks into two, and each of those into two again, and at each fork you must make a decision. Even on the biological level life is not like a pool but like a tree. It does not move towards unity but away from it and the creatures grow further apart as they increase in perfection. Good, as it ripens, becomes continually more different not only from evil but from other good.

742
**Human
Destiny**
Miracles, chap. 14,
para. 21, p. 122.

For God is not merely mending, not simply restoring a *status quo.* Redeemed humanity is to be something more glorious than unfallen humanity.

743
**Human
Destiny**
Mere Christianity, bk. IV,
chap. 4, para. 8,
p. 153.

The whole dance, or drama, or pattern of this three-Personal life is to be played out in each one of us: or (putting it the other way round) each one of us has got to enter that pattern, take his place in that dance. There is no other way to the happiness for which we were made. Good things as well as bad, you know, are caught by a kind of infection. If you want to be wet you must get into the water. If you want joy, power, peace, eternal life, you must get close to or even into, the thing that has them. They are not a sort of prize which God could, if He chose, just hand out to anyone. They are a great fountain of energy and beauty spurting up at the very centre of reality. If you are close to it, the spray will wet you: if you are not, you will remain dry. Once a man is united to God, how could he not live forever? Once a man is separated from God, what can he do but wither and die?

744
**Human
Destiny**
Mere Christianity, bk. IV,
chap. 8, para. 12,
p. 170.

What we have been told is how we men can be drawn into Christ—can become part of that wonderful present which the young Prince of the universe wants to offer to His Father—that present which is Himself and therefore us in Him. It is the only thing we were made for. And there are strange, exciting hints in the Bible that when we are drawn in, a great many other things in Nature will begin to come right. The bad dream will be over: it will be morning.

745
Human Destiny

The Four Loves, chap. 6,
para. 44, pp. 190–191.

For the dream of finding our end, the thing we were made for, in a Heaven of purely human love could not be true unless our whole Faith were wrong. We were made for God. Only by being in some respect like Him, only by being a manifestation of His beauty, lovingkindness, wisdom or goodness, has any earthly Beloved excited our love. It is not that we have loved them too much, but that we did not quite understand what we were loving. It is not that we shall be asked to turn from them, so dearly familiar, to a Stranger. When we see the face of God we shall know that we have always known it. He has been a party to, has made, sustained and moved moment by moment within, all our earthly experiences of innocent love. All that was true love in them was, even on earth, far more His than ours and ours only because His. In Heaven there will be no anguish and no duty of turning away from our earthly Beloveds. First, because we shall have turned already; from the portraits to the Original, from the rivulets to the Fountain, from the creatures He made lovable to Love Himself. But secondly, because we shall find them all in Him. By loving Him more than them we shall love them more than we now do.

746
Human Nature

The Pilgrim's Regress,
Preface, para. 15, p. 13.

We were made to be neither cerebral men nor visceral men, but Men. Not beasts nor angels but Men—things at once rational and animal.

747
Human Nature
God in the Dock, "Dogma and the Universe" (1943), para. 7, pp. 41–42.

We are inveterate poets. Our imaginations awake. Instead of mere quantity, we now have a quality—the sublime. Unless this were so, the merely arithmetical greatness of the galaxy would be no more impressive than the figures in a telephone directory. It is thus, in a sense, from ourselves that the material universe derives its power to over-awe us. To a mind which did not share our emotions, and lacked our imaginative energies, the argument from size would be sheerly meaningless. Men look on the starry heavens with reverence: monkeys do not. The silence of the eternal spaces terrified Pascal, but it was the greatness of Pascal that enabled them to do so. When we are frightened by the greatness of the universe, we are (almost literally) frightened by our own shadows: for these light years and billions of centuries are mere arithmetic until the shadow of man, the poet, the maker of myth, falls upon them. I do not say we are wrong to tremble at his shadow; it is a shadow of an image of God. But if ever the vastness of matter threatens to overcross our spirits, one must remember that it is matter spiritualized which does so. To puny man, the great nebula in Andromeda owes in a sense its greatness.

748
Human Nature
God in the Dock, "Man or Rabbit?" (1946), para. 1, p. 108.

One of the things that distinguishes man from the other animals is that he wants to know things, wants to find out what reality is like, simply for the sake of knowing. When that desire is completely quenched in anyone, I think he has become something less than human.

| 749
Human Nature
Miracles, chap. 7,
para. 17, p. 54. | What we fondly call "primitive" errors do not pass away. They merely change their form. |

| 750
Human Nature
Poems, "Pindar Sang"
(1949), verse 3, p. 16. | We live for a day. What are we? What are we not?
   A man
Is a dream about a shadow. Only when a
   brightness falls from heaven
Can human splendour expand and glow and
   mortal days grow soft. |

| 751
Human Nature
The Four Loves,
Introduction, para. 8,
p. 14. | Man approaches God most nearly when he is in one sense least like God. For what can be more unlike than fullness and need, sovereignty and humility, righteousness and penitence, limitless power and cry for help? |

| 752
Human Situation
Letters to Malcolm:
Chiefly on Prayer, chap.
8, para. 10–11, p. 43. | Does not every movement in the Passion write large some common element in the sufferings of our race? First, the prayer of anguish; not granted. Then He turns to His friends. They are asleep—as ours, or we, are so often, or busy, or away, or preoccupied. Then He faces the Church; the very Church that He brought into existence. It condemns Him. This also is characteristic. In every Church, in every institution, there is something which sooner or later works against the very purpose for which it came into existence. But there seems to be another chance. There is the State; in this case, the Roman state. Its pretensions are far lower than those of the Jewish church, but for that very reason it may be free from local fanaticisms. It claims to be just on a rough, worldly level. Yes, but only so far as is consistent |

with political expediency and *raison d'etat.* One
becomes a counter in a complicated game. But
even now all is not lost. There is still an appeal to
the People—the poor and simple whom He had
blessed, whom He had healed and fed and taught,
to whom He Himself belongs. But they have
become over-night (it is nothing unusual) a
murderous rabble shouting for His blood. There
is, then nothing left but God. And to God, God's
last words are "Why hast thou forsaken me?"
 You see how characteristic, how representative,
it all is. The human situation writ large. These are
among the things it means to be a man. Every
rope breaks when you seize it. Every door is
slammed shut as you reach it. To be like the fox
at the end of the run; the earths all staked.

753
Human Spirit
Miracles, Appendix A,
para. 5, item 4, p. 171.

Some people use "spirit" to mean that relatively
supernatural element which is given to every man
at his creation—the rational element. This is, I
think, the most useful way of employing the
word. Here again it is important to realise that
what is "spiritual" is not necessarily good. A Spirit
(in this sense) can be either the best or the worst
of created things. It is because Man is (in this
sense) a spiritual animal that he can become either
a son of God or a devil.

754
Humanism
Selected Literary Essays,
"Addison" (1945), para.
11–12, pp. 163–164.

The obscurantism of the Humanists is still not
fully recognised. Learning to them meant the
knowledge and imitation of a few rather arbitrarily
selected Latin authors and some even fewer Greek
authors. They despised metaphysics and natural
science; and they despised all the past outside the
favoured periods. They were dominated by a
narrowly ethical purpose. . . . The Humanist
attack is really on metaphysics itself. In Erasmus,

in Rabelais, in the *Utopia* one recognizes the very accent of the angry *belle-lettrist* railing, as he rails in all ages, at "jargon" and "straw-splitting." On this side Pope and Swift are true inheritors of the Humanist tradition. It is easy, of course, to say that Laputa is an attack not on science but on the aberrations of science. I am not convinced. The learning of the Brobdingnagians and the Horses is ruthlessly limited. Nothing that cannot plead the clearest immediate utility—nothing that cannot make two blades of grass grow where one grew before—wins any approval from Swift. . . . The terror expressed at the end of the *Dunciad* is not wholly terror at the approach of ignorance: it is also terror lest the compact little fortress of Humanism should be destroyed, and new knowledge is one of the enemies. Whatever is not immediately intelligible to a man versed in the Latin and French classics appears to them to be charlatanism or barbarity. The number of things they do not want to hear about is enormous.

But Addison wants to hear about everything. He is quite as good a classical scholar as the Tories but he does not live in the Humanist prison.

755
Humanism
English Literature in the Sixteenth Century, Introduction, para. 2, p. 2.

The more we look into the question, the harder we shall find it to believe that humanism had any power of encouraging, or any wish to encourage, the literature that actually arose [in the sixteenth century].

756
Humanism
English Literature in the Sixteenth Century, Introduction, para. 30–31, pp. 20–21.

We read the humanists, in fact, only to learn about humanism; we read the "barbarous" authors in order to be instructed or delighted about any theme they choose to handle. Once we cease to let the humanists' own language beg the question, is it not clear that in this context the "barbarous" is the living and the "classical" the still-born?

It could hardly have been anything but still-born. It is largely to the humanists that we owe the curious conception of the "classical" period before which all was immature or archaic and after which all was decadent. . . . When once this superstition was established it led naturally to the belief that good writing in the fifteenth or sixteenth century meant writing which aped as closely as possible that of the chosen period in the past. All real development of Latin to meet the changing needs of new talent and new subject-matter was thus precluded; with one blow of "his Mace petrific" the classical spirit ended the history of the Latin tongue. This was not what the humanists intended. . . . From that point of view humanism is a great archaizing movement. . . . They succeeded in killing the medieval Latin but not in keeping alive the schoolroom severities of their restored Augustanism. Before they had ceased talking of a rebirth it became evident that they had really built a tomb.

757
Humanism
English Literature in the Sixteenth Century, Introduction, para. 36, p. 24.

Elevation and gravity of language are admirable, or even tolerable, only when they grow from elevation and gravity of thought. To imitate them directly is to manufacture a symptom. The trouble is not that such manufacture is impossible. It is only too possible: even now any clever boy can be taught to write Ciceronian prose. The gestures and accents of magnanimity, laboriously reproduced by little men, clever, meticulous, primed with the *gradus* or the phrase-book, nervously avoiding what is "low," make an ugly spectacle. That was how the humanists came to create a new literary quality—vulgarity. It is hard to point to any

medieval work that is vulgar. When medieval
literature is bad, it is bad by honest, downright
incompetence: dull, prolix, or incoherent. But the
varnish and stucco of some neo-Latin work, the
badness which no man could incur by sheer
defect of talent but only by "endless labour to be
wrong" is a new thing.

758
Humanism
English Literature in the
Sixteenth Century,
Introduction, para. 39,
p. 27.

[The humanist] is too interested in literature,
literature conceived almost exclusively as style, and
style valued chiefly as a model for imitation.

759
Humanism
English Literature in the
Sixteenth Century, bk.
I.II.I, para. 15–16,
p. 132.

It is another instance of that fatal flaw in
humanism which draws a veil over Greek
literature in the very act of discovering it; that
urban and bookish limitation which sees in an
ancient text everything rather than the radical,
obvious, and universal pleasures which it was
intended to give.
. . . How little tendency the humanism of that
time had to kindle poetic imagination or mend
poetic art.

760
Humility
Taliessin Through Logres,
. . . *Arthurian Torso,*
"Williams and the
Arthuriad" (1948),
chap. III, para. 16,
p. 307.

The courtesy of the Emperor has absolutely
decreed that no man can paddle his own canoe
and every man can paddle his fellows', so that the
shy offering and modest acceptance of
indispensable aid shall be the very form of the
celestial etiquette.

761
Humility
Taliessin Through Logres,
. . . Arthurian Torso,
"Williams and the
Arthuriad" (1948),
chap. IV, para. 17,
p. 329.

Of course the whole thing is a kind of make believe or fancy-dress ball. Not only official greatness, as of kings or judges, but what we call real greatness, the greatness of Shakespeare, Erasmus, and Montaigne, is, from a certain point of view, illusory. What then? What but to thank God for the "excellent absurdity" which enables us, if it so happen, to play great parts without pride and little ones without dejection, rejecting nothing through that false modesty which is only another form of pride, and never, when we occupy for a moment the centre of the stage, forgetting that the play would have gone off just as well without us. . . . This is the spirit which ought to govern even the smallest and most temporary assumptions of the higher place; whenever we forgive or permit or teach we should be aware of the "excellent absurdity" but none the less step obediently into our position, assured that if we are some day to come where saints cast down their golden crowns we must here be content both to assume for ourselves and to honour in others crowns of paper and tinsel, most worthy of tender laughter but not of hostile contempt.

762
Humility
Taliessin Through Logres,
. . . Arthurian Torso,
"Williams and the
Arthuriad" (1948),
chap. IV, para. 8, p. 319.

It is not chastening but liberating to know that one has always been almost wholly superfluous; wherever one has done well some other has done all the real work . . . you will do the same for him, perhaps, another day, but you will not know it.

763
Humility
Mere Christianity, bk. III,
chap. 8, para. 13, p. 114.

Do not imagine that if you meet a really humble man he will be what most people call "humble" nowadays: he will not be a sort of greasy, smarmy person, who is always telling you that, of course, he is nobody. Probably all you will think about him is that he seemed a cheerful, intelligent chap who took a real interest in what *you* said to *him*. If you do dislike him it will be because you feel a little envious of anyone who seems to enjoy life so easily. He will not be thinking about humility: he will not be thinking about himself at all.

764
Humility
Mere Christianity, bk. III, chap. 8, para. 14, p. 114.

If anyone would like to acquire humility, I can, I think, tell him the first step. The first step is to realise that one is proud. And a biggish step, too. At least, nothing whatever can be done before it. If you think you are not conceited, it means you are very conceited indeed.

765
Humility
The Horse and His Boy, chap. 14, p. 193.

There was about a second of intense silence. Then Hwin, though shaking all over, gave a strange little neigh, and trotted across to the Lion.

"Please," she said, "you're so beautiful. You may eat me if you like. I'd sooner be eaten by you than fed by anyone else."

"Dearest daughter," said Aslan, planting a lion's kiss on her twitching, velvet nose, "I knew you would not be long in coming to me. Joy shall be yours."

Then he lifted his head and spoke in a louder voice.

"Now Bree," he said, "you poor, proud, frightened Horse, draw near. Nearer still, my son. Do not dare not to dare. Touch me. Smell me. Here are my paws, here is my tail, these are my whiskers. I am a true Beast."

"Aslan," said Bree in a shaken voice, "I'm afraid I must be rather a fool."

"Happy the horse who knows that while he is still young. Or the Human either."

766 **Humility** *Letters to an American Lady* (9 January 1961), para. 5, p. 95.	May God's grace give you the necessary humility. Try not to think—much less, speak—of *their* sins. One's own are a much more profitable theme! And if on consideration, one can find no faults on one's own side, then cry for mercy: for this *must* be a most dangerous delusion.
767 **Humor** *The Screwtape Letters,* Letter XI, para. 5, pp. 51–52.	[Senior devil Screwtape to junior devil Wormwood:] The English . . . take their "sense of humour" so seriously that a deficiency in this sense is almost the only deficiency at which they feel shame. Humour is for them the all-consoling and (mark this) the all-excusing, grace of life. Hence it is invaluable as a means of destroying shame. . . . A thousand bawdy, or even blasphemous, jokes do not help towards a man's damnation so much as his discovery that almost anything he wants to do can be done, not only without the disapproval but with the admiration of his fellows, if only it can get itself treated as a Joke. And this temptation can be almost entirely hidden from your patient by that English seriousness about Humour. Any suggestion that there might be too much of it can be represented to him as "Puritanical" or as betraying a "lack of humour."
768 **Humor** *The Screwtape Letters,* Letter XI, para. 6, p. 52.	[Senior devil Screwtape to junior devil Wormwood:] Flippancy is the best of all. In the first place it is very economical. Only a clever human can make a real Joke about virtue, or indeed about anything else; any of them can be trained to talk as if virtue were funny. Among flippant people the Joke is always assumed to have been made. No one actually makes it; but every serious subject is discussed in a manner

which implies that they have already found a ridiculous side to it. If prolonged, the habit of Flippancy builds up around a man the finest armour plating against the Enemy that I know, and it is quite free from the dangers inherent in the other sources of laughter. It is a thousand miles away from joy; it deadens, instead of sharpening, the intellect; and it excites no affection between those who practise it.

769
Humor
Miracles, chap. 14, para. 29, pp. 127–128.

Almost the whole of Christian theology could perhaps be deduced from the two facts (*a*) That men make coarse jokes, and (*b*) That they feel the dead to be uncanny. The coarse joke proclaims that we have here an animal which finds its own animality either objectionable or funny. Unless there had been a quarrel between the spirit and the organism I do not see how this could be: it is the very mark of the two not being "at home" together. . . . Our feeling about the dead is equally odd. It is idle to say that we dislike corpses because we are afraid of ghosts. You might say with equal truth that we fear ghosts because we dislike corpses. . . . In reality we hate the division which makes possible the conception of either corpse or ghost. Because the thing ought not to be divided, each of the halves into which it falls by division is detestable. . . . Once we accept the Christian doctrine that man was originally a unity and that the present division is unnatural, . . . all the phenomena fall into place.

770
Humor
English Literature in the Sixteenth Century, bk. I.I.I, para. 40, p. 95.

The mixture of farce and terror would be incredible if we did not remember that boys joked most about flogging under Keate, and men joked most about gallows under the old penal code. It is apparently when terrors are over that they become too terrible to laugh at; while they are regnant they are too terrible to be taken with unrelieved gravity. There is nothing funny about Hitler *now.*

771

Humor

The Magician's Nephew,
chap. 10, pp. 118–119.

"Laugh and fear not, creatures. Now that you are no longer dumb and witless, you need not always be grave. For jokes as well as justice come in with speech."

772

Humor

Reflections on the Psalms,
chap. 9, para. 1, p. 90.

A little comic relief in a discussion does no harm, however serious the topic may be. (In my own experience the funniest things have occurred in the gravest and most sincere conversations.)

773

Humor

The Screwtape Letters,
Preface (1960), para. 16,
p. ix.

Humor involves a sense of proportion and a power of seeing yourself from the outside.

774

Husbands

That Hideous Strength,
chap. 4, Section 1,
pp. 76–77.

"Jane, that's the third time you've yawned. You're dropping asleep and I've talked your head off. It comes of being married thirty years. Husbands were made to be talked to. It helps them to concentrate their minds on what they're reading—like the sound of a weir. There!—you're yawning again."

775

Hymns

Christian Reflections,
"On Church Music"
(1949), para. 8, p. 96.

The first and most solid conclusion which (for me) emerges is that both musical parties, the High Brows and the Low, assume far too easily the spiritual value of the music they want.

776

Hymns

Letters of C. S. Lewis (7
December 1950), para. 2,
p. 224.

I naturally *loathe* nearly all hymns; the face and
life of the charwoman in the next pew who revels
in them, teach me that good taste in poetry or
music are *not* necessary to salvation.

777

Hypocrisy

*Letters to an American
Lady* (5 July 1956), para.
2, p. 58.

How difficult it is to avoid having a special
standard for oneself!

778
Identity
Till We Have Faces, part
II, chap. 4, p. 294.

The complaint was the answer. To have heard
myself making it was to be answered. Lightly men
talk of saying what they mean. Often when he
was teaching me to write in Greek the Fox would
say, "Child, to say the very thing you really mean,
the whole of it, nothing more or less or other
than what you really mean; that's the whole art
and joy of words." A glib saying. When the time
comes to you at which you will be forced at last
to utter the speech which has lain at the center of
your soul for years, which you have, all that time,
idiot-like, been saying over and over, you'll not
talk about joy of words. I saw well why the gods
do not speak to us, openly, nor let us answer. Till
that word can be dug out of us, why should they
hear the babble that we think we mean? How can
they meet us face to face till we have faces?

779
Images
A Grief Observed,
chap. IV, para. 15–16,
pp. 76–77.

Images I must suppose, have their use or they
would not have been so popular. (It makes little
difference whether they are pictures and statues
outside the mind or imaginative constructions
within it.) To me, however, their danger is more
obvious. Images of the Holy easily become holy
images—sacrosanct. My idea of God is not a
divine idea. It has to be shattered time after time.
He shatters it Himself. He is the great iconoclast.

Could we not almost say that this shattering is one of the marks of His presence? The Incarnation is the supreme example; it leaves all previous ideas of the Messiah in ruins. And most are "offended" by the iconoclasm; and blessed are those who are not. But the same thing happens in our private prayers.

All reality is iconoclastic.

780

Imagination

Letters of C. S. Lewis (1 July 1921), para. 3, p. 63.

Of landscapes, as of people, one becomes more tolerant after one's twentieth year. (The rate at which we both advance towards a responsible age is indecent.) We learn to look at them, not *in the flat* but *in depth,* as things to be burrowed into. It is not merely a question of lines and colours but of smells, sounds and tastes as well; I often wonder if professional artists don't lose something of the real love of earth by seeing it in eye-sensations only?

781

Imagination

The Letters of C. S. Lewis to Arthur Greeves (8 November 1931), para. 4, p. 430.

[On Greeves's joy in rereading Plato's *Phaedrus*:] You must be enjoying yourself [to] no end. I don't know any greater pleasure than returning to a world of the imagination which one has long forsaken and feeling "After all this is my own."

782

Imagination

The Screwtape Letters, Letter X, para. 2, p. 46.

"All mortals tend to turn into the thing they are pretending to be."

783

Imagination

Selected Literary Essays, "Hamlet: The Prince or the Poem" (1942), para. 22, pp. 104–105.

A child is always thinking about those details in a story which a grown-up regards as indifferent. If when you first told the tale your hero was warned by three little men appearing on the left of the road, and when you tell it again you introduce one little man on the right of the road, the child protests. And the child is right. You think it makes no difference because you are not living the story at all. If you were, you would know better. *Motifs,* machines, and the like are abstractions of literary history and therefore interchangeable: but concrete imagination knows nothing of them.

784
Imagination
Miracles, chap. 7,
para. 16, pp. 52–53.

We are inveterate poets. When a quantity is very great we cease to regard it as a mere quantity. Our imaginations awake. Instead of mere quantity, we now have a quality—the Sublime. . . . Men of sensibility look up on the night sky with awe: brutal and stupid men do not. When the silence of the eternal spaces terrified Pascal, it was Pascal's own greatness that enabled them to do so; to be frightened by the bigness of the nebulae is, almost literally, to be frightened at our own shadow. For light years and geological periods are mere arithmetic until the shadow of man, the poet, the maker of myths, falls upon them. As a Christian I do not say we are wrong to tremble at that shadow, for I believe it to be the shadow of an image of God. But if the vastness of Nature ever threatens to overcrow our spirits, we must remember that it is only Nature spiritualised by human imagination which does so.

785
Imagination
Mere Christianity, bk. IV,
chap. 7, para. 3, p. 161.

Very often the only way to get a quality in reality is to start behaving as if you had it already. That is why children's games are so important. They are always pretending to be grown-ups—playing soldiers, playing shop. But all the time, they are hardening their muscles and sharpening their wits, so that the pretence of being grown-up helps them to grow up in earnest.

786

Imagination

English Literature in the Sixteenth Century, Introduction, para. 89, p. 58.

It is never safe to attribute a man's imaginations too directly to his experience.

787

Imagination

English Literature in the Sixteenth Century, bk. II.II., para. 68, p. 269.

It is always difficult to convince unimaginative readers that anything is invented.

788

Imagination

The Four Loves, chap. 6, para. 47, p. 192.

Those like myself whose imagination far exceeds their obedience are subject to a just penalty; we easily imagine conditions far higher than any we have really reached. If we describe what we have imagined we may make others, and make ourselves, believe that we have really been there.

789

Imagination

Letters to Malcolm: Chiefly on Prayer, chap. 3, para. 9, p. 17.

If the imagination were obedient, the appetites would give us very little trouble.

790

Immortality

Spirits in Bondage, "Dungeon Grates" (1919), pp. 41–42.

We shall keep
Our vision still. One moment was enough
We know we are not made of mortal stuff.
And we can bear all trials that come after
The hate of men and the fool's loud bestial
    laughter
And Nature's rule and cruelties unclean
For we have seen the Glory—we have seen.

791

Immortality

Letters of C. S. Lewis (24 May 1922), para. 1, p. 77.

[A pre-conversion statement:] We [Barfield] then, drifted into a long talk about ultimates. Like me, he has no belief in immortality etc., and always feels materialistic pessimism at his elbow.

792

Incarnation

Christian Reflections,
"Christianity and
Literature" (1939),
chap. 1, para. 5, p. 3.

To believe in the Incarnation at all is to believe
that every mode of human excellence is implicit in
His [Jesus'] historical human character. . . . But if
all had been developed, the limitations of a single
human life would have been transcended and he
would not have been a man; therefore all
excellences save the spiritual remained in varying
degrees implicit.

793

Incarnation

Perelandra, chap. 11,
p. 144.

Every minute it became clearer to him that the
parallel he had tried to draw between Eden and
Perelandra was crude and imperfect. What had
happened on Earth, when Maleldil [God] was
born a man at Bethlehem, had altered the universe
for ever.

794

Incarnation

The Letters of C. S.
Lewis to Arthur Greeves
(26 December 1945),
p. 505.

Something really *new* did happen at Bethlehem:
not an interpretation but an *event*. God became
Man. On the other hand there must be a sense in
which God, being outside time, is changeless and
nothing ever "happens" to Him. I think I should
reply that the event at Bethlehem was a novelty, a
change to the maximum extent to which any
event is a novelty or change: but that *all* time and
all events in it, if we cd. see them all at once and
fully understand them, are a definition or diagram
of what God eternally is. But that is quite
different from saying that the incarnation was
simply an interpretation, or a change in *our*
knowledge. When Pythagoras discovered that the
square on the hypotenuse was equal to the sum
of the squares on the other sides he was
discovering what had been just as true the day
before though no one knew it. But in 50 B.C. the
proposition "God is Man" wd. *not* have been true
in the same sense in wh. it was true in 10 A.D.
because tho' the union of God and Man in Christ

is a timeless fact, in 50 B.C. we hadn't yet got to that bit of time which defines it.

795

Incarnation

Letters of C. S. Lewis
(1947?), para. 3,
pp. 210–211.

God could, had He pleased, have been incarnate in a man of iron nerves, the Stoic sort who lets no sigh escape him. Of His great humility He chose to be incarnate in a man of delicate sensibilities who wept at the grave of Lazarus and sweated blood in Gethsemane. Otherwise we should have missed the great lesson that it is by his *will* alone that a man is good or bad, and that *feelings* are not, in themselves, of any importance. We should also have missed the all-important help of knowing that he has faced all that the weakest of us face, has shared not only the strength of our nature but every weakness of it except sin.

796

Incarnation

Miracles, chap. 14,
para. 1, p. 108.

The central miracle asserted by Christians is the Incarnation. They say that God became Man. Every other miracle prepares for this, or exhibits this, or results from this. Just as every natural event is the manifestation at a particular place and moment of Nature's total character, so every particular Christian miracle manifests at a particular place and moment the character and significance of the Incarnation. There is no question in Christianity of arbitrary interferences just scattered about. It relates not a series of disconnected raids on Nature but the various steps of a strategically coherent invasion—an invasion which intends complete conquest and "occupation." The fitness, and therefore credibility, of the particular miracles depends on their relation to the Grand Miracle; all discussion of them in isolation from it is futile.

797
Incarnation
Miracles, chap. 14,
para. 2, p. 108.

If the thing happened, it was the central event in the history of the Earth.

798
Incarnation
Miracles, chap. 14,
para. 4, pp. 110–111.

The discrepancy between a movement of atoms in an astronomer's cortex and his understanding that there must be a still unobserved planet beyond Uranus is already so immense that the incarnation of God himself is, in one sense, scarcely more startling. We cannot conceive how the Divine Spirit dwelled within the created and human spirit of Jesus: but neither can we conceive how His human spirit, or that of any man, dwells within his natural organism. What we can understand, if the Christian doctrine is true, is that our own composite existence is not the sheer anomaly it might seem to be, but a faint image of the Divine incarnation itself—the same theme in a very minor key. . . both Natural and Supernatural, in which we are living is more multifariously and subtly harmonious than we had suspected. We catch sight of a new key principle—the power of the Higher, just in so far as it is truly higher, to come down, the power of the greater to include the less. Thus solid bodies exemplify many truths of plane geometry, but plane figures not truths of solid geometry: many inorganic propositions are true of organisms but no organic propositions are true of minerals; Montaigne became kittenish with his kitten but she never talked philosophy to him. Everywhere the great enters the little—its power to do so is almost the test of its greatness.

799
Incarnation
Miracles, chap. 14,
para. 5, p. 111.

In the Christian story God descends to reascend. He comes down; . . . down to the very roots and sea-bed of the Nature he has created. But He goes down to come up again and bring the whole ruined world up with Him.

800
Incarnation
Miracles, chap. 14,
para. 6–7, p. 112.

In this descent and re-ascent everyone will recognise a familiar pattern: a thing written all over the world. It is the pattern of all vegetable life. It must belittle itself into something hard, small and deathlike, it must fall into the ground: thence the new life re-ascends. It is the pattern of all animal generation too. There is descent from the full and perfect organisms into the spermatozoon and ovum, and in the dark womb a life at first inferior in kind to that of the species which is being reproduced: then the slow ascent to the perfect embryo, to the living, conscious baby, and finally to the adult. So it is also in our moral and emotional life. The first innocent and spontaneous desires have to submit to the deathlike process of control or total denial: but from that there is a re-ascent to fully formed character in which the strength of the original material all operates but in a new way. Death and Re-birth—go down to go up—it is a key principle. Through this bottleneck, this belittlement, the highroad nearly always lies. . . . The pattern is there in Nature because it was first there in God.

801
Incarnation
Miracles, chap. 14,
para. 21, p. 122.

But once the Son of God, drawn hither not by our merits but by our unworthiness, has put on human nature, then our species (whatever it may have been before) does become in one sense the central fact in all Nature: our species, rising after its long descent, will drag all Nature up with it

because in our species the Lord of Nature is now
included.

802
Incarnation
Miracles, chap. 14,
para. 23, p. 123.

God never undoes anything but evil, never does
good to undo it again. The union between God
and Nature in the Person of Christ admits no
divorce. He will not *go out of* Nature again and
she must be glorified in all ways which this
miraculous union demands.

803
Incarnation
Miracles, chap. 14,
para. 33, p. 131.

The Incarnation . . . illuminates and orders all
other phenomena, explains both our laughter and
our logic, our fear of the dead and our knowledge
that it is somehow good to die, and which at one
stroke covers what multitudes of separate theories
will hardly cover for us if this is rejected.

804
Incarnation
Mere Christianity, bk. II,
chap. 4, para. 8–9, p. 60.

Unfortunately we now need God's help in order
to do something which God, in His own nature,
never does at all—to surrender, to suffer, to
submit, to die. Nothing in God's nature
corresponds to this process at all. So that the one
road for which we now need God's leadership
most of all is a road God, in His own nature, has
never walked. God can share only what He has:
this thing, in His own nature, He has not.

But supposing God became a man—suppose
our human nature which can suffer and die was
amalgamated with God's nature in one person—
then that person could help us. He could
surrender His will, and suffer and die, because He
was man; and He could do it perfectly because
He was God. . . . But we cannot share God's
dying unless God dies; and He cannot die except
by being a man. That is the sense in which He
pays our debt, and suffers for us what He Himself
need not suffer at all.

805

Incarnation

Mere Christianity, bk. IV,
chap. 5, para. 1,
p. 154.

The Son of God became a man to enable men to become sons of God.

806

Incarnation

*The World's Last Night
and Other Essays,* "The
World's Last Night"
(1952), para. 10, p. 99.

The answer of theologians is that the God-Man was omniscient as God, and ignorant as Man. This, no doubt, is true, though it cannot be imagined. Nor indeed can the unconsciousness of Christ in sleep be imagined, not the twilight of reason in his infancy; still less his merely organic life in his mother's womb. But the physical sciences, no less than theology, propose for our belief much that cannot be imagined.

807

Incarnation

Letters of C. S. Lewis
(17 July 1953), para. 1,
p. 250.

You needn't worry about not feeling brave. Our Lord didn't—see the scene in Gethsemane. How thankful I am that when God became man He did not choose to become a man of iron nerves; that would not have helped weaklings like you and me nearly so much.

808

Incarnation

The Last Battle,
chap. 13, pp. 140–141.

"It seems, then," said Tirian, smiling himself, "that the Stable seen from within and the Stable seen from without are two different places."

"Yes," said the Lord Digory. "Its inside is bigger than its outside."

"Yes," said Queen Lucy. "In our world too, a Stable once had something inside it that was bigger than our whole world."

809

Incarnation

The Four Loves, Intro.,
para. 12, p. 17.

Our imitation of God in this life—that is, our willed imitation as distinct from any of the likenesses which He has impressed upon our natures or states—must be an imitation of God incarnate: our model is the Jesus, not only of Calvary, but of the workshop, the roads, the crowds, the clamorous demands and surly oppositions, the lack of all peace and privacy, the interruptions. For this, so strangely unlike anything we can attribute to the Divine life in itself, is apparently not only like, but is, the Divine life operating under human conditions.

810

Incarnation

Letters to Malcolm: Chiefly on Prayer, chap. 8, para. 12, p. 44.

I sometimes wonder if we have even begun to understand what is involved in the very concept of creation. If God will create, He will make something to be, and yet to be not Himself. To be created is, in some sense, to be ejected or separated. Can it be that the more perfect the creature is, the further this separation must at some point be pushed? It is saints and angels, not beasts, who rebel. Inanimate matter sleeps in the bosom of the Father. The "hiddenness" of God perhaps presses most painfully on those who are in another way nearest to Him, and therefore God Himself, made man, will of all men be by God most forsaken? . . . Perhaps there is an anguish, an alienation, a crucifixion involved in the creative act. Yet He who alone can judge judges the far-off consummation to be worth it.

811

Incarnation

Poems, "The Nativity" (1st pub. 1964), p. 122.

Among the oxen (like an ox I'm slow)
I see a glory in the stable grow
Which, with the ox's dullness might at length
　　　Give me an ox's strength.

Among the asses (stubborn I as they)
I see my Saviour where I looked for hay;
So may my beastlike folly learn at least
　　　The patience of a beast.

Among the sheep (I like a sheep have strayed)
I watch the manger where my Lord is laid;
Oh that my baa-ing nature would win thence
    Some woolly innocence!

812

Independence

Letters of C. S. Lewis (17
July 1953), para. 2,
p. 251.

Poor boob—he thought his mind was his own.
Never his own until he makes it Christ's; up till
then, merely a result of heredity, environment, and
the state of his digestion. I became my own only
when I gave myself to Another.

813

Influence

Selected Literary Essays,
"The Literary Impact of
the Authorized Version"
(1950), para. 38, p. 142.

An influence which cannot evade our
consciousness will not go very deep.

814

Inhibitions

Surprised by Joy, chap. 4,
para. 18, p. 69.

It took me as long to acquire inhibitions as others
(they say) have taken to get rid of them. That is
why I often find myself at such cross-purposes
with the modern world: I have been a converted
Pagan living among apostate Puritans.

815

Innocence

The Allegory of Love,
chap. II.III, para. 4,
p. 60.

Innocence is not goodness. Even divine Nature,
even in her prime, cannot make virtue a gift.

816

Innocence

The Allegory of Love,
chap. III.III, para. 13,
p. 133.

Innocence is carried away by the unforeseen.

817

Inspiration

Selected Literary Essays,
"The Vision of John
Bunyan" (1962), para. 4,
p. 147.

It came. I doubt if we shall ever know more of the process called "inspiration" than those two monosyllables tell us.

818

Instinct

The Abolition of Man,
chap. 2, para. 8, 11,
pp. 48, 52.

Telling us to obey instinct is like telling us to obey "people." People say different things: so do instincts. Our instincts are at war. . . . Each instinct, if you listen to it, will claim to be gratified at the expense of all the rest. . . .

The truth finally becomes apparent that neither in any operation with factual propositions nor in any appeal to instinct can the Innovator find the basis for a system of values.

819

Instinct

Christian Reflections,
"On Ethics" (1943?),
para. 15, p. 50.

Our instincts are obviously in conflict. The satisfaction of one demands the denial of another.

820

Interruptions

*The Letters of C. S.
Lewis to Arthur Greeves*
(20 December 1943),
para. 5, p. 499.

The great thing, if one can, is to stop regarding all the unpleasant things as interruptions of one's "own," or "real" life. The truth is of course that what one calls the interruptions are precisely one's real life—the life God is sending one day by day: what one calls one's "real life" is a phantom of one's own imagination. This at least is what I see at moments of insight: but it's hard to remember it all the time.

821

Intolerance

Letters of C. S. Lewis (23
April 1951), para. 3,
p. 229.

I really think that in our days it is the "undogmatic" and "liberal" people who call themselves Christians that are the most arrogant and intolerant. I expect justice and even courtesy from many atheists and, much more, from your people: from Modernists I have to take bitterness and rancour as a matter of course.

822

Introspection

Surprised by Joy,
chap. 14, para. 10,
pp. 218–219.

The surest means of disarming an anger or a lust was to turn your attention from the girl or the insult and start examining the passion itself. The surest way of spoiling a pleasure was to start examining your satisfaction. But if so, it followed that all introspection is in one respect misleading. In introspection we try to look "inside ourselves" and to see what is going on. But nearly everything that was going on a moment before is stopped by the very act of our turning to look at it. Unfortunately this does not mean that introspection finds nothing. On the contrary, it finds precisely what is left behind by the suspension of all our normal activities; and what is left behind is mainly mental images and physical sensations. The great error is to mistake this mere sediment or tract or by-product for the activities themselves. That is how men may come to believe that thought is only unspoken words, or the appreciation of poetry only a collection of mental pictures, when these in reality are what the thought or the appreciation, when interrupted, leave behind—like the swell at sea, working after the wind has dropped. Not, of course, that these activities, before we stopped them by introspection, were unconscious. We do not love, fear, or think without knowing it. Instead of the twofold division into Conscious and Unconscious, we need a threefold division: the Unconscious, the Enjoyed, and the Contemplated.

C. S. Lewis as a young boy. Clive Staples Lewis was born in Belfast, North Ireland, on 29 November 1898.

Top: Little Lea, C. S. Lewis's boyhood home in Belfast, North Ireland, 1905.

Bottom: Members of the Lewis family on the doorstep of Little Lea, Belfast, North Ireland, 1905. Front row (left to right): Warren Lewis, C. S. Lewis, Leonard Lewis (cousin), and Eileen Lewis (cousin). Back row: Agnes Young Lewis (aunt), two maids, Flora Hamilton Lewis (mother), and Albert Lewis (father) with the family dog, Nero.

Above: C. S. Lewis and Warren H. Lewis with their bicycles in front of Glen Machen, the Ewart family home in Belfast, North Ireland, August 1908. The Ewarts were cousins and neighbors of the Lewis family.

Left: Christmas Day party at Little Lea, Belfast, North Ireland, 1908. Standing (left to right): Albert Lewis (father) and Warren Lewis (brother). Seated: Mary Warren Hamilton (maternal grandmother), Ruth Hamilton (partially hidden, cousin), Harley Hamilton (with head in hand, cousin), John Hamilton (below, cousin), C. S. Lewis (above), and Annie Harley Hamilton (aunt).

Friends and relatives at Glen Machen, the Ewart family home in Belfast, North Ireland, summer 1910. Standing (left to right): Arthur Greeves (longtime friend), Gordon Ewart (distant cousin), and C. S. Lewis. Seated: first three unidentified, Lily Greeves (Arthur's sister), and Robert Heard Ewart (distant cousin).

Top: C. S. Lewis with his father, Albert Lewis, who was a solicitor in Belfast, North Ireland. Although undated, the editors estimate that this photograph was taken around the time when C. S. Lewis was preparing for entrance to Oxford University under the tutelage of W. T. Kirkpatrick at Great Bookham, Surrey. Albert Lewis had been a former student of Kirkpatrick, affectionately called "the Great Knock" in Lewis's autobiography.

Bottom: Cadet C. S. Lewis of "E" Company and his roommate, E. F. C. "Paddy" Moore, at Keble College in an Oxford punt, 1917. Moore would be killed during World War I. Lewis later took up lodgings at the Moore home.

C. S. Lewis, July 1919, a little more than a year after his injury at the front during World War I. Taken during the year of the publication of his first book, *Spirits in Bondage*. The Heinemann edition included advertisements for other Heinemann poets such as Siegfried Sassoon, Robert Graves, John Masefield, and John Galsworthy. The young author was classed with a formidable group. Although the book was published under the pseudonym Clive (his first name) Hamilton (his mother's maiden name), the advertisement refers to him as George Lewis.

C. S. Lewis at Stonehenge, 8 April 1925. Taken during the days when he had
applied for a fellowship at Magdalen (pronounced *maudlin*) College, Oxford.

Top: The fellows of Magdalen College, Oxford, 1926. Standing (left to right): Messrs. Longden, ?, C. S. Lewis, C. E. Brownrigg (headmaster of Magdalen College School), Dr. Onions, Mr. Christie (later headmaster of Repton), ?, Dr. M. H. MacKeith, Mr. G. R. Driver M. C., Mr. J. J. Mahley, and Rev. H. E. Salter. Seated: Dr. Herbert Warren, K. C. V. O. (president of Magdalen College), Prof. C. H. Turner, Mr. P. V. H. Benecke, Rev. F. E. Brightman, D. D., Prof. J. A. Smith, Prof. H. L. Bowman, Mr. Dickson, and Mr. Tansley.

Bottom: C. S. Lewis, Mrs. Janie Moore, and Major Warren H. Lewis at The Kilns, Headington, Oxford, 1930. Taken shortly after the Moores and Lewis moved into The Kilns.

Above: The Kilns, Headington, Oxford, Lewis's home for 33 years. It was named after the brick kiln seen to the right of the house.

Left: The entrance to the Eastgate Hotel, where the Inklings first met in Oxford. The Inklings were a literary group comprised of C. S. Lewis, Warren H. Lewis, J. R. R. Tolkien, Charles Williams, and their friends. Courtesy of the editors.

Right: The Eagle and Child Pub, St. Giles Street, Oxford, one of several meeting places of the Inklings. Other meeting places included the Lamb and the Flag Pub and Lewis's rooms at Magdalen College.

Below: The New Building, Magdalen College, Oxford. C. S. Lewis's rooms were at the end on the third floor. The windows look out on the Magdalen Deer Park. During Lewis's years at Magdalen College the park was filled with elm trees, which have since been cut down due to Dutch elm disease. Photo courtesy of the editors.

Above: Magdalen
College tower, Oxford
University. C. S. Lewis
served as fellow and
tutor at Magdalen for 29
years. Courtesy of
Claudia Root; used by
permission.

Left: The pulpit of St.
Mary's, the Oxford
University church. From
this pulpit Lewis
delivered his sermons
"Learning in War-Time"
(22 October 1939) and
"The Weight of Glory"
(8 June 1941). Others
who addressed the
university community
from this pulpit include
Thomas Cranmer, John
Wesley, and John Henry
Newman. Courtesy of
the editors.

Right: Looking across Broad Street into Catte Street, Oxford. The parked bicycles are a familiar sight in Oxford. When Lewis lectured, it was observed that the bicycles would often be parked eight deep as students crowded in to hear him. Courtesy of Claudia Root; used by permission.

Below: St. Stephen's House, Marsden Street, Oxford, former headquarters of the Cowley Fathers, an Anglican monastic order. Lewis would visit here for confession and spiritual counsel. Courtesy of the editors.

C. S. Lewis and Major Warren H. Lewis on vacation in Ireland, 1949.

Top: Entrance to Holy Trinity Church, the parish church of Headington Quarry, Oxford, where the Lewis brothers worshiped. The path in the foreground is where Lewis was struck by the idea of writing letters by a senior devil teaching a junior devil the art of temptation. That idea became Lewis's best-selling book *The Screwtape Letters*. Lewis's funeral service was held here, and he is buried with his brother in the churchyard. Courtesy of the editors.

Bottom: The interior of Holy Trinity Church. Lewis's accustomed pew is behind the front pillar, which obscured his view of the pulpit. Courtesy of Steve Connor, used by permission.

Joy Davidman Lewis, the wife of C. S. Lewis.

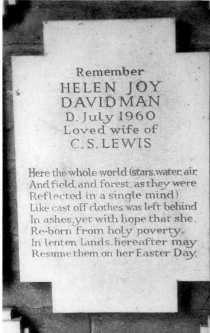

Remember
HELEN JOY
DAVIDMAN
D. July 1960
Loved wife of
C.S.LEWIS

Here the whole world (stars.water. air,
And field, and forest. as they were
Reflected in a single mind)
Like cast off clothes was left behind
In ashes, yet with hope that she,
Re-born from holy poverty,
In lenten lands. hereafter may
Resume them on her Easter Day.

Lower left: Plaque with poem by C. S. Lewis commemorating the death of Joy Davidman Lewis, his wife. Courtesy of Peter Cousin; used by permission.

Top: The Kilns, Headington, Oxford, Lewis's home for 33 years; where he died on 22 November 1963.

Lower right: Grave of C. S. Lewis and his brother, Major Warren H. Lewis, in the yard of Holy Trinity Church, Headington, Oxford.

823
Jargon
Poems, "The Prudent
Jailer" (1947), p. 78.

Stone walls cannot a prison make
Half so secure as rigmarole.

824
Jesus: Creator
Perelandra, chap. 17,
pp. 216–217.

"Each grain, if it spoke, would say, I am at the
centre; for me all things were made. Let no
mouth open to gainsay it. Blessed be He!"

"Each grain is at the centre. The Dust is at the
centre. The Worlds are at the centre. The beasts
are at the centre. The ancient peoples are there.
The race that sinned is there. Tor and Tinidril are
there. The gods are there also. Blessed be He!"

"Where Maleldil is, there is the centre. He is in
every place. Not some of Him in one place and
some in another, but in each place the whole
Maleldil, even in the smallness beyond thought.
There is no way out of the centre save into the
Bent Will which casts itself into the Nowhere.
Blessed be He!"

"Each thing was made for Him. He is the
centre. Because we are with Him, each of us is at
the centre. It is not as in a city of the Darkened
World where they say that each must live for all.
In His city all things are made for each. When He
died in the Wounded World He died not for men,
but for each man. If each man had been the only
man made, He would have done no less. Each

---

thing, from the single grain of Dust to the strongest eldil, is the end and the final cause of all creation and the mirror in which the beam of His brightness comes to rest and so returns to Him. Blessed be He!"

825

Jesus: Creator/Word

Miracles, chap. 10, para. 15, p. 76.

In the New Testament [the] "Son" is identified with the Discourse or Reason or Word which was eternally "with God" and yet also *was* God. He is the all-pervasive principle of concretion or cohesion whereby the universe holds together. All things, and specially Life, arose *within* Him, and within Him all things will reach their conclusion—the final statement of what they have been trying to express.

826

Jesus: Death of

The Weight of Glory, "Membership" (1945), para. 16, p. 117.

It was not for societies or states, that Christ died, but for men.

827

Jesus, Death of

Letters to Malcolm: Chiefly on Prayer, chap. 8, para. 12, p. 44.

The "hiddenness" of God perhaps presses most painfully on those who are in another way nearest to Him, and therefore God Himself, made man, will of all men be by God most forsaken?

828

Jesus: God, Lunatic, or Evil Man

God in the Dock, "Christian Apologetics" (1945), para. 27, p. 101.

When we come to the Incarnation itself, I usually find that some form of the *aut Deus aut malus homo* [either God or a bad man] can be used. The majority of them start with the idea of the "great human teacher" who was deified by his superstitious followers. It must be pointed out how very improbable this is among Jews and how different to anything that happened with Plato, Confucius, Buddha, Mohammed. The Lord's own words and claims (of which many are quite ignorant) must be forced home.

829

Jesus: God, Lunatic, or Evil Man

God in the Dock, "What Are We to Make of Jesus Christ?" (1950), para. 3, pp. 157–158.

On the one side clear, definite moral teaching. On the other, claims which, if not true, are those of a megalomaniac, compared with whom Hitler was the most sane and humble of men. There is no half-way house and there is no parallel in other religions. If you had gone to Buddha and asked him "Are you the son of Bramah?" he would have said, "My son, you are still in the vale of illusion." If you had gone to Socrates and asked, "Are you Zeus?" he would have laughed at you. If you had gone to Mohammed and asked, "Are you Allah?" he would first have rent his clothes and then cut your head off. If you had asked Confucius, "Are you Heaven?" I think he would have probably replied, "Remarks which are not in accordance with nature are in bad taste." The idea of a great moral teacher saying what Christ said is out of the question. In my opinion, the only person who can say that sort of thing is either God or a complete lunatic suffering from that form of delusion which undermines the whole mind of man. If you think you are a poached egg, when you are looking for a piece of toast to suit you, you may be sane, but if you think you are God, there is no chance for you. We may note in passing that He was never regarded as a mere moral teacher. He did not produce that effect on any of the people who actually met Him. He produced mainly three effects—Hatred—Terror—Adoration. There was no trace of people expressing mild approval.

830

Jesus: God, Lunatic, or Evil Man

Mere Christianity, bk. II, chap. 3, para. 11, 13, pp. 55–56.

Jesus . . . told people that their sins were forgiven. . . . This makes sense only if He really was the God whose laws are broken and whose love is wounded in every sin.

. . . I am trying here to prevent anyone saying the really foolish thing that people often say about Him: "I'm ready to accept Jesus as a great moral teacher, but I don't accept His claim to be God." That is the one thing we must not say. A man who was merely a man and said the sort of things Jesus said would not be a great moral teacher. He would either be a lunatic—on a level with the man who says he is a poached egg—or else he would be the Devil of Hell. You can shut Him up for a fool, you can spit at Him and kill Him as a demon; or you can fall at His feet and call Him Lord and God. But let us not come with any patronising nonsense about His being a great human teacher. He has not left that open to us. He did not intend to.

831

Jesus: Relationship to the Father

Mere Christianity, bk. IV, chap. 4, para. 4, p. 151.

We must think of the Son always, so to speak, streaming forth from the Father, like light from a lamp, or heat from a fire, or thoughts from a mind. He is the self-expression of the Father— what the Father has to say. And there never was a time when He was not saying it.

832

Jesus: Savior

God in the Dock, "What Are We to Make of Jesus Christ?" (1950), para. 8–9, p. 160.

"What are we to make of Christ?" There is no question of what we can make of Him, it is entirely a question of what He intends to make of us. You must accept or reject the story.

The things He says are very different from what any other teacher has said. Others say, "This is the truth about the Universe. This is the way you ought to go," but He says, "*I* am the Truth, and the Way, and the Life." He says, "No man can reach absolute reality, except through Me. Try to retain your own life and you will be inevitably ruined. Give yourself away and you will be saved." He says, "If you are ashamed of Me, if, when you hear this call, you turn the other way, I also will look the other way when I come again as God without disguise. If anything whatever is keeping you from God and from Me, whatever it is, throw it away. If it is your eye, pull it out. If it is your hand, cut it off. If you put yourself first you will be last. Come to Me everyone who is carrying a heavy load, I will set that right. Your sins, all of them, are wiped out, I can do that. I am Re-birth, I am Life. Eat Me, drink Me, I am your Food. And finally, do not be afraid, I have overcome the whole Universe." That is the issue.

833
Jesus: Savior
Letters of C. S. Lewis
(1951?), para. 1,
pp. 234–235.

When people object, as you do, that if Jesus was God as well as Man, then He had an unfair advantage which deprives Him for them of all value, it seems to me as if a man struggling in the water shd. refuse a rope thrown to him by another who had one foot on the bank, saying "Oh but you have an unfair advantage." It is because of that advantage that He can help. But all good wishes; we must just differ; in charity I hope. You must not be angry with me for believing, you know; I'm not angry with you.

834
Jesus: Savior
Mere Christianity, bk. II,
chap. 5, para. 1,
p. 62.

The perfect surrender and humiliation were undergone by Christ: perfect because He was God, surrender and humiliation because He was man. Now the Christian belief is that if we somehow share the humility and suffering of Christ we shall also share in His conquest of death and find a new life after we have died and in it become perfect, and perfectly happy, creatures. This means something much more than our trying to follow His teaching. People often ask when the next step in evolution—the step to something beyond man—will happen. But on the Christian view, it has happened already. In Christ a new kind of man appeared: and the new kind of life which began in Him is to be put into us.

835
Jesus: Second Coming
The World's Last Night and Other Essays, "The World's Last Night" (1952), para. 1, p. 93.

It seems to me impossible to retain in any recognisable form our belief in the Divinity of Christ and the truth of the Christian revelation while abandoning, or even persistently neglecting, the promised, and threatened, Return. "He shall come again to judge the quick and the dead," says the Apostles' Creed. "This same Jesus," said the angels in Acts, "shall so come in like manner as ye have seen him go into heaven." "Hereafter," said our Lord himself (by those words inviting crucifixion), "shall ye see the Son of Man . . . coming in the clouds of heaven." If this is not an integral part of the faith once given to the saints, I do not know what is.

836
Jesus: Second Coming
The World's Last Night and Other Essays, "The World's Last Night" (1952), para. 4, pp. 94–95.

For my own part I hate and distrust reactions not only in religion but in everything. Luther surely spoke very good sense when he compared humanity to a drunkard who, after falling off his horse on the right, falls off it the next time on the left. . . . If it [the doctrine of the second coming] has recently been exaggerated, we must now take special care not to overlook it; for that is the side on which the drunk man is now most likely to fall off.

837
Jesus: Second Coming
The World's Last Night and Other Essays, "The World's Last Night" (1952), para. 12, pp. 100–101.

The doctrine of the Second Coming is deeply uncongenial to the whole evolutionary or developmental character of modern thought. We have been taught to think of the world as something that grows slowly towards perfection, something that "progresses" or "evolves." Christian Apocalyptic offers us no such hope. It does not even foretell (which would be more tolerable to our habits of thought) a gradual decay. It foretells a sudden, violent end imposed from without; an extinguisher popped onto the candle, a brick flung at the gramophone, a curtain rung down on the play—"Halt!"

838
Jesus: Second Coming
The World's Last Night and Other Essays, "The World's Last Night" (1952), para. 23, p. 106.

It [the second coming of Christ] is the medicine our condition especially needs.

839
Jesus: Second Coming
The World's Last Night and Other Essays, "The World's Last Night" (1952), para. 26, p. 107.

We must never speak to simple, excitable people about "the Day" without emphasizing again and again the utter impossibility of prediction. We must try to show them that that impossibility is an essential part of the doctrine. If you do not believe our Lord's words, why do you believe in his return at all? And if you do believe them must you not put away from you, utterly and forever, any hope of dating that return? His teaching on the subject quite clearly consisted of three propositions. (1) That he will certainly return. (2) That we cannot possibly find out when. (3) And that therefore we must always be ready for him.

840
Jesus: Second Coming
The World's Last Night and Other Essays, "The World's Last Night" (1952), para. 27, p. 107.

Precisely because we cannot predict the moment, we must be ready at all moments.

841
Jesus: Second Coming
The World's Last Night and Other Essays, "The World's Last Night" (1952), para. 31, p. 110.

What is important is not that we should always fear (or hope) about the End but that we should always remember, always take it into account. An analogy may here help. A man of seventy need not be always feeling (much less talking) about his approaching death: but a wise man of seventy should always take it into account. He would be foolish to embark on schemes which presuppose twenty more years of life: he would be criminally foolish not to make—indeed, not to have made long since—his will. Now, what death is to each man, the Second Coming is to the whole human race.

842
Jesus: Son of God
The Problem of Pain, chap. 1, para. 14, pp. 23–24.

There was a man born among these Jews who claimed to be, or to be the son of, or to be "one with," the Something which is at once the awful haunter of nature and the giver of the moral law. The claim is so shocking—a paradox, and even a horror, which we may easily be lulled into taking too lightly—that only two views of this man are possible. Either he was a raving lunatic of an unusually abominable type, or else He was, and is, precisely what He said. There is no middle way. If the records make the first hypothesis unacceptable, you must submit to the second. And if you do that, all else that is claimed by Christians becomes credible—that this Man, having been killed, was yet alive, and that His death, in some manner incomprehensible to human thought, has effected a real change in our relations to the "awful" and "righteous" Lord, and a change in our favour.

843

Jesus:
Son of God
Christian Reflections,
"The Language of
Religion" (1st pub. 1967),
para. 18, p. 137.

Christians believe that Jesus Christ is the Son of God because He said so. The other evidence about Him has convinced them that He was neither a lunatic nor a quack.

844

Jesus:
Teaching
God in the Dock,
"Dangers of National
Repentance" (1940),
para. 4, p. 191.

The hard sayings of our Lord are wholesome to those only who find them hard.

845

Jesus:
Teaching
Miracles, chap. 14,
para. 2, pp. 108–109.

The historical difficulty of giving for the life, sayings and influence of Jesus any explanation that is not harder than the Christian explanation, is very great. The discrepancy between the depth and sanity and (let me add) *shrewdness* of His moral teaching and the rampant megalomania which must lie behind His theological teaching unless He is indeed God, has never been satisfactorily got over. Hence the non-Christian hypotheses succeed one another with the restless fertility of bewilderment.

846
Jesus:
Teaching
Reflections on the Psalms,
chap. 11, para. 13,
p. 119.

Yet it is, perhaps, idle to speak here of spirit and letter. There is almost no "letter" in the words of Jesus. Taken by a literalist, He will always prove the most elusive of teachers. Systems cannot keep up with that darting illumination. No net less wide than a man's whole heart, nor less fine of mesh than love, will hold the sacred Fish.

847
Jesus:
Unfallen
Letters: C. S. Lewis/Don Giovanni Calabria (10 September 1949), para. 4, p. 57.

Cease not to make mention of me before our common Lord (true God and the only true Man—for all we others, since the Fall of Adam, are but half men).

848
Jesus:
Unfallen
The Four Loves, chap. 3, para. 44, p. 81.

Greed, egoism, self-deception and self-pity are not unnatural or abnormal in the same sense as astigmatism or a floating kidney. For who, in Heaven's name, would describe as natural or normal the man from whom these failings were wholly absent? "Natural," if you like, in a quite different sense; archnatural, unfallen. We have seen only one such Man. And He was not at all like the psychologist's picture of the integrated, balanced, adjusted, happily married, employed, popular citizen. You can't really be very well "adjusted" to your world if it says you "have a devil" and ends by nailing you up naked to a stake of wood.

849
Jews
Letters of C. S. Lewis (1921?), para. 1, p. 58.

[Ed. note: Prior to his conversion, Lewis had some negative ideas about Jews. Note the subsequent change in this attitude. Late in life, he married Joy Davidman Gresham, a Jewish convert to Christianity.] I wonder will you ever get to the end of the Bible; the undesirable "primitives" around you will enable you to appreciate the Hebrews who were class A primitives after all.

850
Jews
The Letters of C. S. Lewis to Arthur Greeves (5 November 1933), para. 7, p. 468.

I might agree that the Allies are partly to blame, but nothing can fully excuse the iniquity of Hitler's persecution of the Jews, or the absurdity of his theoretical position. Did you see that he said "The Jews have made *no contribution to human culture* and in crushing them I am doing the *will of the Lord*." Now as the whole idea of the "Will of the Lord" is precisely what the world owes to the Jews, the blaspheming tyrant has just fixed his absurdity for all to see in a single sentence, and shown that he is as contemptible for his stupidity as he is detestable for his cruelty. For the German people as a whole we ought to have charity: but for dictators, "Nordic" tyrants and so on—well, read the chapter about Mr. Savage in the *Regress* [Lewis's *The Pilgrim's Regress*] and you have my views.

851
Jews
Letters of C. S. Lewis (16 July 1940), para. 2, p. 188.

My enjoyment of the Psalms has been greatly increased lately. The point has been made before, but let me make it again: what an admirable thing it is in the divine economy that the sacred literature of the world shd. have been entrusted to a people whose poetry, depending largely on parallelism, shd. remain poetry in any language you translate it into.

852
Jews
Letters of C. S. Lewis (10 April 1941), para. 2, p. 193.

. . . your Hebraic background, which I envy you.

853

Jews

Letters of C. S. Lewis (14
May 1955), para. 3,
p. 263.

I think myself that the shocking reply to the Syrophenician woman (it came alright in the end) is to remind all us Gentile Christians—who forget it easily enough and even flirt with anti-Semitism—that the Hebrews are spiritually *senior* to us, that God *did* entrust the descendants of Abraham with the first revelation of Himself.

854

Jews

Letters of C. S. Lewis (6
December 1956), para. 2,
p. 272.

I've been much struck in conversation with a Jewess by the extent to which Jews see humour in the O.T. where we don't. Humour varies so much from culture to culture.

855

**Johnson,
Samuel**

*The Letters of C. S.
Lewis to Arthur Greeves*
(22 June 1930), para. 6,
p. 364.

I am delighted to hear that you have taken to Johnson. Yes, isn't it a magnificent style—the very essence of manliness and condensation. I find Johnson very *bracing* when I am in my slack, self pitying mood. The amazing thing is his power of stating platitudes—or what in anyone else wd. be platitudes—so that we really believe them at last and realise their importance. Doesn't it remind you a bit of Handel? As to his critical judgement I think he is always sensible and nearly always wrong. He has no ear for metre and little imagination. I personally get more pleasure from the *Rambler* than from anything else of his & at one time I used to read a Rambler every evening as a nightcap. They are so *quieting* in their brave, sensible dignity.

856

Joy

Perelandra, chap. 6,
p. 83.

"Every joy is beyond all others. The fruit we are eating is always the best fruit of all."

857
**Joy: As
Sehnsucht or
Longing**
The Letters of C. S.
Lewis to Arthur Greeves
(21 March 1916), para.
7, p. 97.

I know quite well that feeling of something
strange and wonderful that ought to happen, and
wish I could think like you that this hope will
someday be fulfilled. . . . Perhaps indeed the
chance of a change into some world of Terreauty
(a word I've coined to mean terror and beauty) is
in reality in some allegorical way daily offered to
us if we had the courage to take it. I mean one
has occasionally felt that this cowardice, this
human loathing of spirits just because they are
such may be keeping doors shut? Who knows?

858
**Joy: As
Sehnsucht or
Longing**
Narrative Poems,
"Dymer" (1st pub. 1926),
verse 10, p. 48.

Can it be possible
That joy flows through and, when the course is
   run
It leaves no change, no mark on us to tell
Its passing? And as poor as we've begun
We end the richest day? What we have won
Can it all die like this? . . . Joy flickers on
The razor-edge of the present and is gone.

859
**Joy: As
Sehnsucht or
Longing**
The Pilgrim's Regress,
Preface, para. 12–13,
pp. 7–8.

"Romanticism" . . . was a particular recurrent
experience which dominated my childhood and
adolescence and which I hastily called "Romantic"
because inanimate nature and marvellous literature
were among the things that evoked it. I still
believe that the experience is common, commonly
misunderstood, and of immense importance: but I
know now that in other minds it arises under
other *stimuli* and is entangled with other
irrelevancies and that to bring it into the forefront
of consciousness is not so easy as I once
supposed. I will now try to describe it sufficiently
to make the following pages intelligible.
   The experience is one of intense longing. . . .
This hunger is better than any other fullness; this

poverty better than all other wealth. And thus it comes about, that if the desire is long absent, it may itself be desired, and that new desiring becomes a new instance of the original desire.

860
Joy: As Sehnsucht or Longing
The Pilgrim's Regress, Preface, para. 17, p. 10.

The human soul was made to enjoy some object that is never fully given—nay, cannot even be imagined as given—in our present mode of subjective and spatio-temporal experience.

861
Joy: As Sehnsucht or Longing
The Pilgrim's Regress, bk. 1, chap. 2, pp. 24–25.

[Ed. note: The "island" in *The Pilgrim's Regress* is the symbol of desire, and desire itself properly understood is the longing for God which is common to all and pursued by some.] Then came the sound of a musical instrument, from behind it seemed, very sweet and very short, as if it were one plucking of a string or one note of a bell, and after it a full, clear voice—and it sounded so high and strange that he thought it was very far away, further than a star. The voice said, Come. Then John . . . saw a green wood full of primroses: and he remembered suddenly how he had gone into another wood to pull primroses, as a child, very long ago—so long that even in the moment of remembering the memory seemed still out of reach. While he strained to grasp it, there came to him from beyond the wood a sweetness and a pang so piercing that instantly he forgot his father's house, and his mother, and the fear of the Landlord, and the burden of the rules. All the furniture of his mind was taken away. A moment later he found that he was sobbing, and the sun had gone in: and what it was that had happened to him he could not quite remember, nor whether it had happened in this wood, or in the other wood when he was a child. It seemed to him that a mist which hung at the far end of the wood had parted for a moment, and through the rift he had seen a calm sea, and in the sea an island. . . . Presently he went home, with a sad excitement upon him, repeating to himself a thousand times, "I know now what I want." The first time that he said it, he was aware that it was not entirely true: but before he went to bed he was believing it.

862

Joy: As Sehnsucht or Longing

The Pilgrim's Regress, bk. 3, chap. 2, pp. 52–53.

"It was what you *really* wanted all the time."

"No, no," cried John. "I know you are wrong there. I grant you, that—that sort of thing—is what I always *get* if I think too long about the Island. But it can't be what I *want*."

"No? Why not?"

"If it is what I wanted, why am I so disappointed when I get it? If what a man really wanted was food, how could he be disappointed when the food arrived?"

863

Joy: As Sehnsucht or Longing

The Pilgrim's Regress, bk. 7, chap. 9, p. 128.

What does not satisfy when we find it, was not the thing we were desiring.

864

Joy: As Sehnsucht or Longing

The Pilgrim's Regress, bk. 3, chap. 9, pp. 156–157.

"What is universal is not the particular picture, but the arrival of some message, not perfectly intelligible, which wakes this desire and sets men longing for something East or West of the world: something possessed, if at all, only in the act of desiring it, and lost so quickly that the craving itself becomes craved; something that tends inevitably to be confused with common or even with vile satisfactions lying close to hand, yet which is able, if any man faithfully live through the dialectic of its successive births and deaths, to lead him at last where true joys are to be found."

865
Joy: As Sehnsucht or Longing
Christian Reflections, "Christianity and Culture" (1940), p. 23n.

I am quite ready to describe *Sehnsucht* as "spilled religion," provided it is not forgotten that the spilled drops may be full of blessing to the unconverted man who licks them up, and therefore begins to search for the cup whence they were spilled. For the drops will be taken by some whose stomachs are not yet sound enough for the full draught.

866
Joy: As Sehnsucht or Longing
The Weight of Glory, "The Weight of Glory" (1941), chap. 1, para. 1, pp. 3–4.

If there lurks in most modern minds the notion that to desire our own good and earnestly to hope for the enjoyment of it is a bad thing, I submit that this notion has crept in from Kant and the Stoics and is no part of the Christian faith. Indeed, if we consider the unblushing promises of reward and the staggering nature of the rewards promised in the Gospels, it would seem that Our Lord finds our desires, not too strong, but too weak. We are half-hearted creatures, fooling about with drink and sex and ambition when infinite joy is offered us, like an ignorant child who wants to go on making mud pies in a slum because he cannot imagine what is meant by the offer of a holiday at the sea. We are far too easily pleased.

867
Joy: As Sehnsucht or Longing
The Weight of Glory,
"The Weight of Glory"
(1941), chap. 1, para. 5,
pp. 6–7.

In speaking of this desire for our own far-off country, which we find in ourselves even now, I feel a certain shyness. I am almost committing an indecency. I am trying to rip open the inconsolable secret in each one of you—the secret which hurts so much that you take your revenge on it by calling it names like Nostalgia and Romanticism and Adolescence; the secret also which pierces with such sweetness that when, in very intimate conversation, the mention of it becomes imminent, we grow awkward and affect to laugh at ourselves; the secret we cannot hide and cannot tell, though we desire to do both. We cannot tell it because it is a desire for something that has never actually appeared in our experience. We cannot hide it because our experience is constantly suggesting it, and we betray ourselves like lovers at the mention of a name. Our commonest expedient is to call it beauty and behave as if that had settled the matter. Wordsworth's expedient was to identify it with certain moments in his own past. But all this is a cheat. If Wordsworth had gone back to those moments in the past, he would not have found the thing itself, but only the reminder of it; what he remembered would turn out to be itself a remembering. The books or the music in which we thought the beauty was located will betray us if we trust to them; it was not *in* them, it only came *through* them, and what came through them was longing. These things—the beauty, the memory of our own past—are good images of what we really desire; but if they are mistaken for the thing itself they turn into dumb idols, breaking the hearts of their worshippers. For they are not the thing itself; they are only the scent of a flower we have not found, the echo of a tune we have not heard, news from a country we have never yet visited. Do you think I am trying to weave a spell? Perhaps I am; but remember your fairy tales. Spells are used for breaking enchantments as well as for inducing them. And you and I have need of the strongest spell that can be found to wake us from the evil enchantment of worldliness which has been laid upon us for nearly a hundred years.

868
Joy: As Sehnsucht or Longing
The Weight of Glory,
"The Weight of Glory"
(1941), chap. 1, para.
11–12, pp. 15–16.

The sense that in this universe we are treated as strangers, the longing to be acknowledged, to meet with some response, to bridge some chasm that yawns between us and reality, is part of our inconsolable secret. And surely, from this point of view, the promise of glory, in the sense described, becomes highly relevant to our deep desire. For glory meant good report with God, acceptance by God, response, acknowledgment, and welcome into the heart of things. The door on which we have been knocking all our lives will open at last.
. . . Apparently, then, our lifelong nostalgia, our longing to be reunited with something in the universe from which we now feel cut off, to be on the inside of some door which we have always seen from the outside, is no mere neurotic fancy, but the truest index of our real situation. And to be at last summoned inside would be both glory and honour beyond all our merits and also the healing of that old ache.

869
Joy: As Sehnsucht or Longing
The Weight of Glory,
"The Weight of Glory"
(1942), chap. 1, para. 14,
p. 18.

The whole man is to drink joy from the fountain of joy.

870
Joy: As Sehnsucht or Longing
Present Concerns: Essays by C. S. Lewis, "Talking About Bicycles" (1946), para. 6–9, p. 68.

"Sounds like a carrot in front of a donkey's nose," said I.

"Even that wouldn't be quite a cheat if the donkey enjoyed the smell of carrots as much as, or more than, the taste. Or suppose the smell raised in the donkey emotions which no actual eating could ever satisfy? Wouldn't he look back (when he was an old donkey, living in the fourth age) and say, 'I'm glad I had that carrot tied in front of my nose. Otherwise I might still have thought eating was the greatest happiness. Now I know there's something far better—the something that came to me in the smell of the carrot. And I'd rather have known that—even if I'm never to get it—than not to have known it, for even to have wanted it is what makes life worth having.'"

"I don't think a donkey would feel like that at all."

"No. Neither a four-legged donkey nor a two-legged one. But I have a suspicion that to feel that way is the real mark of a human."

871
Joy: As Sehnsucht or Longing
The Lion, the Witch and the Wardrobe, chap. 7, p. 64–65.

Perhaps it has sometimes happened to you in a dream that someone says something which you don't understand but in the dream it feels as if it had some enormous meaning—either a terrifying one which turns the whole dream into a nightmare or else a lovely meaning too lovely to put into words, which makes the dream so beautiful that you remember it all your life and are always wishing you could get into that dream again. It was like that now. At the name of Aslan each one of the children felt something jump in his inside. . . . Susan felt as if some delicious smell or some delightful strain of music had just floated by her. And Lucy got the feeling you have when you wake up in the morning and realise that it is the beginning of the holidays or the beginning of summer.

872
Joy: As Sehnsucht or Longing
Narrative Poems, Preface to "Dymer" (1950), para. 5, p. 4.

From at least the age of six, romantic longing—*Sehnsucht*—had played an unusually central part in my experience. Such longing is in itself the very reverse of wishful thinking: it is more like thoughtful wishing.

873
Joy: As Sehnsucht or Longing
Surprised by Joy, chap. 1, para. 4, p. 7.

Once in those very early days my brother brought into the nursery the lid of a biscuit tin which he had covered with moss and garnished with twigs and flowers so as to make it a toy garden or a toy forest. That was the first beauty I ever knew. What the real garden had failed to do, the toy garden did. It made me aware of nature—not, indeed, as a storehouse of forms and colors but as something cool, dewy, fresh, exuberant. I do not think the impression was very important at the moment, but it soon became important in memory. As long as I live my imagination of Paradise will retain something of my brother's toy garden. And every day there were what we called "the Green Hills"; that is, the low line of the Castlereagh Hills which we saw from the nursery windows. They were not very far off but they were, to children, quite unattainable. They taught me longing—Sehnsucht; made me for good or ill, and before I was six years old, a votary of the Blue Flower.

874
Joy: As Sehnsucht or Longing
Surprised by Joy, chap. 1, para. 18, pp. 17–18.

In a sense the central story of my life is about nothing else. . . . it is that of an unsatisfied desire which is itself more desirable than any other satisfaction. I call it Joy, which is here a technical term and must be sharply distinguished both from Happiness and from Pleasure. Joy (in my sense) has indeed one characteristic, and one only, in common with them; the fact that anyone who has experienced it will want it again. Apart from that and considered only in its quality, it might almost equally well be called a particular kind of unhappiness or grief. But then it is a kind we want. I doubt whether anyone who has tasted it would ever, if both were in his power, exchange it for all the pleasures in the world. But then Joy is never in our power and pleasure often is.

875
Joy: As Sehnsucht or Longing
Surprised by Joy, chap. 5, para. 2, p. 72.

Joy is distinct not only from pleasure in general but even from aesthetic pleasure. It must have the stab, the pang, the inconsolable longing.

876
Joy: As Sehnsucht or Longing
Surprised by Joy, chap. 5, para. 10, p. 78.

All Joy reminds. It is never a possession, always a desire for something longer ago or further away or still "about to be."

877
Joy: As Sehnsucht or Longing
Surprised by Joy, chap. 11, para. 6, p. 170.

Joy is not a substitute for sex; sex is very often a substitute for Joy. I sometimes wonder whether all pleasures are not substitutes for Joy.

878
Joy: As Sehnsucht or Longing
Surprised by Joy, chap. 14, para. 11, pp. 219–220.

I saw that all my waitings and watchings for Joy, all my vain hopes to find some mental content on which I could, so to speak, lay my finger and say, "This is it," had been a futile attempt to contemplate the enjoyed. All that such watching and waiting ever *could* find would be either an image (Asgard, the Western Garden, or what not) or a quiver in the diaphragm. I should never have to bother again about these images or sensations. I knew now that they were merely the mental track left by the passage of Joy—not the wave but the wave's imprint on the sand. The inherent dialectic of desire itself had in a way already shown me this; for all images and sensations, if idolatrously mistaken for Joy itself, soon honestly confessed themselves inadequate. All said, in the last resort, "It is not I, I am only a reminder. Look! Look! What do I remind you of?"

879
Joy: As Sehnsucht or Longing
Surprised by Joy, chap. 15, para. 10, p. 238.

But what, in conclusion, of Joy? for that, after all, is what the story has mainly been about. To tell you the truth, the subject has lost nearly all interest for me since I became a Christian. I cannot, indeed, complain, like Wordsworth, that the visionary gleam has passed away. I believe (if the thing were at all worth recording) that the old stab, the old bittersweet, has come to me as often and as sharply since my conversion as at any time of my life whatever. But I now know that the experience, considered as a state of my own mind, had never had the kind of importance I once gave it. It was valuable only as a pointer to something other and outer. While that other was in doubt, the pointer naturally loomed large in my thoughts. When we are lost in the woods the sight of a signpost is a great matter. He who first sees it cries, "Look!" The whole party gathers round and stares. But when we have found the road and are passing signposts every few miles, we shall not stop and stare. They will encourage us and we shall be grateful to the authority that set them up. But we shall not stop and stare, or not much; not on this road, though their pillars are of silver and their lettering of gold. "We would be at Jerusalem."

880
Joy: As Sehnsucht or Longing
Letters of C. S. Lewis
(5 November 1959),
p. 289.

All joy (as distinct from mere pleasure, still more amusement) emphasises our pilgrim status; always reminds, beckons, awakens desire. Our best havings are wantings.

881
Joy: As Sehnsucht or Longing
Letters to Malcolm: Chiefly on Prayer, chap.
17, para. 17, p. 93.

In this world everything is upside down. That which, if it could be prolonged here, would be a truancy, is likest that which in a better country is the End of ends. Joy is the serious business of Heaven.

882
Judgment, The Last
The Last Battle, chap.
14, pp. 153–154.

As they came right up to Aslan one or other of two things happened to each of them. They all looked straight in his face; I don't think they had any choice about that. And when some looked, the expression of their faces changed terribly—it was fear and hatred: except that, on the faces of Talking Beasts, the fear and hatred lasted only for a fraction of a second. You could see that they suddenly ceased to be *Talking* Beasts. They were just ordinary animals. And all the creatures who looked at Aslan in that way swerved to their right, his left, and disappeared into his huge black shadow, which (as you have heard) streamed away to the left of the doorway. The children never saw

---

them again. I don't know what became of them. But the others looked in the face of Aslan and loved him, though some of them were very frightened at the same time. And all these came in at the Door, in on Aslan's right. There were some queer specimens among them. Eustace even recognised one of those very Dwarfs who had helped to shoot the Horses. But he had no time to wonder about that sort of thing (and anyway it was no business of his) for a great joy put everything else out of his head.

883
Jungian Criticism
Selected Literary Essays,
"Psycho-Analysis and
Literary Criticism"
(1942), para. 30–31,
pp. 299–300.

The emotional power of Jung's essay [on "Mind and the Earth"] is, as far as it goes, a proof that he is quite right in claiming that certain images, in whatever material they are embodied, have a strange power to excite the human mind. Every sentence he writes helps to prove this. At the same time we may be cautious about accepting his explanation, since there are some grounds for suspecting that the argument seems plausible not because of its real cogency but because of the powerful emotions it arouses. Has Jung, in fact, worked us into a state of mind in which almost anything, provided it was dim, remote, long buried, and mysterious, would seem (for the moment) an adequate explanation of the "leap in our blood" which responds to great myth?

. . . Jung has not explained the pleasure of entertaining primordial images but exhibited the pleasure of meditating on them and of entertaining, in the process, one particular primordial image, which itself needs explanation as much as any of the others. The *idea* that our sorrow is part of the world's sorrow is, in certain moods, moving enough: the mere *fact* that lots of other people have had toothache does not make toothache less painful.

884
Keats, John:
Endymion
The Letters of C. S.
Lewis to Arthur Greeves
(8 November 1931),
para. 3, p. 429.

I am inclined to think that when Keats wrote Endymion he was not v. certain of his own intention: that he faltered between the myth as his imagination set it before him (full of meaning, but not meaning necessarily decipherable by Keats' intellect) and between various ideas of conscious meanings of his own invention, wh., considering his age and education, were possibly confused and even shallow. There is thus some confusion throughout: and this, along with another fault, prevents it from being a perfect poem.

The other fault is the lack of spiritual experience. He knows about the hunting for "it" and longing and wandering: but he has, as yet, no real idea of what it wd. be if you found it. Hence while Endymion's description to Peona of his unrest, and Endymion's journeying under earth and sea, are wonderful, his actual meetings with Cynthia are (to me) failures: not because they are erotic but because they are erotic in a rather commonplace way—all gasps and exclamations and a sort of suburban flirtatious air. It is horrible to use such words of Keats, but I think he would be the first to agree.

885

Kilns, The

*The Letters of C. S.
Lewis to Arthur Greeves*
(24 December 1930),
para. 6, p. 398.

This house has a good night atmosphere about it: in the sense that I have never been in a place where one was *less* likely to get the creeps: a place *less* sinister. Good life must have been lived here before us. If it is haunted, it is haunted by good spirits.

886

King James Version

*English Literature in the
Sixteenth Century,* bk.
II.I.II, para. 13, p. 215.

The Authorized Version, in fact, haunts our prose not as Mr Eliot haunts modern poetry or as Macaulay used to haunt journalists, but much more as Homer haunts the prose of Plato; that is, as something set apart, like plums in a cake or lace on a frock, not like wine mixing in water. As the metre and dialect set every scrap of Homer apart from the Plato in which it is embedded, so the archaism and sanctity tend to set apart the fragments of scripture embedded in English literature. I am not of course denying that it has some influence of the deeper and less obtrusive kind, but the wonder is that it has so little.

887

Kipling, Rudyard

Selected Literary Essays,
"Kipling's World" (1948),
para. 1–2, 3, 5,
pp. 232–234.

Kipling is intensely loved and hated. Hardly any reader likes him a little.

. . . One moment I am filled with delight at the variety and solidity of his imagination; and then, at the very next moment, I am sick, sick to death, of the whole Kipling world. Of course, one can reach temporary saturation point with any author; there comes an evening when even Boswell or Virgil will do no longer. But one parts from them as a friend: one knows one will want them another day; and in the interval one thinks of them with pleasure. But I mean something quite different from that; I mean a real disenchantment, a recoil which makes the Kipling world for the moment, not dull (it is never that), but unendurable—a heavy, glaring, suffocating monstrosity. . . .

The first cause for my sudden recoil from Kipling, I take to be not the defect but the excess of his art. . . . Sometimes the story has been so compressed that in the completed version it is not quite told. . . . But even when this is not so, the art overreaches itself in another way. Every sentence that did not seem to Kipling perfectly and triumphantly good has been removed. As a result the style tends to be too continuously and obtrusively brilliant. The result is a little fatiguing. Our author gives us no rest: we are bombarded with felicities till they deafen us. There is no elbow room, no leisureliness. We need roughage as well as nourishment in a diet; but there is no roughage in a Kipling story—it is all unrelieved vitamins from the first word to the last. . . .

The fault of which I am here accusing Kipling is one which only a great artist could commit.

888

Kipling, Rudyard

Selected Literary Essays, "Kipling's World" (1948), para. 7, 9, 11, 21, pp. 235, 237, 245.

Kipling is first and foremost the poet of work.

. . . What Kipling chiefly communicates—and it is, for good and for ill, one of the strongest things in the world—is the peculiar relation which men who do the same work have to that work and to one another.

. . . We who are of one trade (whether journalists, soldiers, galley slaves, Indian Civilians, or what you will) know so many things that the outsiders will never, never understand. . . . "We belong." It is a bond which in real life sometimes proves stronger than any other.

. . . I think that nearly all his work (for there are a few, and very valuable exceptions), at all periods is dominated by one master passion. What he loves better than anything in the world is the intimacy within a closed circle—even if it be only a circle of shared misery.

889
Knowledge
Christian Reflections,
"Religion: Reality or
Substitute" (1941),
para. 9, p. 41.

Authority, reason, experience; on these three, mixed in varying proportions all our knowledge depends. The authority of many wise men in many different times and places forbids me to regard the spiritual world as an illusion. My reason, showing me the apparently insoluble difficulties of materialism and proving that the hypothesis of a spiritual world covers far more of the facts with far fewer assumptions, forbids me again. My experience even of such feeble attempts as I have made to live the spiritual life does not lead to the results which the pursuit of an illusion ordinarily leads to, and therefore forbids me yet again. I am not now saying that no one's reason and no one's experience produce different results. I am only trying to put the whole problem the right way round, to make it clear that the value given to the testimony of any feeling must depend on our whole philosophy, not our whole philosophy on a feeling.

890
Knowledge
Taliessin Through Logres,
. . . Arthurian Torso,
"Williams and the
Arthuriad" (1948), chap.
IV, para. 35, p. 340.

Though flesh (in a sense) "knows what spirit knows," only "spirit knows it knows." Only when we look back from supernature do we see what nature really meant.

891
Knowledge
Christian Reflections, "De
Futilitate" (address given
during WW II, 1st pub.
1967), para. 12, p. 62.

The physical sciences, then, depend on the validity of logic just as much as metaphysics or mathematics. If popular thought feels "science" to be different from all other kinds of knowledge because science is experimentally verifiable, popular thought is mistaken. Experimental verification is not a new kind of assurance coming in to supply the deficiencies of mere logic. We should therefore abandon the distinction between scientific and non-scientific thought. The proper distinction is between logical and non-logical thought. I mean, the proper distinction for our present purpose: that purpose being to find whether there is any class of thoughts which has objective value, which is not *merely* a fact about how the human cortex behaves. For that purpose we can make no distinction between science and other logical exercises of thought, for if logic is discredited science must go down along with it.

892
Knox, John
English Literature in the Sixteenth Century, bk. II.I.I, para. 58, 64, pp. 198, 202.

Knox is already becoming the *enfant terrible* of Calvinism; and in the *Admonition* we see both why and how. He imagined that his error lay in just the opposite direction. He thought himself a timid temporizing, culpably gentle preacher. . . . One is tempted to say that no equal instance of self-ignorance is recorded until the moment at which Johnson pronounced himself "a very polite man."

. . . It might be supposed that to read a body of work so occasional, so little varied in subject-matter, and so fierce in temper, was a hard task. In reality, the surprising thing is that it is not harder. He has humour: in places he even has tenderness. . . . It is safe and dependable prose; a better prose than any (except Tyndale's) which we have met in this chapter. It is not the style that keeps readers away from John Knox.

893
Labels
Reflections on the Psalms,
chap. 11, para. 2, p. 109.

I have been suspected of being what is called a Fundamentalist. That is because I never regard any narrative as unhistorical simply on the ground that it includes the miraculous.

894
Lamb,
Charles
Letters to Children (16 January 1954), para. 2, p. 37.

You'll find his letters as good as his essays: indeed they are almost exactly the same, only more of it.

895
Language
God in the Dock,
" 'Horrid Red Things' "
(1944), para. 9, p. 71.

All language, except about objects of sense, is metaphorical through and through. To call God a "Force" (that is, something like a wind or a dynamo) is as metaphorical as to call Him a Father or a King. On such matters we can make our language more polysyllabic and duller: we cannot make it more literal. The difficulty is not peculiar to theologians. Scientists, poets, psychoanalysts, and metaphysicians are all in the same boat.

896
Language
*Present Concerns: Essays
by C. S. Lewis,* "Prudery
and Philology" (1955),
para. 4, p. 88.

Mere description is impossible. Language forces
you to an implicit comment.

897
Language
*Present Concerns: Essays
by C. S. Lewis,* "Prudery
and Philology" (1955),
para. 5, pp. 88–89.

We are sometimes told that everything in the
world can come into literature. This is perhaps
true in some sense. But it is a dangerous truth
unless we balance it with the statement that
nothing can go into literature except words, or (if
you prefer) that nothing can go in except by
becoming words. And words, like every other
medium, have their own proper powers and
limitations.

898
Language
Studies in Words, chap.
1, para. 8, p. 6.

I have an idea of what is good and bad language.
. . . Language is an instrument for communication.
The language which can with the greatest ease
make the finest and most numerous distinctions of
meaning is the best. It is better to have *like* and
love than to have *aimer* for both. It was better to
have the older English distinction between "I
haven't got indigestion" (I am not suffering from it
at the moment) and "I don't have indigestion" (I
am not a dyspeptic) than to level both, as America
has now taught most Englishmen to do, under "I
don't have."

899
Language
The Four Loves, chap. 1,
para. 5, p. 12.

Of course language is not an infallible guide, but
it contains, with all its defects, a good deal of
stored insight and experience. If you begin by
flouting it, it has a way of avenging itself later on.
We had better not follow Humpty Dumpty in
making words mean whatever we please.

900
Language
Studies in Words, chap.
2, para. 1, p. 313.

Language exists to communicate whatever it can communicate. Some things it communicates so badly that we never attempt to communicate them by words if any other medium is available.

901
Language
Studies in Words, chap.
2, para. 3, p. 314.

One of the most important and effective uses of language is the emotional. It is also, of course, wholly legitimate. We do not talk only in order to reason or to inform. We have to make love and quarrel, to propitiate and pardon, to rebuke, console, intercede, and arouse. "He that complains," said Johnson, "acts like a man, like a social being." The real objection lies not against the language of emotion as such, but against language which, being in reality emotional, masquerades—whether by plain hypocrisy or subtler self-deceit—as being something else.

902
Language
Christian Reflections,
"The Language of
Religion" (1st pub. 1967),
para. 3, p. 130.

The superiority of the Scientific description clearly consists in giving for the coldness of the night a precise quantitative estimate which can be tested by an instrument. The test ends all disputes. If the statement survives the test, then various inferences can be drawn from it with certainty: e.g., various effects on vegetable and animal life can be predicted. It is therefore of use in what Bacon calls "operation." We can take action on it. On the other hand it does not, of itself, give us any information about the quality of a cold night, does not tell us what we shall be feeling if we go out of doors. If, having lived all our lives in the tropics, we didn't know what a hard frost was like, the thermometer reading would not of itself inform us. Ordinary language would do that better—"Your ears will ache"—"You'll lose the feeling in your fingers"—"You'll feel as if your ears were coming off."

903
Language
Christian Reflections,
"The Language of
Religion" (1st pub. 1967),
para. 12, p. 135.

I think Poetic language does convey information, but it suffers from two disabilities in comparison with Scientific. (1) It is verifiable or falsifiable only to a limited degree and with a certain fringe of vagueness. . . . In that sense, Scientific statements are, as people say now, far more easily "cashed." But the poet might of course reply that it always will be easier to cash a cheque for 30 shillings than one for 1,000 pounds, that the scientific statements are cheques, in one sense, for very small amounts, giving us, out of the teeming complexity of every concrete reality only "the common measurable features." (2) Such information as Poetic language has to give can be received only if you are ready to meet it half-way. It is no good holding a dialectical pistol to the poet's head and demanding how the deuce a river could have hair, or thought be green, or a woman a red rose.

904
Language
Christian Reflections,
"The Language of
Religion" (1st pub. 1967),
para. 20, p. 138.

To be incommunicable by Scientific language is, so far as I can judge, the normal state of experience.

905
Language
Christian Reflections,
"The Language of
Religion" (1st pub. 1967),
para. 23, p. 140.

The very essence of our life as conscious beings, all day and every day, consists of something which cannot be communicated except by hints, similes, metaphors, and the use of those emotions (themselves not very important) which are pointers to it.

906
Latimer,
Hugh
English Literature in the
Sixteenth Century, bk.
II.I.I, para. 52,
pp. 192–194.

Hugh Latimer's character may be ambiguous or even repellent: his sermons, in their own kind, are resounding successes, "though, to be sure, not very theological." . . . He is one of the purest examples in English of the "popular" preacher in the fullest—if you will, the lowest—sense of that word. . . . He is full of anecdotes, jibes, digression, and simple vituperation; he takes his hearers into his confidence, explains how this or that illustration came into his head, forgets himself and recalls himself; all sounds as if it were extemporaneous. We should probably be naive if we took the style at its face value. An appearance of casualness ("I am no orator as Brutus is") is one of the rhetorician's weapons: and I suspect that everything which seems to fall by chance from Latimer's lips is consciously devised to hold the attention and undermine the resistance of the audience. He establishes intimacy with them in order to sway them. . . . The mere strength and pith and urgency of his sentences, in that age so given to verbiage, is a literary virtue. He is as importunate as Hazlitt. He would have been a fine broadcaster.

907
Law
The Pilgrim's Regress, bk.
8, chap. 8, pp. 152–153.

"Nothing leads back to him which did not at first proceed from him."

". . . The Landlord has circulated other things besides the Rules. What use are Rules to people who cannot read?"

"But nearly everyone can."

"No one is born able to read: so that the starting point for all of us must be a picture and not the Rules. And there are more than you suppose who are illiterate all their lives, or who, at the best, never learn to read well."

"And for those people the pictures are the right thing?"

"I would not quite say that. The pictures alone are dangerous, and the Rules alone are dangerous. That is why the best thing of all is to find Mother Kirk at the beginning, and to live from infancy with a third thing which is neither the Rules nor the pictures and which was brought into the country by the Landlord's Son. That, I say, is the best: never to have known the quarrel between the Rules and the pictures. But it very rarely happens. The Enemy's agents are everywhere at work, spreading illiteracy in one district and blinding men to the pictures in another. . . . As often as men become Pagans again, the Landlord again sends them pictures and stirs up sweet desire and so leads them back to Mother Kirk even as he led the actual Pagans long ago. There is, indeed, no other way."

". . . The Landlord succeeded in getting a lot of messages through."

". . . These pictures woke desire."

". . . And then the Pagans made mistakes. They would keep on trying to get the same picture again: and if it didn't come, they would make copies of it for themselves. Or even if it did come they would try to get out of it not desire but satisfaction."

908

Law

Taliessin Through Logres, . . . Arthurian Torso, "Williams and the Arthuriad" (1948), chap. IV, para. 7, p. 318.

Law can only kill till gospel comes to transcend it; the king's head on the coins is a death's head unless the economic life is ruled by the spirit.

909
Lawrence,
D. H.
Selected Literary Essays,
"What Chaucer Really
Did to 'Il Filostrato'"
(1932), para. 21, p. 44.

For real stagnancy and isolation we must turn to the decorative lakes dug out far inland at such a mighty cost by Mr George Moore; to the more popular corporation swimming-baths of Dr Marie Stopes; or to the teeming marshlands of the late D. H. Lawrence, whose depth the wisest knows not and on whose bank the hart gives up his life rather than plunge in.

910
Lawrence,
D.H.
Selected Literary Essays,
"Four-Letter Words"
(1961), para. 16, p. 174.

It looks as if no nation, age, or class has commonly used four-letter words to "move desire." If that is so, those who thought Lawrence's vocabulary—we are not discussing his over-all tendency—a grave moral danger were presumably mistaken. But still less does it appear that such words have been used for a reverential and (in the old sense) "enthusiastick" treatment of sex. They are the vocabulary either of farce or of vituperation; either innocent, or loaded with the very opposite evil to that which prudes suspect—with a gnostic or Swiftian contempt for the body. Lawrence's usage is not to be reckoned a return to nature from some local or recent inhibition. It is, for good or ill, as artificial, as remote from the linguistic soil, as Euphuism or, a closer comparison, the most desperate parts of *Lyrical Ballads.* Here, as in them, the words may be earthy; this use of them is not. It is a rebellion against language. *Lady Chatterley* has made short work of a prosecution by the Crown. It still has to face more formidable judges. Nine of them, and all goddesses.

911
Laymen
Mere Christianity, bk. III,
chap. 3, para. 3, p. 79.

Some Christians—those who happen to have the right talents—should be economists and statesmen, and . . . all economists and statesmen should be Christians, and . . . their whole efforts in politics and economics should be directed to putting "Do as you would be done by" into action. If that happened, and if we others were really ready to take it, then we should find the Christian solution for our own social problems pretty quickly. . . . The job is really on us, on the laymen.

912

Leadership

Prince Caspian, chap. 11, p. 144.

He led them to the right of the dancing trees— whether they were still dancing nobody knew, for Lucy had her eyes on the Lion and the rest had their eyes on Lucy.

913

Lewis, Albert (C. S. Lewis's Father)

Letters of C. S. Lewis (27 October 1929), para. 2, p. 138.

One of the best things he ever said was the day before I left—four days before his death. As I came in, the day nurse said, "I've just been telling Mr Lewis that he's exactly like my father." Papy: "And how am I like your father?" Nurse, "Why, he's a pessimist." Papy (after a pause): "I suppose he has several daughters."

914

Lewis, C. S.: The Abolition of Man

Letters to an American Lady (20 February 1955), para. 1, p. 39.

I'm so pleased about the *Abolition of Man,* for it is almost my favorite among my books but in general has been almost totally ignored by the public.

915

Lewis, C. S.: Evangelistic Writing

God in the Dock, "Rejoinder to Dr Pittenger" (1958), para. 13, p. 181.

Most of my books are evangelistic.

374

916
**Lewis, C. S.:
His Writing**
*The Letters of C. S.
Lewis to Arthur Greeves*
(4 December 1932),
para. 1, p. 445.

I think I see, from your criticisms, that you like a much more correct, classical, and elaborate manner than I. I aim chiefly at being idiomatic and racy, basing myself on Malory, Bunyan, and Morris, tho' without archaisms: and would usually prefer to use ten words, provided they are honest native words and idiomatically ordered, than one "literary word." To put the thing in a nutshell you want "The man of whom I told you" and I want "The man I told you of."

917
**Lewis, C. S.:
His Writing**
*The Letters of C. S.
Lewis to Arthur Greeves*
(January 1943), para. 2,
p. 495.

As you will have noticed I've been having great luck with my books lately, and it wd. be affectation to pretend I hadn't got much pleasure out of it: but the catch is it increases the amount of letters one has to write almost beyond endurance.

918
**Lewis, C. S.:
His Writing**
God in the Dock, "God in the Dock" (1948),
para. 9, p. 244.

My own work has suffered very much from the incurable intellectualism of my approach. The simple, emotional appeal ("Come to Jesus") is still often successful. But those who, like myself, lack the gift for making it, had better not attempt it.

919
**Lewis, C. S.:
His Writing**
*Letters: C. S. Lewis/Don
Giovanni Calabria*
(14 January 1949),
para. 3-4, pp. 51, 53.

As for my own work, I would not wish to deceive you with vain hope. I am now in my fiftieth year. I feel my zeal for writing, and whatever talent I originally possessed, to be decreasing; nor (I believe) do I please my readers as I used to. I labour under many difficulties. My house is unquiet and devastated by women's quarrels. I have *to dwell in the tents of Kedar.* My aged mother [his "adopted" mother Mrs. Janie Moore], worn out by long infirmity, is my daily care. Pray for me, Father, that I ever bear in mind that profoundly true maxim: "if thou wish to bring others peace, keep thyself in peace."

These things I write not as complaints but lest you should believe I am writing books. If it shall please God that I write more books, blessed be He. If it shall please Him not, again, blessed be He. Perhaps it will be the most wholesome thing for my soul that I lose both fame and skill lest I were to fall into that evil disease, vainglory.

920
Lewis, C. S.:
His Writing
Letters of C. S. Lewis
(22 December 1954),
p. 259.

[Referring to a Christmas gift of specially bound copies of his *Surprised by Joy* and *Mere Christianity* from his publisher:] I never had a handsomer present. . . . Perhaps these two charming volumes will teach me at last to have for the bodies of my own books the same reverence I have for the bodies of all other books. For it is a curious fact that I never can regard them as being really *books*; the boards and print, in however mint a condition, remain a mere pretence behind which one sees the scratchy, inky old MS.

921
Lewis, C. S.:
His Writing
Letters to Children
(6 December 1960),
para. 1-5, pp. 94–95.

1. Why did I become a writer? Chiefly, I think, because my clumsiness or fingers prevented me from making things in any other way. . . .

2. What "inspires" my books? Really I don't know. Does anyone know where exactly an idea comes from? With me all fiction *begins with* pictures in my head. But where the pictures come from I couldn't say.

3. Which of my books do I think most "representational"? Do you mean (a.) Most representative, most typical, most characteristic? or (b.) Most full of "representations" i.e. images? But whichever you mean, surely this is a question not for me but for my readers to decide. Or do you mean simply which do I like best? Now, the

answer wd. be *Till We Have Faces* and *Perelandra*.
4. I have, as usual, dozens of "plans" for books, but I don't know which, if any, of these will come off. Very often a book of mine gets written when I'm tidying a drawer and come across notes for a plan rejected by me years ago and now suddenly realize I can do it after all. This, you see, makes predictions rather difficult!
5. I enjoy writing fiction more than writing anything else. Wouldn't anyone?

922
Lewis, C. S.:
Letters to Malcolm: Chiefly on Prayer
Letters: C. S. Lewis/Don Giovanni Calabria
(5 January 1953), para. 4, p. 73.

I invite your prayers about a work which I now have in hand. I am trying to write a book about private prayers for the use of the laity, especially for those who have been recently converted to the Christian faith and so far are without any sustained and regular habit of prayer. I tackled the job because I saw many no doubt very beautiful books written on this subject of prayer for the religious but few which instruct tiros and those still babes (so to say) in the Faith. I find many difficulties nor do I definitely know whether God wishes me to complete this task or not.

923
Lewis, C. S.:
The Lion, the Witch and the Wardrobe
Letters of C. S. Lewis
(5 March 1951), para. 3, p. 228.

I am glad you all liked *The Lion*. A number of mothers, and still more, schoolmistresses, have decided that it is likely to frighten children, so it is not selling very well. But the real children like it, and I am astonished how some *very* young ones seem to understand it. I think it frightens some adults, but v. few children.

924
Lewis, C. S.:
*The Lion, the
Witch and the
Wardrobe*
*Letters: C. S. Lewis/Don
Giovanni Calabria* (13
September 1951), para.
4–5, p. 65.

I am sending you my tale recently translated into
Italian in which, frankly, I have rather played than
worked. I have given my imagination free rein yet
not, I hope, without regard for edification—for
building up both my neighbour and myself.
I do not know whether you will like this kind of
trifle. But if you do not, perhaps some boy or girl
will like it from among your "good children." [Ed.
note: Lewis's correspondent ran a home for
orphans.]

925
Lewis, C. S.:
*Mere
Christianity*
Letters of C. S. Lewis
(15 May 1941), p. 193.

[Referring to the radio talks that would later
become part of *Mere Christianity*, Lewis here
writes to Sister Penelope, who would speak after
him:] We ought to meet about the BBC talks if
nothing else, as I'm giving four in August. Mine
are *praeparatio evangelica* rather than evangelism,
an attempt to convince people that there is a
moral law, that we disobey it, and that the
existence of a Lawgiver is at least very probable
and also (*unless* you add the Christian doctrine of
the Atonement) that this imports despair rather
than comfort.

926
**Lewis, C. S.:
"Mere
Christianity"
in His Books**
Letters of C. S. Lewis
(16 March 1955),
para. 1, p. 262.

I have always in my books been concerned simply
to put forward "mere" Christianity.

927
Lewis, C. S.:
Out of the
Silent Planet
Letters of C. S. Lewis
9 July 1939), para. 1,
pp. 166–167.

The letter [at the end of *Out of the Silent Planet*] is pure fiction and the "circumstances which put the book out of date" are merely the way of preparing for a sequel. But the danger of "Westonism" I meant to be real. What set me about writing the book was the discovery that a pupil of mine took all that dream of interplanetary colonization quite seriously, and the realization that thousands of people in one way and another depend on some hope of perpetuating and improving the human race for the whole meaning of the universe—that a "scientific" hope of defeating death is a real rival to Christianity.

928
Lewis, C. S.:
Out of the
Silent Planet
Letters of C. S. Lewis
9 July 1939), para. 2,
p. 167.

You will be both grieved and amused to hear that out of about 60 reviews [of *Out of the Silent Planet*] only 2 showed any knowledge that my idea of the fall of the Bent One was anything but an invention of my own. But if there only was someone with a richer talent and more leisure I think that this great ignorance might be a help to the evangelisation of England; any amount of theology can now be smuggled into people's minds under cover of romance without their knowing it.

929
Lewis, C. S.:
Out of the
Silent Planet
Letters of C. S. Lewis
August 1960?), p. 295.

My *Out of the Silent Planet* has no factual basis and is a critique of our own age only as any Christian work is implicitly a critique of any age. I was trying to redeem for genuinely imaginative purposes the form popularly known in this country as "science-fiction" . . . ; just as . . . *Hamlet* redeemed the popular revenge play.

930
Lewis, C. S.:
Perelandra
Letters of C. S. Lewis
(9 November 1941),
p. 195.

I've got Ransom to Venus and through his first conversation with the "Eve" of that world; a difficult chapter. I hadn't realized till I came to write it all the *Ave-Eva* business. I may have embarked on the impossible. This woman has got to combine characteristics which the Fall has put poles apart—she's got to be in some ways like a Pagan goddess and in other ways like the Blessed Virgin. But, if one can get even a fraction of it into words, it is worth doing.

931
Lewis, C. S.:
The Pilgrim's Regress
The Letters of C. S.
Lewis to Arthur Greeves
(25 March 1933),
para. 9, p. 452.

Dents say they will have *Pilgrim's Regress* out by the end of May. I have successfully resisted a foolish idea they had of an illustrated edition—whose price wd. of course have killed any sale it might hope for. But it *is* going to be decorated by a map on the end leaf which I had great fun in drawing the sketch for. I suppose you have no objection to my dedicating the book to you? It is yours by every right—written in your house, read to you as it was written, and celebrating (at least in the most important parts) an experience which I have more in common with you than anyone else. By the bye, you will be interested to hear that in finally revising the MS I did adopt many of your corrections, or at least made alterations where you objected. So if the book is a ghastly failure I shall always say "Ah it's this Arthur business."

932
Lewis, C. S.:
The Pilgrim's Regress
The Letters of C. S.
Lewis to Arthur Greeves
(13 June 1933), para. 6,
p. 454.

I had an extremely kind letter from Reid about the book [*The Pilgrim's Regress*]. I think it is going to be at least as big a failure as *Dymer,* and am consequently trying to take to heart all the things I wrote you when you were bowled over by Reid's decision on your first novel—not entirely without success. [See the first entry under

"Ambition" for an excerpt of the letter Lewis refers to.]

933 **Lewis, C. S.:** *The Pilgrim's Regress* *Letters of C. S. Lewis* (8 November 1939), p. 170.	The Tableland [in *The Pilgrim's Regress*] represents *all* high and dry states of mind, of which High Anglicanism then seemed to me to be one—most of the representatives of it whom I had then met being v. harsh people who called themselves scholastics and appeared to be inspired more by hatred of their fathers' religion than anything else.
934 **Lewis, C. S.:** *The Pilgrim's Regress* *Letters of C. S. Lewis* (19 January 1953), pp. 248–249.	I don't wonder that you got fogged in *Pilgrim's Regress*. It was my first religious book and I didn't then know how to make things easy. I was not even trying to very much, because in those days I never dreamed I would become a "popular" author and hoped for no readers outside a small "highbrow" circle. Don't waste your time over it any more. The *poetry* is my own.
935 **Lewis, C. S.:** *The Screwtape Letters* *Letters of C. S. Lewis* (20 July 1940), p. 188.	After the service was over—one could wish these things came more seasonably—I was struck by an idea for a book which I think might be both useful and entertaining. It would be called "As one Devil to another" and would consist of letters from an elderly retired devil to a young devil who has just started work on his first "patient." The idea would be to give all the psychology of temptation from the other point of view.
936 **Lewis, C. S.:** *The Screwtape Letters* *God in the Dock*, "Cross-Examination" (1963), para. 33, 35, p. 263.	Of all my books, there was only one I did not take pleasure in writing. . . . *The Screwtape Letters*. They were dry and gritty going. At the time, I was thinking of objections to the Christian life, and decided to put them into the form, "That's what the devil would say." But making goods "bad" and bads "good" gets to be fatiguing.

937
Lewis, C. S.:
That Hideous Strength
Letters of C. S. Lewis
(28 May 1945), para. 1,
p. 207.

I'm glad you recognized the N.I.C.E. as not being quite the fantastic absurdity some people think. I hadn't myself thought that any of the people in contemporary rackets were *really* dabbling in magic; I had supposed that to be a romantic addition of my own. But there you are. The trouble about writing satire is that the real world always anticipates you, and what were meant for exaggerations turn out to be nothing of the sort.

938
Lewis, C. S.:
That Hideous Strength
Letters of C. S. Lewis
(31 January 1946),
para. 1, p. 209.

That Hideous Strength has been unanimously damned by all reviewers.

939
Lewis, C. S.:
Till We Have Faces
Letters of C. S. Lewis
(10 February 1957),
para. 1–5, pp. 273–274.

An author doesn't necessarily understand the meaning of his own story better than anyone else, so I give my account of *Till We Have Faces* simply for what it is worth. The "levels" I am conscious of are these.

(1) A work of (supposed) historical imagination. . . . Much that you take as allegory was intended solely as realistic detail. . . .

(2) Psyche is an instance of the *anima naturaliter Christiana* making the best of the Pagan religion she is brought up in and thus being guided (but always "under the cloud," always in terms of her own imaginations or that of her people) towards the true God. She is in some ways like Christ because every good man or woman is like Christ. What else could they be like? But of course my interest is primarily in Orual.

(3) Orual is (not a symbol) but an instance, a

"case" of human affection in its natural condition, true, tender, suffering, but in the long run tyrannically possessive and ready to turn to hatred when the beloved ceases to be its possession. What such love particularly cannot stand is to see the beloved passing into a sphere where it cannot follow. All this I hoped would stand as a mere story in its own right. But—

(4) Of course I had always in mind its close parallel to what is probably happening at this moment in at least five families in your home town. Someone becomes a Christian, or in a family nominally Christian already, does something like becoming a missionary or entering a religious order. The others suffer a sense of outrage. What they love is being taken from them. The boy must be mad. And the conceit of him! Or: is there something in it after all? . . . Now I, as a Christian, have a good deal of sympathy with those jealous, suffering, puzzled people (for they do suffer, and out of their suffering much of the bitterness against religion arises). I believe the thing is common.

940

Lewis, Joy Davidman Gresham

Letters to an American Lady (16 November 1956), para. 2, p. 63.

You may as well know (but don't talk of it, for all is still uncertain) that I may soon be, in rapid succession, a bridegroom and a widower. There may, in fact, be a deathbed marriage.

941
Lewis, Joy Davidman Gresham
Letters to an American Lady (17 January 1957), para. 1, p. 65.

I have married a lady suffering from cancer. I think she will weather it this time: after that, life under the sword of Damocles. Very little chance (not exactly *none*) of a permanent escape. I acquire two schoolboy stepsons. My brother and I have been coping with them for their Christmas holidays. Nice boys, but gruelling work for 2 old bachelors! I'm dead tired now.

942
Lewis, Joy Davidman Gresham
Letters: C. S. Lewis/Don Giovanni Calabria (15 December 1959), para. 2–3, p. 101.

Now, after two years' remission, my wife's mortal illness has returned. May it please the Lord that, whatever is His will for the body, the minds of both of us may remain unharmed; that faith unimpaired may strengthen us, contrition soften us and peace make us joyful.

And that, up to now, has happened; nor would you readily believe what joys we sometimes experience in the midst of troubles. What wonder? For has He not promised comfort to those who mourn? [Ed. note: the addressee is Don Luigi Pedrollo.]

943
Lewis, Joy Davidman Gresham
A Grief Observed, chap. III, para. 29, pp. 55–56.

A good wife contains so many persons in herself. What was H. [Joy] not to me? She was my daughter and my mother, my pupil and my teacher, my subject and my sovereign; and always, holding all these in solution, my trusty comrade, friend, shipmate, fellow-soldier. My mistress; but at the same time all that any man friend (and I have good ones) has ever been to me. Perhaps more. If we had never fallen in love we should have none the less been always together, and created a scandal.

944
Liberty
Christian Reflections,
"The Poison of
Subjectivism" (1943),
para. 22, p. 81.

The very idea of freedom presupposes some objective moral law which overarches rulers and ruled alike. Subjectivism about values is eternally incompatible with democracy. We and our rulers are of one kind only so long as we are subject to one law. But if there is no Law of Nature, the *ethos* of any society is the creation of its rulers, educators and conditioners; and every creator stands above and outside his own creation.

945
Liberty
Taliessin Through Logres,
. . . *Arthurian Torso,*
"Williams and the
Arthuriad" (1948),
chap. IV, para. 14,
p. 326.

[Said of the House of Taliessin in William's poetry:] Slavery there becomes freedom and dominion becomes service. As willed necessity is freedom, so willed hierarchy becomes equality.

946
Liberty
The Screwtape Letters,
"Screwtape Proposes a
Toast" (1959), para. 18,
pp. 160–161.

[Senior devil Screwtape in a speech at the "Annual Dinner of the Tempters' Training College for Young Devils":] Hidden in the heart of this striving for Liberty there was also a deep hatred of personal freedom. That invaluable man Rousseau first revealed it. In his perfect democracy, you remember, only the state religion is permitted, slavery is restored, and the individual is told that he has really willed (though he didn't know it) whatever the Government tells him to do. From that starting point, via Hegel (another indispensable propagandist on our side) we easily contrived both the Nazi and the Communist state.

947
Life
Letters of C. S. Lewis (8
February 1956), para. 1,
p. 266.

Actually it seems to me that one can hardly say anything either bad enough or good enough about life.

948
Life and Death
Letters of C. S. Lewis
(7 April 1922), para. 1,
p. 73.

I wish life and death were not the only alternatives, for I don't like either; one could imagine a via media.

949
Literalism
Christian Reflections,
"Christianity and
Culture" (1940), chap. 2,
Section III, para. 6.3,
pp. 31–32.

In practical life a certain amount of "reading between the lines" is necessary: if we took every letter and every remark simply at its face value we should soon find ourselves in difficulties. On the other hand, most of us have known people with whom "reading between the lines" became such a mania that they overlooked the obvious truth of every situation and lived in the perpetual discovery of mares' nests; and doctors tell us of a form of lunacy in which the simplest remark uttered in the patient's presence becomes to him evidence of a conspiracy and the very furniture of his cell takes on an infinitely sinister significance.

950
Literary Criticism
Christian Reflections,
"Christianity and
Literature" (1939),
chap. 1, para. 11, p. 7.

An author should never conceive himself as bringing into existence beauty or wisdom which did not exist before, but simply and solely as trying to embody in terms of his own art some reflection of eternal Beauty and Wisdom. Our criticism would therefore from the beginning group itself with some existing theories of poetry against others. It would have affinities with the primitive or Homeric theory in which the poet is the mere pensioner of the Muse. It would have affinities with the Platonic doctrine of a transcendent Form partly imitable on earth; and remoter affinities with the Aristotelian doctrine of [mimesis] and the Augustan doctrine about the imitation of Nature and the Ancients. It would be

opposed to the theory of genius as, perhaps,
generally understood; and above all it would be
opposed to the idea that literature is self-
expression.

**51
Literary
Criticism**
*The Personal Heresy: A
Controversy,* chap. 5,
para. 17, p. 113.

It is by art or skill that the poets contrive to utter
concretely what it is that they want to say; but
the thing said is not "Art"—it is something more
like a remark. The skill which went to the
utterance of it has all the privileges of art; it is
exempt (like plumbing or boot-blacking) from
moral and logical criticism, and it is best judged
by fellow artists. To claim similar immunities for
the thing said is a confusion. I will let the plumber
tell me how culpable his predecessor was in
allowing my scullery to get flooded; I will not let
him decide *whether* it is flooded, still less whether
it ought to be.

**52
Literary
Criticism**
Selected Literary Essays,
"High Brows and Low
Brows" (1939), para.
20–21, pp. 276–277.

The great authors of the past wrote to entertain
the leisure of their adult contemporaries, and a
man who cared for literature needed no spur and
expected no good conduct marks for sitting down
to the food provided for him. Boys at school were
taught to read Latin and Greek poetry by the
birch, and discovered the English poets as
accidentally and naturally as they now discover
the local cinema. Most of my own generation,
and many, I hope, of yours, tumbled into
literature in that fashion. Of each of us some great
poet made a rape when we still wore Eton collars.
Shall we be thought immodest if we claim that
most of the books we loved from the first were
good books and our earliest loves are still
unrepented? If so, that very fact bears witness to
the novelty of the modern situation; to us, the

claim that we have always liked Keats is no prouder than the claim that we have always liked bacon and eggs.

For there are changes afoot. I foresee the growth of a new race of readers and critics to whom, from the very outset, good literature will be an accomplishment rather than a delight, and who will always feel, beneath the acquired taste, the backward tug of something else which they feel merit in resisting. Such people will not be content to say that some books are bad or not very good; they will make a special class of "lowbrow" art which is to be vilified, mocked, quarantined, and sometimes (when they are sick or tired) enjoyed. They will be sure that what is popular must always be bad, thus assuming that human taste is *naturally* wrong, that it needs not only improvement and development but veritable conversion. For them a good critic will be, as the theologians say, essentially a "twice-born" critic, one who is regenerate and washed from his Original Taste. They will have no conception, because they have had no experience, of spontaneous delight in excellence.

953
Literary Criticism

Christian Reflections, "Christianity and Culture" (1940), section III, para. 8, p. 31.

A bad book is to be deemed a real evil in so far as it can be shown to prompt to sensuality, or pride, or murder, or to conflict with the doctrine of Divine Providence, or the like. The other dyslogistic terms dear to critics (vulgar, derivative, cheap, precious, academic, affected, bourgeois, Victorian, Georgian, "literary," etc.) had better be kept strictly on the taste side of the account. In discovering what attitudes are present you can be as subtle as you like. But in your theological and ethical condemnation (as distinct from your dislike of the taste) you had better be very un-subtle. Yo had better reserve it for plain mortal sins, and plain atheism and heresy. For our passions are always urging us in the opposite direction, and if we are not careful criticism may become a mere excuse for taking revenge on books whose smell we dislike by erecting our temperamental antipathies into pseudo-moral judgements.

954
Literary Criticism
Christian Reflections, "Christianity and Culture" (1940), section III, para. 11, p. 34.

A great deal (not all) of our literature was made to be read lightly, for entertainment. If we do not read it, in a sense, "for fun" and with our feet on the fender, we are not using it as it was meant to be used, and all our criticism of it will be pure illusion. For you cannot judge any artifact except by using it as it was intended. It is no good judging a butter-knife by seeing whether it will saw logs. Much bad criticism, indeed, results from the efforts of critics to get a work-time result out of something that never aimed at producing more than pleasure.

955
Literary Criticism
A Preface to "Paradise Lost," chap. 9, para. 2–3, pp. 62–64.

The things which separate one age from another are superficial. Just as, if we stripped the armour off a medieval knight or the lace off a Caroline courtier, we should find beneath them an anatomy identical with our own, so, it is held, if we strip off from Virgil his Roman imperialism, from Sidney his code of honour, from Lucretius his Epicurean philosophy, and from all who have it their religion, we shall find the Unchanging Human Heart, and on this we are to concentrate. I held this theory myself for many years, but I have now abandoned it. I continue, of course, to admit that if you remove from people the things that make them different, what is left must be the same, and that the Human Heart will certainly appear as Unchanging if you ignore its changes.

. . . Instead of stripping the knight of his armour you can try to put his armour on yourself; instead of seeing how the courtier would look without his lace, you can try to see how you would feel *with* his lace; that is, with his honour, his wit, his royalism, and his gallantries out of the *Grand Cyrus*. I had much rather know what I should feel like if I adopted the beliefs of Lucretius than how Lucretius would have felt if he had never entertained them. The possible Lucretius in myself interests me more than the possible C. S. Lewis in Lucretius. There is in G. K. Chesterton's *Avowals and Denials* a wholly admirable essay called *On Man: Heir of All the Ages*. An heir is one who inherits and "any man who is cut off from the past . . . is a man most unjustly disinherited.". . . You must, so far as in you lies, become an Achaean chief while reading Homer, a medieval knight while reading Malory, and an eighteenth century Londoner while reading Johnson. Only thus will you be able to judge the work "in the same spirit that its author writ" and to avoid chimerical criticism.

956
Literary Criticism
Selected Literary Essays,
"Psycho-Analysis and
Literary Criticism"
(1942), para. 1, p. 286.

The genuinely critical question [is] "Why, and How, should we read this?"

957
Literary Criticism
English Literature in the
Sixteenth Century, bk.
III.I, para. 95, p. 379.

[Speaking of the fragmentary state of Spenser's *Faerie Queene*:] There is a stage in the invention of any long story at which the outsider would see nothing but chaos. Numerous alternatives, written, half-written, and unwritten (the latter possibly the most influential of all) ferment together. Passages which no longer fit the main scheme are retained because they seem too good to lose: they will be harmonized somehow later on if the author lives to complete his work. Eve a final revision often leaves ragged edges; unnoticed by generations of readers but pointed out in the end by professional scholars. There is a psychological law which makes it harder for the author to detect them than for the scholar. To the scholar an event in fiction is as firm a *datum* as an event in real life: he did not choose and cannot change it. The author has chosen it and changed it and seen it in its molten condition passing from one shape to another. It has as many rivals for its place in his memory as it had for its place in the final text.

958
Literary
Criticism
Letters to an American Lady (31 March 1954), para. 1, p. 30.

I'm sick of our Abracadabrist poets. What gives the show away is that their professed admirers give quite contradictory interpretations of the same poem—I'm prepared to believe that an unintelligible picture is really a very good horse if all its admirers tell me so; but when one says it's a horse, and the next that it's a ship, and the third that it's an orange, and the fourth that it's Mt. Everest, I give it up.

959
Literary
Criticism
Studies in Words, chap. 2, para. 28–32, 36, p. 326–329, 331.

When we write criticism we have to be continually on our guard. . . . If we honestly believe a work to be very bad we cannot help hating it. The function of criticism, however, is "to get ourselves out of the way and let humanity decide"; not to discharge our hatred but to expose the grounds for it; not to vilify faults but to diagnose and exhibit them. Unfortunately to express our hatred and to revenge ourselves is easier and more agreeable. Hence there is a tendency to select our pejorative epithets with a view not to their accuracy but to their power of hurting. . . .

The best protection against this is to remind ourselves again and again what the proper function of pejorative words is. The ultimate, simplest and most abstract, is *bad* itself. The only good purpose for ever departing from that monosyllable when we condemn anything is to be more specific, to answer the question "Bad in what way?"

. . . I would be very glad if I could transfer to even one reader my conviction that *adverse* criticism, far from being the easiest, is one of the hardest things in the world to do well. And that for two reasons.

. . . When we try to define the badness of a work, we usually end by calling it bad on the strength of characteristics which we can find also in good work.

. . . The other difficulty lies within. . . . What we think thoroughly bad, we hate. . . . We may dislike the author personally, he and we may belong to opposed literary "parties" or factions. The book before us becomes a symbol of *l'infame*. Hence a perpetual danger of what is called criticism (judgement) becoming mere action—a blow delivered in a battle. But if it does, we are lost as critics.

. . . I think we must get it firmly fixed in our minds that the very occasions on which we should most like to write a slashing review are precisely those on which we had much better hold our tongues. The very desire is a danger signal. . . . The strength of our dislike is itself a probable symptom that all is not well within; that some raw place in our psychology has been touched, or else that some personal or partisan motive is secretly at work.

960
**Literary
Criticism**
*An Experiment in
Criticism*, chap. 11,
para. 9, pp. 110–111.

The very fact that people, or even any one person, can well and truly read, and love for a lifetime, a book we had thought bad, will raise the suspicion that it cannot really be as bad as we thought. Sometimes, to be sure, our friend's mistress remains in our eyes so plain, stupid and disagreeable that we can attribute his love only to the irrational and mysterious behaviour of hormones; similarly, the book he likes may continue to seem so bad that we have to attribute his liking to some early association or other psychological accident. But we must, and should, remain uncertain. Always, there may be something in it that we can't see.

961
**Literary
Criticism**
*Of Other Worlds: Essays
and Stories*, "On
Criticism" (1st pub.
1966), para. 7, p. 46.

The author is not the worst, but the best, judge of his critics. Ignorant as he may be of his book's value, he is at least an expert on its content.

962
**Literary
Criticism**
*Of Other Worlds: Essays
and Stories*, "On
Criticism" (1st pub.
1966), para. 8. p. 47.

Negative statements are of course particularly dangerous for the lazy or hurried reviewer. And here, at once, is a lesson for us all as critics. One passage out of the whole *Faerie Queene* will justify you in saying that Spenser sometimes does so-and-so: only an exhaustive reading and an unerring memory will justify the statement that he never does so. This everyone sees. What more easily escapes one is the concealed negative in statements apparently positive: for example in any statement that contains the predicate "new." One says lightly that something which Donne or Sterne or Hopkins did was new: thus committing oneself to the negative that no one had done it before.

But this is beyond one's knowledge. Again, things we are all apt to say about the growth or development of a poet may often imply the negative that he wrote nothing except what has come down to us—which no one knows. We have not seen the contents of his waste paper basket. If we had, what now looks like an abrupt change in his manner from poem A to poem B might turn out not to have been abrupt at all.

963
Literary Criticism
Of Other Worlds: Essays and Stories, "On Criticism," para. 11, p. 48.

Nearly all critics are prone to imagine that they know a great many facts relevant to a book which in reality they don't know. The author inevitably perceives their ignorance because he (often he alone) knows the real facts. This critical vice may take many different forms.

Nearly all reviewers assume that your books were written in the same order in which they were published and all shortly before publication. There was a very good instance of this lately in the reviews of Tolkien's *Lord of the Rings.* Most critics assumed (this illustrates a different vice) that it must be a political allegory and a good many thought that the master Ring must "be" the atomic bomb. Anyone who knew the real history of the composition knew that this was not only erroneous, but impossible; chronologically impossible. Others assumed that the mythology of his romance had grown out of his children's story *The Hobbit.* This, again, he and his friends knew to be mainly false. Now of course nobody blames the critics for not knowing these things: how should they? The trouble is that they don't know they don't know. A guess leaps into their minds and they write it down without even noticing that it is a guess.

964
Literary Criticism
Studies in Medieval and
Renaissance Literature,
"The Genesis of a
Medieval Book" (1966),
para. 28, p. 38.

In my opinion all criticism should be of books, not of authors.

965
Literary History
Letters of C. S. Lewis
(31 March 1928),
para. 1, p. 125.

My studies in the XVIth century—you will remember my idea of a book about Erasmus— have carried me much further back than I anticipated. Indeed it is the curse and the fascination of literary history that there are no real beginnings. Take what point you will for the start of some new chapter in the mind and imaginations of man, and you will invariably find that it has always begun a bit earlier; or rather, it branches so imperceptibly out of something else that you are forced to go back to the something else. The only satisfactory opening for any study is the first chapter of Genesis.

966
Literary History
The Allegory of Love,
chap. VI.I, para. 2,
p. 234.

There are few absolute beginnings in literary history, but there is endless transformation.

967
Literary History
Studies in Medieval and
Renaissance Literature,
"Tasso" (1940s?), para. 5,
p. 115.

At the moment, we live in the full tide of the most violent counter-romanticism that has ever been seen.

968
**Literary
History**
*English Literature in the
Sixteenth Century*, bk.
III.I, para. 21, p. 331.

To judge between one *ethos* and another, it is necessary to have got inside both, and if literary history does not help us to do so it is a great waste of labour.

969
**Literary
History**
*Studies in Medieval and
Renaissance Literature*,
"Edmund Spenser,
1552–99" (1954),
para. 22, p. 134.

One of the great uses of literary history is to keep on reminding us that while man is constantly acquiring new powers he is also constantly losing old ones.

970
Literature
The Allegory of Love,
chap. III.III, para. 10,
p. 130.

There is nothing in literature which does not, in some degree, percolate into life.

971
Literature
*Present Concerns: Essays
by C. S. Lewis*, "Is
English Doomed?"
(1944), pp. 29–30.

The true aim of literary studies is to lift the student out of his provincialism by making him "the spectator," if not of all, yet of much, "time and existence." The student, or even the schoolboy, who has been brought by good (and therefore mutually disagreeing) teachers to meet the past where alone the past still lives, is taken out of the narrowness of his own age and class into a more public world. He is learning the true *Phaenomenologie des Geistes*; discovering what varieties there are in Man. "History" alone will not do, for it studies the past mainly in secondary authorities. It is possible to "do History" for years without knowing at the end what it felt like to be an Anglo-Saxon *eorl*, a cavalier, an eighteenth-

century country gentleman. The gold behind the
paper currency is to be found, almost exclusively,
in literature. In it lies deliverance from the tyranny
of generalizations and catchwords. Its students
know (for example) what diverse realities—
Launcelot, Baron Bradwardine, Mulvaney—hide
behind the word *militarism*.

972
Literature
*An Experiment in
Criticism*, Epilogue,
para. 13–14,
pp. 137–138.

Each of us by nature sees the whole world from
one point of view with a perspective and a
selectiveness peculiar to himself. And even when
we build disinterested fantasies, they are saturated
with, and limited by, our own psychology. To
acquiesce in this particularity on the sensuous
level—in other words, not to discount
perspective—would be lunacy. We should then
believe that the railway line really grew narrower
as it receded into the distance. But we want to
escape the illusions of perspective on higher levels
too. We want to see with other eyes, to imagine
with other imaginations, to feel with other hearts,
as well as with our own. We are not content to
be Leibnitzian monads. We demand windows.
Literature as Logos is a series of windows, even of
doors. One of the things we feel after reading a
great work is "I have got out." Or from another
point of view, "I have got in"; pierced the shell of
some other monad and discovered what it is like
inside.

Good reading, therefore, though it is not
essentially an affectional or moral or intellectual
activity, has something in common with all three.
In love we escape from our self into one other. In
the moral sphere, every act of justice or charity
involves putting ourselves in the other person's
place and thus transcending our own competitive

particularity. In coming to understand anything we are rejecting the facts as they are for us in favour of the facts as they are. The primary impulse of each is to maintain and aggrandise himself. The secondary impulse is to go out of the self, to correct its provincialism and heal its loneliness. In love, in virtue, in the pursuit of knowledge, and in the reception of the arts, we are doing this. Obviously this process can be described either as an enlargement or as a temporary annihilation of the self. But that is an old paradox; "he that loseth his life shall save it."

973
Literature
An Experiment in Criticism, Epilogue, para. 17–18, pp. 140–141.

The man who is contented to be only himself, and therefore less a self, is in prison. My own eyes are not enough for me, I will see through those of others. Reality, even seen through the eyes of many, is not enough. I will see what others have invented. Even the eyes of all humanity are not enough. I regret that the brutes cannot write books. Very gladly would I learn what face things present to a mouse or a bee: more gladly still would I perceive the olfactory world charged with all the information and emotion it carries for a dog.

Literary experience heals the wound, without undermining the privilege, of individuality. There are mass emotions which heal the wound; but they destroy the privilege. In them our separate selves are pooled and we sink back into sub-individuality. But in reading great literature I become a thousand men and yet remain myself. Like the night sky in the Greek poem, I see with a myriad eyes, but it is still I who see. Here, as in worship, in love, in moral action, and in knowing, I transcend myself; and am never more myself than when I do.

974 **Literature,** **Classic** *Selected Literary Essays,* "De Descriptione Temporum" (1955), para. 22, p. 13.	It is my settled conviction that in order to read Old Western literature aright you must suspend most of the responses and unlearn most of the habits you have acquired in reading modern literature.

975 **Literature,** **Contemporary** *Rehabilitations,* "Our English Syllabus" (1st pub. 1939), para. 14, p. 91.	There is an intrinsic absurdity in making current literature a subject of academic study, and the student who wants a tutor's assistance in reading the works of his own contemporaries might as well ask for a nurse's assistance in blowing his own nose.

976 **Liturgiology** *Letters to Malcolm:* *Chiefly on Prayer,* chap. 1, para. 2, pp. 3–4.	There is no subject in the world (always excepting sport) on which I have less to say than liturgiology.

977 **Longing** *The Weight of Glory,* "The Weight of Glory" (1942), para. 13, pp. 16–17.	If we take the imagery of Scripture seriously, if we believe that God will one day *give* us the Morning Star and cause us to *put on* the splendour of the sun, then we may surmise that both the ancient myths and the modern poetry, so false as history, may be very near the truth as prophecy. At present we are on the outside of the world, the wrong side of the door. We discern the freshness and purity of morning, but they do not make us fresh and pure. We cannot mingle with the splendours we see. But all the leaves of the New Testament are rustling with the rumour that it will not always be so. Some day, God willing, we shall get *in.* When human souls have become as perfect in voluntary obedience as the inanimate creation is in its lifeless obedience, then they will put on its

glory, or rather that greater glory of which nature is only the first sketch.

978
Longing
Till We Have Faces, bk. 1, chap. 7, p. 76.

"Do you think it all meant nothing, all the longing? The longing for home? For indeed it now feels not like going, but like going back. All my life the god of the Mountain has been wooing me. Oh, look up once at least before the end and wish me joy. I am going to my lover. Do you not see now—?"

979
Love
Mere Christianity, bk. III, chap. 9, para. 5, p. 116.

The rule for all of us is perfectly simple. Do not waste time bothering whether you "love" your neighbour; act as if you did. As soon as we do this we find one of the great secrets. When you are behaving as if you loved someone, you will presently come to love him. If you injure someone you dislike, you will find yourself disliking him more. If you do him a good turn, you will find yourself disliking him less.

980
Love
The World's Last Night and Other Essays, "The World's Last Night" (1952), para. 30, p. 109.

Perfect love, we know, casteth out fear. But so do several other things—ignorance, alcohol, passion, presumption, and stupidity. It is very desirable that we should all advance to that perfection of love in which we shall fear no longer; but it is very undesirable, until we have reached that stage, that we should allow any inferior agent to cast out our fear.

981
Love
The Four Loves, chap. 2, para. 14, p. 33.

Need-love cries to God from our poverty; Gift-love longs to serve, or even to suffer for, God; Appreciative love says: "We give thanks to thee for thy great glory." Need-love says of a woman "I cannot live without her"; Gift-love longs to give

her happiness, comfort, protection—if possible,
wealth; Appreciative love gazes and holds its
breath and is silent, rejoices that such a wonder
should exist even if not for him, will not be
wholly dejected by losing her, would rather have it
so than never to have seen her at all.

982
Love
The Four Loves, chap. 2,
para. 33, pp. 41–42.

All natural affections . . . can become rivals to
spiritual love: but they can also be preparatory
imitations of it, training (so to speak) of the
spiritual muscles which Grace may later put to a
higher service; as women nurse dolls in childhood
and later nurse children.

983
Love
A Grief Observed, chap.
1, para. 12, p. 7.

If God were a substitute for love we ought to
have lost all interest in Him. Who'd bother about
substitutes when he has the thing itself? But that
isn't what happens. We both knew we wanted
something besides one another—quite a different
kind of something, a quite different kind of want.
You might as well say that when lovers have one
another they will never want to read, or eat—or
breathe.

984
Love
Poems, "Infatuation"
(1st pub. 1964), para. 1,
p. 73.

Body and soul most fit for love can best
Withstand it. I am ill, and cannot rest,
Therefore I'm caught. Disease is amorous, health
At love's door has the pass both in and out.

985
Love: Abuses
The Great Divorce,
chap. 11, pp. 96–97.

"There's something in natural affection which will
lead it on to eternal love more easily than natural
appetite could be led on. But there's also
something in it which makes it easier to stop at
the natural level and mistake it for the heavenly."

Brass is mistaken for gold more easily than clay is. And if it finally refuses conversion its corruption will be worse than the corruption of what ye call the lower passions. It is a stronger angel, and therefore, when it falls, a fiercer devil."

986
Love: Abuses
The Four Loves, chap. 6, para. 5, pp. 166–167.

The rebellious slogan "All for love" is really love's death warrant (date of execution, for the moment, left blank).

987
Love: Being Lovable
The Four Loves, chap. 3, para. 20, p. 65.

"If you would be loved, be lovable," said Ovid. That cheery old reprobate only meant, "If you want to attract the girls you must be attractive," but his maxim has a wider application. The amorist was wiser in his generation than Mr Pontifex and King Lear.

988
Love: Charity
Mere Christianity, bk. III, chap. 9, para. 10, p. 117.

Christian Love, either towards God or towards man, is an affair of the will.

989
Love: Charity
Mere Christianity, bk. III, chap. 9, para. 2, p. 115.

Love, in the Christian sense, does not mean an emotion. It is a state not of the feelings but of the will; that state of the will which we have naturally about ourselves, and must learn to have about other people.

990
Love: Charity
Letters of C. S. Lewis (18 February 1954), para. 1, p. 255.

Charity means love. It is called Agape in the New Testament to distinguish it from Eros (sexual love), Storge (family affection) and Philia (friendship). So there are 4 kinds of love, all good in their proper place, but Agape is the best because it is the kind God has for us and is good in all circumstances.

991

Love: Charity

Letters of C. S. Lewis (18 February 1954), para. 1, p. 256.

Agape is all giving, not getting. Read what St. Paul says about it in First Corinthians Chap. 13. Then look at a picture of Agape in action in St. Luke, Chap. 10, vv. 30–35. And then, better still, look at Matthew Ch. 25, vv. 31–46; from which you see that Christ counts all that you do for *this* baby exactly as if you had done it for Him when He was a baby in the manger at Bethlehem; you are in a sense sharing in the things His mother did for Him. Giving money is only *one* way of showing charity; to give time and toil is far better and (for most of us) harder.

992

Love: Charity

The Four Loves, chap. 6, para. 13, p. 169.

To love at all is to be vulnerable. Love anything, and your heart will certainly be wrung and possibly be broken. If you want to make sure of keeping it intact, you must give your heart to no one, not even to an animal. Wrap it carefully round with hobbies and little luxuries; avoid all entanglements; lock it up safe in the casket or coffin of your selfishness. But in that casket—safe, dark, motionless, airless—it will change. It will not be broken; it will become unbreakable, impenetrable, irredeemable. The alternative to tragedy, or at least to the risk of tragedy, is damnation. The only place outside Heaven where you can be perfectly safe from all the dangers and perturbations of love is Hell.

993

Love: Charity

The Four Loves, chap. 6, para. 14, p. 170.

Christ did not teach and suffer that we might become, even in the natural loves, more careful of our own happiness. If a man is not uncalculating towards the earthly beloveds whom he has seen, he is none the more likely to be so towards God whom he has not. We shall draw nearer to God, not by trying to avoid the sufferings inherent in all loves, but by accepting them and offering them to Him; throwing away all defensive armour. If our hearts need to be broken, and if He chooses this as the way in which they should break, so be it.

994 **Love: Charity** *Letters of C. S. Lewis* (undated), para. 2, p. 269.	The love we are commanding [sic] to have for God and our neighbour is a state of the *will*, not of the affections (though if they ever also play their part so much the better).
995 **Love: Dangers** *The Four Loves,* chap. 1, para. 13, p. 17.	"Love ceases to be a demon only when he ceases to be a god"; which of course can be re-stated in the form "begins to be a demon the moment he begins to be a god." This balance seems to me an indispensable safeguard. If we ignore it the truth that God is love may slyly come to mean for us the converse, that love is God.
996 **Love: Dangers** *The Four Loves,* chap. 3, para. 46, p. 83.	Love, having become a god, becomes a demon.
997 **Love: God's** **Love for Us** *The Problem of Pain,* chap. 3, para. 8, 13, pp. 41, 46.	He [God] has paid us the intolerable compliment of loving us, in the deepest, most tragic, most inexorable sense. . . . Love, in its own nature, demands the perfecting of the beloved; . . . mere "kindness" which tolerates anything except suffering in its object is, in that respect, at the opposite pole from Love.

998
Love: God's Love for Us
The Problem of Pain,
chap. 3, para. 13–14,
pp. 46–47.

Of all powers he [God] forgives most, but he condones least: he is pleased with little, but demands all.

. . . In awful and surprising truth, we are the objects of His love. You asked for a loving God: you have one. The great spirit you so lightly invoked, the "lord of terrible aspect," is present: not a senile benevolence that drowsily wishes you to be happy in your own way, not the cold philanthropy of a conscientious magistrate, not the care of a host who feels responsible for the comfort of his guests, but the consuming fire Himself, the Love that made the worlds, persistent as the artist's love for his work and despotic as a man's love for a dog, provident and venerable as a father's love for a child, jealous, inexorable, exacting as love between the sexes. . . . It is certainly a burden of glory not only beyond our deserts but also, except in rare moments of grace, beyond our desiring.

999
Love: God's Love for Us
The Problem of Pain,
chap. 3, para. 18, p. 53.

The call is not only to prostration and awe; it is to a reflection of the Divine life, a creaturely participation in the Divine attributes which is far beyond our present desires. We are bidden to "put on Christ," to become like God. That is, whether we like it or not, God intends to give us what we need, not what we now think we want. Once more, we are embarrassed by the intolerable compliment, by too much love, not too little.

1000
Love: God's Love for Us
The Problem of Pain,
chap. 6, para. 7,
pp. 96–97.

We are perplexed to see misfortune falling upon decent, inoffensive, worthy people. . . . God, who made these deserving people, may really be right when He thinks that their modest prosperity and the happiness of their children are not enough to make them blessed: that all this must fall from them in the end, and that if they have not learned to know Him they will be wretched. And therefore He troubles them, warning them in advance of an insufficiency that one day they will have to discover. The life to themselves and their families stands between them and the recognition of the need; He makes that life less sweet to them. I call this a Divine humility because it is a poor thing to strike our colours to God when the ship is going down under us; a poor thing to come to Him as a last resort, to offer up "our own" when it is no longer worth keeping. If God were proud He would hardly have us on such terms: but He is not proud, He stoops to conquer, He will have us even though we have shown that we prefer everything else to Him, and come to Him because there is "nothing better" now to be had.

1001

Love: God's Love for Us

Miracles, chap. 7, para. 14, p. 52.

If it is maintained that anything so small as the Earth must, in any event, be too unimportant to merit the love of the Creator, we reply that no Christian ever supposed we did merit it. Christ did not die for men because they were intrinsically worth dying for, but because He is intrinsically love, and therefore loves infinitely.

1002

Love: God's Love for Us

Letters of C. S. Lewis (13 June 1951), para. 6, p. 233.

Continue seeking Him with seriousness. Unless he wanted you, you would not be wanting Him.

1003
Love: God's Love for Us
Mere Christianity, bk. III, chap. 9, para. 10, p. 118.

Though our feelings come and go, His love for us does not. It is not wearied by our sins, or our indifference; and, therefore, it is quite relentless in its determination that we shall be cured of those sins, at whatever cost to us, at whatever cost to Him.

1004
Love: God's Love for Us
The World's Last Night and Other Essays, "Religion and Rocketry" (1958), para. 12, p. 87.

We must surely believe that the divine charity is as fertile in resource as it is measureless in condescension. To different diseases, or even to different patients sick with the same disease, the great Physician may have applied different remedies; remedies which we should probably not recognize as such even if we ever heard of them.

1005
Love: God's Love for Us
The Four Loves, chap. 1, para. 2–3, 8, pp. 11–12, 14–15.

Divine Love is Gift-love. The Father gives all He is and has to the Son. The Son gives Himself back to the Father, and gives Himself to the world, and for the world to the Father, and thus gives the world (in Himself) back to the Father too.

And what, on the other hand, can be less like anything we believe of God's life than Need-love? He lacks nothing, but our Need-love, as Plato saw, is "the son of Poverty." It is the accurate reflection in consciousness of our actual nature. We are born helpless. As soon as we are fully conscious we discover loneliness. We need others physically, emotionally, intellectually; we need them if we are to know anything, even ourselves. . . . A very strange corollary follows. Man approaches God most nearly when he is in one sense least like God. For what can be more unlike than fullness and need, sovereignty and humility, righteousness and penitence, limitless power and a cry for help? This paradox staggered me when I first ran into it.

1006 **Love: God's** **Love for Us** *The Four Loves,* chap. 6, para. 21, p. 176.	God, who needs nothing, loves into existence wholly superfluous creatures in order that he may love and perfect them.

1007 **Love: God's** **Love for Us** *The Four Loves,* chap. 6, para. 21, p. 176.	He creates the universe, already foreseeing—or should we say "seeing"? there are no tenses in God—the buzzing cloud of flies about the cross, the flayed back pressed against the uneven stake, the nails driven through the mesial nerves, the repeated torture of back and arms as it is time after time, for breath's sake, hitched up. If I may dare the biological image, God is a "host" who deliberately creates His own parasites; causes us to be that we may exploit and "take advantage of" Him. Herein is love. This is the diagram of Love Himself, the inventor of all loves.

1008 **Love: God's** **Love for Us** *Letters of C. S. Lewis* (undated), para. 1, p. 231.	God loves us; not because we are loveable but because He is love, not because he needs to receive but because He delights to give.

1009 **Love: Our** **Love for God** *The Great Divorce,* chap. 11, pp. 92–93.	"Human beings can't make one another really happy for long. . . . You cannot love a fellow-creature fully till you love God. . . . No natural feelings are high or low, holy or unholy, in themselves. They are all holy when God's hand is on the rein. They all go bad when they set up on their own and make themselves into false gods."

1010
**Love: Our
Love for God**
The Great Divorce,
chap. 11, p. 97.

"Every natural love will rise again and live forever in this country [heaven]: but none will rise again until it has been buried."

1011
**Love: Our
Love for God**
*Taliessin Through Logres,
. . . Arthurian Torso,*
"Williams and the
Arthuriad" (1948),
chap. IV, para. 15,
pp. 326–327.

An old saint, being asked whether it is easy or hard to love God, replied: "It is easy *to those who do it.*"

1012
**Love: Our
Love for God**
Mere Christianity, bk. III,
chap. 8, para. 11, p. 113.

To love and admire anything outside yourself is to take one step away from utter spiritual ruin; though we shall not be well so long as we love and admire anything more than we love and admire God.

1013
**Love: Our
Love for God**
Letters to Children
(6 May 1955), p. 52.

God knows quite well how hard we find it to love Him more than anyone or anything else, and He won't be angry with us as long as we are trying. And He will help us.

1014
**Love: Our
Love for God**
*Letters to an American
Lady* (18 August 1956),
p. 61.

I think God wants us to love Him more, not to love creatures (even animals) less. We love everything in one way too much (i.e. at the expense of our love for Him) but in another way we love everything too little.

No person, animal, flower, or even pebble, has ever been loved too much—i.e. more than every one of God's works deserves.

1015
Love: Our
Love for God
The Four Loves, chap. 1,
para. 7, p. 13.

Every Christian would agree that a man's spiritual health is exactly proportional to his love for God.

1016
Love: Our
Love for God
The Four Loves, chap. 2,
para. 9, pp. 30–31.

Moral principles (conjugal fidelity, filial piety, gratitude, and the like) may preserve the relationship for a lifetime. But where Need-love is left unaided we can hardly expect it not to "die on us" once the need is no more. That is why the world rings with the complaints of mothers whose grown-up children neglect them and of forsaken mistresses whose lovers' love was pure need— which they have satisfied. Our Need-love for God is in a different position because our need of Him can never end either in this world or in any other. But our awareness of it can, and then the Need-love dies too.

1017
Love: Our
Love for Jesus
Letters to Children, (26
October 1963), p. 111.

If you continue to love Jesus, nothing much can go wrong with you, and I hope you may always do so.

1018
Love:
Priorities
God in the Dock,
"Some Thoughts" (1948),
para. 7, p. 150.

Because we love something else more than this world we love even this world better than those who know no other.

410

1019
Love:
Priorities
Letters of C. S. Lewis
8 November 1952),
para. 11, p. 248.

When I have learnt to love God better than my earthly dearest, I shall love my earthly dearest better than I do now. In so far as I learn to love my earthly dearest at the expense of God and *instead* of God, I shall be moving towards the state in which I shall not love my earthly dearest at all. When first things are put first, second things are not suppressed but increased.

1020
Love:
Priorities
The Four Loves, chap. 6,
para. 15, pp. 170–171.

It is probably impossible to love any human being simply "too much." We may love him too much *in proportion* to our love for God; but it is the smallness of our love for God, not the greatness of our love for the man, that constitutes the inordinacy. . . . But the question whether we are loving God or the earthly Beloved "more" is not, so far as concerns our Christian duty, a question about the comparative intensity of two feelings. The real question is, which (when the alternative comes) do you serve, or choose, or put first? To which claim does your will, in the last resort, yield?

1021
Love:
Priorities
Letters to Malcolm:
Chiefly on Prayer,
chap. 4, para. 14, p. 22.

We must aim at what St. Augustine (is it?) calls "ordinate loves." Our deepest concern should be for first things, and our next deepest for second things, and so on down to zero—to total absence of concern for things that are not really good, nor means to good, at all.

1022
Love:
Romantic
Letters of C. S. Lewis
o Arthur Greeves
12 October 1915),
para. 5, p. 85.

You ask me whether I have ever been in love: fool as I am, I am not quite such a fool as all that. But if one is only to talk from first-hand experience on any subject, conversation would be a very poor business. But though I have no personal experience of the thing they call love, I have what is better—the experience of Sapho [sic], of

Euripides of Catullus of Shakespeare of Spenser of Austen of Bronte of, of—anyone else I have read. We see through their eyes. And as the greater includes the less, the passion of a great mind includes all the qualities of the passion of a small one. Accordingly, we have every right to talk about it.

**1023
Love:
Romantic**
Mere Christianity, bk. III, chap. 6, para. 9, p. 99.

Love as distinct from "being in love" is not merely a feeling. It is a deep unity, maintained by the will and deliberately strengthened by habit; reinforced by (in Christian marriages) the grace which both partners ask, and receive, from God. They can have this love for each other even at those moments when they do not like each other; as you love yourself even when you do not like yourself. They can retain this love even when each would easily, if they allowed themselves, be "in love" with someone else. "Being in love" first moved them to promise fidelity: this quieter love enables them to keep the promise. It is on this love that the engine of marriage is run: being in love was the explosion that started it.

**1024
Love:
Romantic**
A Grief Observed, chap. IV, para. 30, p. 84.

This is one of the miracles of love; it gives—to both, but perhaps especially to the woman—a power of seeing through its own enchantments and yet not being disenchanted.

**1025
Love:
Romantic**
God in the Dock, "We Have No Right to Happiness" (1963), para. 25, p. 321.

When two people achieve lasting happiness, this is not solely because they are great lovers but . because they are also—I must put it crudely— good people; controlled, loyal, fairminded, mutually adaptable people.

1026
Loyalty
The World's Last Night and Other Essays,
"Religion and Rocketry"
(1958), para. 15 p. 91.

Our loyalty is due not to our species but to God. . . . It is spiritual, not biological, kinship that counts.

1027
Lust
The Letters of C. S. Lewis to Arthur Greeves (29 May 1918), para. 9, p. 218.

[Ed. note: a pre-conversion statement:] Yes, after all our old conversations I *can* feel otherwise about the lusts of the flesh: is not desire merely a kind of sugar-plum that nature gives us to make us breed, as she does the beetles and toads so that both we and they may beget more creatures to struggle in the same net: Nature, or the common order of things, has really produced in man a sort of Frankenstein who is learning to shake her off. For man alone of all things can master his instincts.

1028
Lust
Letters of C. S. Lewis (10 June 1930), p. 141.

The idea of female beauty is the erotic stimulus for women as well as men. . . . i.e., a lascivious man thinks about women's bodies, a lascivious woman thinks about her own. *What* a world we live in!

1029
Lust
Christian Reflections, "Christianity and Culture (1940), Section III, para. 12, p. 35.

Eros "ceases to be a devil only when it ceases to be a god."

1030
Luther, Martin
Selected Literary Essays, "Donne and Love Poetry" (1938), para. 13, pp. 116–117.

When we turn from the religious works of More to Luther's *Table Talk* we are at once struck by the geniality of the latter. If Luther is right, we have waked from nightmare into sunshine: if he is wrong, we have entered into a fools' paradise. The burden of his charge against the Catholics is that they have needlessly tormented us with scruples.

1031
Lyly, John
English Literature in the Sixteenth Century, bk. II.III, para. 57, 59, 64, pp. 312–314, 316–317.

We now come to Lyly (c. 1553–1606) himself, an author once unjustly celebrated for a style which he did not invent, and now inadequately praised for his real, and very remarkable, achievement. . . .

Euphues itself is related to Lyly's literary career rather as the Preface of the *Lyrical Ballads* is related to Wordsworth's; each marking a temporary aberration, a diversion of the author from his true path, which by its unfortunate celebrity confuses our impression of his genius. . . . He gets some post in the Revels and also at St. Paul's choir school; officially to teach the children Latin (judging by his own verses, he did it very badly), but unofficially to be dramatist, trainer, and producer to what is, in effect, a theatrical company. To that world of "revels," of pretty, pert, highly trained boys who sing elegant poems to delicious music and enact stories that are "ten leagues beyond man's life," in dialogue of exquisite and artificial polish, Lyly belongs. There he does (though with much financial discontent) the work that he was born to do.

. . . Lyly as a dramatist is the first writer since the great medievals whose taste we can trust. . . . Having conceived the imaginary world in which most of his plays are set . . . he brings everything into keeping. He is consistently and exquisitely artificial. . . . The lightness of Lyly's touch, the delicacy, the blessed unreality were real advances in civilization. . . . It is on these bubble-like comedies, not on *Euphues* nor on his anti-Martinist pamphlet *Pappe with a Hatchet,* that Lyly's fame must rest. And they are good, not despite, but by means of, his style. It is the perfect instrument for his purpose, and he can make it pert, grave, tragic, or rapturously exalted. . . . Here is the "Golden" literature at last.

1032
Macdonald, George
The Letters of C. S. Lewis to Arthur Greeves (10 October 1929), para. 2, p. 313.

I am slowly reading a book that we have known *about,* but not known, for many a long day— Macdonald's *Diary of an Old Soul.* How I would have scorned it once! I strongly advise you to try it. He seems to know everything and I find my own experience in it constantly: as regards the literary quality, I am coming to like even his clumsiness. There is a delicious home-spun, earthy flavour about it, as in George Herbert. Indeed *for me* he is better than Herbert.

1033
Macdonald, George
The Letters of C. S. Lewis to Arthur Greeves (31 August 1930), para. 4, pp. 388–389.

As you said in one of your letters, his novels have great and almost intolerable faults. His only real form is the symbolical fantasy like *Phantastes* or *Lilith.* This is what he always writes: but unfortunately, for financial reasons, he sometimes has to *disguise* it as ordinary Victorian fiction. Hence what you get is a certain amount of the real Macdonald linked (as Mezentius linked live men to corpses)—linked onto a mass of quite worthless "plot." . . . Yet the gold is so good that it carries off the dross. . . . I know nothing that gives me such a feeling of spiritual healing, of being washed, as to read G. Macdonald.

1034
Macdonald, George
George MacDonald: An Anthology, Preface, para. 8, pp. 13–14.

His peace of mind came not from building on the future but from resting in what he called "the holy Present." . . . He appears to have been a sunny, playful man, deeply appreciative of all really beautiful and delicious things that money can buy, and no less deeply content to do without them. It is perhaps significant—it is certainly touching— that his chief recorded weakness was a Highland love of finery; and he was all his life hospitable as only the poor can be.

1035
Macdonald, George
George MacDonald: An Anthology, Preface, para. 14, pp. 18–19.

One very effective way of silencing the voice of conscience is to impound in an *Ism* the teacher through whom it speaks: the trumpet no longer seriously disturbs our rest when we have murmured "Thomist," "Barthian" or "Existentialist." And in MacDonald it is always the voice of conscience that speaks. He addresses the will: the demand for obedience, for "something to be neither more nor less nor other than *done*" is incessant. Yet in that very voice of conscience every other faculty somehow speaks as well—intellect and imagination and humour and fancy and all the affections; and no man in modern times was perhaps more aware of the distinction between law and Gospel, the inevitable failure of mere morality. The Divine Sonship is the key-conception which unites all the different elements of this thought. I dare not say that he is never in error; but to speak plainly I know hardly any other writer who seems to be closer, or more continually close, to the Spirit of Christ Himself. Hence his Christ-like union of tenderness and severity. Nowhere else outside the New Testament have I found terror and comfort so intertwined.

1036
**Macdonald,
George**
*George MacDonald:
An Anthology,* Preface,
para. 15, p. 20.

He hopes, indeed, that all men will be saved; but that is because he hopes that all will repent.

1037
**Macdonald,
George**
*George MacDonald:
An Anthology,* Preface,
para. 16, p. 20.

I have never concealed the fact that I regarded him as my master; indeed I fancy I have never written a book in which I did not quote from him. But it has not seemed to me that those who have received my books kindly take even now sufficient notice of the affiliation. Honesty drives me to emphasise it. And even if honesty did not—well, I am a don, and "source-hunting" (*Quellenforschung*) is perhaps in my marrow.

1038
**Machiavelli:
The Prince**
*English Literature in the
Sixteenth Century,*
Introduction, para. 74,
p. 51.

It would be unreasonable . . . to pass over in silence the *Prince* (1513) of Machiavelli, for there the repudiation of medieval principles goes farthest. But for that very reason Machiavelli is not very important. He went too far. Everyone answered him, everyone disagreed with him. The book's success was a success of scandal. To readers who seriously sought instruction in the art of tyranny he could, after all, reveal only the secrets which all men knew. Not to be, but to seem, virtuous—it is a formula whose utility we all discovered in the nursery.

1039
**Marlowe,
Christopher**
*English Literature in the
Sixteenth Century,* bk.
III.III.III, para. 12–13,
pp. 486–488.

Marlowe's greatest poetical achievement is the two sestiads of his unfinished *Hero and Leander.* This is a more perfect work than any of his plays, not because their poetry is always inferior to it but because in it the poetry and the theme are at one. Here, and here only, he found matter to which his genius was entirely adequate. For Marlowe is our great master of the material imagination; he writes best about flesh, gold, gems, stone, fire, clothes, water, snow, and air. . . . The monotonous megalomania of his heroes argues as much penury as depravity in the poet. They utter screaming follies very largely because he cannot think of anything more relevant or probable for them to say. But what incapacitated him as a tragedian qualified him magnificently as a writer of erotic epyllion. This was the work he was born to do. In this form his sole business was to make holiday from all facts and all morals in a world of imagined deliciousness where all beauty was sensuous and all sensuality was beautiful. . . . Nothing could be simpler or more obvious than such a project, but this does not mean that it was easy to execute. Most attempts of the sort have been failures: Shakespeare himself . . . largely failed in *Venus and Adonis*. . . . We may, no doubt, condemn the whole genre on moral grounds: but if it is to be written at all it demands powers which hardly any poet possesses.

. . . I do not know that any other poet has rivalled its peculiar excellence.

1040
Marriage
The Screwtape Letters,
Letter XVIII, para. 6,
pp. 83–84.

[Senior devil Screwtape to junior devil Wormwood:] Humans who have not the gift of continence can be deterred from seeking marriage as a solution because they do not find themselves "in love," and, thanks to us, the idea of marrying with any other motive seems to them low and cynical. Yes, they think that. They regard the intention of loyalty to a partnership for mutual help, for the preservation of chastity, and for the transmission of life, as something lower than a storm of emotion.

1041
Marriage
Mere Christianity, bk. III,
chap. 6, para. 2–3,
pp. 95–96.

The Christian idea of marriage is based on Christ's words that a man and wife are to be regarded as a single organism. . . . The male and the female were made to be combined together in pairs, not simply on the sexual level, but totally combined. The monstrosity of sexual intercourse outside marriage is that those who indulge in it are trying to isolate one kind of union (the sexual) from all the other kinds of union which were intended to go along with it and make up the total union. The Christian attitude does not mean that there is anything wrong about sexual pleasure, any more than about the pleasure of eating. It means that you must not isolate that pleasure and try to get it by itself, any more than you ought to try to get the pleasures of taste without swallowing and digesting, by chewing things and spitting them out again.

As a consequence, Christianity teaches that marriage is for life.

1042
Marriage
The Horse and His Boy,
chap. 15, p. 216.

Aravis also had many quarrels (and, I'm afraid even fights) with Cor, but they always made it up again: so that years later, when they were grown up they were so used to quarrelling and making it up again that they got married so as to go on doing it more conveniently.

1043
Marriage
The Four Loves, chap. 5,
para. 26, p. 148.

Christian writers (notably Milton) have sometimes spoken of the husband's headship with a complacency to make the blood run cold. We must go back to our Bibles. The husband is the head of the wife just in so far as he is to her what Christ is to the Church. He is to love her as Christ loved the Church—read on—*and give his life for her* (*Eph.* V, 25). This headship, then, is

most fully embodied not in the husband we
should all wish to be but in him whose marriage
is most like a crucifixion; whose wife receives
most and gives least, is most unworthy of him,
is—in her own mere nature—least lovable.

1044
Marriage
A Grief Observed,
chap. IV, para. 32,
pp. 57–58.

There is, hidden or flaunted, a sword between the
sexes till an entire marriage reconciles them. It is
arrogance in us to call frankness, fairness, and
chivalry "masculine" when we see them in a
woman; it is arrogance in them, to describe a
man's sensitiveness or tact or tenderness as
"feminine." But also what poor, warped fragments
of humanity most mere men and mere women
must be to make the implications of that
arrogance plausible. Marriage heals this. Jointly
the two become fully human. "In the image of
God created He *them*." Thus, by a paradox, this
carnival of sexuality leads us out beyond our
sexes.

1045
Marriage or Singleness
*Letters to an American
Lady* (8 November
1962), para. 1,
pp. 109–110.

I nominally have [a place of my own] and am
nominally master of the house, but things seldom
go as I would have chosen. The truth is that the
only alternatives are either solitude (with all its
miseries and dangers, both moral and physical) or
else all the rubs and frustrations of a joint life.
The second, even at its worst seems to me far the
better. I hope one is rewarded for all the stunning
replies one thinks of one does not utter! But alas,
even when we don't *say* them, more comes out in
our look, our manner, and our voice. An
elaborately patient silence can be very provoking!
We are *all* fallen creatures and *all* very hard to live
with.

1046
Marxism

Present Concerns: Essays
by C. S. Lewis, "Modern
Man and His Categories
of Thought" (1946),
para. 7, pp. 64–65.

Proletarianism, in its various forms ranging from strict Marxism to vague "democracy" . . . [is] self-satisfied to a degree perhaps beyond the self-satisfaction of any recorded aristocracy. They are convinced that whatever may be wrong with the world it cannot be themselves. Someone else must be to blame for every evil. Hence, when the existence of God is discussed, they by no means think of Him as their Judge. On the contrary, they are His judges. If He puts up a reasonable defence they will consider it and perhaps acquit Him. They have no feelings of fear, guilt, or awe. They think, from the very outset, of God's duties to them, not their duties to Him. And God's duties to them are conceived not in terms of salvation but in purely secular terms—social security, prevention of war, a higher standard of life. "Religion" is judged exclusively by its contribution to these ends.

1047
Masculine

That Hideous Strength,
chap. 14, section 5,
p. 316.

"The male you could have escaped, for it exists only on the biological level. But the masculine none of us can escape. What is above and beyond all things is so masculine that we are all feminine in relation to it. You had better agree with your adversary quickly."

"You mean I shall have to become a Christian?" said Jane.

"It looks like it," said the Director.

1048
Masculine

God in the Dock,
"Priestesses in the
Church?" (1948),
para. 12, pp. 238–239.

It is painful, being a man, to have to assert the privilege, or the burden, which Christianity lays upon my own sex. I am crushingly aware how inadequate most of us are, in our actual and historical individualities, to fill the place prepared for us. But it is an old saying in the army that you salute the uniform not the wearer. Only one wearing the masculine uniform can (provisionally, and till the *Parousia*) [Footnote: "The future return of Christ in glory to judge the living and the dead."] represent the Lord to the Church: for we are all, corporately and individually, feminine to Him. We men may often make very bad priests. That is because we are insufficiently masculine. It is no cure to call in those who are not masculine at all. A given man may make a very bad husband; you cannot mend matters by trying to reverse the roles. He may make a bad male partner in a dance. The cure for that is that men should more diligently attend dancing classes; not that the ballroom should henceforward ignore distinctions of sex and treat all dancers as neuter. That would, of course, be eminently sensible, civilized, and enlightened, but, once more, "not near so much like a Ball."

1049
Materialism and Christianity
God in the Dock, "Man or Rabbit?" (1946?), para. 4, p. 110.

The Christian and the Materialist hold different beliefs about the universe. They can't both be right. The one who is wrong will act in a way which simply doesn't fit the real universe. Consequently, with the best will in the world, he will be helping his fellow creatures to their destruction.

1050
Materialism, Philosophical
God in the Dock, "Dogma and the Universe" (1943), para. 3, p. 39.

If anything emerges clearly from modern physics, it is that nature is not everlasting. The universe had a beginning, and will have an end. But the great materialistic systems of the past all believed in the eternity, and thence in the self-existence of matter.

1051
Maturity
An Experiment in
Criticism, chap. 7,
para. 23, p. 72.

The process of growing up is to be valued for what we gain, not for what we lose.

1052
Maturity
An Experiment in
Criticism, chap. 2,
para. 11, p. 12.

Excellence in our response to books, like excellence in other things, cannot be had without experience and discipline, and therefore cannot be had by the very young.

1053
Maturity
An Experiment in
Criticism, chap. 7,
para. 25, p. 73.

Nothing is more characteristically juvenile than contempt for juvenility: . . . youth's characteristic chronological snobbery.

1054
Memory
The Letters of C. S.
Lewis to Arthur Greeves
(16 November 1915),
para. 4, p. 87.

Why is it that one can never think of the past without wanting to go back?

1055
Memory
Letters of C. S. Lewis (31
August 1921), para. 1,
pp. 71–72.

I still feel that the real value of such a holiday is still to come, in the images and ideas which we have put down to mature in the cellarage of our brains, thence to come up with a continually improving bouquet. Already the hills are getting higher, the grass greener, and the sea bluer than they really were; and thanks to the deceptive working of happy memory our poorest stopping places will become haunts of impossible pleasure and Epicurean repast.

1056

Memory

Present Concerns: Essays by C. S. Lewis, "Talking About Bicycles" (1946), para. 21, p. 71.

Wordsworth, you see, was Enchanted. He got delicious gleams of memory from his early youth and took them at their face value. He believed that if he could have got back to certain spots in his own past he would find there the moment of joy waiting for him. You are Disenchanted. You've begun to suspect that those moments, of which the memory is now so ravishing, weren't at the time quite so wonderful as they now seem. You're right. They weren't. Each great experience is

"a whisper
Which Memory will warehouse as a shout."
[Footnote: From an unpublished poem by Owen Barfield.]

But what then? Isn't the warehousing just as much a fact as anything else? Is the vision any less important because a particular kind of polarized light between past and present happens to be the mechanism that brings it into focus? Isn't it a fact about mountains—as good a fact as any other—that they look purple at a certain distance?

1057

Memory

Letters to Malcolm: Chiefly on Prayer, chap. 22, para. 15, pp. 121–122.

Memory as we now know it is a dim foretaste, a mirage even, of a power which the soul, or rather Christ in the soul (He went to "prepare a place" for us), will exercise hereafter. It need no longer be intermittent. Above all, it need no longer be private to the soul in which it occurs. I can now communicate to you the fields of my boyhood—they are building-estates to-day—only imperfectly, by words. Perhaps the day is coming when I can take you for a walk through them.

1058
Memory
Letters to Malcolm:
Chiefly on Prayer,
chap. 22, para. 17,
p. 122.

The dullest of us knows how memory can transfigure; how often some momentary glimpse of beauty in boyhood is

   a whisper
Which memory will warehouse as a shout.

Don't talk to me of the "illusions" of memory. Why should what we see at the moment be more "real" than what we see from ten years' distance?

1059
Memory
Letters to Malcolm:
Chiefly on Prayer,
chap. 22, para. 17,
p. 122.

Traherne's "orient and immortal wheat" or Wordsworth's landscape "apparelled in celestial light" may not have been so radiant in the past when it was present as in the remembered past. That is the beginning of the glorification. One day they will be more radiant still. Thus in the sense-bodies of the redeemed the whole New Earth will arise. The same, yet not the same, as this. It was sown in corruption, it is raised in incorruption.

1060
Memory
Letters to Malcolm:
Chiefly on Prayer,
chap. 22, para. 18,
p. 123.

The strangest discovery of a widower's life is the possibility, sometimes, of recalling with detailed and uninhibited imagination, with tenderness and gratitude, a passage of carnal love, yet with no re-awakening of concupiscence. And when it occurs (it must not be sought) awe comes upon us. It is like seeing nature itself rising from its grave. What was sown in momentariness is raised in still permanence. What was sown as a becoming, rises as being. Sown in subjectivity, it rises in objectivity. The transitory secret of two is now a chord in the ultimate music.

1061
Mercy
God in the Dock, "The Humanitarian Theory of Punishment" (1949), para. 13, p. 294.

The essential act of mercy was to pardon; and pardon in its very essence involves the recognition of guilt and ill-desert in the recipient. If crime is only a disease which needs cure, not sin which deserves punishment, it cannot be pardoned. How can you pardon a man for having a gumboil or a club foot? But the Humanitarian theory wants simply to abolish Justice and substitute Mercy for it. This means that you start being "kind" to people before you have considered their rights, and then force upon them supposed kindnesses which no one but you will recognize as kindnesses and which the recipient will feel as abominable cruelties. You have overshot the mark. Mercy, detached from Justice, grows unmerciful. That is the important paradox. As there are plants which will flourish only in mountain soil, so it appears that Mercy will flower only when it grows in the crannies of the rock of Justice: transplanted to the marshlands of mere Humanitarianism, it becomes a man-eating weed, all the more dangerous because it is still called by the same name as the mountain variety.

1062
Metaphor
The Allegory of Love, chap. II.III, para. 6, p. 60.

Every metaphor is an allegory in little.

1063
Metaphor
Miracles, chap. 10, para. 10, p. 72.

It is a serious mistake to think that metaphor is an optional thing which poets and orators may put into their work as a decoration and plain speakers can do without. The truth is that if we are going to talk at all about things which are not perceived by the senses, we are forced to use language metaphorically. Books on psychology or

economics or politics are as continuously
metaphorical as books of poetry or devotion.
There is no other way of talking, as every
philologist is aware. . . . All speech about
supersensibles is, and must be, metaphorical in the
highest degree.

1064
Metaphor
Miracles, chap. 10,
para. 19, p. 79.

Christian doctrines which are "metaphorical" . . .
mean something which is just as "supernatural" or
shocking after we have removed the ancient
imagery as it was before. . . . These things not
only cannot be asserted—they cannot even be
presented for discussion—without metaphor. We
can make our speech duller; we cannot make it
more literal.

1065
Middle Ages
Letters of C. S. Lewis (7
June 1934), para. 3,
p. 156.

This is a point I would press on anyone dealing
with the Middle Ages, that the first essential is to
read the relevant classics over and over: the key to
everything—allegory, courtly love, etc.—is there.
After that the two things to know really well are
the *Divine Comedy* and the *Romance of the Rose.*
The student who has really digested these (I don't
claim to be such a person myself!) with good
commentaries, and who also knows the Classics
and the Bible (including the *apocryphal* New
Testament) has the game in his hands and can
defeat over and over again those who have simply
burrowed in obscure parts of the actual middle
ages.

1066
Middle Ages
Letters of C. S. Lewis (7
June 1934), para. 4,
p. 157.

Remember (this has been all-important to me) that
what you want to know about the Middle Ages
will often not be in a book on the Middle Ages,
but in the early chapters of some history of
general philosophy or science.

1067
Middle Ages
The Discarded Image,
chap. 1, para. 8, p. 5.

[The medieval mind had an] overwhelmingly bookish or clerkly character. . . . When we speak of the Middle Ages as the ages of authority we are usually thinking about the authority of the Church. But they were the age not only of her authority, but of authorities. If their culture is regarded as a response to environment, then the elements in that environment to which it responded most vigorously were manuscripts.

1068
Middle Ages
The Discarded Image,
chap. 1, para. 14–15, 18,
pp. 10, 12.

At his most characteristic, medieval man was not a dreamer nor a wanderer. He was an organiser, a codifier, a builder of systems. He wanted "a place for everything and everything in the right place." Distinction, definition, tabulation were his delight. Though full of turbulent activities, he was equally full of the impulse to formalise them. War was (in intention) formalised by the art of heraldry and the rules of chivalry; sexual passion (in intention), by an elaborate code of love. . . . There was nothing which medieval people liked better, or did better, than sorting out and tidying up. Of all our modern inventions I suspect that they would most have admired the card index.

. . . The perfect examples are the *Summa* of Aquinas and Dante's *Divine Comedy*; as unified and ordered as the Parthenon or the *Oedipus Rex,* as crowded and varied as a London terminus on a bank holiday.

. . . This Model of the Universe is a supreme medieval work of art . . . in a sense the central work, that in which most particular works were embedded, to which they constantly referred, from which they drew a great deal of their strength.

1069
Middle Ages:
Art/Literature
The Discarded Image,
chap. 5, section A,
para. 13, p. 101.

Medieval art was deficient in perspective, and poetry followed suit. Nature, for Chaucer, is all foreground; we never get a landscape. And neither poets nor artists were much interested in the strict illusionism of later periods.

1070
Middle Ages:
Literature
The Discarded Image,
chap. 8, para. 10–13,
pp. 204–205.

The Model universe of our ancestors had a built-in significance. And that in two senses; as having "significant form" (it is an admirable design) and as a manifestation of the wisdom and goodness that created it. There was no question of waking it into beauty or life. Ours, most emphatically, was not the wedding garment, nor the shroud. The achieved perfection was already there. The only difficulty was to make an adequate response.

This, if accepted, will perhaps go far to explain some characteristics of medieval literature.

It may, for example, explain both its most typical vice and its most typical virtue. The typical vice, as we all know, is dulness; sheer, unabashed, prolonged dulness, where the author does not seem to be even trying to interest us. . . . The writer feels everything to be so interesting in itself that there is no need for him to make it so. The story, however badly told, will still be worth telling; the truths, however badly stated, still worth stating. He expects the subject to do for him nearly everything he ought to do himself. . . .

And yet, I believe, it is also connected with the characteristic virtue of good medieval work. What this is, anyone can feel if he turns from the narrative verse of, say, Chapman or Keats to the best parts of Marie de France or Gower. What will strike him at once is the absence of strain. In the Elizabethan or Romantic examples we feel that the poet has done a great deal of work; in the medieval, we are at first hardly aware of a poet at all. The writing is so limpid and effortless that the story seems to be telling itself. You would think, till you tried, that anyone could do the like. But in reality no story tells itself. Art is at work. But it is the art of people who, no less than the bad medieval authors, have a complete confidence in the intrinsic value of their matter. The telling is for the sake of the tale; in Chapman or Keats we feel that the tale is valued only as an opportunity for the lavish and highly individual treatment.

1071
Miracles
God in the Dock,
"Miracles" (1942),
para. 1, 3, pp. 25–27.

Seeing is not believing. This is the first thing to get clear in talking about miracles. Whatever experiences we may have, we shall not regard them as miraculous if we already hold a philosophy which excludes the supernatural. . . . The senses are not infallible. . . . Experience by itself proves nothing. If a man doubts whether he is dreaming or waking, no experiment can solve his doubt, since every experiment may itself be part of the dream. Experience proves this, or that, or nothing, according to the preconceptions we bring to it. . . .

The experience of a miracle in fact requires two conditions. First we must believe in a normal stability of nature, which means we must recognize that the data offered by our senses recur in regular patterns. Secondly, we must believe in some reality beyond Nature.

1072
Miracles
God in the Dock,
"Miracles" (1942),
para. 7, p. 29.

The miracles in fact are a retelling in small letters of the very same story which is written across the whole world in letters too large for some of us to see.

1073
Miracles
Miracles, chap. 1,
para. 2, p. 3.

Every event which might claim to be a miracle is, in the last resort, something presented to our senses, something seen, heard, touched, smelled, or tasted. And our senses are not infallible. If anything extraordinary seems to have happened, we can always say that we have been the victims of an illusion. If we hold a philosophy which excludes the supernatural, this is what we always shall say. What we learn from experience depends on the kind of philosophy we bring to experience.

1074
Miracles
Miracles, chap. 8,
para. 7–8, pp. 58–60.

This perhaps helps to make a little clearer what the laws of Nature really are. We are in the habit of talking as if they caused events to happen; but they have never caused any event at all. . . .

It is therefore inaccurate to define a miracle as something that breaks the laws of Nature. It doesn't. If I knock out my pipe I alter the position of a great many atoms: in the long run, and to an infinitesimal degree, of all the atoms there are. Nature digests or assimilates this event with perfect ease and harmonises it in a twinkling with all other events. It is one more bit of raw material for the laws to apply to, and they apply.

. . . If God creates a miraculous spermatozoon in the body of a virgin, it does not proceed to break any laws. The laws at once take it over. Nature is ready. Pregnancy follows, according to all the normal laws, and nine months later a child is born. We see every day that physical nature is not in the least incommoded by the daily inrush of events from biological nature or from psychological nature. If events ever come from beyond Nature altogether, she will be no more incommoded by them. Be sure she will rush to the point where she is invaded, as the defensive forces rush to a cut in our finger, and there hasten to accommodate the newcomer. The moment it enters her realm it obeys all her laws. Miraculous wine will intoxicate, miraculous conception will lead to pregnancy, inspired books will suffer all the ordinary processes of textual corruption, miraculous bread will be digested. The divine art of miracle is not an art of suspending the pattern to which events conform but of feeding new events into that pattern.

1075
Miracles
Miracles, chap. 8, para. 10, p. 61.

By definition, miracles must of course interrupt the usual course of Nature; but if they are real they must, in the very act of so doing, assert all the more the unity and self-consistency of total reality at some deeper level.

1076
Miracles
Miracles, chap. 8, para. 10, pp. 61–62.

If what we call Nature is modified by supernatural power, then we may be sure that the capability of being so modified is of the essence of Nature—that the total events, if we could grasp it, would turn out to involve, by its very character, the possibility of such modifications. If Nature brings forth miracles then doubtless it is as "natural" for her to do so when impregnated by the masculine force beyond her as it is for a woman to bear children to a man. In calling them miracles we do not mean that they are contradictions or outrages; we mean that, left to her own resources, she could never produce them.

1077
Miracles
Miracles, chap. 15, para. 1, p. 132.

The fitness of the Christian miracles and their difference from these mythological miracles, lies in the fact that they show invasion by a Power which is not alien. They are what might be expected to happen when she is invaded not simply by a god, but by the God of Nature: by a Power which is outside her jurisdiction not as a

foreigner but as a sovereign. They proclaim that
He who has come is not merely a king, but *the*
King, her King and ours.

1078
Miracles
Miracles, chap. 15,
para. 2, p. 132.

I am in no way committed to the assertion that
God has never worked miracles through and for
Pagans or never permitted created supernatural
beings to do so.

1079
Miracles
Miracles, chap. 15,
para. 2, p. 133.

Sometimes the credibility of the miracles is in an
inverse ratio to the credibility of the religion. Thus
miracles are (in late documents, I believe) recorded
of the Buddha. But what could be more absurd
than that he who came to teach us that Nature is
an illusion from which we must escape should
occupy himself in producing effects on the
Natural level—that he who comes to wake us
from a nightmare should *add* to the nightmare?
The more we respect his teaching the less we
could accept his miracles. But in Christianity, the
more we understand what God it is who is said
to be present and the purpose for which He is
said to have appeared, the more credible the
miracles become. That is why we seldom find the
Christian miracles denied except by those who
have abandoned some part of the Christian
doctrine. The mind which asks for a non-
miraculous Christianity is a mind in process of
relapsing from Christianity into mere "religion."

1080
Miracles
Miracles, chap. 15,
para. 4, pp. 134–135.

In all these miracles alike the incarnate God does
suddenly and locally something that God has done
or will do in general. Each miracle writes for us in
small letters something that God has already
written, or will write in letters almost too large to
be noticed, across the whole canvas of Nature.

They focus at a particular point either God's actual, or His future, operations on the universe.

1081
Miracles
Miracles, chap. 15, para. 6, pp. 135–136.

Another way of expressing the real character of the miracles would be to say that though isolated from other actions, they are not isolated in either of the two ways we are apt to suppose. They are not, on the one hand, isolated from other Divine acts: they do close and small and, as it were, in focus what God at other times does so large that men do not attend to it. Neither are they isolated exactly as we suppose from other human acts: they anticipate powers which all men will have when they also are "sons" of God and enter into that "glorious liberty." Christ's isolation is not that of a prodigy but of a pioneer. He is the first of His kind; He will not be the last.

1082
Miracles
Miracles, chap. 16, para. 14, p. 150.

In the Walking on the Water we see the relations of spirit and Nature so altered that Nature can be made to do whatever spirit pleases. This new obedience of Nature is, of course, not to be separated even in thought from spirit's own obedience to the Father of Spirits. Apart from that proviso such obedience by Nature, if it were possible, would result in chaos: the evil dream of Magic arises from finite spirit's longing to get that power without paying that price.

1083
Miracles
Miracles, chap. 17, para. 5, pp. 167–168.

You are probably quite right in thinking that you will never see a miracle done: . . . They come on great occasions: they are found at the great ganglions of history—not of political or social history, but of that spiritual history which cannot be fully known by men. If your own life does not happen to be near one of those ganglions, how should you expect to see one? If we were heroic

missionaries, apostles, or martyrs, it would be a
different matter. But why you or I? Unless you live
near a railway, you will not see trains go past your
windows. How likely is it that you or I will be
present when a peace-treaty is signed, when a
great scientific discovery is made, when a dictator
commits suicide? That we should see a miracle is
even less likely. Nor, if we understand, shall we be
anxious to do so. "Nothing almost sees miracles
but misery." Miracles and martyrdoms tend to
bunch about the same areas of history—areas we
have naturally no wish to frequent.

1084
Missions
Christian Reflections,
"Christianity and
Culture" (1940), chap. 2,
para. 18, p. 17.

If we are to convert our heathen neighbours, we
must understand their culture.

1085
Money
Perelandra, chap. 4,
p. 48.

This now appeared to him as a principle of far
wider application and deeper moment. This itch
to have things over again, as if life were a film
that could be unrolled twice or even made to
work backwards . . . was it possibly the root of
all evil? No: of course the love of money was
called that. But money itself—perhaps one valued
it chiefly as a defence against chance, a security
for being able to have things over again, a means
of arresting the unrolling of the film.

1086
Money
Mere Christianity, bk. IV,
chap. 10, para. 11,
p. 180.

One of the dangers of having a lot of money is
that you may be quite satisfied with the kinds of
happiness money can give and so fail to realise
your need for God. If everything seems to come
simply by signing checks, you may forget that you
are at every moment totally dependent on God.

1087
Moral Relapse
*The Letters of C. S.
Lewis to Arthur Greeves*
(13 August 1930),
para. 3, p. 376.

One of the worst things about a moral relapse—
to me—is that it throws such a shadow back on
the time before during which you thought you
were getting on quite well. Having found
oneself—for the hundredth time—back where one
started, it seems so obvious that one has never
really moved at all: and that what seemed progress
was only [a] dream, or even the irrelevant result of
circumstances or physical condition.

1088
Moralists
The Screwtape Letters,
Letter XXIII, p. 107.

[Senior devil Screwtape to junior devil
Wormwood:] We . . . distract men's minds from
Who He [Jesus] is, and what He did. We first
make Him solely a teacher . . . all great moralists
are sent [by God], not to inform men, but to
remind them, to restate the primeval moral
platitudes.

1089
Morality
The Problem of Pain,
chap. 1, para. 11,
pp. 21–22.

Morality, like numinous awe, is a jump; in it, man
goes beyond anything that can be "given" in the
facts of experience. And it has one characteristic
too remarkable to be ignored. The moralities
accepted among men may differ—though not, at
bottom, so widely as is often claimed—but they
all agree in prescribing a behaviour which their
adherents fail to practise. All men alike stand
condemned, not by alien codes of ethics, but by
their own, and all men therefore are conscious of
guilt.

1090
Morality
The Problem of Pain,
chap. 4, p. 65.

God may be more than moral goodness: He is
not less. The road to the promised land runs past
Sinai. The moral law may exist to be transcended:
but there is no transcending it for those who have
not first admitted its claims upon them, and then
tried with all their strength to meet that claim,

and fairly and squarely faced the fact of their failure.

1091
Morality
Christian Reflections "On Ethics" (1943?), chap. 4, para. 27, p. 56.

In thus recalling men to traditional morality I am not of course maintaining that it will provide an answer to every particular moral problem with which we may be confronted. M. Sartre seems to me to be the victim of a curious misunderstanding when he rejects the conception of general moral rules on the ground that such rules may fail to apply clearly to all concrete problems of conduct. Who could ever have supposed that by accepting a moral code we should be delivered from all questions of casuistry? Obviously it is moral codes that create questions of casuistry, just as the rules of chess create chess problems. The man without a moral code, like the animal, is free from moral problems. The man who has not learned to count is free from mathematical problems. A man asleep is free from all problems. Within the framework of general human ethics problems will, of course, arise and will sometimes be solved wrongly. This possibility of error is simply the symptom that we are awake, not asleep, that we are men, not beasts or gods. If I were pressing on you a panacea, if I were recommending traditional ethics as a means to some end, I might be tempted to promise you the infallibility which I actually deny. But that, you see, is not my position. I send you back to your nurse and your father, to all the poets and sages and law givers, because, in a sense, I hold that you are already there whether you recognize it or not: that there is really no ethical alternative: that those who urge us to adopt new moralities are only offering us the mutilated or expurgated text of a book which we already possess in the original manuscript. They all wish us to depend on them instead of on that original, and then to deprive us of our full humanity. Their activity is in the long run always directed against our freedom.

1092
Morality
Christian Reflections,
"The Poison of
Subjectivism" (1943),
chap. 6, para. 8–10,
pp. 74–75.

Let us get two propositions written into our minds with indelible ink.

(1) The human mind has no more power of inventing a new value than of planting a new sun in the sky or a new primary colour in the spectrum.

(2) Every attempt to do so consists in arbitrarily selecting some one maxim of traditional morality, isolating it from the rest, and erecting it into an *unum necessarium.*

1093
Morality
On Stories, "The Novels
of Charles Williams"
(1949), para. 16, p. 27.

Morality has spoiled literature often enough: we all remember what happened to some nineteenth-century novels. The truth is, it is very bad to reach the stage of thinking deeply and frequently about duty unless you are prepared to go a stage further. The Law, as St Paul first clearly explained, only takes you to the school gates. Morality exists to be transcended. We act from duty in the hope that someday we shall do the same acts freely and delightfully.

1094
Morality
Mere Christianity, bk. I,
chap. 1, para. 11, p. 21.

First, . . . human beings, all over the earth, have this curious idea that they ought to behave in a certain way, and cannot really get rid of it. Secondly, . . . they do not in fact behave in that way. They know the Law of Nature; they break it. These two facts are the foundation of all clear thinking about ourselves and the universe we live in.

1095
Morality
Mere Christianity, bk. I;
chap. 2, para. 2, 4,
pp. 22–23.

This thing that judges between two instincts, that decides which should be encouraged, cannot itself be either of them. You might as well say the sheet of music which tells you, at a given moment, to play one note on the piano and not another, is itself one of the notes on the keyboard. The Moral Law tells us the tune we have to play: our instincts are merely the keys.

. . . There is none of our impulses which the Moral Law may not sometimes tell us to suppress, and none which it may not sometimes tell us to encourage. . . . Strictly speaking, there are no such things as good and bad impulses. Think once again of a piano. It has not got two kinds of notes on it, the "right" notes and the "wrong" ones. Every single note is right at one time and wrong at another.

1096
Morality
Mere Christianity, bk. I,
chap. 2, para. 5,
pp. 23–24.

The most dangerous thing you can do is to take any one impulse of your own nature and set it up as the thing you ought to follow at all costs. There is not one of them which will not make us into devils if we set it up as an absolute guide.

1097
Morality
Mere Christianity, bk. I,
chap. 2, para. 6–7,
pp. 24–25.

"Isn't what you call the Moral Law just a social convention, something that is put into us by education?"

. . . If no set of moral ideas were truer or better than any other, there would be no sense in preferring civilised morality to savage morality, or Christian morality to Nazi morality. In fact, of course, we all do believe that some moralities are better than others. . . . The moment you say that one set of moral ideas can be better than another, you are, in fact, measuring them both by a standard . . . comparing them both with some

Real Morality, admitting that there is such a thing as a real Right, independent of what people think, and that some people's ideas get nearer to that real Right than others.

1098
Morality
God in the Dock, "Cross-Examination" (1963), para. 44, p. 265.

Moral collapse follows upon spiritual collapse.

1099
More, Sir Thomas
English Literature in the Sixteenth Century, bk. II.I.I, para. 30, p. 180.

Great claims have in modern times been made for More's English prose; I can accept them only with serious reservations. . . . The man who sits down and reads fairly through fifty pages of More will find many phrases to admire; but he will also find an invertebrate length of sentence, a fumbling multiplication of epithets, and an almost complete lack of rhythmical vitality. . . . Its chief cause is the fact that More never really rose from a legal to a literary conception of clarity and completeness. He multiplies words in a vain endeavour to stop up all possible chinks, where a better artist forces his conceptions on us by the light and heat of intellect and emotion in which they burn. He thus loses the advantages both of full writing and of concise writing. There are no lightning thrusts: and, on the other hand, no swelling tide of thought and feeling. The style is stodgy and dough-like. As for the good phrases, the reader will already have divined their nature. They come when More is in his homeliest vein: their race and pith and mere Englishry are the great redeeming feature of his prose. . . . Nearly all that is best in More is comic or close to comedy.

1100
More, Sir Thomas
English Literature in the Sixteenth Century, bk. II.I.I, para. 31, pp. 180–181.

We think of More, and rightly, as a humanist and a saintly man. On the one hand, he is the writer of the *Utopia,* the friend of Erasmus, the man whose house became a sort of academy. On the other, he is the man who wanted to be a Carthusian, who used a log of wood for his bolster and wore the hair, the martyr who by high example refused the wine offered him on his way to execution. The literary tragedy is that neither of these sides to his character found nearly such perfect expression in his writings as they deserved. The *Utopia* ought to have been only a beginning: his fertility of mind, his humour, and his genius for dialogue ought to have been embodied in some great work, some *colloquies* meatier than those of Erasmus, some satiric invention more gravely droll than Rabelais. As for his sanctity, to live and die like a saint is no doubt a better thing than to write like one, but it is not the same thing; and More does not write like a saint.

1101
More, Sir Thomas:
Supplication of Souls
English Literature in the Sixteenth Century, bk. II.I.I, para. 20, pp. 172–173.

The *Supplication of Souls* . . . illustrates a further stage in the degradation of the idea of purgatory. In Fisher the pain has been separated from any spiritual purification, but the torments had at least been inflicted by angels. In More this last link with heaven is severed. The attendants (if that is the right word) are now devils. "Our keepers," say the imprisoned souls, "are such as God kepe you from, cruell damned spirites, odious enemies and despitefull tormentours, and theyr companye more horrible and grieuous to vs than is the payn itself and the intollerable tourmente that they doo vs, wherewith from top to toe they cease not to teare vs." The length of the sentence has thus become the sole difference between purgatory and hell.

Purgatory is a department of hell. And More's humour, continued even here, somehow increases the horror. Instead of the psalms and litanies which resounded on the sunlit terraces of Dante's mountain from souls "contented in the flame," out of the black fire which More has imagined, mixed with the howls of unambiguous physical torture, come peals of harsh laughter. All is black, salt, macabre. I make the point not to disgrace a man before whom the best of us must stand uncovered, but because the age we are studying cannot be understood without it. This sort of thing, among others, was what the old religion had come to mean in the popular imagination during the reign of Henry VIII: this was one of the things a man left behind in becoming a Protestant.

1102
More, Sir Thomas:
Utopia
English Literature in the
Sixteenth Century, bk.
II.I.I, para. 14–15,
pp. 168–169.

The *Utopia* has its serious, even its tragic, elements. It is, as its translator Robinson says, "fruteful and profitable." But it is not a consistently serious philosophical treatise, and all attempts to treat it as such break down sooner or later. . . . The truth surely is that as long as we take the *Utopia* for a philosophical treatise it will "give" wherever we lean our weight. It is, to begin with, a dialogue: and we cannot be certain which of the speakers, if any, represents More's considered opinion. . . . The whole book [may be] only a satiric glass to reveal our own avarice by contrast and is not meant to give us directly practical advice.

These puzzles may give the impression that the *Utopia* is a confused book: and if it were intended as a serious treatise it would be very confused indeed. On my view, however, it appears confused only so long as we are trying to get out of it what it never intended to give. It becomes intelligible and delightful as soon as we take it for what it is—a holiday work, a spontaneous overflow of intellectual high spirits, a revel of debate, paradox, comedy and (above all) of invention, which starts many hares and kills none. It is written by More the translator of Lucian and friend of Erasmus, not More the chancellor or the ascetic. Its place on our shelves is close to *Gulliver* and *Erewhon,* within reasonable distance of Rabelais, a long way from the *Republic* or *New Worlds for Old.*

1103
More, Sir Thomas:
Utopia
English Literature in the
Sixteenth Century, bk.
II.I.I, para. 16, p. 170.

[*Utopia*] has no place in the history of political philosophy: in the history of prose fiction it has a very high place indeed.

1104
Mornings
Letters to an American
Lady (30 September
1958), p. 78.

I am a barbarously early riser. . . . I love the empty, silent, dewy, cobwebby hours.

1105
Motives
Letters to an American
Lady (28 March 1961),
para. 1, p. 97.

Humans are very seldom either totally sincere or totally hypocritical. Their moods change, their motives are mixed, and they are often themselves quite mistaken as to what their motives are.

1106
Mystery
A Grief Observed,
chap. IV, para. 38,
p. 89.

The best is perhaps what we understand least.

1107
Mysticism
Letters to Malcolm:
Chiefly on Prayer,
chap. 12, para. 8,
p. 65.

The true religion gives value to its own mysticism; mysticism does not validate the religion in which it happens to occur.

1108
Myth
The Pilgrim's Regress,
bk. 9, chap. 5, p. 171.

"Child, if you will, it *is* mythology. It is but truth, not fact: an image, not the very real. But then it is My mythology. The words of Wisdom are also myth and metaphor: but since they do not know themselves for what they are, in them the hidden myth is master, here it should be servant: and it is but of man's inventing. This is My inventing, this is the veil under which I have chosen to appear even from the first until now. For this end I made your senses and for this end your imagination, that you might see My face and live. What would you have? Have you not heard among the pagans the story of Semele? Or was there any age in any land when men did not know that corn and wine were the blood and body of a dying and yet living God?

1109
Myth
Selected Literary Essays,
"Shelley, Dryden, and Mr
Eliot" (1939), para. 34,
p. 205.

Myth is . . . like manna; it is to each man a different dish and to each the dish he needs.

1110
Myth and
Christianity
God in the Dock, "Myth
Became Fact" (1944),
para. 11, pp. 66–67.

Now as myth transcends thought, Incarnation transcends myth. The heart of Christianity is a myth which is also a fact. The old myth of the Dying God, *without ceasing to be myth* comes down from the heaven of legend and imagination to the earth of history. It *happens*—at a particular date, in a particular place, followed by definable historical consequences. We pass from a Balder or an Osiris, dying nobody knows when or where, to a historical Person crucified (it is all in order) *under Pontius Pilate.* By becoming fact it does not cease to be myth: that is the miracle.

1111
Myth and Christianity
God in the Dock, "Myth Became Fact" (1944), para. 13, p. 67.

Those who do not know that this great myth became Fact when the Virgin conceived are, indeed to be pitied. But Christians also need to be reminded . . . that what became Fact was a Myth, that it carries with it into the world of Fact all the properties of a myth. God is more than a god, not less; Christ is more than Balder, not less. We must not be ashamed of the mythical radiance resting on our theology.

1112
Nashe, Thomas

English Literature in the Sixteenth Century, bk. III.II.I, para. 24, 27, pp. 410–412.

Thomas Nashe (1567–1601) is undoubtedly the greatest of the Elizabethan pamphleteers, the perfect literary showman, the juggler with words who can keep a crowd spell-bound by sheer virtuosity. The subject, in his sort of writing, is unimportant. . . .

Wherever it came from, the style which appears in *Pierce Penilesse* offered the Elizabethan reader a new sort of pleasure. . . . It is very easy to see the faults of *Piers*; its shapeless garrulity, the reckless inconsistency of its attitudes, and the author's nasty pleasure in describing cruelty. It is more useful to try to see why it was once liked, for this was the most popular of Nashe's works and was even, if we can trust his own statement, translated into French. Its appeal is almost entirely to that taste for happy extravagance in language and triumphant impudence of tone, which the Elizabethans have, perhaps, bequeathed rather to their American than to their English descendants. . . . Throughout the work Nashe's phrasing has the vividness of a clown's red nose.

**1113
Nashe,
Thomas**
*English Literature in the
Sixteenth Century,* bk.
III.II.I, para. 28, p. 413.

[The Nashe-Harvey quarrel:] You must come to them as to a ferocious game: if you are looking for serious debate you will find them unreadable. The very qualities which we should blame in an ordinary controversialist are the life and soul of Nashe. He is unfair, illogical, violent, extravagant, coarse: but then that is the joke. . . . Nashe's satire . . . always has Dryden's unanswerable ease and gusto, seems to cost the writer nothing, kills with nonchalance.

**1114
Nationalism**
The Four Loves, chap. 2,
para. 34, p. 42.

Of course [healthy] patriotism . . . is not in the least aggressive. It asks only to be let alone. It becomes militant only to protect what it loves. In any mind which has a pennyworth of imagination it produces a good attitude towards foreigners. How can I love my home without coming to realise that other men, no less rightly, love theirs? Once you have realised that the Frenchmen like *café complet* just as we like bacon and eggs— why, good luck to them and let them have it. The last thing we want is to make everywhere else just like our own home. It would not be home unless it were different.

**1115
Nationalism**
The Four Loves, chap. 2,
para. 37-38, pp. 44–45.

Patriotism . . . is not a sentiment but a belief: a firm, even prosaic belief that our own nation, in sober fact, has long been, and still is markedly superior to all others. I once ventured to say to an old clergyman who was voicing this sort of patriotism, "But, sir, aren't we told that *every* people thinks its own men the bravest and its own women the fairest in the world?" He replied with total gravity—he could not have been graver if he had been saying the Creed at the altar—"Yes, but in England it's true." To be sure, this conviction had not made my friend (God rest his soul) a

villain; only an extremely lovable old ass. It can
however produce asses that kick and bite. On the
lunatic fringe it may shade off into that popular
Racialism which Christianity and science equally
forbid.

1116

Natural Gifts, Danger of

Mere Christianity, bk. IV, chap. 10, para. 11–14, pp. 180–182.

Natural gifts carry with them a . . . danger. If you
have sound nerves and intelligence and health and
popularity and a good upbringing, you are likely
to be quite satisfied with your character as it is.
"Why drag God into it?" you may ask. . . . Often
people who have all these natural kinds of
goodness cannot be brought to recognise their
need for Christ at all until, one day, the natural
goodness lets them down and their self-
satisfaction is shattered. In other words, it is hard
for those who are "rich" in this sense to enter the
Kingdom.

It is very different for the nasty people—the
little, low, timid, warped, thin-blooded, lonely
people, or the passionate, sensual, unbalanced
people. If they make any attempt at goodness at
all, they learn, in double quick time, that they
need help. It is Christ or nothing for them. . . .

There is either a warning or an encouragement
here for every one of us. If you are a nice
person—if virtue comes easily to you—beware!
Much is expected from those to whom much is
given. If you mistake for your own merits what
are really God's gifts to you through nature, and if
you are contented with simply being nice, you are
still a rebel: and all those gifts will only make
your fall more terrible. . . . The Devil was an
archangel once; his natural gifts were as far above
yours as yours are above those of a chimpanzee.

But if you are a poor creature—poisoned by a
wretched up-bringing in some house full of vulgar
jealousies and senseless quarrels—saddled, by no

choice of your own, with some loathsome sexual perversion—nagged day in and day out by an inferiority complex that makes you snap at your best friends—do not despair. He knows all about it. You are one of the poor whom He blessed. He knows what a wretched machine you are trying to drive. Keep on. Do what you can. One day (perhaps in another world, but perhaps far sooner than that) he will fling it on the scrapheap and give you a new one.

1117
Naturalism
Miracles, chap. 5, para. 5, p. 36.

When men say "I ought" they certainly think they are saying something, and something true, about the nature of the proposed action, and not merely about their own feelings. But if Naturalism is true, "I ought" is the same sort of statement as "I itch" or "I'm going to be sick."

1118
Naturalism
Miracles, chap. 5, para. 6–8, pp. 36–37.

The Naturalist can, if he chooses, brazen it out. He can say . . . "all ideas of good and evil are hallucinations—shadows cast on the outer world by the impulses which we have been conditioned to feel." Indeed many Naturalists are delighted to say this.

But then they must stick to it; and fortunately (though inconsistently) most real Naturalists do not. A moment after they have admitted that good and evil are illusions, you will find them exhorting us to work for posterity, to educate, revolutionise, liquidate, live and die for the good of the human race. . . . They write with indignation like men proclaiming what is good in itself and denouncing what is evil in itself, and not at all like men recording that they personally like mild beer but some people prefer bitter. Yet if the "oughts" of Mr. [H. G.] Wells and, say, Franco are both equally the impulses which Nature has

conditioned each to have and both tell us nothing
about any objective right or wrong, whence is all
the fervour? Do they remember while they are
writing thus that when they tell us we "ought to
make a better world" the words "ought" and
"better" must, on their own showing, refer to an
irrationally conditioned impulse which cannot be
true or false any more than a vomit or a yawn?

My idea is that sometimes they do forget. That
is their glory. Holding a philosophy which
excludes humanity, they yet remain human. At the
sight of injustice they throw all their Naturalism
to the winds and speak like men.

1119
Naturalism
Miracles, chap. 5,
para. 10, p. 38.

There is no escape. . . . If we are to continue to
make moral judgments (and whatever we say we
shall in fact continue) then we must believe that
the conscience of man is not a product of Nature.
It can be valid only if it is an offshoot of some
absolute moral wisdom, a moral wisdom which
exists absolutely "on its own" and is not a
product of non-moral, non-rational Nature.

1120
Naturalism
Miracles, chap. 17,
para. 1, p. 164.

We all have Naturalism in our bones and even
conversion does not at once work the infection
out of our system. Its assumptions rush back upon
the mind the moment vigilance is relaxed.

1121
Nature
Miracles, chap. 4,
para. 12, p. 31.

God and Nature have come into a certain
relation. They have, at the very least, a relation—
almost, in one sense, a common frontier—in every
human mind.

1122
Nature
Miracles, chap. 9,
para. 7, pp. 66–67.

You must have tasted, however briefly, the pure
water from beyond the world before you can be
distinctly conscious of the hot, salty tang of
Nature's current. To treat her as God, or as

Everything, is to lose the whole pith and pleasure of her. Come out, look back, and then you will see . . . this astonishing cataract of bears, babies, and bananas: this immoderate deluge of atoms, orchids, oranges, cancers, canaries, fleas, gases, tornadoes and toads. How could you ever have thought that this was the ultimate reality? How could you ever have thought that it was merely a stage-set for the moral drama of men and women? She is herself. Offer her neither worship nor contempt. Meet her and know her. If we are immortal, and if she is doomed (as the scientists tell us) to run down and die, we shall miss this half-shy and half-flamboyant creature, this ogress, this hoyden, this incorrigible fairy, this dumb witch. But the theologians tell us that she, like ourselves, is to be redeemed. The "vanity" to which she was subjected was her disease, not her essence. She will be cured, but cured in character: not tamed (Heaven forbid) nor sterilised. We shall still be able to recognise our old enemy, friend, play-fellow and foster-mother, so perfected as to be not less, but more, herself. And that will be a merry meeting.

1123
Nature
Present Concerns: Essays by C. S. Lewis, "On Living in an Atomic Age" (1948), para. 5, p. 74.

Nature does not, in the long run, favour life. If Nature is all that exists—in other words, if there is no God and no life of some quite different sort somewhere outside Nature—then all stories will end in the same way: in a universe from which all life is banished without possibility of return. It will have been an accidental flicker, and there will be no one even to remember it.

1124
Nature
Present Concerns: Essays by C. S. Lewis, "On Living in an Atomic Age" (1948), para. 8–11, pp. 75–78.

Let us begin by supposing that Nature is all that exists. Let us suppose that nothing ever has existed or ever will exist except this meaningless play of atoms in space and time: that by a series of hundredth chances it has (regrettably) produced things like ourselves—conscious beings who now know that their own consciousness is an accidental result of the whole meaningless process and is therefore itself meaningless. . . .

In this situation there are, I think, three things one might do:

(1) You might commit suicide. . . .

(2) You might decide simply to have as good a time as possible. The universe is a universe of nonsense, but since you are here, grab what you can. Unfortunately, however, there is, on these terms, so very little left to grab—only the coarsest sensual pleasures. . . .

(3) You may defy the universe. You may say, "Let it be irrational, I am not. Let it be merciless, I will have mercy. By whatever curious chance it has produced me, now that I am here I will live according to human values. I know the universe will win in the end, but what is that to me? I will go down fighting. . . ."

I suppose that most of us, in fact, while we remain materialists, adopt a more or less uneasy alternation between the second and the third attitude . . . All Naturalism leads us to this in the end—to a quite final and hopeless discord between what our minds claim to be and what they really must be if Naturalism is true. . . . It is when one has faced this preposterous conclusion that one is at last ready to listen to the voice that whispers: "But suppose we really are spirits? Suppose we are not the offspring of Nature?"

1125
Nature
Present Concerns: Essays by C. S. Lewis, "On Living in an Atomic Age" (1948), para. 12, pp. 78–79.

If Nature when fully known seems to teach us (that is, if the sciences teach us) that our own minds are chance arrangements of atoms, then there must have been some mistake; for if that were so, then the sciences themselves would be chance arrangements of atoms and we should have no reason for believing in them. There is only one way to avoid this deadlock. We must go back to a much earlier view. We must simply accept it that we are spirits, free and rational beings, at present inhabiting an irrational universe, and must draw the conclusion that we are *not derived from it.* We are strangers here. We come from somewhere else. Nature is not the only thing that exists. There is "another world," and that is where we come from. And that explains why we do not feel at home here. A fish feels at home in the water. If we "belonged here" we should feel at home here. All that we say about "Nature red in tooth and claw," about death and time and mutability, all our half-amused, half-bashful attitude to our own bodies, is quite inexplicable on the theory that we are simply natural creatures. If this world is the only world, how did we come to find its laws either so dreadful or so comic? If there is no straight line elsewhere, how did we discover that Nature's line is crooked?

1126
Nature
Present Concerns: Essays by C. S. Lewis, "On Living in an Atomic Age" (1948), para. 13, p. 79.

What, then, is Nature, and how do we come to be imprisoned in a system so alien to us? Oddly enough, the question becomes much less sinister the moment one realizes that Nature is not all. Mistaken for our mother, she is terrifying and even abominable. But if she is only our sister—if she and we have a common Creator—if she is our sparring partner—then the situation is quite tolerable.

1127
Nature
The Four Loves, chap. 2,
para. 21–24, pp. 35–37.

If you take nature as a teacher she will teach you exactly the lessons you had already decided to learn; this is only another way of saying that nature does not teach. The tendency to take her as a teacher is obviously very easily grafted on to the experience we call "love of nature." But it is only a graft. While we are actually subjected to them, the "moods" and "spirits" of nature point no morals. Overwhelming gaiety, insupportable grandeur, sombre desolation are flung at you. Make what you can of them, if you must make at all. The only imperative that nature utters is, "Look. Listen. Attend." . . .

What nature-lovers—whether they are Wordsworthians or people with "dark gods in their blood"—get from nature is an iconography, a language of images. I do not mean simply visual images; it is the "moods" or "spirits" themselves— the powerful expositions of terror, gloom, jocundity, cruelty, lust, innocence, purity—that are the images. In them each man can clothe his own belief. We must learn our theology or philosophy elsewhere (not surprisingly, we often learn them from theologians and philosophers).

But when I speak of "clothing" our belief in such images I do not mean anything like using nature for similes or metaphors in the manner of the poets. Indeed I might have said "filling" or "incarnating" rather than clothing. Many people— I am one myself—would never, but for what nature does to us, have had any content to put into the words we must use in confessing our faith. Nature never taught me that there exists a God of glory and of infinite majesty. I had to learn that in other ways. But nature gave the word *glory* a meaning for me.

. . . Nature does not teach. A true philosophy may sometimes validate an experience of nature;

an experience of nature cannot validate a
philosophy. Nature will not verify any theological
or metaphysical proposition (or not in the manner
we are now considering); she will help to show
what it means.

1128
**Nature and
Christianity**
The Four Loves, chap. 2,
para. 27, p. 39.

Nature cannot satisfy the desires she arouses nor
answer theological questions nor sanctify us. Our
real journey to God involves constantly turning
our backs on her; passing from the dawn-lit fields
into some poky little church, or (it might be)
going to work in an East End parish. But the love
of her has been a valuable and, for some people,
an indispensable initiation.

1129
**Nature and
Christianity**
The Four Loves, chap. 2,
para. 28, p. 39.

Say your prayers in a garden early, ignoring
steadfastly the dew, the birds and the flowers, and
you will come away overwhelmed by its freshness
and joy; go there in order to be overwhelmed
and, after a certain age, nine times out of ten
nothing will happen to you.

1130
**Nature and
Religion**
Christian Reflections,
"Christianity and
Culture" (1940), para. 32,
p. 22.

There is an easy transition from Theism to
Pantheism; but there is also a blessed transition in
the other direction. For some souls I believe, for
my own I remember, Wordsworthian
contemplation can be the first and lowest form of
recognition that there is something outside
ourselves which demands reverence. To return to
Pantheistic errors about the nature of this
something would, for a Christian, be very bad.
But once again, for "the man coming up from
below" the Wordsworthian experience is an
advance. Even if he goes no further he has
escaped the worst arrogance of materialism: if he
goes on he will be converted.

1131
Nature and Religion
The Four Loves, chap. 2, para. 26, p. 38.

There are worms in the belly as well as primroses in the wood. Try to reconcile them, or show that they don't really need reconciliation, and you are turning from direct experience of nature—our present subject—to metaphysics or theodicy or something of that sort. That may be a sensible thing to do; but I think it should be kept distinct from the love of nature. While we are on that level, while we are still claiming to speak of what nature has directly "said" to us, we must stick to it. We have seen an image of glory. We must not try to find a direct path through it and beyond it to an increasing knowledge of God. The path peters out almost at once. Terrors and mysteries, the whole depth of God's counsels and the whole tangle of the history of the universe, choke it. We can't get through; not that way. We must make a *detour*—leave the hills and woods and go back to our studies, to church, to our Bibles, to our knees. Otherwise the love of nature is beginning to turn into a nature religion. And then, even if it does not lead us to the Dark Gods, it will lead us to a great deal of nonsense.

1132
Nature, Laws of
God in the Dock, "The Laws of Nature" (1945), para. 4–5, p. 77.

The laws of physics, I understand, decree that when one billiards ball (A) sets another billiards ball (B) in motion, the momentum lost by A exactly equals the momentum gained by B. This is a *Law.* That is, this is the pattern to which the movement of the two billiards balls must conform. Provided, of course that something sets ball A in motion. And here comes the snag. The *law* won't set it in motion. It is usually a man with a cue who does that. But a man with a cue would send us back to free-will, so let us assume that it was lying on a table in a liner and that what set it in motion was a lurch of the ship. In that case it was not the law which produced the movement; it was a wave. And that wave, though it certainly moved *according* to the laws of physics, was not moved by them. It was shoved by other waves, and by winds, and so forth. And however far you traced the story back you would never find the *laws* of Nature causing anything.

The dazzlingly obvious conclusion now arose, in my mind: *in the whole history of the universe the laws of Nature have never produced a single event.* They are the pattern to which every event must conform, provided only that it can be induced to happen.

1133
Necessary Evils
The Weight of Glory, "Membership" (1945), para. 4, p. 109.

Do not let us mistake necessary evils for good.

1134
Newspapers
Present Concerns: Essays by C. S. Lewis, "After Priggery—What?" (1945), para. 11, p. 59.

To abstain from reading—and . . . from buying— a paper which you have once caught telling lies seems a very moderate form of asceticism. Yet how few practice it.

1135
Newspapers
Letters to an American Lady (26 October 1955), para. 2, p. 47.

I never read the papers. Why does anyone? They're nearly all lies, and one has to wade thru' such reams of verbiage and "write up" to find out even what they're saying.

1136
Newspapers
Letters to Malcolm: Chiefly on Prayer, chap. 6, para. 2, p. 29.

One wouldn't condemn a dog on newspaper extracts.

1137

Nonsense

The Four Loves, chap. 2,
para. 41, p. 48.

Nonsense draws evil after it.

1138

Nonsense

A Grief Observed,
chap. 4, para. 25, p. 81.

[Lewis was grieving the death of his wife:] Can a mortal ask questions which God finds unanswerable? Quite easily, I should think. All nonsense questions are unanswerable. How many hours are there in a mile? Is yellow square or round? Probably half the questions we ask—half our great theological and metaphysical problems— are like that.

1139

Nostalgia

The Letters of C. S. Lewis to Arthur Greeves (1 October 1931), para. 4, pp. 424–425.

I think I have got over *wishing* for the past back again. I look at it this way. The delights of those days were given to lure us into the world of the Spirit, as sexual rapture is there to lead to offspring and family life. They were nuptial ardours. To ask that they should return, or should remain, is like wishing to prolong the honeymoon at an age when a man should rather be interested in the careers of his growing sons. They have done their work, those days and led on to better things.

1140

Novella

English Literature in the Sixteenth Century, bk. II.III, para. 52, p. 309.

The *novella* seems to have little connexion with later developments of fiction. It is an elaboration of the oral anecdote. . . . In English its historical function was not to produce higher forms of fiction but to serve as a dung or compost for the popular drama.

1141

Novels

The Letters of C. S. Lewis to Arthur Greeves (27 March 1932), p. 442.

I personally enjoy a novel only in so far as it fails to be a novel pure and simple and escapes from the eternal love business into some philosophical, religious, fantastic, or farcical region.

1142
Novelty
The Screwtape Letters,
Letter XXV, para. 4,
p. 117.

The pleasure of novelty is by its very nature more subject than any other to the law of diminishing returns. And continued novelty costs money, so that the desire for it spells avarice or unhappiness or both. And again, the more rapacious this desire, the sooner it must eat up all the innocent sources of pleasure.

1143
Obedience
Letters of C. S. Lewis (26 March 1940), para. 1, p. 179.

You can't begin training a child to command until it has reason and age enough to command someone or something without absurdity. You can at once begin training it to obey; that is teaching it the art of obedience *as such*—without prejudice to the views it will hold later on as to who should obey whom, or when, or how much . . . since it is perfectly obvious that every human being is going to spend a great deal of his life in obeying.

1144
Obedience
The Weight of Glory, "Membership" (1945), para. 9, p. 113.

Obedience is the road to freedom, humility the road to pleasure, unity the road to personality.

1145
Obedience
Taliessin Through Logres, . . . Arthurian Torso, "Williams and the Arthuriad" (1948), chap. IV, para. 33, pp. 338–339.

The Father can be well pleased in that Son only who adheres to the Father when apparently forsaken. The fullest grace can be received by those only who continue to obey during the dryness in which all grace seems to be withheld.

1146

Obedience

Letters of C. S. Lewis
(7 December 1950),
para. 4, p. 225.

Obedience is the key to all doors; *feelings* come (or don't come) and go as God pleases. We can't produce them at will, and mustn't try.

1147

One Way

The Pilgrim's Regress,
bk. 8, chap. 8, p. 155.

"*One* road leads home and a thousand roads lead into the wilderness."

1148

Opinion, Popular

The Problem of Pain,
chap. 9, para. 6, p. 134.

I take a very low view of "climates of opinion." In his own subject every man knows that all discoveries are made and all errors corrected by those who ignore the "climate of opinion."

1149

Opposition

The Personal Heresy: A Controversy, chap. 3, para. 1, p. 49.

A friend of mine once described himself as being "hungry for rational opposition." The words seemed to me to hit off very happily the state of a man who has published doctrines which he knows to be controversial, and yet finds no one to voice the general disagreement he is looking for. . . . In such matters to find an opponent is almost to find a friend.

1150

Order from Chaos

Present Concerns: Essays by C. S. Lewis, "Modern Man and His Categories of Thought" (1946), para. 6, pp. 63–64.

To the modern man it seems simply natural that an ordered cosmos should emerge from chaos, that life should come out of the inanimate, reason out of instinct, civilization out of savagery, virtue out of animalism. This idea is supported in his mind by a number of false analogies: the oak coming from the acorn, the man from the spermatozoon, the modern steamship from the primitive coracle. The supplementary truth that every acorn was dropped by an oak, every spermatozoon derived from a man, and the first boat by something so much more complex than itself as a man of genius, is simply ignored. The modern mind accepts as a formula for the universe in general the principle "Almost nothing may be expected to turn into almost everything" without noticing that the parts of the universe under our direct observation tell a quite different story.

1151
Ordered Life
Reflections on the Psalms, chap. 6, para. 8, p. 59.

The Order of the Divine mind, embodied in the Divine Law, is beautiful. What should a man do but try to reproduce it, so far as possible, in his daily life?

1152
Originality
Selected Literary Essays, "Donne and Love Poetry" (1938), para. 21, p. 122.

Of all literary virtues "originality," in the vulgar sense, has . . . the shortest life.

1153
Originality
The Weight of Glory, "Membership" (1945), para. 19, pp. 119–120.

I have wanted to try to expel that quite unchristian worship of the human individual . . . I mean the pestilent notion (one sees it in literary criticism) that each of us starts with a treasure called "Personality" locked up inside him, and that to expand and express this, to guard it from interference, to be "original," is the main end of life. This is Pelagian, or worse, and it defeats even itself. No man who values originality will ever be original. But try to tell the truth as you see it, try to do any bit of work as well as it can be done for the work's sake, and what men call originality will come unsought. Even on that level, the submission of the individual to the function is already beginning to bring true Personality to birth.

1154
**Orwell,
George:
1984 and
*Animal Farm***
On Stories, "George
Orwell" (1955),
para. 3–4, 10–11, 13–14,
pp. 101–104.

What puzzles me is the marked preference of the public for *1984* [over *Animal Farm*]. For it seems to me (apart from its magnificent, and fortunately detachable, Appendix on "Newspeak") to be merely a flawed, interesting book; but the *Farm* is a work of genius which may well outlive the particular and (let us hope) temporary conditions that provoked it.

To begin with, it is very much the shorter of the two. This in itself would not, of course, show it to be the better. I am the last person to think so. Callimachus, to be sure, thought a great book a great evil, but then I think Callimachus a great prig. My appetite is hearty and when I sit down to read I like a square meal. But in this instance the shorter book seems to do all that the longer one does; and more. The longer book does not justify its greater length. There is dead wood in it.

. . . The great sentence "All animals are equal but some are more equal than others" bites deeper than the whole of *1984*.

. . . Paradoxically, when Orwell turns all his characters into animals he makes them more fully human.

. . . Here, despite the animal disguise, we feel we are in a real world.

. . . Finally, *Animal Farm* is formally almost perfect; light, strong, balanced. There is not a sentence that does not contribute to the whole. The myth says all the author wants it to say and (equally important) it doesn't say anything else. Here is an *objet d'art* as durably satisfying as a Horatian ode or a Chippendale chair.

1155

Outsiders

The Weight of Glory,
"The Inner Ring" (1944),
para. 15, p. 103.

The torture allotted to the Danaids in the classical underworld, that of attempting to fill sieves with water, is the symbol not of one vice but of all vices. It is the very mark of a perverse desire that it seeks what is not to be had. The desire to be inside the invisible line illustrates this rule. As long as you are governed by that desire you will never get what you want. You are trying to peel an onion: if you succeed there will be nothing left. Until you conquer the fear of being an outsider, an outsider you will remain.

| 1156 | St. Paul . . . approved of capital punishment—he says "the magistrate bears the sword and should bear the sword." It is recorded that the soldiers who came to St. John Baptist asking, "What shall we do?" were not told to leave the army. When Our Lord Himself praised the Centurion He never hinted that the military profession was in itself sinful. This has been the general view of Christendom. Pacifism is a v. recent and local variation. We must of course respect and tolerate Pacifists, but I think their view erroneous. |

1156

Pacifism

Letters of C. S. Lewis
(8 November 1952),
para. 9, p. 248.

St. Paul . . . approved of capital punishment—he says "the magistrate bears the sword and should bear the sword." It is recorded that the soldiers who came to St. John Baptist asking, "What shall we do?" were not told to leave the army. When Our Lord Himself praised the Centurion He never hinted that the military profession was in itself sinful. This has been the general view of Christendom. Pacifism is a v. recent and local variation. We must of course respect and tolerate Pacifists, but I think their view erroneous.

1157

Pain

God in the Dock, "Evil
and God" (1941), para. 2,
p. 22.

Evil may seem more urgent to us than it did to the Victorian philosophers—favoured members of the happiest class in the happiest country in the world at the world's happiest period. But it is no more urgent for us than for the great majority of monotheists all down the ages. The classic expositions of the doctrine that the world's miseries are compatible with its creation and guidance by a wholly good Being come from Boethius waiting in prison to be beaten to death and from St Augustine meditating on the sack of Rome.

1158
Pain
God in the Dock,
"Vivisection" (1947),
para. 3, p. 225.

If we find a man giving pleasure it is for us to prove (if we criticise him) that his action is wrong. But if we find a man inflicting pain it is for him to prove that his action is right. If he cannot, he is a wicked man.

1159
Pain
Letters of C. S. Lewis
(31 January 1952),
para. 1, pp. 237–238.

That suffering is not *always* sent as a punishment is clearly established for believers by the book of Job and by John IX. 1–4. That it *sometimes* is, is suggested by parts of the Old Testament and Revelation. It wd. certainly be most dangerous to assume that any given pain was penal. I believe that all pain is contrary to God's will, absolutely but not relatively. When I am taking a thorn out of my own finger (or a child's finger) the pain is "absolutely" contrary to my will; i.e. if I could have chosen a situation without pain I would have done so. But I *do* will what caused the pain, relatively to the given situation; i.e. granted the thorn I prefer the pain to leaving the thorn where it is. A mother spanking a child would be in the same position; she would rather cause it this pain than let it go on pulling the cat's tail, but she would like it better if no situation which demands a smack had arisen.

1160
Pain
Letters of C. S. Lewis
(1 November 1954),
para. 2, p. 257.

Do you know, the suffering of the innocent is *less* of a problem to me v. often than that of the wicked. It sounds absurd; but I've met so many innocent sufferers who seem to be gladly offering their pain to God in Christ as part of the Atonement, so patient, so meek, even so at peace, and so unselfish that we can hardly doubt they are being, as St. Paul says, "made perfect by suffering." On the other hand I meet selfish egoists in whom suffering seems to produce only

resentment, hate, blasphemy, and more egoism.
They are the real problem.

1161
Pain
Letters of C. S. Lewis
(29 April 1959),
para. 1, p. 285.

We are not necessarily doubting that God will do
the best for us; we are wondering how painful the
best will turn out to be.

1162
Pain
A Grief Observed,
chap. 3, para. 19,
pp. 50–51.

[Lewis was grieving the death of his wife:] What
do people mean when they say "I am not afraid
of God because I know He is good?" Have they
never even been to a dentist?

1163
Pain
Poems, "As the Ruin
Falls" (1st pub. 1964),
pp. 109–110.

All this is flashy rhetoric about loving you.
I never had a selfless thought since I was born.
I am mercenary and self-seeking through and
     through:
I want God, you, all friends, merely to serve my
     turn.

Peace, re-assurance, pleasure, are the goals I seek,
I cannot crawl one inch outside my proper skin:
I talk of love—a scholar's parrot may talk
     Greek—
But, self-imprisoned, always end where I begin.

Only that now you have taught me (but how late)
     my lack.
I see the chasm. And everything you are was
     making
My heart into a bridge by which I might get back
From exile, and grow man. And now the bridge is
     breaking.

For this I bless you as the ruin falls. The pains
You give me are more precious than all other
     gains.

1164
Pantheism
God in the Dock,
"Rejoinder to Dr
Pittenger" (1958),
para. 10, p. 181.

I freely admit that, believing both, I have stressed the transcendence of God more than His immanence. I thought, and think, that the present situation demands this. I see around me no danger of Deism but much of an immoral, naive and sentimental pantheism. I have often found that it was in fact the chief obstacle to conversion.

1165
Parliament
The Allegory of Love,
chap. IV.II, para. 12,
p. 172.

Some politicians hold that the only way to make a revolutionary safe is to give him a seat in Parliament.

1166
Patriotism
The Four Loves, chap. 2,
para. 33, p. 41.

As the family offers us the first step beyond self-love, so this [patriotism] offers us the first step beyond family selfishness.

1167
Paul, St.
Selected Literary Essays,
"High Brows and Low"
(1939), para. 13, p. 271.

St Paul, despite some passages of striking beauty, seems to me to write badly.

1168
Peace
God in the Dock,
"Delinquents in the
Snow" (1957), para. 14,
p. 309.

Not all kinds of peace are compatible with all kinds of goodwill, nor do all those who say "Peace, peace" inherit the blessing promised to the peacemakers. [Footnote: Jeremiah vi. 14; viii. 11 and Matthew v. 9]

1169
Peer Pressure
The Weight of Glory,
"The Inner Ring" (1944),
para. 7, p. 98.

Freud would say, no doubt, that the whole thing is a subterfuge of the sexual impulse. I wonder whether the shoe is not sometimes on the other foot. I wonder whether, in ages of promiscuity, many a virginity has not been lost less in obedience to Venus than in obedience to the lure of the caucus. For of course, when promiscuity is the fashion, the chaste are outsiders. They are ignorant of something that other people know. They are uninitiated. And as for lighter matters, the number who first smoked or first got drunk for a similar reason is probably very large.

1170

Persecution

Letters: C. S. Lewis/Don Giovanni Calabria (20 September 1947), para. 4, pp. 33, 35.

I could well believe that it is God's intention, since we have refused milder remedies, to compel us into unity, by persecution even and hardship. Satan is without doubt nothing else than a hammer in the hand of a benevolent and severe God. For all, either willingly or unwillingly, do the will of God: Judas and Satan as tools or instruments, John and Peter as sons.

1171

Persecution

Letters: C. S. Lewis/Don Giovanni Calabria (20 September 1947), para. 3, p. 33.

Those who suffer the same things from the same people for the same Person can scarcely not love each other.

1172

Personhood

The Weight of Glory, "Membership" (1945), para. 17, p. 118.

We shall then first be true persons when we have suffered ourselves to be fitted into our places. We are marble waiting to be shaped, metal waiting to be run into a mould.

1173

Perspective

God in the Dock, "On the Reading of Old Books" (1944), para. 4, p. 202.

Every age has its own outlook. It is specially good at seeing certain truths and specially liable to make certain mistakes. We all, therefore, need the books that will correct the characteristic mistakes of our own period. And that means the old books.

1174
Pessimism
Surprised by Joy, chap. 7,
para. 20, pp. 116–117.

It is true that when a pessimist's life is threatened he behaves like other men; his impulse to preserve life is stronger than his judgment that life is not worth preserving. But how does this prove that the judgment was insincere or even erroneous? A man's judgment that whisky is bad for him is not invalidated by the fact that when the bottle is at hand he finds desire stronger than reason and succumbs. Having once tasted life, we are subjected to the impulse of self-preservation. Life, in other words, is as habit-forming as cocaine. What then? If I still held creation to be "a great injustice" I should hold that this impulse to retain life aggravates the injustice. If it is bad to be forced to drink the potion, how does it mend matters that the potion turns out to be an addiction drug? Pessimism cannot be answered so. Thinking as I then thought about the universe, I was reasonable in condemning it. At the same time I now see that my view was closely connected with a certain lopsidedness of temperament. I had always been more violent in my negative than in my positive demands. Thus, in personal relations, I could forgive much neglect more easily than the least degree of what I regarded as interference. At table I could forgive much insipidity in my food more easily than the least suspicion of what seemed to me excessive or inappropriate seasoning. In the course of life I could put up with any amount of monotony far more patiently than even the smallest disturbance, bother, bustle, or what the Scotch call *kurfuffle*. Never at any age did I clamor to be amused; always and at all ages (where I dared) I hotly demanded not to be interrupted. The pessimism, or cowardice, which would prefer nonexistence itself to even the mildest unhappiness was thus merely the generalization of all these pusillanimous preferences. And it remains true that I have, almost all my life, been quite unable to feel that horror of nonentity, of annihilation, which, say, Dr Johnson felt so strongly. I felt it for the first time only in 1947. But that was after I had long been reconverted and thus begun to know what life really is and what would have been lost by missing it.

1175
Philosophy: Dualism
God in the Dock,
"Evil and God" (1941),
para. 4–5, p. 22.

Dualism is a truncated metaphysic.
The moral difficulty is that Dualism gives evil a positive, substantive, self-consistent nature, like that of good.

1176
Philosophy, Essence of
Surprised by Joy,
chap. 14, para. 17,
p. 225.

Once, when he [Dom Bede Griffiths] and Barfield were lunching in my room I happened to refer to philosophy as "a subject." "It wasn't a *subject* to Plato," said Barfield, "it was a way."

1177
Philosophy, Good and Bad
The Weight of Glory,
"Learning in War-Time"
(1939), para. 10, p. 28.

Good philosophy must exist, if for no other reason, because bad philosophy needs to be answered.

1178
Planning
Letters to Malcolm:
Chiefly on Prayer,
chap. 7, para. 9, p. 38.

A world where the future is unknown cannot be inconsistent with planned and purposive action since we are actually planning and purposing in such a world now and have been doing so for thousands of years.

1179
Plato
Rehabilitations, "The
Idea of an 'English
School,'" para. 8, p. 64.

To lose what I owe to Plato and Aristotle would
be like the amputation of a limb.

1180
Plato
*English Literature in the
Sixteenth Century,* bk.
III.I, para. 106, p. 386.

Plato's thought is at bottom otherworldly,
pessimistic, and ascetic; far more ascetic than
Protestantism. The natural universe is, for Plato, a
world of shadows, of Helens false as Spenser's
false Florimell (*Rep.* 586 A-C); the soul has come
into it at all only because she lost her wings in a
better place (*Phaedr.* 246 D-248 E); and the life of
wisdom, while we are here, is a practice or
exercise of death (*Phaed.* 80 D-81 A).

1181
**Platonism and
Christianity**
*Studies in Medieval and
Renaissance Literature,*
"Edmund Spenser,
1552-99" (1954),
para. 36, p. 144.

[Protestant Christianity and Platonism:] Both
systems are united with one another and cut off
from some—not all—modern thought by their
conviction that Nature, the totality of phenomena
in space and time, is not the only thing that
exists: is, indeed, the least important thing.
Christians and Platonists both believe in an
"other" world. They differ, at least in emphasis,
when they describe the relations between that
other world and Nature. For a Platonist the
contrast is usually that between an original and a
copy, between the real and the merely apparent,
between the clear and the confused: for a
Christian, between the eternal and the temporary,
or the perfect and the partially spoiled. The
essential attitude of Platonism is aspiration or
longing: the human soul, imprisoned in the
shadowy, unreal world of Nature, stretches out its
hands and struggles towards the beauty and reality
of that which lies (as Plato says) "on the other

side of existence." Shelley's phrase "the desire of the moth for the star" sums it up. In Christianity, however, the human soul is not the seeker but the sought: it is God who seeks, who descends from the other world to find and heal Man; the parable about the Good Shepherd looking for and finding the lost sheep sums it up.

1182
Poetic Revolutions
Studies in Medieval and Renaissance Literature, "Tasso" (1940s?), para. 3, p. 113.

In romantic England poetic rebellions are usually anti-romantic; in France it is the romantics who rebel.

1183
Poetry
The Allegory of Love, chap. V.I, para. 18, p. 221.

Doubtless it is a rule in poetry that if you do your own work well, you will find you have done also work you never dreamed of.

1184
Poetry
Taliessin Through Logres, . . . Arthurian Torso, "Williams and the Arthuriad" (1948), chap. V, para. 17, pp. 350–351.

[For Williams] poetry no doubt was a way of approaching God: but a poetry directly and consciously subordinated to the ends of edification usually becomes bad poetry. . . . He thought nothing more ridiculous and disastrous than any attempted subjection of the natural playfulness of Caucasia to some kind of quasi-sacramental gravity.

1185
Poetry
Selected Literary Essays, "Hero and Leander" (1952), para. 21, p. 73.

Heaven forbid that we should never read—and praise—any poems less than perfect.

1186
Poetry
*English Literature in the
Sixteenth Century,* bk.
III.I, para. 93, p. 377.

Great subjects do not make great poems; usually,
indeed, the reverse.

1187
Poetry
Reflections on the Psalms,
chap. 1, para. 8, p. 5.

It seems to me appropriate, almost inevitable, that
when that great Imagination which in the
beginning, for Its own delight and for the delight
of men and angels and (in their proper mode) of
beasts, had invented and formed the whole world
of Nature, submitted to express Itself in human
speech, that speech should sometimes be poetry.
For poetry too is a little incarnation, giving body
to what had been before invisible and inaudible.

1188
Poetry
Studies in Words (1960),
chap. 12, para. 7, 9,
pp. 317–318.

Poetry most often communicates emotions, not
directly, but by creating imaginatively the grounds
for those emotions. It therefore communicates
something more than emotion; only by means of
that something more does it communicate the
emotion at all. . . .

This, which is eminently true of poetry, is true
of all imaginative writing. One of the first things
we have to say to a beginner who has brought us
his MS. is, "Avoid all epithets which are merely
emotional. It is no use *telling* us that something
was 'mysterious' or 'loathsome' or 'awe-inspiring'
or 'voluptuous.' Do you think your readers will
believe you just because you say so? You must go
quite a different way to work. By direct
description, by metaphor and simile, by secretly
evoking powerful associations, by offering the
right stimuli to our nerves (in the right degree and
the right order), and by the very beat and vowel-
melody and length and brevity of your sentences,
you must bring it about that we, we readers, not

you, exclaim 'how mysterious!' or 'loathsome' or whatever it is. Let me taste for myself, and you'll have no need to *tell* me how I should react to the flavour."

1189
Poetry
Studies in Words (1960),
chap. 12, para. 12,
p. 319.

The poet's route to our emotions lies through our imaginations.

1190
Poetry,
Ancient and
Modern
Studies in Medieval and
Renaissance Literature,
"Edmund Spenser,
1552–99" (1954),
para. 35, p. 143.

In the earliest times theology, science, history, fiction, singing, instrumental music, and dancing were all a single activity. Traces of this can still be found in Greek poetry. Then the different arts which had once all been elements of *poesis* developed and became more different from one another, and drew apart (the enormous gains and losses of this process perhaps equal one another). Poetry became more and more unlike prose. It is now so unlike it that the number of those who can read it is hardly greater than the number of those who write it.

1191
Poetry,
Modern
Selected Literary Essays,
"De Descriptione
Temporum" (1955),
para. 15, p. 9.

I do not see how anyone can doubt that modern poetry is not only a greater novelty than any other "new poetry" but new in a new way, almost in a new dimension.

1192
Poets and
Poetry
English Literature in the
Sixteenth Century, bk.
III.I, para. 17, p. 328.

"Look in thy heart and write" is good counsel for poets; but when a poet looks in his heart he finds many things there besides the actual. That is why, and how, he is a poet.

1193
Poets,
Metaphysical
English Literature in the
Sixteenth Century,
Epilogue, II, para. 4,
p. 540.

The Metaphysicals were making no absolute innovation when they deliberately produced poetic shocks by coupling what was sacred, august, remote, or inhuman with what was profane, humdrum, familiar, and social, so that God is asked to "batter" a heart, Christ's "stretched sinews" become fiddlestrings, cherubs have breakfasts, stars are a patrol, and snow puts a periwig on bald woods. The novelty lay in doing this sort of thing more often, and perhaps more violently, than previous poets had done, and indeed making it almost the mainstay of their poetics.

1194
Political
Power
The Abolition of Man,
chap. 3, para. 4. p. 70.

Each generation exercises power over its successors: and each, in so far as it modifies the environment bequeathed to it and rebels against tradition, resists and limits the power of its predecessors. This modifies the picture which is sometimes painted of a progressive emancipation from tradition and a progressive control of natural processes resulting in a continual increase of human power. In reality, of course, if any one age really attains, by eugenics and scientific education, the power to make its descendants what it pleases, all men who live after it are the patients of that power. They are weaker, not stronger: for though we may have put wonderful machines in their hands we have pre-ordained how they are to use them.

1195
Politics
The Weight of Glory,
"Membership" (1945),
para. 4, p. 109.

A sick society must think much about politics, as a sick man must think much about his digestion.

1196
Politics and Christianity

God in the Dock, Part II, 'Meditation on the Third Commandment," para. 7, p. 199.

M. Maritain has hinted at the only way in which Christianity (as opposed to schismatics blasphemously claiming to represent it) can influence politics. Nonconformity has influenced modern English history not because there was a Nonconformist Party but because there was a Nonconformist conscience which all parties had to take into account. . . . He who converts his neighbour has performed the most practical Christian-political act of all.

1197
Politics, Christians in

God in the Dock, 'Meditation on the Third Commandment" (1941), para. 1, 4–5, pp. 196–198.

From many letters to *The Guardian* [Footnote: a weekly Anglican newspaper], and from much that is printed elsewhere, we learn of the growing desire for a Christian "party," a Christian "front," or a Christian "platform" in politics. Nothing is so earnestly to be wished as a real assault by Christianity on the politics of the world: nothing, at first sight, so fitted to deliver this assault as a Christian party.

. . . It remains to ask how the resulting situation will differ from that in which Christians find themselves today.

It is not reasonable to suppose that such a Christian Party will acquire new powers of leavening the infidel organization to which it is attached. Why should it? Whatever it calls itself, it will represent, not Christendom, but a part of Christendom. The principle which divides it from its brethren and unites it to its political allies will not be theological. It will have no authority to speak for Christianity; it will have no more power than the political skill of its members gives it to control the behaviour of its unbelieving allies. But there will be a real, and most disastrous, novelty. It will be not simply a *part* of Christendom, but *a part claiming to be the whole.* By the mere act of calling itself the Christian Party it implicitly accuses all Christians who do not join it of apostasy and betrayal. It will be exposed, in an aggravated degree, to that temptation which the Devil spares none of us at any time—the temptation of claiming for our favourite opinions that kind and degree of certainty and authority which really belongs only to our Faith.

1198

Possessiveness

The Four Loves, chap. 3, para. 30, pp. 71–72.

But it is not only children who react thus. Few things in the ordinary peacetime life of a civilised country are more nearly fiendish than the rancour with which a whole unbelieving family will turn on the one member of it who has become a Christian, or a whole lowbrow family on the one who shows signs of becoming an intellectual. This is not, as I once thought, simply the innate and, as it were, disinterested hatred of darkness for light. A church-going family in which one has gone atheist will not always behave any better. It is the reaction to a desertion, even to robbery. Someone or something has stolen "our" boy (or girl). He who was one of Us has become one of Them. What right had anybody to do it? He is *ours.*

1199

Post-Christian Europe

God in the Dock, "Is Theism Important?" (1952), para. 1, p. 172.

When grave persons express their fear that England is relapsing into Paganism, I am tempted to reply, "Would that she were." For I do not think it at all likely that we shall ever see Parliament opened by the slaughtering of a garlanded white bull in the House of Lords or Cabinet Ministers leaving sandwiches in Hyde Park as an offering for the Dryads. If such a state of affairs came about, then the Christian apologist would have something to work on. For a Pagan, as history shows, is a man eminently convertible to Christianity. He is essentially the pre-Christian,

or sub-Christian, religious man. The post-Christian
man of our day differs from him as much as a
divorcée differs from a virgin.

1200
**Post-Christian
Europe**
Selected Literary Essays,
"De Descriptione
Temporum" (1955),
para. 8, pp. 4–5.

The christening of Europe seemed to all our
ancestors, whether they welcomed it themselves as
Christians, or, like Gibbon, deplored it as
humanistic unbelievers, a unique, irreversible
event. But we have seen the opposite process. Of
course the un-christening of Europe in our time is
not quite complete; neither was her christening in
the Dark Ages. But roughly speaking we may say
that whereas all history was for our ancestors
divided into two periods, the pre-Christian and
the Christian, and two only, for us it falls into
three—the pre-Christian, the Christian, and what
may reasonably be called the post-Christian. This
surely must make a momentous difference. I am
not here considering either the christening or the
un-christening from a theological point of view. I
am considering them simply as cultural changes.
When I do that, it appears to me that the second
change is even more radical than the first.
Christians and Pagans had much more in common
with each other than either has with a post-
Christian. The gap between those who worship
different gods is not so wide as that between
those who worship and those who do not. . . .
Surely Seneca and Dr Johnson are closer together
than Burton and Freud?

1201
**Post-Christian
Europe**
Selected Literary Essays,
"De Descriptione
Temporum" (1955),
para. 16, p. 10.

[It is a] false idea that the historical process allows
mere reversal; that Europe can come out of
Christianity "by the same door as in she went"
and find herself back where she was. It is not
what happens. A post-Christian man is not a
Pagan; you might as well think that a married

woman recovers her virginity by divorce. The post-Christian is cut off from the Christian past and therefore doubly from the Pagan past.

1202
Post-Christian Man
Letters: C. S. Lewis/Don Giovanni Calabria (17 March 1953), para. 4–7, p. 81.

What you say about the present state of mankind is true: indeed, it is even worse than you say.

For they neglect not only the law of Christ but even the Law of Nature as known by the Pagans. For now they do not blush at adultery, treachery, perjury, theft and the other crimes which I will not say Christian Doctors, but the pagans and the barbarous have themselves denounced.

They err who say "the world is turning pagan again." Would that it were! The truth is that we are falling into a much worse state.

"Post-Christian man" is not the same as "pre-Christian man." He is as far removed as virgin is from widow: there is nothing in common except want of a spouse: but there is a great difference between a spouse-to-come and a spouse lost.

1203
Post-Christian Man
Letters: C. S. Lewis/Don Giovanni Calabria (15 September 1953), para. 2–3, p. 89.

Regarding the moral condition of our times (since you bid me prattle on) I think this. Older people, as we both are, are always "praisers of times past." They always think the world is worse than it was in their young days. Therefore we ought to take care lest we go wrong. But, with this proviso, certainly I feel that very grave dangers hang over us. This results from the apostasy of the great part of Europe from the Christian faith. Hence a worse state than the one we were in before we received the Faith. For no one returns from Christianity to the same state he was in before Christianity but into a worse state: the difference between a pagan and an apostate is the difference between an unmarried woman and an adulteress. For faith perfects nature but faith lost corrupts nature.

Therefore many men of our time have lost not only the supernatural light but also the natural light which pagans possessed.

But God, who is the God of mercies, even now has not altogether cast off the human race. In younger people, although we may see much cruelty and lust, yet at the same time do we not see very many sparks of virtues which perhaps our own generation lacked? How much courage, how much concern for the poor do we see! We must not despair. And (among us) a not inconsiderable number are now returning to the Faith.

1204
Power
Boxen: The Imaginary World of the Young C. S. Lewis (1905–1913), "History of Animal-Land," II.I, p. 48.

[Ed. note: from fiction written at about age 9.] The emancipation of the Commons would have been a good thing had they used their power, thus gained, well. But unhappily they used it exceedingly badly: they had no sympathy with persons who were not in the same rank of life, or did not fall in with their ideas.

1205
Power
Boxen: The Imaginary World of the Young C. S. Lewis (1905–1913), "Boxen: or Scenes from Boxonian City Life," chap. X, p. 82.

[Ed. note: from fiction written at about age 12 to 14.] "The bird actually blackmailed me. And now he wants me to get him a cliqueship."

"Well," said the stranger, "get him one. Our object is to place the new Clique under an obligation to us."

1206
Power
The Allegory of Love, chap. IV.II, para. 21, p. 188.

The descent to hell is easy, and those who begin by worshipping power soon worship evil.

1207
Prayer
Letters of C. S. Lewis
(1933?), p. 155.

Since I have begun to pray, I find my extreme view of personality changing. My own empirical self is becoming more important, and this is exactly the opposite of self-love. You don't teach a seed how to die into treehood by throwing it into the fire: and it has to become a good seed before it's worth burying.

1208
Prayer
Letters of C. S. Lewis
(3 December 1959),
para. 1, p. 290.

It is quite useless knocking at the door of heaven for earthly comfort; it's not the sort of comfort they supply there.

1209
Prayer
*Letters to Malcolm:
Chiefly on Prayer,*
chap.11, para. 10, p. 60.

For most of us the prayer in Gethsemane is the only model. Removing mountains can wait.

1210
**Prayer:
Answers**
Letters of C. S. Lewis
(21 February 1932),
para. 2, p. 149.

The efficacy of prayer is, at any rate, no *more* of a problem than the efficacy of *all* human acts. i.e., if you say "It is useless to pray because Providence already knows what is best and will certainly do it," then why is it not equally useless (and for the same reason) to try to alter the course of events in any way whatever?

1211
**Prayer:
Answers**
God in the Dock,
"Scraps" (1945), para. 4,
p. 217.

"Praying for particular things," said I, "always seems to me like advising God how to run the world. Wouldn't it be wiser to assume that He knows best?" "On the same principle," said he, "I suppose you never ask a man next to you to pass the salt, because God knows best whether you ought to have salt or not. And I suppose you never take an umbrella, because God knows best

---

whether you ought to be wet or dry." "That's quite different," I protested. "I don't see why," said he. "The odd thing is that He should let us influence the course of events at all. But since He lets us do it in one way I don't see why He shouldn't let us do it in the other."

1212

Prayer:

Answers

Christian Reflections,
"Petitionary Prayer: A
Problem Without an
Answer" (1953),
chap. 12, para. 8, p. 144.

I must often be glad that certain past prayers of my own were not granted.

1213

Prayer:

Answers

The World's Last Night
and Other Essays,
"The Efficacy of Prayer"
(1959), para. 6, pp. 4–5.

Prayer is request. The essence of request, as distinct from compulsion, is that it may or may not be granted. And if an infinitely wise Being listens to the requests of finite and foolish creatures, of course He will sometimes grant and sometimes refuse them.

1214

Prayer:

Answers

The World's Last Night
and Other Essays,
"The Efficacy of Prayer"
(1959), para. 7, p. 5.

There are, no doubt, passages in the New Testament which may seem at first sight to promise an invariable granting of our prayers. But that cannot be what they really mean. For in the very heart of the story we meet a glaring instance to the contrary. In Gethsemane the holiest of all petitioners prayed three times that a certain cup might pass from Him. It did not. After that the idea that prayer is recommended to us as a sort of infallible gimmick may be dismissed.

1215
Prayer:
Answers

The World's Last Night and Other Essays, "The Efficacy of Prayer" (1959), para. 19–21, pp. 10–11.

Our act, when we pray, must not, any more than all our other acts, be separated from the continuous act of God Himself, in which alone all finite causes operate.

It would be even worse to think of those who get what they pray for as a sort of court favorites, people who have influence with the throne. The refused prayer of Christ in Gethsemane is answer enough to that. And I dare not leave out the hard saying which I once heard from an experienced Christian: "I have seen many striking answers to prayer and more than one that I thought miraculous. But they usually come at the beginning: before conversion, or soon after it. As the Christian life proceeds, they tend to be rarer. The refusals, too, are not only more frequent; they become more unmistakable, more emphatic."

Does God then forsake just those who serve him best? Well, He who served Him best of all said, near His tortured death, "Why hast thou forsaken me?" When God becomes man, that Man, of all others, is least comforted by God, at His greatest need. There is a mystery here which, even if I had the power, I might not have the courage to explore. Meanwhile, little people like you and me, if our prayers are sometimes granted, beyond all hope and probability, had better not draw hasty conclusions to our own advantage. If we were stronger, we might be less tenderly treated. If we were braver, we might be sent, with far less help, to defend far more desperate posts in the great battle.

1216
Prayer:
Answers

Letters to Malcolm: Chiefly on Prayer, chap. 5, para. 16, p. 28.

If God had granted all the silly prayers I've made in my life, where should I be now?

1217
Prayer:
Answers
Letters to Malcolm:
Chiefly on Prayer,
chap. 9, para. 5, p. 48.

We have long since agreed that if our prayers are granted at all they are granted from the foundation of the world. God and His acts are not in time. Intercourse between God and man occurs at particular moments for the man, but not for God. If there is—as the very concept of prayer presupposes—an adaptation between the free actions of men in prayer and the course of events, this adaptation is from the beginning inherent in the great single creative act. Our prayers are heard—don't say "have been heard" or you are putting God into time—not only before we make them but before we are made ourselves.

1218
Prayer:
Answers
Letters to Malcolm:
Chiefly on Prayer,
chap. 12, para. 10, p. 60.

It seems to me we must conclude that such promises [as in Mark 11:24] about prayer with faith refer to a degree or kind of faith which most believers never experience. A far inferior degree is, I hope, acceptable to God. Even the kind that says "Help thou my unbelief" may make way for a miracle. Again, the absence of such faith as insures the granting of the prayer is not even necessarily a sin; for Our Lord had no such assurance when he prayed in Gethsemane.

1219
Prayer:
Communion
with God
Poems, "Footnote to All
Prayers" (1933), p. 129.

Take not, oh Lord, our literal sense. Lord, in Thy great,
Unbroken speech our limping metaphor translate.

1220

Prayer: Communion with God

The World's Last Night and Other Essays, "The Efficacy of Prayer" (1959), para. 16, p. 8.

Prayer is either a sheer illusion or a personal contact between embryonic, incomplete persons (ourselves) and the utterly concrete Person. Prayer in the sense of petition, asking for things, is a small part of it; confession and penitence are its threshold, adoration its sanctuary, the presence and vision and enjoyment of God its bread and wine. In it God shows Himself to us. That He answers prayers is a corollary—not necessarily the most important one—from that revelation. What He does is learned from what He is.

1221

Prayer: Communion with God

Poems, "Prayer" (1st pub. 1964), pp. 122–123.

Master, they say that when I seem
    To be in speech with you,
Since you make no replies, it's all a dream
    —One talker aping two.

They are half right, but not as they
    Imagine; rather, I
Seek in myself the things I meant to say,
    And lo! the wells are dry.

Then, seeing me empty, you forsake
    The Listener's rôle, and through
My dead lips breathe and into utterance wake
    The thoughts I never knew.

And thus you neither need reply
    Nor can; thus, while we seem
Two talking, thou art One forever, and I
    No dreamer, but thy dream.

1222

Prayer: Communion with God

Letters to Malcolm: Chiefly on Prayer, chap. 15, para. 15–17, pp. 81–82.

The dramatic person could not tread the stage unless he concealed a real person; unless the real and unknown I existed, I would not even make mistakes about the imagined me. And in prayer this real I struggles to speak, for once, from his real being, and to address, for once, not the other actors, but—what shall I call Him? The Author, for He invented us all? The Producer, for He controls all? Or the Audience, for He watches, and will judge, the performance?

The attempt is not to escape from space and time and from my creaturely situation as a subject facing objects. It is more modest: to re-awake the awareness of that situation. If that can be done, there is no need to go anywhere else. This situation itself is, at every moment, a possible theophany. Here is the holy ground: the Bush is burning now.

. . . The prayer preceding all prayers is "May it be the real I who speaks. May it be the real Thou that I speak to." Infinitely various are the levels from which we pray. Emotional intensity is in itself no proof of spiritual depth. If we pray in terror we shall pray earnestly; it only proves that terror is an earnest emotion. Only God Himself can let the bucket down to the depths in us. And, on the other side, He must constantly work as the iconoclast. Every idea of Him we form, He must in mercy shatter. The most blessed result of prayer would be to rise thinking "But I never knew before, I never dreamed . . ." I suppose it was at such a moment that Thomas Aquinas said of all his own theology, "It reminds me of straw."

1223
Prayer:
Confession
Letters to Malcolm:
Chiefly on Prayer,
chap. 4, para. 15, p. 22,

We must lay before Him what is in us, not what ought to be in us.

1224
Prayer:
Distractions
Letters to Malcolm:
Chiefly on Prayer,
chap. 4, para. 18, p. 23.

If we lay all the cards on the table, God will help us to moderate the excesses. But the pressure of things we are trying to keep out of our mind is a hopeless distraction. As someone said, "No noise is so emphatic as one you are trying not to listen to."

1225
Prayer: Duty
Letters to Malcolm:
Chiefly on Prayer,
chap. 21, para. 11–15,
pp. 114–116.

If we were perfected, prayer would not be a duty, it would be delight. Some day, please God, it will be. The same is true of many other behaviours which now appear as duties. If I loved my neighbor as myself, most of the actions which are now my moral duty would flow out of me as spontaneously as song from a lark or fragrance from a flower. Why is this not so yet? Well, we know, don't we? Aristotle has taught us that delight is the "bloom" on an unimpeded activity. But the very activities for which we were created are, while we live on earth, variously impeded: by evil in ourselves or in others. Not to practise them is to abandon our humanity. To practise them spontaneously and delightfully is not yet possible. This situation creates the category of duty, the whole specifically moral realm.

It exists to be transcended. Here is the paradox of Christianity. As practical imperatives for here and now the two great commandments have to be translated "Behave *as if* you loved God and man." For no man can love because he is told to. Yet obedience on this practical level is not really obedience at all. And if a man really loved God and man, once again this would hardly be obedience; for if he did, he would be unable to help it. Thus the command really says to us, "Ye must be born again." Till then, we have duty, morality, the Law. A schoolmaster, as St. Paul says, to bring us to Christ. We must expect no more of

it than of a schoolmaster; we must allow it no
less. . . .

But the school-days, please God, are numbered.
There is no morality in Heaven. The angels never
knew (from within) the meaning of the word
ought, and the blessed dead have long since gladly
forgotten it. This is why Dante's Heaven is so
right, and Milton's, with its military discipline so
silly.

. . . In the perfect and eternal world the Law
will vanish. But the results of having lived
faithfully under it will not.

I am therefore not really deeply worried by the
fact prayer is at present a duty, and even an
irksome one.

1226
**Prayer:
Petition**
Letters of C. S. Lewis
(16 April 1940), para. 4,
p. 183.

The practical problem about charity (in one's
prayer) is very hard work, isn't it? When you pray
for Hitler and Stalin how do you actually teach
yourself to make the prayer real? The two things
that help me are (*a*) A continual grasp of the idea
that one is only joining one's feeble little voice to
the perpetual intercession of Christ who died for
these very men. (*b*) A recollection, as firm as I can
make it, of all one's own cruelty; wh. might have
blossomed under different conditions into
something terrible. You and I are not at bottom
so different from these ghastly creatures.

1227
**Prayer:
Petition**
Letters of C. S. Lewis
(1951?), p. 226.

In praying for people one dislikes I find it helpful
to remember that one is joining in *His* prayer for
them.

1228 **Prayer:** **Petition** *Letters to Malcolm:* *Chiefly on Prayer,* chap. 5, para. 8–9, p. 26.	The petition, then, is not merely that I may patiently suffer God's will but also that I may vigorously do it. . . . "Thy will be *done*—by me—now" brings one back to brass tacks.
1229 **Prayer:** **Petition** *Letters to Malcolm:* *Chiefly on Prayer,* chap. 11, para. 14–15, p. 61.	Our Lord descends into the humiliation of being a suitor, of praying on His own behalf, in Gethsemane. But when He does so the certitude about His Father's will is apparently withdrawn. After that it would be no true faith—it would be idle presumption—for us, who are habitually suitors and do not often rise to the level of servants, to imagine that we shall have any assurance which is not an illusion—or correct only by accident—about the event of our prayers. Our struggle is—isn't it?—to achieve and retain faith on a lower level. To believe that, whether He can grant them or not, God will listen to our prayers, will take them into account. Even to go on believing that there is a Listener at all.
1230 **Prayer:** **Timing/** **Habits** *Letters of C. S. Lewis* (22 November 1931), para. 1, p. 144.	"Dean's Prayers"—which I have before described to you, lasts about a quarter of an hour. I then breakfast in Common Room with the Dean's Prayer party. [Ed. note: The newly converted Lewis readily observed the habit of prayer both solitary and communal.]
1231 **Prayer:** **Timing/** **Habits** *Letters to an American* *Lady* (20 February 1955), para. 1, p. 38.	I don't think we ought to try to keep up our normal prayers when we are ill and over-tired. I would not say this to a beginner who still has the habit to form. But you are past that stage. One mustn't make the Christian life into a punctilious system of *law,* like the Jewish [for] two reasons (1)

It raises scruples when we don't keep the routine
(2) It raises presumption when we do.

1232
**Prayer:
Timing/
Habits**
*Letters to Malcolm:
Chiefly on Prayer,*
chap. 3, para. 7,
pp. 16–17.

And, talking of sleepiness, I entirely agree with
you that no one in his senses, if he has any power
of ordering his own day, would reserve his chief
prayers for bed-time—obviously the worst possible
hour for any action which needs concentration.
The trouble is that thousands of unfortunate
people can hardly find any other. Even for us,
who are the lucky ones, it is not always easy. My
own plan, when hard pressed, is to seize any time,
and place, however unsuitable, in preference to
the last waking moment. On a day of travelling—
with, perhaps, some ghastly meeting at the end of
it—I'd rather pray sitting in a crowded train than
put it off till midnight when one reaches a hotel
bedroom with aching head and dry throat and
one's mind partly in a stupor and partly in a whirl.
On other, and slightly less crowded, days a bench
in a park, or a back street where one can pace up
and down, will do.

1233
Preaching
*Present Concerns: Essays
by C. S. Lewis,* "Modern
Man and His Categories
of Thought" (1946),
para. 11, p. 66.

Where God gives the gift, the "foolishness of
preaching" [Footnote: 1 Corinthians 1:21] is still
mighty. But best of all is a team of two; one to
deliver the preliminary intellectual barrage, and the
other to follow up with a direct attack on the
heart.

1234
Preaching
God in the Dock, "Cross-
Examination" (1963),
para. 46, p. 265.

I believe that there are many accommodating
preachers, and too many practitioners in the
church who are not believers. Jesus Christ did not
say "Go into all the world and tell the world that
it is quite right." The Gospel is something
completely different. In fact, it is directly opposed
to the world.

1235
Predestination
Letters of C. S. Lewis
(3 August 1953),
para. 3, p. 252.

I think we must take a leaf out of the scientists' book. They are quite familiar with the fact that for example, Light has to be regarded *both* as a wave and as a stream of particles. No-one can make these two views consistent. Of course reality must be self-consistent; but till (if ever) we can *see* the consistency it is better to hold two inconsistent views than to ignore one side of the evidence. The real inter-relation between God's omnipotence and Man's freedom is something we can't find out. Looking at the Sheep and the Goats, every man can be quite sure that every kind act he does will be accepted by Christ. Yet equally, we all do feel sure that all the good in us comes from Grace. We have to leave it at that. I find the best plan is to take the Calvinist view of my own virtues and other people's vices; and the other view of my own vices and other people's virtues. But tho' there is much to be puzzled about, there is nothing to be *worried* about. It is plain from Scripture that, in whatever sense the Pauline doctrine is true, it is not true in any sense which excludes its (apparent) opposite. You know what Luther said, "Do you doubt if you are chosen? Then say your prayers and you may conclude that you are."

1236
Prejudice
*Studies in Medieval and
Renaissance Literature,*
"Edmund Spenser,
1552–99" (1954),
para. 28, p. 138.

There is a great difference between rejecting something you have known from the inside and rejecting something (as uneducated people tend to do) simply because it happens to be out of fashion in your own time. It is like the difference between a mature and travelled man's love for his own country and the cocksure conviction of an ignorant adolescent that his own village (which is the only one he knows) is the hub of the universe and does everything in the Only Right Way. For our own age, with all its accepted ideas, stands to the vast extent of historical time much as one village stands to the whole world.

1237
**Preten-
tiousness**
The Four Loves, chap. 4, para. 33, p. 109.

We all appear as dunces when feigning an interest in things we care nothing about.

1238
Pride
Christian Reflections, "Christianity and Culture" (1940), para. 4, p. 14.

A man is never so proud as when striking an attitude of humility.

1239
Pride
Present Concerns: Essays by C. S. Lewis, "After Priggery—What?" (1945), para. 1, p. 56.

To avoid a man's society because he is poor or ugly or stupid may be bad; but to avoid it because he is wicked—with the all but inevitable implication that you are less wicked (at least in some respect)—is dangerous and disgusting.

1240
Pride
Letters of C. S. Lewis (15 May 1952), para. 3, p. 241.

Yes, pride is a perpetual nagging temptation. Keep on knocking it on the head, but don't be too worried about it. As long as one knows one is proud one is safe from the worst form of pride.

1241
Pride
The Screwtape Letters, "Screwtape Proposes a Toast" (1959), para. 23, pp. 162–163.

No man who says *I'm as good as you* believes it. He would not say it if he did. The St. Bernard never says it to the toy dog, nor the scholar to the dunce, nor the employable to the bum, nor the pretty woman to the plain. The claim to equality, outside the strictly political field, is made only by those who feel themselves to be in some way inferior. What it expresses is precisely the itching,

smarting, writhing awareness of an inferiority
which the patient refuses to accept.
And therefore resents. Yes, and therefore resents
every kind of superiority in others; denigrates it;
wishes its annihilation. Presently he suspects every
mere difference of being a claim to superiority.

1242
Pride
Poems, "Infatuation"
(1st pub. 1964),
para. 8, p. 75.

I longed last night to make her know the truth
That none of them has told her. Flushed with
    youth,
Dazed with a half-hour triumph, she held the
    crowd.
She loved the boys that buzzed on her like flies,
She loved the envy in the woman's eyes,
Faster she talked. I longed to cry aloud,
"What, has no brother told you yet, with whom
With what, you share the power that makes you
    proud?"

1243
Priorities
God in the Dock, "First
and Second Things"
(1942), para. 7, p. 280.

You can't get second things by putting them first;
you can get second things only by putting first
things first.

1244
Priorities
God in the Dock, "First
and Second Things"
(1942), para. 10, p. 281.

Perhaps civilization will never be safe until we care
for something else more than we care for it.

1245
Priorities
Letters of C. S. Lewis
(23 April 1951), para. 2,
p. 228.

Put first things first and we get second things
thrown in: put second things first and we lose
both first and second things.

1246

Priorities

Reflections on the Psalms,
chap. 5, para. 7,
pp. 48–49.

There is a stage in a child's life at which it cannot separate the religious from the merely festal character of Christmas or Easter. I have been told of a very small and very devout boy who was heard murmuring to himself on Easter morning a poem of his own composition which began "Chocolate eggs and Jesus risen." This seems to me, for his age, both admirable poetry and admirable piety. But of course the time will soon come when such a child can no longer effortlessly and spontaneously enjoy that unity. He will become able to distinguish the spiritual from the ritual and festal aspect of Easter; chocolate eggs will no longer be sacramental. And once he has distinguished he must put one or the other first. If he puts the spiritual first he can still taste something of Easter in the chocolate eggs; if he puts the eggs first they will soon be no more than any other sweetmeat. They have taken on an independent, and therefore a soon withering, life.

1247

Progress

The Allegory of Love,
chap. I.I, para. 1, p. 1.

Humanity does not pass through phases as a train passes through stations: being alive, it has the privilege of always moving yet never leaving anything behind. Whatever we have been, in some sort we are still.

1248

Progress

God in the Dock, "Evil and God" (1941), para. 1, p. 21.

If things can improve, this means that there must be some absolute standard of good above and outside the cosmic process to which that process can approximate. There is no sense in talking of "becoming better" if better means simply "what we are becoming"—it is like congratulating yourself on reaching your destination and defining destination as "the place you have reached."

1249 **Progress** *The World's Last Night and Other Essays*, "The World's Last Night" (1952), para. 13, p. 101.	In my opinion, the modern conception of Progress or Evolution (as popularly imagined) is simply a myth, supported by no evidence whatever.
1250 **Progress** *God in the Dock*, "Is Progress Possible?" (1958), para. 1, p. 311.	I care far more how humanity lives than how long. Progress, for me, means increasing goodness and happiness of individual lives. For the species, as for each man, mere longevity seems to me a contemptible ideal.
1251 **Prose** *English Literature in the Sixteenth Century*, bk. II.III, para. 1, p. 273.	Nothing in literature is so "desperately mortal" as a stylish prose. On the other hand, the prose of men who are intent upon their matter and write only to be understood tends, not quite fairly, to gain from the passage. . . . Decoration externally laid on and inorganic, is now hardly tolerated except in the human face.
1252 **Protestantism** *English Literature in the Sixteenth Century*, Introduction, para. 50–51, pp. 33–34.	On the Protestant view one could not, and by God's mercy need not, expiate one's sins. Theologically, Protestantism was either a recovery, or a development, or an exaggeration (it is not for the literary historian to say which) of Pauline theology. . . . In the mind of a Tyndale or Luther, as in the mind of St Paul himself, this theology was by no means an intellectual construction made in the interests of speculative thought. It springs directly out of a highly specialized religious experience. . . . The experience is that of catastrophic conversion. The man who has passed through it feels like one who has waked from nightmare into ecstasy. Like an accepted lover, he feels that he has done nothing, and never could have done anything, to deserve such astonishing

happiness. Never again can he "crow from the
dunghill of desert." All the initiative has been on
God's side; all has been free, unbounded grace.
And all will continue to be free, unbounded
grace. His own puny and ridiculous efforts would
be as helpless to retain the joy as they would have
been to achieve it in the first place. Fortunately
they need not. Bliss is not for sale, cannot be
earned. "Works" have no "merit," though of
course faith, inevitably, even unconsciously, flows
out into works of love at once. He is not saved
because he does works of love: he does works of
love because he is saved. It is faith alone that has
saved him: faith bestowed by sheer gift. From this
buoyant humility, this farewell to the self with all
its good resolutions, anxiety, scruples, and motive-
scratchings, all the Protestant doctrines originally
sprang.

For it must be clearly understood that they
were at first doctrines not of terror but of joy and
hope: indeed, more than hope, fruition, for as
Tyndale says, the converted man is already tasting
eternal life. The doctrine of predestination, says
the XVIIth Article, is "full of sweet, pleasant and
unspeakable comfort to godly persons." . . . Relief
and buoyancy are the characteristic notes. In a
single sentence of the *Tischreden* Luther tosses the
question aside for ever. Do you doubt whether
you are elected to salvation? Then say your
prayers, man, and you may conclude that you are.
It is as easy as that.

1253
Psalms
Letters of C. S. Lewis
(16 July 1940), para. 2,
p. 188.

My enjoyment of the Psalms has been greatly
increased lately. The point has been made before,
but let me make it again: what an admirable thing
it is in the divine economy that the sacred
literature of the world shd. have been entrusted to
a people whose poetry, depending largely on

---

parallelism, shd. remain poetry in any language you translate it into.

1254 **Psalms** Reflections on the Psalms, chap. 5, para. 4, p. 45.	The most valuable thing the Psalms do for me is to express that same delight in God which made David dance.
1255 **Psalms** Reflections on the Psalms, chap. 5, para. 10, p. 52.	There . . . I find an experience fully God-centered, asking of God no gift more urgently than His presence, the gift of Himself, joyous to the highest degree, and unmistakably real.
1256 **Psalms:** **Imprecatory** Reflections on the Psalms, chap. 3, para. 6, p. 22.	At the outset I felt sure, and I feel sure still, that we must not either try to explain them away or to yield for one moment to the idea that, because it comes in the Bible, all this vindictive hatred must somehow be good and pious. We must face both facts squarely. The hatred is there—festering, gloating, undisguised—and also we should be wicked if we in any way condoned or approved it, or (worse still) used it to justify similar passions in ourselves. Only after these two admissions have been made can we safely proceed.
1257 **Psychiatrists** Letters of C. S. Lewis (1947), para. 6, p. 211.	Keep clear of psychiatrists unless you know that they are also Christians. Otherwise they start with the assumption that your religion is an illusion and try to "cure" it: and this assumption they make not as professional psychologists but as amateur philosophers.
1258 **Purgatory** English Literature in the Sixteenth Century, bk. II.I.I, para. 8, p. 163.	A modern tends to see purgatory through the eyes of Dante: so seen, the doctrine is profoundly religious. That purification must, in its own nature, be painful, we hardly dare to dispute.

1259
Purgatory
Letters to Malcolm:
Chiefly on Prayer,
chap. 20, para. 7–10,
pp. 108–109.

I believe in Purgatory.

Mind you, the Reformers had good reasons for throwing doubt on "the Romish doctrine concerning Purgatory" as that Romish doctrine had then become. . . .

The right view returns magnificently in Newman's *Dream.* There, if I remember it rightly, the saved soul, at the very foot of the throne, begs to be taken away and cleansed. It cannot bear for a moment longer "With its darkness to affront that light." Religion has reclaimed Purgatory.

Our souls *demand* Purgatory, don't they? Would it not break the heart if God said to us, "It is true, my son, that your breath smells and your rags drip with mud and slime, but we are charitable here and no one will upbraid you with these things, nor draw away from you. Enter into the joy"? Should we not reply, "With submission, sir, and if there is no objection, I'd *rather* be cleaned first." "It may hurt, you know"—"Even so, sir."

1260
Puritanism
Selected Literary Essays,
"Donne and Love
Poetry" (1938), para. 15,
p. 116.

We have come to use the word "Puritan" to mean what should rather be called "rigorist" or "ascetic," and we tend to assume that the sixteenth-century Puritans were "puritanical" in this sense. Calvin's rigorist theocracy at Geneva lends colour to the error. But there is no understanding the period of the Reformation in England until we have grasped the fact that the quarrel between the Puritans and the Papists was not primarily a quarrel between rigorism and indulgence, and that, in so far as it was, the rigorism was on the Roman side. . . . The idea that a Puritan was a repressed and repressive person would have astonished Sir Thomas More and Luther about equally. . . . Puritan theology, so far from being grim and gloomy, seemed to More to err in the direction of fantastic optimism.

1261
Puritanism
English Literature in the Sixteenth Century,
Introduction, para. 52, p. 34.

Nearly every association which now clings to the word *puritan* has to be eliminated when we are thinking of the early Protestants. Whatever they were, they were not sour, gloomy, or severe; nor did their enemies bring any such charge against them. . . . For More, a Protestant was one "dronke of the new must of lewd lightnes of minde and vayne gladnesse of harte." . . . Luther, he said, had made converts precisely because "he spiced al the poison" with "libertee." . . . Protestantism was not too grim, but too glad, to be true.

1262
Puritanism
English Literature in the Sixteenth Century,
Introduction, para. 63, p. 44.

The [English sixteenth-century] puritan party, properly so called, insisted on Calvin's system of church government as well as on his general theology. They themselves would not have admitted a distinction between the two. They taught that a system—as they called it, a *platfourme*—of church government could be found in the New Testament and was binding on all believers till the end of the world. To a modern reader, examining the texts on which they based this theory, it appears one of the strangest mirages which have ever deceived the human mind: only explicable, if at all, by the strong enchantment of the master's exploits at Geneva.

1263
Puritanism
Studies in Medieval and Renaissance Studies,
"Edmund Spenser, 1552-99" (1954), para. 2, pp. 121–122.

By purity the Elizabethan Puritan meant not chastity but "pure" theology and, still more, "pure" church discipline. That is, he wanted an all-powerful Presbyterian Church, a church stronger than the state, set up in England, on the

---

model of Calvin's church at Geneva. Knox in Scotland loudly demanded, and at least one English Puritan hinted, that this should be done by armed revolution. Calvin, the great successful doctrinaire who had actually set up the "new order," was the man who had dazzled them all. We must picture these Puritans as the very opposite of those who bear that name today: as young, fierce, progressive intellectuals, very fashionable and up-to-date. They were not teetotallers; bishops, not beer, were their special aversion. And humanists in this context means simply "classicists"—men very interested in Greek, but more interested in Latin, and far more interested in the "correct" or "classical" style of Latin than in what the Latin authors said. They wanted English drama to observe the (supposedly) Aristotelian "unities," and some of them wanted English poets to abandon rhyme—a nasty, "barbarous" or "Gothic" affair—and use classical metres in English. There was no necessary enmity between Puritans and humanists. They were often the same people, and nearly always the same sort of people: the young men "in the Movement," the impatient progressives demanding a "clean sweep." And they were united by a common (and usually ignorant) hatred for everything medieval: for scholastic philosophy, medieval Latin, romance, fairies, and chivalry.

1264
Puritanism: Sexuality
Studies in Medieval and Renaissance Literature, "Tasso" (1940s?), para. 9, p. 117.

Asceticism is far more characteristic of Catholicism than of the Puritans. Celibacy and the praise of virginity are Catholic: the honour of the marriage bed is Puritan.

1265
**Puritanism:
Sexuality**
*English Literature in the
Sixteenth Century,*
Introduction, para. 52,
p. 35.

To be sure, there are standards by which the early Protestants could be called "puritanical"; they held adultery, fornication, and perversion for deadly sins. But then so did the Pope. If that is puritanism, all Christendom was then puritanical together. So far as there was any difference about sexual morality, the Old Religion was the more austere. The exaltation of virginity is a Roman, that of marriage, a Protestant, trait.

1266
Purity
Mere Christianity, bk. IV,
chap. 2, para. 14–15,
p. 144.

The instrument through which you see God is your whole self. And if a man's self is not kept clean and bright, his glimpse of God will be blurred—like the Moon seen through a dirty telescope. That is why horrible nations have horrible religions: they have been looking at God through a dirty lens.

   God can show Himself as He really is only to real men. And that means not simply to men who are individually good, but to men who are united together in a body, loving one another, helping one another, showing Him to one another. For that is what God meant humanity to be like; like players in one band, or organs in one body.

1267
Purpose
Till We Have Faces,
part 2, chap. 4, p. 308.

I ended my first book with the words *no answer.* I know now, Lord, why you utter no answer. You are yourself the answer. Before your face questions die away. What other answer would suffice?

1268

**Questions:
Moral,
Philosophical,
and
Theological**

A Grief Observed,
chap. IV, para. 25, p. 81.

Can a mortal ask questions which God finds unanswerable? Quite easily, I should think. All nonsense questions are unanswerable. How many hours are there in a mile? Is yellow square or round? Probably half the questions we ask—half our great theological and metaphysical problems—are like that.

1269

**Questions:
Moral,
Philosophical,
and
Theological**

A Grief Observed,
chap. IV, para. 28, p. 83.

Heaven will solve our problems, but not, I think, by showing us subtle reconciliations between all our apparently contradictory notions. The notions will all be knocked from under our feet. We shall see that there never was any problem.

1270	If only one had time to read a little more: we
Reading	either get shallow & broad or narrow and deep.

The Letters of C. S. Lewis to Arthur Greeves (2 March 1919), para. 5, p. 249.

1271	If we must find out what bad men are writing,
Reading	and must therefore buy their papers, and therefore

Present Concerns: Essays by C. S. Lewis, "After Priggery—What?" (1945), para. 11, p. 60.

enable their papers to exist, who does not see that this supposed necessity of observing the evil is just what maintains the evil? It may in general be dangerous to ignore an evil; but not if the evil is one that perishes by being ignored.

1272	An unliterary man may be defined as one who
Reading	reads books once only. . . .

Of Other Worlds: Essays and Stories, "On Stories" (1947), para. 24–25, pp. 17–18.

   The re-reader is looking not for actual surprises (which can come only once) but for a certain surprisingness. The point has often been misunderstood. . . . In the only sense that matters the surprise works as well the twentieth time as the first. It is the *quality* of unexpectedness, not the *fact* that delights us. It is even better the second time . . . in literature. We do not enjoy a story fully at the first reading. Not till the curiosity, the sheer narrative lust, has been given its sop and laid asleep, are we at leisure to savour the real beauties. Till then, it is like wasting great wine on a ravenous natural thirst which merely wants cold wetness. The children understand this well when they ask for the same story over and over again, and in the same words. They want to have again the "surprise" of discovering that what seemed Little-Red-Riding-Hood's grandmother is really the wolf. It is better when you know it is coming: free from the shock of actual surprise you can attend better to the intrinsic surprisingness of the *peripeteia*.

1273
Reading
Old Books

Studies in Medieval and Renaissance Literature, "De Audiendis Poetis" (late 1950s?; 1st pub. 1966), para. 5–7, pp. 2–3.

There are two ways of enjoying the past, as there are two ways of enjoying a foreign country. One man carries his Englishry abroad with him and brings it home unchanged. Wherever he goes he consorts with the other English tourists. By a good hotel he means one that is like an English hotel. He complains of the bad tea where he might have had excellent coffee. . . .

But there is another sort of travelling and another sort of reading. You can eat the local food and drink the local wines, you can share the foreign life, you can begin to see the foreign country as it looks, not to the tourist, but to its inhabitants. You can come home modified, thinking and feeling as you did not think and feel before. So with the old literature. You can go beyond the first impression that a poem makes on your modern sensibility. By study of things outside the poem, by comparing it with other poems, by steeping yourself in the vanished period, you can then re-enter the poem with eyes more like those of the natives; now perhaps seeing that the associations you gave to the old words were false, that the real implications were different than you supposed.

. . . I am writing to help the second sort of reading. Partly, of course, because I have a historical motive. I am a man as well as a lover of poetry: being human, I am inquisitive, I want to know as well as to enjoy. But even if enjoyment alone were my aim I should still choose this way, for I should hope to be led by it to newer and fresher enjoyments, things I could never have met in my own period, modes of feeling, flavours, atmospheres, nowhere accessible but by a mental journey into the real past. I have lived nearly sixty years with myself and my own century and am not so enamoured of either as to desire no glimpse of a world beyond them.

1274

Reality

Letters to Malcolm: Chiefly on Prayer, chap. 15, para. 12, p. 80.

We should never ask of anything "Is it real?," for everything is real. The proper question is "A real *what*?," e.g., a real snake or real *delirium tremens?*

1275

Reason

Selected Literary Essays, "Bluspels and Flalansferes: A Semantic Nightmare" (1939), para. 23. p. 265.

It must not be supposed that I am in any sense putting forward the imagination as the organ of truth. We are not talking of truth, but of meaning: meaning which is the antecedent condition both of truth and falsehood, whose antithesis is not error but nonsense. I am a rationalist. For me, reason is the natural organ of truth; but imagination is the organ of meaning. Imagination, producing new metaphors or revivifying old, is not the cause of truth, but its condition. It is, I confess, undeniable that such a view indirectly implies a kind of truth or rightness in the imagination itself.

1276 **Reason** A Preface to "Paradise Lost," chap. II, para. 4, p. 11.	*Reasoning* is never, like poetry, judged *from the outside* at all. The critique of a chain of reasoning is itself a chain of reasoning: the critique of a tragedy is not itself a tragedy.

1277 **Reason** The Abolition of Man, chap. 2, para. 19, p. 60.	An open mind, in questions that are not ultimate, is useful. But an open mind about ultimate foundations either of Theoretical or Practical Reason is idiocy. If a man's mind is open on these things, let his mouth at least be shut.

1278 **Reason** Miracles, chap. 3, para. 5–6, pp. 14–15.	All possible knowledge, then, depends on the validity of reasoning. If the feeling of certainty which we express by words like *must be* and *therefore* and *since* is a real perception of how things outside our own minds really "must" be, well and good. But if this certainty is merely a feeling *in* our own minds and not a genuine insight into realities beyond them—if it merely represents the way our minds happen to work—then we can have no knowledge. Unless human reasoning is valid no science can be true. It follows that no account of the universe can be true unless that account leaves it possible for our thinking to be a real insight. A theory which explained everything else in the whole universe but which made it impossible to believe that our thinking was valid, would be utterly out of court. For that theory would itself have been reached by thinking, and if thinking is not valid that theory would, of course, be itself demolished. It would have destroyed its own credentials. It would be an argument which proved that no argument was sound—a proof that there are no such things as proofs—which is nonsense.

1279

Reason

Miracles, chap. 3,
para. 26, p. 21.

If . . . a proof that there are no proofs is
nonsensical, so is a proof that there are proofs.
Reason is our starting point. There can be no
question either of attacking or defending it. If by
treating it as a mere phenomenon you put
yourself outside it, there is then no way, except by
begging the question, of getting inside again.

1280

Reason

Miracles, chap. 4,
para. 2, pp. 25–26.

At [the] frontier [where Reason and Nature meet]
we find a great deal of traffic but it is all one-way
traffic. It is a matter of daily experience that
rational thoughts induce and enable us to alter the
course of Nature—of physical nature when we
use mathematics to build bridges, or of psychological nature when we apply arguments to
alter our own emotions. . . . On the other hand,
Nature is quite powerless to produce rational
thought: not that she never modifies our thinking
but that the moment she does so, it ceases (for
that very reason) to be rational. For, as we have
seen, a train of thought loses all rational
credentials as soon as it can be shown to be
wholly the result of non-rational causes. When
Nature, so to speak, attempts to do things to
rational thoughts she only succeeds in killing
them. That is the peculiar state of affairs at the
frontier. Nature can only raid Reason to kill; but
Reason can invade Nature to take prisoners and
even to colonise. Every object you see before you
at this moment—the walls, ceiling, and furniture,
the book, your own washed hands and cut fingernails, bears witness to the colonisation of Nature
by Reason: for none of this matter would have
been in these states if Nature had had her way.

1281 **Reason** *Miracles,* chap. 3, para. 31, pp. 23–24.	Reason is given before Nature and on reason our concept of Nature depends. . . . Our whole idea of Nature depends . . . on the thinking we are actually doing, not *vice-versa.* This is the prime reality, on which the attribution of reality to anything else rests. If it won't fit into Nature, we can't help it. We will certainly not, on that account, give it up. If we do, we should be giving up Nature too.
1282 **Reason** *Mere Christianity,* bk. II, chap. 3, para. 4, pp. 52–53.	There is a difficulty about disagreeing with God. He is the source from which all your reasoning power comes: you could not be right and He wrong any more than a stream can rise higher than its own source. When you are arguing against Him you are arguing against the very power that makes you able to argue at all: it is like cutting off the branch you are sitting on.

1283
Reason
Poems, "Reason" (1st
pub. 1964), p. 81.
	Set on the soul's acropolis the reason stands
	A virgin, arm'd, commercing with celestial light,
	And he who sins against her has defiled his own
	Virginity: no cleansing makes his garment white;
	So clear is reason. But how dark, imagining,
	Warm, dark, obscure and infinite, daughter of
	    Night:
	Dark is her brow, the beauty of her eyes with
	    sleep
	Is loaded, and her pains are long, and her delight.

1284 **Rebellion:** **Against God** *Spirits in Bondage,* "De Profundis," p. 34.	O universal strength, I know it well It is but froth of folly to rebel For thou art Lord and hast the keys of Hell.

1285
Redemption
See also conversion,
eternal life, salvation.

The Problem of Pain,
chap. 8, para. 1,
pp. 118–19.

Some will not be redeemed. There is no doctrine which I would more willingly remove from Christianity than this, if it lay in my power. But it has the full support of Scripture and, specially, of Our Lord's own words; it has always been held by Christendom; and it has the support of reason. If a game is played, it must be possible to lose it. If the happiness of a creature lies in self-surrender, no one can make that surrender but himself (though many can help him to make it) and he may refuse. I would pay any price to be able to say truthfully "All will be saved." But my reason retorts, "Without their will, or with it?" If I say "Without their will" I at once perceive a contradiction; how can the supreme voluntary act of self-surrender be involuntary? If I say "With their will," my reason replies "How if they *will not* give in?"

1286
Reformation
*English Literature in the
Sixteenth Century,* bk.
II.I.I, para. 1, p. 157.

In England, as elsewhere, the Reformation was a process that occurred on three planes: firstly in the thought and conscience of the individual, secondly in the intertangled realms of ecclesiastical and political activity, and thirdly on the printed page.

1287
Reincarnation
*The Dark Tower &
Other Stories,* "The Dark
Tower" (1939–40;
1st pub. 1977), p. 29.

"You don't believe in reincarnation?"
  "Of course not. I'm a Christian."

1288
Religion
*The Letters of C. S.
Lewis to Arthur Greeves*
26 January 1930),
para. 4, pp. 333–334.

All private reading has ceased, except for 20 minutes before bed (if alone) when I drink a cup of cocoa and try to wash the day off with Macdonalds Diary of an Old Soul. I shall soon have finished it and must look round for another book. Luckily the world is full of books of that general type: that is another of the beauties of coming, I won't say, to religion but to an attempt at religion—one finds oneself on the main road with all humanity, and can compare notes with an endless succession of previous travellers. It is emphatically coming home: as Chaucer says "Returneth *home* from worldly vanitee."

1289

Religion and Domestic Life

The Letters of C. S. Lewis to Arthur Greeves (22 June 1930), para. 2, pp. 362–363.

It is terrible to find how little progress one's philosophy and charity have made when they are brought to the test of domestic life.

1290

Religion, Dangers of

The Screwtape Letters, "Screwtape Proposes a Toast" (1961), para. 41, pp. 171–172.

[Senior devil Screwtape in a speech at the "Annual Dinner of the Tempters' Training College for Young Devils":] It will be an ill day for us if what most humans mean by "religion" ever vanishes from the Earth. It can still send us the truly delicious sins. The fine flower of unholiness can grow only in the close neighbourhood of the Holy. Nowhere do we tempt so successfully as on the very steps of the altar.

1291

Resurrection: Jesus

Miracles, chap. 16, para. 2, pp. 143–144.

The Resurrection is the central theme in every Christian sermon reported in the Acts. The Resurrection, and its consequences were the "gospel" or good news which the Christians brought: what we call the "gospels," the narratives of Our Lord's life and death, were composed later for the benefit of those who had already accepted the *gospel*. They were in no sense the basis of Christianity: they were written for those already converted. The miracle of the Resurrection, and the theology of that miracle, comes first: the

biography comes later as a comment on it.
Nothing could be more unhistorical than to pick
out selected sayings of Christ from the gospels
and to regard those as the datum and the rest of
the New Testament as a construction upon it. The
first fact in the history of Christendom is a
number of people who say they have seen the
Resurrection.

1292

Resurrection: Jesus and the Saved

Miracles, chap. 16, para. 12, p. 149.

The records represent Christ . . . as withdrawing
six weeks later, into some different mode of
existence. It says—He says—that He goes "to
prepare a place for us." This presumably means
that He is about to create that whole new Nature
which will provide the environment or conditions
for His glorified humanity and, in Him, for ours.
. . . It is not the picture of an escape from any and
every kind of Nature into some unconditioned
and utterly transcendent life. It is the picture of a
new human nature and a new Nature in general,
being brought into existence. . . . The old field of
space, time, matter, and the senses is to be
weeded, dug, and sown for a new crop. We may
be tired of that old field: God is not.

1293

Resurrection: the Saved

Poems, "The Naked Seed" (1933), p. 117.

Oh, thou that art unwearying, that dost neither
sleep
       Nor slumber, who didst take
All care for Lazarus in the careless tomb, oh keep
       Watch for me till I wake.
If thou think for me what I cannot think, if thou
       Desire for me what I
Cannot desire, my soul's interior Form, though
       now
       Deep-buried, will not die,
—No more than the insensible dropp'd seed
       which grows

> Through winter ripe for birth
> Because, while it forgets, the heaven remembering
>   throws
>   Sweet influence still on earth,
> —Because the heaven, moved moth-like by thy
>   beauty, goes
>   Still turning round the earth.

1294

**Resurrection:
the Saved**

Perelandra, chap. 3,
p. 32.

A sceptical friend of ours called McPhee was arguing against the Christian doctrine of the resurrection of the human body. I was his victim at the moment and he was pressing on me in his Scots way with such questions as "So you think you're going to have guts and a palate for ever in a world where there'll be no eating, and genital organs in a world without copulation? Man, ye'll have a grand time of it!" When Ransom suddenly burst out with great excitement, "Oh, don't you see, you ass, that there's a difference between a trans-sensuous life and a non-sensuous life?" That, of course, directed McPhee's fire to him. What emerged was that in Ransom's opinion the present functions and appetites of the body would disappear, not because they were atrophied but because they were, as he said "engulfed."

1295

**Resurrection:
the Saved**

*The Letters of C. S.
Lewis to Arthur Greeves*
(19 August 1947),
para. 1, pp. 510–511.

I agree that we don't know what a spiritual body is. But I don't like *contrasting* it with (your words) "an actual, physical body." This suggests that the spiritual body wd. be the opposite of "actual"—i.e. some kind of vision or imagination. And I do think most people imagine it as something that *looks* like the present body and isn't really there. Our Lord's eating the boiled fish seems to put the boots on that idea, don't you think? I suspect the distinction is the other way round—that it is

---

something compared with which our present
bodies are half real and phantasmal.

1296 **Resurrection:** **the Saved** *Miracles,* chap. 16, para. 15, p. 151.	The general resurrection involves the reverse process universalised—a rush of matter towards organisation at the call of spirits which require it. It is presumably a foolish fancy (not justified by the words of Scripture) that each spirit should recover those particular units of matter which he ruled before. For one thing, they would not be enough to go round: we all live in second-hand suits and there are doubtless atoms in my chin which have served many another man, many a dog, many an eel, many a dinosaur. Nor does the unity of our bodies even in this present life, consist in retaining the same particles. My form remains one, though the matter in it changes continually. I am, in that respect like a curve in a waterfall.
1297 **Resurrection:** **the Saved** *Miracles,* chap. 16, para. 19, p. 153.	It must indeed be emphasised throughout that we know and can know very little about the New Nature. The task of the imagination here is not to forecast it but simply, by brooding on many possibilities, to make room for a more complete and circumspect agnosticism. It is useful to remember that even now senses responsive to different vibrations would admit us to quite new worlds of experience: that a multi-dimensional space would be different, almost beyond recognition, from the space we are now aware of, yet not discontinuous from it: that time may not always be for us, as it now is, unilinear and irreversible: that other parts of Nature might some day obey us as our cortex now does. It is useful not because we can trust these fancies to give us

any positive truths about the New Creation but because they teach us not to limit, in our rashness, the vigour and variety of the new crops which this old field might yet produce. We are therefore compelled to believe that nearly all we are told about the New Creation is metaphorical. But not quite all. That is just where the story of the Resurrection suddenly jerks us back like a tether. The local appearances, the eating, the touching, the claim to be corporeal, must be either reality or sheer illusion. The New Nature is, in the most troublesome way, interlocked at some points with the Old.

1298
Resurrection: the Saved
Miracles, chap. 16, para. 21, p. 155.

A new Nature is being not merely made but made out of an old one. We live amid all the anomalies, inconveniences, hopes, and excitements of a house that is being rebuilt.

1299
Resurrection: the Saved and Animals
Letters to an American Lady (26 November 1962), pp. 110–111.

My stuff about animals came long ago in *The Problem of Pain.* I ventured the supposal—it could be nothing more—that as we are raised *in* Christ, so at least some animals are raised *in* us. Who knows, indeed, but that a great deal even of the inanimate creation is raised *in* the redeemed souls who have, during this life, taken its beauty into themselves? That may be the way in which the "new heaven and the new earth" are formed. Of course we can only guess and wonder. But these particular guesses arise in me, I trust, from taking seriously the resurrection of the body: a doctrine which now-a-days is very soft pedalled by nearly all the faithful—to our great impoverishment. Not that you and I have now much reason to rejoice in having bodies! Like old automobiles, aren't they? where all sorts of apparently different things keep going wrong, but what they add up to is the plain fact that the machine is wearing out. Well, it was not meant to last forever. Still, I have a kindly feeling for the old rattle-trap. Through it God showed me that whole side of His beauty which is embodied in colour, sound, smell and size. No doubt it has often led me astray: but not half so often, I suspect, as my soul has led *it* astray. For the spiritual evils which we share with the devils (pride, spite) are far worse than what we share with the beasts: and sensuality really arises more from the imagination than from the appetites; which, if left merely to their own animal strength, and not elaborated by our imagination, would be fairly easily managed. But this is turning into a sermon!

1300
Revelation
The Problem of Pain, chap. 1, p. 15.

If the universe is so bad, or even half so bad, how on earth did human beings ever come to attribute it to the activity of a wise and good Creator? Men are fools, perhaps; but hardly so foolish as that. The direct inference from black to white, from evil flower to virtuous root, from senseless work to a workman infinitely wise, staggers belief. The spectacle of the universe as revealed by experience can never have been the ground of religion: it must always have been something in spite of which religion, acquired from a different source, was held.

1301
Reverence
The Allegory of Love, chap. III.V, para. 3, p. 144.

Whatever claims reverence risks ridicule.

1302 **Rights** *Selected Literary Essays,* "Kipling's World" (1948), para. 14, 240.	If all men stood talking of their rights before they went up a mast or down a sewer or stoked a furnace or joined an army, we should all perish; nor while they talked of their rights would they learn to do these things. . . . The man preoccupied with his own rights is not only a disastrous, but a very unlovely object; indeed, one of the worst mischiefs we do by treating a man unjustly is that we force him to be thus preoccupied.
1303 **Romance** **(as a Literary** **Genre)** *Spenser's Images of Life,* chap. IX.I, para. 2, p. 120.	Just as a lobster wears its skeleton outside, so the characters in Romance wear their character outside. For it is their story that is their character.
1304 **Ruskin, John** *Selected Literary Essays,* "The Literary Impact of the Authorised Version" (1950), para. 29, p. 138.	A structure descending from Cicero through the prose of Hooker, Milton, and Taylor, and then enriched with romantic colouring for which Homer and the Bible are laid under contribution—that seems to me the formula for Ruskin's style.

1305 **Salvation** See also conversion, eternal life, redemption. *Christian Reflections,* *Christianity and* *Culture" (1940), section I,* *para. 4, p. 14.*	The glory of God, and, as our only means to glorifying Him, the salvation of human souls, is the real business of life.
1306 **Salvation** *Christian Reflections,* *"Christianity and* *Culture" (1940), section* *II, para. 4, p. 26.*	The salvation of souls is a means to the glorifying of God because only saved souls can duly glorify Him.
1307 **Salvation** *The Weight of Glory,* *"Membership" (1945),* *para. 19, p. 120.*	Christianity is not, in the long run, concerned either with individuals or communities . . . but a new creature.
1308 **Salvation** *Taliessin Through Logres,* *. . . Arthurian Torso,* *"Williams and the* *Arthuriad" (1948), chap.* *III, para. 16, p. 307.*	"He saved others, himself he cannot save" is a *definition* of the Kingdom. All salvation, everywhere and at all times, in great things or in little, is vicarious.

1309
Salvation
The Lion, the Witch and the Wardrobe, chap. 12, p. 124.

"Please—Aslan," said Lucy, "can anything be done to save Edmund?"

"All shall be done," said Aslan.

1310
Salvation
Mere Christianity, bk. II, chap. 5, para. 2, p. 62.

There are three things that spread the Christ life to us: baptism, belief, and that mysterious action which different Christians call by different names—Holy Communion, the Mass, the Lord's Supper.

1311
Salvation
Mere Christianity, bk. IV, chap. 1, para. 10–13, 15–16, pp. 137–140.

The point in Christianity which gives us the greatest shock is the statement that by attaching ourselves to Christ, we can "become Sons of God." . . . God has brought us into existence and loves us and looks after us, and in that way is like a father. But when the Bible talks of our "becoming" Sons of God, obviously it must mean something different. . . .

One of the creeds says that Christ is the Son of God, "begotten, not created"; and it adds "begotten by his Father before all worlds."

. . . To beget is to become the father of: to create is to make. And the difference is this. When you beget, you beget something of the same kind as yourself. A man begets human babies. . . . But when you make, you make something of a different kind from yourself. . . . A man makes a wireless set—or he may make something more like himself than a wireless set: say, a statue. If he is a clever enough carver he may make a stature which is very like a man indeed. But, of course, it is not a real man; it only looks like one. It cannot breathe or think. It is not alive.

Now that is the first thing to get clear. What God begets is God; just as what man begets is man. What God creates is not God; just as what man makes is not man. That is why men are not Sons of God in the sense that Christ is. They may be like God in certain ways, but they are not things of the same kind. They are more like statues or pictures of God. . . .

. . . What man, in his natural condition, has not got, is Spiritual life—the higher and different sort of life that exists in God. . . .

And that is precisely what Christianity is about. This world is a great sculptor's shop. We are the statues and there is a rumour going round the shop that some of us are some day going to come to life.

1312
Salvation
Mere Christianity, bk. IV, chap. 5, para. 8, pp. 156–157.

What, then, is the difference which He [Jesus] has made to the whole human mass? It is just this; that the business of becoming a son of God, of being turned from a created thing into a begotten thing, of passing over from the temporary biological life into timeless "spiritual" life, has been done for us. Humanity is already "saved" in principle. We individuals have to appropriate that salvation. But the really tough work—the bit we could not have done for ourselves—has been done for us. We have not got to try to climb up into spiritual life by our own efforts; it has already come down into the human race. If we will only lay ourselves open to the one Man in whom it was fully present, and who, in spite of being God, is also a real man, He will do it in us and for us.

1313
Salvation
Mere Christianity, bk. IV, chap. 10, para. 15–16, p. 182.

We must not suppose that even if we succeeded in making everyone nice we should have saved their souls. A world of nice people, content in their own niceness, looking no further, turned away from God, would be just as desperately in need of salvation as a miserable world—and might even be more difficult to save.

For mere improvement is no redemption, though redemption always improves people even here and now and will, in the end, improve them to a degree we cannot yet imagine. God became man to turn creatures into sons: not simply to produce better men of the old kind but to produce a new kind of man.

1314
Salvation
Mere Christianity, bk. IV, chap. 11, para. 1, 4, 7, pp. 183, 185–186.

Christ's work of making New Men [is like] . . . turning a horse into a winged creature. . . . It is not mere improvement but Transformation.

It is a change that goes off in a totally different direction—a change from being creatures of God to being sons of God. The first instance appeared in Palestine two thousand years ago.

. . . I have called Christ the "first instance" of the new man. But of course He is something more than that. He is not merely a new man, one specimen of the species, but *the* new man. He is the origin and centre and life of all the new men.

1315
Salvation
Mere Christianity, bk. IV, chap. 10, para. 17, p. 183.

What can you ever really know of other people's souls—of their temptations, their opportunities, their struggles? One soul in the whole creation you do know: and it is the only one whose fate is placed in your hands. If there is a God, you are, in a sense, alone with Him. You cannot put Him off with speculations about your next door neighbours or memories of what you have read in books. What will all that chatter and hearsay count (will you even be able to remember it?) when the anaesthetic fog which we call "nature" or "the real world" fades away and the Presence in which you have always stood becomes palpable, immediate, and unavoidable?

1316
Sanctification
God in the Dock, "Man
or Rabbit?" (1946),
para. 10, p. 112.

All the rabbit in us is to disappear—the worried, conscientious, ethical rabbit as well as the cowardly and sensual rabbit. We shall bleed and squeal as the handfuls of fur come out; and then, surprisingly, we shall find underneath it all a thing we have never yet imagined: a real Man, an ageless god, a son of God, strong, radiant, wise, beautiful, and drenched in joy.

1317
Sanctification
Miracles, chap. 15,
para. 5, p. 135.

Whatever may have been the powers of unfallen man, it appears that those of redeemed Man will be almost unlimited. Christ, re-ascending from His great dive, is bringing up Human Nature with Him. Where He goes, it goes too. It will be made "like Him."

1318
Sanctification
Miracles, Appendix A,
para. 6, p. 172.

The regenerate man is *totally* different from the unregenerate, for the regenerate life, the Christ that is formed in him, transforms every part of him: in it his spirit, soul and body will all be reborn. Thus if the regenerate life is not a *part* of the man, this is largely because where it arises at all it cannot rest till it becomes the whole man. . . . The regenerate man will find his soul eventually harmonised with his spirit by the life of Christ that is in him.

1319
Sanctification
Mere Christianity, bk. IV,
chap. 7, para. 11, p. 164.

Put right out of your head the idea that these are only fancy ways of saying that Christians are to read what Christ said and try to carry it out—as a man may read what Plato or Marx said and try to carry it out. They mean something much more than that. They mean that a real Person, Christ, here and now, in that very room where you are saying your prayers, is doing things to you. It is not a question of a good man who died two thousand years ago. It is a living Man, still as much a man as you, and still as much God as He was when He created the world, really coming and interfering with your very self; killing the old natural self in you and replacing it with the kind of self He has. At first, only for moments. Then for longer periods. Finally, if all goes well, turning you permanently into a different sort of thing; into a new little Christ, a being which, in its own small way, has the same kind of life as God; which shares in His power, joy, knowledge and eternity.

1320

Sanctification

Mere Christianity, bk. IV, chap. 7, para. 12, p. 165.

I cannot, by direct moral effort, give myself new motives. After the first few steps in the Christian life we realise that everything which really needs to be done in our souls can be done only by God.

1321

Satan

Poems, "Wormwood" (1933), p. 87.

Thou only art alternative to God, oh, dark
    And burning island among spirits, tenth
    hierarch,
Wormwood, immortal Satan, Ahriman, alone
    Second to Him to whom no second else were
    known. . . .
All that seemed earth is Hell, or Heaven. God is:
    thou art:
The rest, illusion. How should man live save as
    glass
To let the white light without flame, the Father,
    pass
Unstained: or else—opaque, molten to thy desire,
Venus infernal starving in the strength of fire!

Lord, open not too often my weak eyes to this.

1322
Satan
A Preface to "Paradise
Lost," chap. 13, para. 2,
p. 95.

We know from his [Milton's] prose works that he believed everything detestable to be, in the long run, also ridiculous; and mere Christianity commits every Christian to believing that "the Devil is (in the long run) an ass."

1323
Satan
A Preface to "Paradise
Lost," chap. 13, para. 3,
pp. 96–97.

[Commenting on Milton's Satan in *Paradise Lost*:] His revolt is entangled in contradictions from the very outset, and he cannot even raise the banner of liberty and equality without admitting in a tell-tale parenthesis that "Orders and Degrees Jarr not with liberty" (v, 789). He wants hierarchy and does not want hierarchy. Throughout the poem he is engaged in sawing off the branch he is sitting on, not only in the quasi-political sense already indicated, but in a deeper sense still, since a creature revolting against a creator is revolting against the source of his own powers—including even his power to revolt.

1324
Satan
A Preface to "Paradise
Lost," chap. 13, para. 4,
p. 97.

[Commenting on Milton's Satan in *Paradise Lost*:] He has become more a Lie than a Liar, a personified self-contradiction.

1325
Satan
A Preface to "Paradise
Lost," chap. 13, para. 6,
p. 99.

[Commenting on Milton's Satan in *Paradise Lost*:] What we see in Satan is the horrible co-existence of a subtle and incessant intellectual activity with an incapacity to understand anything. This doom he has brought upon himself; in order to avoid seeing one thing he has, almost voluntarily, incapacitated himself from seeing at all. And thus, throughout the poem, all his torments come, in a sense, at his own bidding, and the Divine judgement might have been expressed in the words "thy will be done." He says "Evil be thou my good" (which includes "Nonsense be thou my sense") and his prayer is granted.

**1326
Satan**
A Preface to "Paradise Lost," chap. 13, para. 9, pp. 102–103.

[Commenting on Milton's Satan in *Paradise Lost*:] To admire Satan, then, is to give one's vote not only for a world of misery, but also for a world of lies and propaganda, of wishful thinking, of incessant autobiography. Yet the choice is possible. Hardly a day passes without some slight movement towards it in each one of us. That is what makes *Paradise Lost* so serious a poem. The thing is possible, and the exposure of it is resented. Where *Paradise Lost* is not loved, it is deeply hated.

**1327
Satan**
The Weight of Glory, "Membership" (1945), para. 3, p. 118.

Like a good chess player he is always trying to manoeuvre you into a position where you can save your castle only by losing your bishop.

**1328
Sayers, Dorothy**
On Stories, "A Panegyric for Dorothy L. Sayers" (1958), para. 2, 4, pp. 92–93.

She aspired to be, and was, at once a popular entertainer and a conscientious craftsman: like (in her degree) Chaucer, Cervantes, Shakespeare, or Moliere. I have an idea that, with a very few exceptions, it is only such writers who matter much in the long run.
. . . She never sank the artist and the entertainer in the evangelist.

**1329
Scholarship**
The Weight of Glory, "Learning in War-Time" (1939), para. 9, pp. 27–28.

The intellectual life is not the only road to God, nor the safest, but we find it to be a road, and it may be the appointed road for us. Of course it will be so only so long as we keep the impulse pure and disinterested. That is the great difficulty. As the author of the *Theologia Germanica* says,

we may come to love knowledge—*our* knowing—
more than the thing known: to delight not in the
exercise of our talents but in the fact that they are
ours, or even in the reputation they bring us.
Every success in the scholar's life increases this
danger. If it becomes irresistible, he must give up
his scholarly work. The time for plucking out the
right eye has arrived.

1330
Science and Christianity
The Weight of Glory,
"Is Theology Poetry?"
(1944), para. 24,
pp. 91–92.

When I accept Theology I may find difficulties, at
this point or that, in harmonising it with some
particular truths which are imbedded in the
mythical cosmology derived from science. But I
can get in, or allow for, science as a whole.
Granted that Reason is prior to matter and that
the light of that primal Reason illuminates finite
minds. I can understand how men should come,
by observation and inference, to know a lot about
the universe they live in. If, on the other hand, I
swallow the scientific cosmology as a whole, then
not only can I not fit in Christianity, but I cannot
even fit in science. If minds are wholly dependent
on brains, and brains on bio-chemistry, and bio-
chemistry (in the long run) on the meaningless
flux of the atoms, I cannot understand how the
thought of those minds should have any more
significance than the sound of the wind in the
trees. And this is to me the final test. This is how
I distinguish dreaming and waking. When I am
awake I can, in some degree, account for and
study my dream. The dragon that pursued me last
night can be fitted into my waking world. I know
that there are such things as dreams: I know that
I had eaten an indigestible dinner: I know that a
man of my reading might be expected to dream
of dragons. But while in the nightmare I could
not have fitted in my waking experience. The
waking world is judged more real because it can

thus contain the dreaming world: the dreaming world is judged less real because it cannot contain the waking one. For the same reason I am certain that in passing from the scientific point of view to the theological, I have passed from dream to waking. Christian theology can fit in science, art, morality, and the sub-Christian religious. The scientific point of view cannot fit in any of these things, not even science itself.

1331
Science and Christianity
Miracles, chap. 7, para. 11, p. 51.

No man was, I suppose, ever so mad as to think that man, or all creation, *filled* the Divine Mind; if we are a small thing to space and time, space and time are a much smaller thing to God. It is a profound mistake to imagine that Christianity ever intended to dissipate the bewilderment and even the terror, the sense of our own nothingness, which come upon us when we think about the nature of things. It comes to intensify them. Without such sensations there is no religion. Many a man, brought up in the glib profession of some shallow form of Christianity, who comes through reading Astronomy to realise for the first time how majestically indifferent most reality is to man, and who perhaps abandons his religion on that account, may at that moment be having his first genuinely religious experience.

1332
Scots
Letters of C. S. Lewis (postmarked 13 April 1929), pp. 133–134.

I have just seen what is the trouble about all this Scotchness. When you want to be typically English you pretend to be very hospitable and honest, and hearty. When you want to be typically Irish you try to be very witty and dashing and fanciful. . . . But the typically Scotch attitude consists not in being loud or quiet, or merry or sad, but just in being *Scotch*.

1333
**Scott,
Sir Walter**
Poems, "To Roy
Campbell" (1939), p. 66.

A right branch on the old European tree
Of valour, truth, freedom, and courtesy,
A man (though often slap-dash in his art)
Civilized to the centre of his heart,
A man who, old and cheated and in pain,
Instead of snivelling, got to work again,
Work without end and without joy, to save
His honour, and go solvent to the grave;
Yet even so, wrung from his failing powers,
One book of his would furnish ten of ours
With characters and scenes.

1334
**Scott,
Sir Walter**
Selected Literary Essays,
"Shelley, Dryden, and Mr
Eliot" (1939), para.
18–20, pp. 217–218.

Whatever may be said against Scott's style or his contrived (and often ill-contrived) plots it will not touch the essential glory of the Waverley Novels. That glory is in my opinion, twofold.

First, these novels almost created that historical sense which we now all take for granted, and by which we often condemn Scott himself. . . . He, first of men, taught us the feeling for period. . . . If we are now so conscious of period, that we feel more difference between decades than our ancestors felt between centuries, we owe this, for good or ill, to Scott.

Secondly, the novels embody . . . immensely valuable qualities of mind. . . . They have those virtues of which no age is in more desperate need than our own. They have their own essential rectitude. They slur some things; they exaggerate nothing. Minor frailties are never worked up into enormous sins, nor petty distresses into factitious tragedies. Everything is in proportion. Consider what either Dickens on the one hand, or George Moore on the other, would have made of Effie Deans. Then turn back to Scott and breathe the air of sense.

| 1335 **Self-Concept** *The Problem of Pain,* chap. 4, para. 3, p. 57. | Unless Christianity is wholly false, the perception of ourselves which we have in moments of shame must be the only true one. |

| 1336 **Self-Control** *Prince Caspian,* chap. 11, p. 143. | And so at last they got on the move. Lucy went first, biting her lip and trying not to say all the things she thought of saying to Susan. But she forgot them when she fixed her eyes on Aslan. |

| 1337 **Self-Description** *Selected Literary Essays,* "De Descriptione Temporum" (1955), para. 22, pp. 13–14. | If a live dinosaur dragged its slow length into the laboratory, would we not all look back as we fled? What a chance to know at last how it really moved and looked and smelled and what noises it made! And if the Neanderthaler could talk, then, though his lecturing technique might leave much to be desired, should we not almost certainly learn from him some things about him which the best modern anthropologist could never have told us? He would tell us without knowing he was telling. One thing I know: I would give a great deal to hear any ancient Athenian, even a stupid one, talking about Greek tragedy. He would know in his bones so much that we seek in vain. At any moment some chance phrase might, unknown to him, show us where modern scholarship had been on the wrong track for years. Ladies and gentlemen, I stand before you somewhat as that Athenian might stand. I read as a native texts you must read as foreigners. You see why I said that the claim was not really arrogant; who can be proud of speaking fluently his mother tongue or knowing his way about his father's house? . . . Where I fail as a critic, I may yet be useful as a specimen. I would even dare to go further. Speaking not only for myself but for all other Old Western men whom you may meet, I would say, |

use your specimens while you can. There are not
going to be many more dinosaurs.

1338
Self-Giving
The Problem of Pain,
chap. 10, para. 10,
pp. 152–153.

In self-giving, if anywhere, we touch a rhythm not
only of all creation but of all being. For the
Eternal Word also gives Himself in sacrifice; and
that not only on Calvary. For when He was
crucified He "did that in the wild weather of His
outlying provinces which He had done at home
in glory and gladness" [Footnote: George
Macdonald. *Unspoken Sermons*: 3rd Series, pp.
11, 12]. From before the foundation of the world
He surrenders begotten Deity back to begetting
Deity in obedience. . . . From the highest to the
lowest, self exists to be abdicated and, by that
abdication, becomes the more truly self, to be
thereupon yet the more abdicated, and so forever.
. . . This is not a heavenly law which we can
escape by remaining earthly, nor an earthly law
which we can escape by being saved. What is
outside the system of self-giving is not earth, nor
nature, nor ordinary life, but simply and solely
Hell. Yet even Hell derives from this law such
reality as it has. That fierce imprisonment in the
self is but the obverse of the self-giving which is
absolute reality.

1339
Self-Image
Letters of C. S. Lewis (20
June 1952), para. 1,
p. 242.

I would prefer to combat the "I'm special" feeling
not by the thought "I'm no more special than
anyone else," but by the feeling "Everyone is as
special as me."

1340
Self-Image
Till We Have Faces, bk.
1, chap. 10, pp. 111–112.

"Don't you think the things people are most
ashamed of are the things they can't help?"
    I thought of my ugliness and said nothing.

533

1341
Selfishness
Till We Have Faces, bk.
1, chap. 14, p. 165.

The look in her face now was one I did not understand. I think a lover—I mean, a man who loved—might look so on a woman who had been false to him. And at last she said,

"You are indeed teaching me about kinds of love I did not know. It is like looking into a deep pit. I am not sure whether I like your kind better than hatred."

1342
Selfishness
Till We Have Faces, bk.
I, chap. 14, p. 167.

"The sun is almost down," she said. "Go. You have saved your life; go and live it as you can."

1343
Sermon on the Mount
God in the Dock,
"Rejoinder to Dr
Pittenger" (1958),
para. 13, p. 182.

As to "caring for" the Sermon on the Mount, if "caring for" here means "liking" or enjoying, I suppose no one "cares for" it. Who can *like* being knocked flat on his face by a sledge-hammer? I can hardly imagine a more deadly spiritual condition than that of the man who can read that passage with tranquil pleasure. This is indeed to be "at ease in Zion."

1344
Servanthood
*Letters: C. S. Lewis/Don
Giovanni Calabria* (27
March 1948), chap. 4,
para. 5–7, pp. 45, 47.

I believe that the men of this age (and among them you Father, and myself) think too much about the state of nations and the situation of the world. Does not the author of *The Imitation* warn us against involving ourselves too much with such things?

We are not kings, we are not senators. Let us beware lest, while we torture ourselves in vain about the fate of Europe, we neglect either Verona or Oxford.

In the poor man who knocks at my door, in my ailing mother, in the young man who seeks my advice, the Lord Himself is present: therefore let us wash His feet. [Ed. note: Verona is the home city of Lewis's correspondent.]

1345
**Shakespeare,
William**
Selected Literary Essays,
"Variation in Shakespeare
and Others" (1939),
para. 2, p. 75.

Where Milton marches steadily forward, Shakespeare behaves rather like a swallow. He darts at the subject and glances away; and then he is back again before your eyes can follow him. It is as if he kept on having tries at it, and being dissatisfied. He darts image after image at you and still seems to think that he has not done enough. He brings up a whole light artillery of mythology, and gets tired of each piece almost before he has fired it. He wants to see the object from a dozen different angles; if the undignified word is pardonable, he *nibbles,* like a man trying a tough biscuit now from this side and now from that. You can find the same sort of contrast almost anywhere between these two poets.

1346
**Shakespeare,
William**
Selected Literary Essays,
"Variation in Shakespeare
and Others" (1939),
para. 3, p. 76.

You see . . . how simple, how all of one piece, like the clean growth of a tulip, the Milton is: how diversified—more like a chrysanthemum—is the Shakespeare. . . . Milton gives you a theme developing: Shakespeare plays variations on a theme that remains the same.

1347
**Shakespeare,
William**
Selected Literary Essays,
"Variation in Shakespeare
and Others" (1939),
para. 9, p. 81.

The mark of Shakespeare (and it is quite enough for one mortal man) is simply this: to have combined two species of excellence which are not, in a remarkable degree, combined by any other artist, namely the imaginative splendour of the highest type of lyric and the realistic presentation of human life and character.

1348
**Shakespeare,
William**
Selected Literary Essays,
"Variation in Shakespeare
and Others" (1939),
para. 9, p. 83.

It is only in Shakespeare's plays that we call the characters, as well as the author, poets. No one describes Clytemnestra as a poet. The poetry belongs to Aeschylus. . . . But Shakespeare makes you believe that Othello and Macbeth really spoke as we hear them.

1349
Shakespeare, William

English Literature in the Sixteenth Century, Introduction, para. 61, p. 44.

All our lifetime the current has been setting towards licence. In Elizabeth's reign it was the opposite. Nothing seems to have been more saleable, more *come il faut*, than the censorious. We are overwhelmed by floods of morality from very young, very ignorant, and not very moral men. The glib harshness is to us a little repulsive: but it won applause then as easily as attacks on Victorianism, romanticism, or nostalgia have won it in our own century. The gentleness and candour of Shakespeare's mind has impressed all his readers. But it impresses us still more the more we study the general tone of sixteenth-century literature. He is gloriously anomalous.

1350
Shakespeare, William:
Hamlet

Selected Literary Essays, "Hamlet: The Prince or the Poem?" (1942), para. 7, p. 92.

"Most certainly an artistic failure." All argument is for that conclusion—until you read or see *Hamlet* again. And when you do, you are left saying that if this is failure, then failure is better than success. We want more of these "bad" plays. From our first childish reading of the ghost scenes down to those golden minutes which we stole from marking examination papers on *Hamlet* to read a few pages of *Hamlet* itself, have we ever known the day or the hour when its enchantment failed? . . . It has a taste of its own, an all-pervading relish which we recognize even in its smallest fragments, and which, once tasted, we recur to. When we want that taste, no other book will do instead.

1351
**Shakespeare,
William:**
Hamlet
Selected Literary Essays,
"Hamlet: The Prince or
the Poem?" (1942),
para. 12, 21, pp. 97, 103.

Hamlet for me is no more separable from his
ghost than Macbeth from his witches, Una from
her lion, or Dick Whittington from his cat. The
Hamlet formula, so to speak, is not "a man who
has to avenge his father" but "a man who has
been given a task by a ghost." Everything else
about him is less important than that.
. . . The critics, or most of them, have at any
rate kept constantly before us the knowledge that
in this play there is greatness and mystery. They
were never entirely wrong. Their error, on my
view, was to put the mystery in the wrong place—
in Hamlet's motives rather than in that darkness
which enwraps Hamlet and the whole tragedy and
all who read or watch it. It is a mysterious play in
the sense of being a play about mystery.

1352
**Shakespeare,
William:**
Hamlet
Selected Literary Essays,
"Hamlet: The Prince or
the Poem?" (1942),
para. 19, 21, pp. 101,
104.

I believe that we read Hamlet's speeches with
interest chiefly because they describe so well a
certain spiritual region through which most of us
have passed and anyone in his circumstances
might be expected to pass.
. . . The real and lasting mystery of our human
situation has been greatly depicted.

1353
**Shakespeare,
William:**
Hamlet
Selected Literary Essays,
"Hamlet: The Prince or
the Poem?" (1942),
para. 20, pp. 102–103.

I would not cross the room to meet Hamlet. It
would never be necessary. He is always where I
am. The method of the whole play is much nearer
to Mr Eliot's own method in poetry than Mr
Eliot suspects. Its true hero is man—haunted
man—man with his mind on the frontier of two
worlds, man unable either quite to reject or quite
to admit the supernatural, man struggling to get
something done as man has struggled from the
beginning, yet incapable of achievement because
of his inability to understand either himself or his

fellows or the real quality of the universe which has produced him.

1354 **Shakespeare,** **William:** *Hamlet* Selected Literary Essays, "Hamlet: The Prince or the Poem?" (1942), para. 22, p. 104.	[Hamlet is] a pale man in black clothes (would that our producers would ever let him appear!) with his stockings coming down, a dishevelled man whose words make us at once think of loneliness and doubt and dread, of waste and dust and emptiness, and from whose hands, or from our own, we feel the richness of heaven and earth and the comfort of human affection slipping away.

1355 **Shakespeare,** **William:** *King Lear* The Four Loves, chap. 3, para. 19, pp. 64–65.	It would be absurd to say that Lear is lacking in Affection. In so far as Affection is Need-love he is half-crazy with it. Unless, in his own way, he loved his daughters he would not so desperately desire their love. The most unlovable parent (or child) may be full of such ravenous love. But it works to their own misery and everyone else's. The situation becomes suffocating. If people are already unlovable a continual demand on their part (as of right) to be loved—their manifest sense of injury, their reproaches, whether loud and clamorous or merely implicit in every look and gesture of resentful self-pity—produce in us a sense of guilt (they are intended to do so) for a fault we could not have avoided and cannot cease to commit. They seal up the very fountain for which they are thirsty. If ever, at some favoured moment, any germ of Affection for them stirs in us, their demand for more and still more petrifies us again. And of course such people always desire the same proof of our love; we are to join their side, to hear and share their grievance against someone else. If my boy really loved me he would see how selfish his father is . . . if my brother loved me he would make a party with me against my sister . . .

if you loved me you wouldn't let me be treated like this.

1356

Shakespeare, William:

The Merchant of Venice

Selected Literary Essays, "Hamlet: The Prince or the Poem?" (1942), para. 11, pp. 95–96.

A good example of the kind of play which can be twisted out of recognition by character criticism is the *Merchant of Venice.* . . . The real play is not so much about men as about metals. . . . The important thing about Bassanio is that he can say, "Only my blood speaks to you in my veins," and again, "all the wealth I had Ran in my veins." . . . The whole contrast is between the crimson and organic wealth in his veins, the medium of nobility and fecundity, and the cold, mineral wealth in Shylock's counting-house. . . . The "naughty world" of finance exists in the play chiefly that we may perceive the light of the "good deed," or rather of the good state, which is called Belmont.

1357

Shakespeare, William:

Sonnets

English Literature in the Sixteenth Century, bk. III.III.III, para. 33, pp. 504–505.

When we read the whole sequence through at a sitting (as we ought sometimes to do) we have a different experience. From its total plot, however ambiguous, however particular, there emerges something not indeed common or general like the love expressed in many individual sonnets but yet, in a higher way, universal. The main contrast in the *Sonnets* is between the two loves, that "of comfort" and that "of despair." The love "of despair" demands all: the love "of comfort" asks, and perhaps receives, nothing. Thus the whole sequence becomes an expanded version of Blake's "The Clod and the Pebble." And so it comes about that, however the thing began—in perversion, in convention, even (who knows?) in fiction—Shakespeare, celebrating the "Clod" as no man has celebrated it before or since, ends by

---

expressing simply love, the quintessence of all
loves whether erotic, parental, filial, amicable, or
feudal. Thus from extreme particularity there is a
road to the highest universality. The love is, in the
end, so simply and entirely love that our *cadres*
are thrown away and we cease to ask what kind.
However it may have been with Shakespeare in
his daily life, the greatest of the sonnets are
written from a region in which love abandons all
claims and flowers into charity: after that it makes
little odds what the root was like. They open a
new world of love poetry; as new as Dante's and
Petrarch's had been in their day. . . . The self-
abnegation, the "naughting," in the *Sonnets* never
rings false. This patience, this anxiety (more like a
parent's than a lover's) to find excuses for the
beloved, this clear-sighted and wholly
unembittered resignation, this transference of the
whole self into another self without the demand
for a return, have hardly a precedent in profane
literature. In certain senses of the word "love,"
Shakespeare is not so much our best as our only
love poet.

1358
Shakespeare,
William:
Sonnets
English Literature in the
Sixteenth Century, bk.
III.III.III, para. 36,
p. 508.

They very seldom present or even feign to present
passionate thought growing and changing in the
heat of a situation; they are not dramatic. The end
of each is clearly in view from the beginning, the
theme already chosen. Instead of a single
developing thought we get what musicians call an
"arrangement," what we might call a pattern or
minuet, of thoughts and images. . . . It is partly
responsible for that immense pleasurableness
which we find in the *Sonnets* even where their
matter is most painful: and also for their curious
stillness or tranquillity. Shakespeare is always

standing back a little from the emotions he treats. He left it to his created persons, his Lears and Othellos, to pour out raw experience, scalding hot. In his own person he does not do so. He sings (always sings, never talks) of shame and degradation and the divided will, but it is as if he sang from above, moved and yet not moved; a Golden, Olympian poet.

1359
Shakespeare, William: *The Winter's Tale*
Selected Literary Essays, "William Morris" (1937), para. 6, p. 224.

In the *Winter's Tale* the Pygmalion myth or resurrection myth in the last act is the substance and the characters, motives, and half-hearted attempts at explanation which surround it are the shadow.

1360
Shelley, Percy
Selected Literary Essays, "Shelley, Dryden, and Mr Eliot" (1939), para. 1, p. 187.

Few poets have suffered more than Shelley from the modern dislike of the Romantics. It is natural that this should be so. His poetry is, to an unusual degree, entangled in political thought, and in a kind of political thought now generally unpopular. His belief in the natural perfectibility of man justly strikes the Christian reader as foolishness; while, on the other hand, the sort of perfection he has in view is too ideal for dialectical materialists. His writings are too generous for our cynics; his life is too loose for our "humanist" censors. Almost every recent movement of thought in one way or another serves to discredit him. From some points of view, this reaction cannot be regarded as wholly unfortunate. There is much in Shelley's poetry that has been praised to excess; much even that deserves no praise at all. . . . He is not a *safe* poet.

1361
Shelley, Percy
Selected Literary Essays,
"Shelley, Dryden, and
Mr Eliot" (1939), para.
16–17, 19, pp. 197–198.

It is simply not true to say that Shelley conceives the human soul as a naturally innocent and divinely beautiful creature, interfered with by external tyrants. On the contrary no other heathen writer comes nearer to stating and driving home the doctrine of original sin.

. . . When Shelley looks at and condemns the oppressor he does so with the full consciousness that he also is a man just like that: the evil is within as well as without; all are wicked. . . .

We mistake Shelley wholly if we do not understand that for him, as certainly as for St Paul, humanity in its merely natural or "given" condition is a body of death. It is true that the conclusion he draws is very different from that of St Paul. To a Christian, conviction of sin is a good thing because it is the necessary preliminary to repentance; to Shelley it is an extremely dangerous thing. It begets self-contempt, and self-contempt begets misanthropy and cruelty. . . . The man who has once seen the darkness within himself will soon seek vengeance on others; and in *Prometheus* self-contempt is twice mentioned as an evil. I do not think we can seriously doubt that Shelley is right. If a man will not become a Christian, it is very undesirable that he should become aware of the reptilian inhabitants in his own mind. To know how bad we are, in the condition of mere nature, is an excellent recipe for becoming much worse.

1362
Shelley, Percy
Selected Literary Essays,
"Shelley, Dryden, and
Mr Eliot" (1939),
para. 21, p. 199.

Shelley produces works which, though not perfect, are in one way more satisfactory than any of Dryden's longer pieces: that is to say, they display a harmony between the poet's real and professed intention, they answer the demands of their forms, and they have unity of spirit. Shelley is at home in his best poems, his clothes, so to speak, fit him, as Dryden's do not. The faults are faults of execution, such as over-elaboration, occasional verbosity, and the like: mere stains on the surface. The faults in Dryden are fundamental discrepancies between the real and the assumed poetic character, or radical vices in the design: diseases at the heart. Shelley could almost say with Racine, "When my plan is made my poem is done"; with Dryden the plan itself usually foredooms the poem's failure.

1363
Shelley, Percy: *Prometheus Unbound*
Selected Literary Essays, "Shelley, Dryden, and Mr Eliot" (1939), para. 33, 36, 38, pp. 205, 207–208.

The resulting whole is the greatest long poem in the nineteenth century, and the only long poem of the highest kind in that century which approaches to perfection.

. . . For my own part I believe that no poet has felt more keenly, or presented more weightily the necessity for a complete unmaking and remaking of man, to be endured at the dark bases of his being. I do not know the book (in profane literature) to which I should turn for a like expression of what von Hugel would have called the "costingness" of regeneration. . . .

The fourth act I shall not attempt to analyse. It is an intoxication, a riot, a complicated and uncontrollable splendour, long, and yet not too long, sustained on the note of ecstasy such as no other English poet, perhaps no other poet, has given us. It can be achieved by more than one artist in music: to do it in words has been, I think, beyond the reach of nearly all.

1364
Sidney,
Sir Philip
English Literature in the
Sixteenth Century, bk.
III.I, para. 11, p. 324.

Even at this distance Sidney is dazzling. He is that rare thing, the aristocrat in whom the aristocratic ideal is really embodied. Leicester's nephew, Pembroke's brother-in-law, and eligible *parti* for a princess, painted by Veronese, poet and patron of poets, statesman, knight, captain—fate has dealt such hands before, but they have very seldom been so well played.

1365
Sidney,
Sir Philip
English Literature in the
Sixteenth Century, bk.
III.I, para. 13, p. 326.

Sidney knows, what few Drab poets ever learned, that verse must carry the smallest possible cargo of words which exist solely for the sake of other words.

1366
Sidney,
Sir Philip:
Arcadia
English Literature in the
Sixteenth Century, bk.
III.I, para. 32, 36–37,
pp. 335, 338.

Even when we have added the heroic to the amatory and realized that the pastoral is quite subordinate, we have still left out one of the elements that go to make the *Arcadia*. Sidney is not merely a lover and a knight; he is also a moralist, a scholar, and a man of affairs. He aspires to teach not only virtue but prudence. He often exchanges his poetical prose for that style which the ancients called *politike;* and he dearly loves a debate or a set speech. . . . It is significant that the whole story moves neither to a martial nor an amorous, but to a forensic, climax; the great trial scene almost fills the fifth book. . . .

Pamela and Philoclea . . . are true natives of Arcadia. . . . To idealize discreetly, to go beyond Nature yet on Nature's lines, to paint dreams which have not come through the ivory gate, to embody what reality hints, forms such as "Nature, often erring, yet shewes she would faine make"— this is a very rare achievement. And Sidney has almost done it. . . .

Yet characterization is not Sidney's main interest. The heart of the *Arcadia*, the thing for which it exists, which wrung from Milton even in his anger an admission of its "wit and worth," is its nobility of sentiment. We can almost say of Sidney as Johnson said of Richardson, "You must read him for the sentiment."

1367
Sidney,
Sir Philip:
Arcadia
English Literature in the Sixteenth Century, bk. III.I, para. 38, p. 339.

The *Arcadia* is a kind of touchstone. What a man thinks of it, far more than what he thinks of Shakespeare or Spenser or Donne, tests the depth of his sympathy with the sixteenth century. It is . . . a work of distillation. It gathers up what a whole generation wanted to say. . . . It is— medieval, Protestant, pastoral, Stoical, Platonic.

1368
Sidney,
Sir Philip:
Arcadia
English Literature in the Sixteenth Century, bk. III.I, para. 42, p. 342.

Theoretically we are all pagans in Arcadia. . . . Nevertheless, Christian theology is always breaking in. . . . The convention was well understood, and very useful. In such works the gods are God *incognito* and everyone is in on the secret. Paganism is the religion of poetry through which the author can express, at any moment, just so much or so little of his real religion as his art requires.

1369
Sidney,
Sir Philip:
Astrophel and Stella
English Literature in the Sixteenth Century, bk. III.I, para. 19, p. 329.

There is so much careless writing in *Astrophel and Stella* that malicious quotation could easily make it appear a failure. Sidney can hiss like a serpent ("Sweet swelling lips well maist thou swell"), gobble like a turkey ("Moddels such be wood globes"), and quack like a duck ("But God wot, wot not what they mean"). But *non ego paucis*. With all its faults this work towers above everything that had been done in poetry, south of the Tweed, since Chaucer died. The fourth song alone, with its hurried and (as it were) whispered metre, its inimitable refrain, its perfect selection of images, is enough to raise Sidney above all his contemporaries. Here at last a situation is not merely written about: it is created, presented, so as to compel our imaginations.

**1370
Sidney,
Sir Philip:**
*Astrophel and
Stella*
English Literature in the
Sixteenth Century, bk.
III.I, para. 20, p. 330.

Considered historically, then, and in relation to his predecessors, Sidney is one of our most important poets. Nothing which that century had yet produced could have led us to predict the music, passion, and eloquence of *Astrophel and Stella*.

**1371
Sidney,
Sir Philip:**
*Defence of
Poesie*
English Literature in the
Sixteenth Century, bk.
III.I, para. 44, p. 343.

The *Defence of Poesie* or *Apology for Poetry,* as the two quartos of 1595 respectively name it, is, I suppose, universally accepted as the best critical essay in English before Dryden; and it is not obvious that Dryden wrote anything so good. In his comments on individual writers he is no doubt happier than Sidney, but in the theory of poetry he is much less consistent and complete. He lives from hand to mouth. Sidney's theory, for good or ill, springs organically from his whole attitude to life. If we want to refute it we must grub up the roots.

**1372
Sin**
Letters: C. S. Lewis/Don
Giovanni Calabria
(26 December 1951),
para. 8, p. 69.

You write much about your own sins. Beware . . . lest humility should pass over into anxiety or sadness. It is bidden us to "rejoice and always rejoice." Jesus has cancelled the handwriting which was against us. Lift up our hearts!

1373
Sin
Mere Christianity,
chap. 5, para. 14,
pp. 94–95.

The sins of the flesh are bad, but they are the least bad of all sins. All the worst pleasures are purely spiritual: the pleasure of putting other people in the wrong, of bossing and patronising and spoiling sport, and back-biting; the pleasures of power, of hatred. For there are two things inside me, competing with the human self which I must try to become. They are the Animal self, and the Diabolical self. The Diabolical self is the worse of the two. That is why a cold, self-righteous prig who goes regularly to church may be far nearer to hell than a prostitute. But, of course, it is better to be neither.

1374
Sin
The Four Loves, chap. 4,
para. 39, pp. 111–112.

The worst sins of men are spiritual.

1375
Sin
*Letters to Malcolm:
Chiefly on Prayer,*
chap. 13, para. 4, p. 69.

A question at once arises. Is it still God speaking when a liar or a blasphemer speaks? In one sense, almost Yes. Apart from God he could not speak at all; there are no words not derived from the Word; no acts not derived from Him who is *Actus purus.* And indeed the only way in which I can make real to myself what theology teaches about the heinousness of sin is to remember that every sin is the distortion of an energy breathed into us—an energy which, if not thus distorted, would have blossomed into one of those holy acts whereof "God did it" and "I did it" are both true descriptions. We poison the wine as He decants it into us; murder a melody He would play with us as the instrument. We caricature the self-portrait He would paint. Hence all sin, whatever else it is, is sacrilege.

1376 **Sin** *Letters to Malcolm:* *Chiefly on Prayer,* chap. 18, para. 13, pp. 97–98.	I've been reading Alexander Whyte. Morris lent him to me. He was a Presbyterian divine of the last century, whom I'd never heard of. Very well worth reading, and strangely broad-minded— Dante, Pascal, and even Newman, are among his heroes. But I mention him at the moment for a different reason. He brought me violently face to face with a characteristic of Puritanism which I had almost forgotten. For him, one essential symptom of the regenerate life is a permanent, and permanently horrified, perception of one's natural and (it seems) unalterable corruption. The true Christian's nostril is to be continually attentive to the inner cesspool.
1377 **Sin,** **Shame over** *Letters to Malcolm:* *Chiefly on Prayer,* chap. 18, para. 16, p. 99.	I have found (to my regret) that the degrees of shame and disgust which I actually feel at my own sins do not at all correspond to what my reason tells me about their comparative gravity. . . . Our emotional reactions to our own behaviour are of limited ethical significance.
1378 **Sincerity** *Selected Literary Essays,* "Donne and Love Poetry" (1938), para. 3, pp. 107–108.	[Said of "Petrarchan" sonneteers:] To accuse them of insincerity is like calling an oyster insincere because it makes its disease into a pearl.
1379 **Sincerity** *A Preface to "Paradise* *Lost,"* Chapter 11, para. 12, p. 79.	We are not "so grossly ignorant of human nature as not to know that precept may be very sincere where practice is very imperfect."

1380
**Sixteenth-
Century
England**
*English Literature in the
Sixteenth Century,*
Introduction, para. 96,
p. 63.

[The sixteenth century saw] a growing restriction and loss of liberty: Calvinism and Constellation both threatening free will, sovereignty threatening political freedom, humanism imposing new prohibitions on vocabulary and spontaneous emotion. The tight, starched ruff in an Elizabethan portrait, combined with the heroic or villainous energy of the face that rises above it, is no bad symbol.

1381
**Sixteenth-
Century
Literature**
*English Literature in the
Sixteenth Century,*
Introduction, para. 1,
p. 1.

The rough outline of our literary history in the sixteenth century is not very difficult to grasp. At the beginning we find a literature still medieval in form and spirit. . . . Their prose is clumsy, monotonous, garrulous; their verse either astonishingly tame and cold or, if it attempts to rise, the coarsest fustian. In both mediums we come to dread a certain ruthless emphasis; bludgeon-work. Nothing is light, or tender, or fresh. All the authors write like elderly men. The mid-century is an earnest, heavy-handed, commonplace age: a drab age. Then, in the last quarter of the century, the unpredictable happens. With startling suddenness we ascend. Fantasy, conceit, paradox, colour, incantation return. Youth returns. The fine frenzies of ideal love and ideal war are readmitted. Sidney, Spenser, Shakespeare, Hooker—even, in a way, Lyly—display what is almost a new culture: that culture which was to last through most of the seventeenth century and to enrich the very meanings of the words *England* and *Aristocracy*. Nothing in the earlier history of our period would have enabled the sharpest observer to foresee this transformation.

1382
**Sixteenth-
Century
Literature**
*English Literature in the
Sixteenth Century*, bk.
I.II.I, para. 1, p. 120.

From the varied excellence of the fourteenth century to the work of the early sixteenth it is a history of decay; so that in turning from the Scotch poetry of the age to the English we pass from civilization to barbarism.

1383
**Sixteenth-
Century
Literature**
*English Literature in the
Sixteenth Century*, bk.
II.II, para. 22, p. 237.

The grand function of the Drab Age poets was to build a firm metrical highway out of the late medieval swamp.

1384
**Sixteenth-
Century
Literature**
*English Literature in the
Sixteenth Century*, bk.
II.II, para. 67,
pp. 268–269.

Though the mind sickens at the task of dragging all these poetasters back to the cruel light, our labour will not have been wasted if we are now cured of some false notions about the Drab Age. It is not a period during which the genial spring of a "Renaissance" gradually ripens poetry towards its "Golden" summer. In this age there was no such advance; save in metrical smoothness, there was a decline. The earliest Drab poetry, that of Wyatt, was the best. . . . He, soon heavily reinforced by Surrey, inaugurated the vogue of the poulter's measure. Nor is there any indication that humanism or the Italians had a tendency to arrest the decline. Except on Surrey it is doubtful whether they were good influences. . . . It has, of course, been suggested that Henry VIII (that hard-worked whipping boy) was responsible for the Drab Age by cutting off the heads of scholars or poets. But who (save Surrey) were the promising poets that he killed? It is not clear that our poetry would be much the poorer if he had beheaded nearly every writer mentioned in this chapter.

1385
**Sixteenth-
Century
Literature**
*English Literature in the
Sixteenth Century,* bk.
II.II, para. 69, p. 271.

Drab poetry, Golden poetry, and metaphysical poetry alike are dominated by an impulse which is the direct opposite of Worsworthianism, naturalism, or expressionism. The poets are never concerned solely to communicate an experience; they are also concerned—usually more concerned—to fabricate a novel, attractive, intricate object, a dainty device. They would hardly have understood how a modern can use words like "pretty" and "clever" in dispraise of a poem.

1386
**Sixteenth-
Century
Literature**
*English Literature in the
Sixteenth Century,* bk.
III.I, para. 8–9,
pp. 322–323.

The Golden poetics [late sixteenth century], it will be seen, are by no means free from confusion. But it is, in my opinion, the claim to inspiration and to limitless freedom of invention, and not the occasional Horatianisms about following Nature, that really provide the key; . . . for we are of a higher birth than nature and her masters by divine right. . . .

The change which English poetry underwent at the hands of the Golden poets was twofold: a great change in power (a change from worse to better) and a slighter change in character. "Drab" does not mean "bad," but most Drab poetry had been bad in fact. The Golden poets rejected some of its metres almost entirely, set a new standard of melody for those they retained, and purged its vocabulary. The change in character was, as I have said, slighter. The chief merit of good Drab—plain statement which carries the illusion of the speaking voice—was not lost, but it becomes very subordinate. The main effort is directed towards richness, to a poetry which no one could mistake for speech; and this is increasingly so as the Golden Age proceeds. With the Golden manner there goes, usually, a Golden matter; ideally ardent lovers or ideally heroic wars in an ideally flowery and fruitful landscape are the staple.

1387
Sixteenth-Century Literature
English Literature in the Sixteenth Century, bk. III.I, para. 36, p. 341.

The Elizabethans had neither the romantic, nor the scientific, reverence for nature. Her beauties were, for them, not degraded but raised by being forced into real service to, or fanciful connexion with, the needs and moods of humanity. Their outlook was anthropocentric to a degree now hardly imaginable. . . . The Romantic poet wishes to be absorbed into Nature, the Elizabethan, to absorb her.

1388
Sixteenth-Century Literature
English Literature in the Sixteenth Century, bk. III.II.I, para. 38, p. 418.

Somehow or other during the later part of the sixteenth century Englishmen learned to write.

1389
Sixteenth-Century Literature
English Literature in the Sixteenth Century, bk. III.III.I, para. 9, p. 467.

The Golden poets are chiefly poets who write for their living and have to face frank criticism: courtiers who versified at odd moments tended to be Drab.

1390
Sixteenth-Century Literature
English Literature in the Sixteenth Century, bk. III.III.III, para. 54, p. 523.

It would be wrong not to notice that Golden poetry also has its limitations, which become its vices when it attempts matter beyond its reach. That failure of reach is what distinguishes it from certain other styles—the style of Homer, Dante, or Chaucer; for they could handle anything. The Golden style not only fails but becomes ludicrous,

---

even odious, when it attempts to present heroic action occurring in the real world.

1391
Sixteenth-Century Literature
English Literature in the Sixteenth Century, Epilogue, III, para. 7, pp. 557–558.

When we look back on the sixteenth century our main impression must be one of narrow escapes and unexpected recoveries. It looked as if our culture was going to be greatly impoverished. Yet somehow the "upstart" Tudor aristocracy produced a Sidney and became fit to patronize a Spenser, an Inigo Jones, an early Milton. Somehow such an apparent makeshift as the Elizabethan church became the church of Hooker, Donne, Andrewes, Taylor, and Herbert. We stole most of the honey which the humanists were carrying without suffering very much from their stings. . . .

One great loss had indeed been suffered by poetry. I have already noticed how the Golden style was limited in its range by its own extreme poeticalness. It must now be added that the Metaphysical style was equally, though diversely, limited. If the one was too rich, the other was too subtle and ebullient, to tell a plain tale. Hence, between the two, huge territories that had once flourished under the rule of poetry were in effect ceded to prose. They have not been recovered. . . . I do not suppose that the sixteenth century differs in these respects from any other arbitrarily selected stretch of years. It illustrates well enough the usual complex, unpatterned historical process; in which, while men often throw away irreplaceable wealth, they not infrequently escape what seemed inevitable dangers, not knowing that they have done either nor how they did it.

1392
Sixteenth-Century Literature

Studies in Medieval and Renaissance Literature, "Edmund Spenser, 1552-99" (1954), para. 9, p. 127.

When Spenser and Sidney began writing, English poetry was in a deplorable condition. Short histories of literature sometimes give the impression that the "Revival of Learning" began from the first to exercise a quickening influence upon our literature. I find no evidence that this was so. Nearly all the good poetry of the sixteenth century is crowded into its last twenty years (except in Scotland, where it comes at the beginning of the century and is overwhelmingly medieval in character). In England, until Sidney and Spenser arose, the last poet of real importance had been Sir Thomas Wyatt, who died in 1542: and his poetry, at its best, owes at least as much to the Middle Ages as the Revival of Learning. Between Wyatt and Spenser there extends a period in which it looks as though English poetry were never going to rise again even half so high as it had already risen in the Middle Ages.

1393
Sixteenth-Century Religion

English Literature in the Sixteenth Century, Introduction, para. 57, p. 38.

[The Elizabethan's] ubiquitous piety . . . is, indeed, best seen in the writers who are not dealing with religion; in Tusser, the chroniclers, Shakespeare, or Hakluyt's voyagers. In all these we find the assumption, unemphasized because it is unquestioned, that every event, every natural fact, and every institution, is rooted in the supernatural. Every change of wind at sea, every change of dynasty at home, all prosperity and all adversity, is unhesitatingly referred to God. The writers do not argue about it; they know. It is probable that the actual religion of most Englishmen in the earlier part of the century was of a similar kind.

1394
Skelton, John
English Literature in the Sixteenth Century, bk.
I.I.I, para. 45, p. 97.

Beside Dunbar, Skelton is not a *writer* at all. In a poem by Skelton anything may happen, and Skelton has no more notion than you what it will be. That is his charm; the charm of the amateur.

1395
Skelton, John
English Literature in the Sixteenth Century, bk.
I.II.I, para. 18, 21,
pp. 133, 135.

John Skelton (1464–1529) is the only poet of that age who is still read for pleasure. . . . The merit of Skelton lies not in innovation but in using well an established tradition for a purpose to which it is excellently suited.

1396
Skelton, John
English Literature in the Sixteenth Century, bk.
I.II.I, para. 24, 27, 28,
pp. 136, 139, 140.

The problem about the source of Skeltonics sinks into insignificance beside the critical problem. A form whose only constant attribute is rhyme ought to be intolerable: it is indeed the form used by every clown scribbling on the wall in an inn yard. How then does Skelton please? It is, no doubt, true to say that he sometimes does not. Where the poem is bad on other grounds the Skeltonics make it worse.

. . . The Skeltonic, which defies all the rules of art, pleases (on a certain class of subjects) because—and when—this helter-skelter artlessness symbolizes something in the theme. Childishness, dipsomania, and a bird are the themes on which we have found it successful. When it attempts to treat something fully human and adult—as in the Flodden poem—it fails.

. . . He is very near the borders of art. He is saved by the skin of his teeth. No one wishes the poems longer, and a few more in the same vein would be intolerable.

1397
Skelton, John
English Literature in the Sixteenth Century, bk.
I.II.I, para. 25, p. 138.

[Skelton's] *Philip Sparrow* is our first great poem of childhood. . . . It is indeed the lightest—the most like a bubble—of all the poems I know. It would break at a touch: but hold your breath,

---

watch it, and it is almost perfect. The Skeltonics are essential to its perfection. Their prattling and hopping and their inconsequence, so birdlike and so childlike, are the best possible embodiment of the theme. We should not, I think, refuse to call this poem great; perfection in light poetry, perfect smallness, is among the rarest of literary achievements.

1398
Skelton, John
English Literature in the Sixteenth Century, bk. I.II.I, para. 32, p. 142.

[Skelton's work,] at its best, dances round or through our critical defences by its extreme unpretentiousness—an unpretentiousness quite without parallel in our literature. But I think there is more nature than art in this happy result. Skelton does not know the peculiar powers and limitations of his own manner, and does not reserve it, as an artist would have done, for treating immature or disorganized states of consciousness. When he happens to apply it to such states, we may get delightful poetry: when to others, verbiage. There is no building in his work, no planning, no reason why any piece should stop just where it does (sometimes his repeated *envoys* make us wonder if it is going to stop at all), and no kind of assurance that any of his poems is exactly the poem he intended to write. Hence his intimacy. He is always in undress. Hence his charm, the charm of the really gifted amateur (a very different person from the hard working inferior artist).

1399
Skepticism
Christian Reflections, "De Futilitate" (WW II; 1st pub. 1967), para. 10, p. 61.

We are always prevented from accepting total scepticism because it can be formulated only by making a tacit exception in favour of the thought we are thinking at the moment—just as the man who warns the newcomer "Don't trust anyone in this office" always expects you to trust him at that moment.

1400

Skepticism

Christian Reflections,
"Modern Theology and
Biblical Criticism" (1959),
para. 25, p. 162.

Everywhere, except in theology, there has been a vigorous growth of scepticism about scepticism itself.

1401

Sleep

Letters to an American
Lady (27 November
1953), p. 23.

About sleep: do you find that the great secret (if one can do it) is not to *care* whether you sleep? Sleep is a jade who scorns her suitors but woos her scorners.

1402

Sloth

Letters: C. S. Lewis/Don
Giovanni Calabria
(10 September 1949),
para. 1, p. 55.

[Speaking of a delay in answering a letter:] Nothing else was responsible for it except the perpetual labour of writing and (lest I should seem to exonerate myself too much) a certain Accidia [sloth], an evil disease and, I believe, of the Seven Deadly Sins that one which in me is the strongest—though few believe this of me.

1403

Smoking

Letters of C. S. Lewis
(13 March 1956),
para. 1, p. 267.

You'll find my views about drinks in *Christian Behaviour* [see *Mere Christianity*, bk. 3, chap. 2]. . . . Smoking is much harder to justify. I'd like to give it up but I'd find this v. hard, i.e. I can abstain, but I can't concentrate on anything else while abstaining—not smoking is a whole time job.

1404

Snobbery

Letters of C. S. Lewis
(30 March 1927),
para. 1, p. 113.

When snobbery consists *only* of the admiring look upward and *not* of the contemptuous look downward, one need not be hard on it. A laugh—no unfriendly laugh—is the worst that it deserves. After all, this kind of snobbery is half of it mere romance.

1405

Sonnet Sequence

English Literature in the Sixteenth Century, bk. III.I, para. 16, p. 327.

The first thing to grasp about the sonnet sequence is that it is not a way of telling a story. It is a form which exists for the sake of prolonged lyrical meditation, chiefly on love but relieved from time to time by excursions into public affairs, literary criticism, compliment, or what you will. External events—a quarrel, a parting, an illness, a stolen kiss—are every now and then mentioned to provide themes for the meditation. Thus you get an island, or (if the event gives matter for more than one piece) an archipelago, of narrative in the lyrical sea.

1406

Sonnet Sequence

English Literature in the Sixteenth Century, bk. III.III.III, para. 17, pp. 490–491.

The sonneteers wrote not to tell their own love stories, not to express whatever in their own loves was local and peculiar, but to give us others, the inarticulate lovers, a voice. The reader was to seek in a sonnet not what the poet felt but what he himself felt, what all men felt. A good sonnet (*mutatis mutandis* and *salva reverentia*) was like a good public prayer: the test is whether the congregation can "join" and make it their own, not whether it provides interesting materials for the spiritual biography of the compiler. . . . The whole body of sonnet sequences is much more like an erotic liturgy than a series of erotic confidences.

1407

Spenser, Edmund

English Literature in the Sixteenth Century, bk. III.I, para. 107, p. 387.

Spenser . . . assumed from the outset that the truth about the universe was knowable and in fact known. If that were so, then of course you would expect agreements between the great teachers of all ages just as you expect agreements between the reports of different explorers. The agreements are the important thing, the useful and interesting thing. Differences, far from delighting us as precious manifestations of some unique temper or culture, are mere errors which can be neglected. Such intellectual optimism may be mistaken; but granted the mistake, a sincere and serious poet is bound to be, from our point of view, a syncretist. I believe that Sidney and Shakespeare are in this respect like Spenser, and to grasp this is one of the first duties of their critics. I do not think Shakespeare wrote a single line to express "his" ideas. What some call his philosophy, he would have called common knowledge.

1408

Spenser, Edmund

English Literature in the Sixteenth Century, bk. III.I, para. 112–113, pp. 389, 391.

Spenser is an essentially narrative poet. No one loves him who does not love his story; outside the proems to the books and cantos he scarcely writes a line that is not for the story's sake. His style is to be judged as the style of a story-teller.

. . . Thus, while he touches hands with the pure Golden poets, he also touches hands with Chaucer, Byron, and Crabbe. Wordsworth acknowledged him as a model.

1409

Spenser, Edmund

English Literature in the Sixteenth Century, bk. III.I, para. 115, p. 391.

Those who wish to attack Spenser will be wise to concentrate on his style. There alone he is seriously vulnerable.

1410

Spenser, Edmund

Studies in Medieval and Renaissance Studies, "Edmund Spenser, 1552–99" (1954), para. 1–3, pp. 121–122.

In 1569 Spenser entered Pembroke Hall at Cambridge. The most interesting thing about his university career is that he passed through it without becoming attached to either of the two intellectual movements by which Cambridge was then agitated.

We can hardly help calling them "Puritanism" and "humanism." . . .

There are some possible signs (but all

ambiguous) in Spenser's *Shepheards Calendar* (1579) that he was once or twice nearly captured by the Puritans, but it certainly did not last long. What is more remarkable is that he never surrendered to humanism, though he clearly lived in a humanistic circle of the narrowest sort. His friend Gabriel Harvey—a very grotesque creature and, to judge from his surviving records, a textbook case of the Inferiority Complex—disapproved of the whole design of *The Faerie Queene*. He complained that in it "Hobgoblin" was stealing the garland from "Apollo": in other words, that medieval romance was winning the day against classicism. . . . Nothing is more impressive about Spenser than his reaction to these humanist friends. He did neither of the two things we should expect. He never quarrelled with them; and he never took the slightest notice of their advice. He remained a faithful friend to Harvey (who had few friends); and he devoted his whole poetical career to a revival, or prolongation, of those medieval motifs which humanism wished to abolish.

1411
Spenser, Edmund
Studies in Medieval and Renaissance Literature, "Edmund Spenser, 1552-99" (1954), para. 9, pp. 127–128.

[Spenser] was not a man laying the coping stone on an edifice of good poetry already half-built; he was a man struggling by his own exertions out of a horrible swamp of dull verbiage, ruthlessly over-emphatic metre, and screaming rhetoric.

1412
Spenser, Edmund:
Epithalamion
Studies in Medieval and
Renaissance Literature,
"Edmund Spenser,
1552-99" (1954),
para. 13, pp. 129-130.

The *Epithalamion* . . . belongs to a different world, and indeed there is no poem in English at all like it. It traces the whole bridal day and night from the moment at which the bride is awaked to the moment at which the tired lovers fall asleep and the stars pour down good influences on the child they have engendered and on all their descendants yet to be. Into this buoyant poem Spenser has worked all the diverse associations of marriage, actual and poetic, Pagan and Christian: summer, landscape, neighbours, pageantry, religion, riotous eating and drinking, sensuality, moonlight—are all harmonized. . . . Those who have attempted to write poetry will know how very much easier it is to express sorrow than joy. That is what makes the *Epithalamion* matchless. Music has often reached that jocundity; poetry, seldom.

1413
Spenser, Edmund: *The Faerie Queene*
English Literature in the
Sixteenth Century, bk.
III.I, para. 108, p. 387.

Spenser expected his readers to find in it not his philosophy but their own experience—everyone's experience—loosened from its particular contexts by the universalizing power of allegory.

1414
Spenser, Edmund: *The Faerie Queene*
English Literature in the
Sixteenth Century, bk.
III.I, para. 114, p. 391.

The more nearly Spenser approaches to drama the less he succeeds. He does not know the rhetoric of the passions and substitutes that of the schools. This is because he is not the poet of passions but of moods. I use that word to mean those prolonged states of the "inner weather" which may colour our world for a week or even a month. That is what Spenser does best. In reading him we are reminded not of falling in love but of being in love; not of the moment which brought despair but of the despair which followed it; not of our sudden surrenders to temptation but of our habitual vices; not of religious conversion but of the religious life. Despite the apparent remoteness of his scenes, he is, far more than the dramatists, the poet of ordinary life, of the thing that goes on. Few of us have been in Lear's situation or Hamlet's: the houses and bowers and gardens of the *Faerie Queene,* both good and evil, are always at hand.

1415
Spenser, Edmund: *The Faerie Queene*
Studies in Medieval and Renaissance Literature, "Edmund Spenser, 1552–99" (1954), para. 17, p. 132.

For *The Faerie Queene* he invented his new nine-line stanza which has wholly different qualities. The more complex interlacing of the rhymes and, still more, the concluding alexandrine, which gives to each stanza the effect of a wave falling on a beach, combine to make it slower, weightier, more stately. Of all Spenser's innovations his stanza is perhaps the most important. It makes all his resemblances to the Italians merely superficial. It dictates the peculiar tone of *The Faerie Queene.* Milton, who knew and loved both Spenser and Spenser's models, described it as "sage and solemn tunes." A brooding solemnity—now deeply joyful, now sensuous, now melancholy, now loaded with dread—is characteristic of the poem at its best.

1416
Spenser, Edmund: *The Faerie Queene*
Studies in Medieval and Renaissance Literature, "Edmund Spenser, 1552–99" (1954), para. 18, pp. 132–133.

From the time of its publication down to about 1914 it was everyone's poem—the book in which many and many a boy first discovered that he liked poetry; a book which spoke at once, like Homer or Shakespeare or Dickens, to every reader's imagination. Spenser did not rank as a hard poet like Pindar, Donne, or Browning. How we have lost that approach I do not know. And unfortunately *The Faerie Queene* suffers even more than most great works from being approached through the medium of commentaries and "literary history." These all demand from us a sophisticated, self-conscious frame of mind. But then, when we have used all these aids, we discover that the poem itself demands exactly the opposite response. Its primary appeal is to the most naive and innocent tastes: to that level of our consciousness which is divided only by the thinnest veil from the immemorial lights and glooms of the collective Unconscious itself. It demands of us a child's love of marvels and dread of bogies, a boy's thirst for adventures, a young man's passion for physical beauty. If you have lost or cannot re-arouse these attitudes, all the commentaries, all your scholarship about "the Renaissance" or "Platonism" or Elizabeth's Irish policy, will not avail. The poem is a great palace, but the door into it is so low that you must stoop to go in. No prig can be a Spenserian. It is of course much more than a fairy-tale, but unless we can enjoy it as a fairy-tale first of all, we shall not really care for it.

1417

Spenser, Edmund: *The Faerie Queene*

Spenser's Images of Life, Introduction, para. 1, p. 1.

The Faerie Queene is perhaps the most difficult poem in English. Quite how difficult, I am only now beginning to realize after forty years of reading it. For one thing, it demands for its full enjoyment a double response. But in this, of course, it is like most old literature. Falstaff is both a funny fat man and an ironic comment on the world he inhabits; *Hamlet,* both a profound exploration of death and a rousing melodrama; the *Divina commedia,* both a mimesis of the whole spiritual life and first-class science fiction. Neither a prig nor a simpleton can fully appreciate any of these, but either can get something from all of them.

1418

Spenser, Edmund: *The Faerie Queene*

Spenser's Images of Life, Introduction, para. 13, pp. 9–11.

Spenser lived in a society that had inherited this whole complex of iconographical traditions. . . . If we want to know whether an artist could work under such iconographical chains, with their innumerable fine links of predetermined detail, we have only to look for our answer to Botticelli. Far from imprisoning, iconography was for him an inheritance that set him free to be an artist. His art is original—but only as art. Accepting traditional images, he loads them with wisdom from the philosophers and disposes them in divine compositions. And so, in my opinion, does Spenser.

1419

Spenser, Edmund: *The Faerie Queene*

Spenser's Images of Life, chap. III.5, para. 1, p. 61.

A general reflection on the form of *The Faerie Queene*. Its characteristic thickness of texture is not a matter of local complexities (though there are plenty of those), so much as of resonances sounding at large throughout the poem. Widely separated passages may at any time turn out to be interconnected, and the connection will perhaps depend on descriptive details that at first seemed insignificant. Carelessness over such details, therefore, can vitiate far more that the interpretation of the passage immediately concerned. Reading *The Faerie Queene* is like following out the threads of a tapestry so intricately woven that a single mistake may tear the whole fabric.

1420

Spenser, Edmund: *The Faerie Queene*

Spenser's Images of Life, chap. IV.1, para. 2–3, pp. 64–66.

The image of evil . . . in all three poets [Marlowe, Shakespeare, and Milton] . . . appears as *energy*— lawless and rebellious energy, no doubt, but nevertheless energy, abounding and upsurging. From this, I believe, springs the difficulty these poets have in making the good a fit antagonist for the evil. It is why Tamburlaine's victims are nonentities and Faustus' good angel a mere stick; why Richmond seems so pale beside Richard III; and why Milton's God has a popularity rating lower than his Satan.

When we turn to the image of evil in Spenser, we find a very noticeable difference. For in *The Faerie Queene* evil does not usually appear as energy.

1421

Spenser, Edmund: *The Faerie Queene*

Spenser's Images of Life, chap. VIII, para. 1, p. 113.

Adverse criticism of the stories in *The Faerie Queene* is usually based on a false expectation. Both the complaints against "faceless knights" and those against "characters with no insides" come alike from readers who are looking for a novelistic interest. But it is quite wrong to approach the poem with this demand; for Spenser never meant to supply it. Occasionally, of course, he makes a very brief approach to the kind of fiction now valued in the novel. . . . We should never concentrate, however, on passages such as these. It is always a great mistake to value a work of one kind for its occasional slight approximations to some other kind which happens to be preferred. If we can't learn to like a work of art for what it is, we had best give it up. There is no point in trying to twist it or force it into a form it was never meant to have. And certainly to read *The Faerie Queene* as a novel is perverse and unrewarding enough. It is like going to a Mozart opera just for the spoken bits.

1422

Spenser, Edmund: *The Faerie Queene*

Spenser's Images of Life, chap. VIII, para. 5, p. 116.

A story of this kind is in a way more like a symphony than a novel. Corresponding to the themes of the musical form, the literary form has images, which may be delicious or threatening or cryptic or grotesque, but which are always richly expressive of mood. The images are in every possible relation of contrast, mutual support, development, variation, half-echo, and the like, just as the musical themes are. But the ostensible connection between them all—what keeps the meddling intellect quiet—is here provided by the fact that they are all *happening* to someone. They are all worked into the experience or the world of the characters "whose" story it is. That, no more and no less, is the *raison d'être* of characters in the characterless story.

1423

Spenser, Edmund: *The Faerie Queene*

Spenser's Images of Life, chap. X.2, para. 8, p. 140.

The poem is not an epic. It is rather a pageant of the universe, or of Nature, as Spenser saw it. The vision is a religious but not a mystical one. For the poet's basic religion, the religion that underlies the forms of his imagination, is simply the worship of "the glad Creator." Beyond that, perhaps, he was not much inclined to go. . . . It is, as we say, a comment on life. But it is still more a celebration of life: of order, fertility, spontaneity, and jocundity. It is, if you like, Spenser's Hymn to Life. Perhaps this is why *The Faerie Queene* never loses a reader it has once gained. (For that is one of the first critical facts about the poem.) Once you have become an inhabitant of its world, being tired of it is like being tired of London, or of life.

1424

Spiritual Growth

Prince Caspian, chap. 10, p. 136.

"Welcome, child," he said.

"Aslan," said Lucy, "you're bigger."

"That is because you are older, little one," answered he.

"Not because you are?"

"I am not. But every year you grow, you will find me bigger."

1425
Spiritual
Growth
The World's Last Night and Other Essays, "The World's Last Night" (1952), para. 36, p. 113.

Women sometimes have the problem of trying to judge by artificial light how a dress will look by daylight. That is very like the problem of all of us: to dress our souls not for the electric lights of the present world but for the daylight of the next. The good dress is the one that will face that light. For that light will last longer.

1426
Spiritual
Growth
Letters to Malcolm: Chiefly on Prayer, chap. 6, para. 14–16, p. 34.

"If our heart condemn us, God is greater than our heart." And equally, if our heart flatter us, God is greater than our heart. I sometimes pray not for self-knowledge in general but for just so much self-knowledge at the moment as I can bear and use at the moment; the little daily dose.

Have we any reason to suppose that total self-knowledge, if it were given us, would be for our good? Children and fools, we are told, should never look at half-done work; and we are not yet, I trust, even half-done. You and I wouldn't, at all stages, think it wise to tell a pupil exactly what we thought of his quality. It is much more important that he should know what to do next. . . .

The unfinished picture would so like to jump off the easel and have a look at itself!

1427
Spirituality
Miracles, chap. 16, para. 31–32, p. 163.

Where our fathers, peering into the future, saw gleams of gold, we see only the mist, white, featureless, cold and never moving.

The thought at the back of all this negative spirituality is really one forbidden to Christians. They, of all men, must not conceive spiritual joy and worth as things that need to be rescued or tenderly protected from time and place and matter and the senses. Their God is the God of corn and oil and wine. He is the glad Creator. He has become Himself incarnate. The sacraments have been instituted. Certain spiritual gifts are offered us only on condition that we perform certain bodily acts. After that we cannot really be in doubt of His intention. To shrink back from all that can be called Nature into negative spirituality is as if we ran away from horses instead of learning to ride.

1428
Stereotypes
Selected Literary Essays,
"De Descriptione
Temporum" (1955),
para. 2, p. 2.

A stereotyped image can obliterate a man's own experience.

1429
Story
*Of Other Worlds: Essays
and Stories,* "On Stories"
(1947), para. 26, p. 18.

I should like to be able to believe that I am here in a very small way contributing . . . to the encouragement . . . of story that can mediate imaginative life to the masses while not being contemptible to the few.

1430
Story
*Of Other Worlds: Essays
and Stories,* "On Stories"
(1947), para. 26, p. 18,

To be stories at all they must be series of events: but it must be understood that this series—the *plot,* as we call it—is only really a net whereby to catch something else. The real theme may be, and perhaps usually is, something that has no sequence in it, something other than a process and much more like a state or quality. Giantship, otherness, the desolation of space, are examples that have crossed our path.

1431
Story
*Of Other Worlds: Essays
and Stories,* "On Stories"
(1947), para. 29–30,
pp. 20–21.

If the author's plot is only a net, and usually an imperfect one, a net of time and event for catching what is not really a process at all, is life much more? . . .

In life and art both, as it seems to me, we are always trying to catch in our net of successive

---

moments something that is not successive. Whether in real life there is any doctor who can teach us how to do it, so that at last either the meshes will become fine enough to hold the bird, or we be so changed that we can throw our nets away and follow the bird to its own country, is not a question for this essay. But I think it is sometimes done—or very, very nearly done—in stories. I believe the effort to be well worth making.

1432
Students
The Letters of C. S. Lewis to Arthur Greeves (6 December 1931), para. 8, p. 434.

Indeed this is the best part of my job. In every given year the pupils I really like are in a minority; but there is hardly a year in which I do not make some real friend. I am glad that people become more and more one of the sources of pleasure as I grow older.

1433
Style
Selected Literary Essays, "High and Low Brows" (1939), para. 13, p. 271.

There is no class of books which can be "good in their own way" without bothering about style.

1434
Style
English Literature in the Sixteenth Century, bk. II.III, para. 63, p. 315.

No style can be good in the mouth of a man who has nothing, or nonsense, to say.

1435
Style
English Literature in the Sixteenth Century, bk. III.I, para. 39, p. 340.

A sentence is too long either when length makes it obscure or unpronounceable, or else when the matter is too little to fill it.

1436
Style
Letters to Children
(11 September 1958),
para. 1, p. 81.

[Lewis was advising a young author regarding style:] A strict allegory is like a puzzle with a solution: a great romance is like a flower whose smell reminds you of something you can't quite place. I think the something is "the whole *quality* of life as we actually experience it."

1437
Style
The Screwtape Letters,
preface (1960), para. 26,
p. xiv.

At bottom, every ideal of style dictates not only how we should say things but what sort of things we may say.

1438
Style
God in the Dock, "Before
We Can Communicate"
(1961), para. 10, p. 256.

In the very process of eliminating from your matter all that is technical, learned, or allusive, you will discover, perhaps for the first time, the true value of learned language: namely, brevity. It can say in ten words what popular speech can hardly get into a hundred.

1439
Style
Selected Literary Essays,
"The Vision of John
Bunyan" (1962), para. 20,
p. 151.

It is always dangerous to talk too long about style. It may lead one to forget that every single sentence depends for its total effect on the place it has in the whole.

1440
Suffering
Taliessin Through Logres,
. . . *Arthurian Torso*,
"Williams and the
Arthuriad" (1948), chap.
V, para. 33, p. 359.

Christians naturally think more often of what the world has inflicted on the saints; but the saints also inflict much on the world. Mixed with the cry of martyrs, the cry of nature wounded by Grace also ascends—and presumably to heaven. That cry has indeed been legitimized for all believers by the words of the Virgin Mother herself—"Son, why hast thou thus dealt with us? Behold, thy father and I have sought thee sorrowing."

1441
Surrender
Mere Christianity, bk. IV,
chap. 8, para. 4, p. 167.

Christ says "Give me All. I don't want so much of
your time and so much of your money and so
much of your work: I want You. I have not come
to torment your natural self, but to kill it. . . . I
will give you a new self instead. In fact, I will give
you Myself: my own will shall become yours."

1442
Surrey, Earl of (Henry Howard)
English Literature in the
Sixteenth Century, bk.
II.II, para. 19, p. 235.

Metrically, he is one of the great road-makers. If
we adopted the ludicrous principle of judging
poets not by their own work but by their utility
to their successors, he would have to rank not
only above Wyatt but above Chaucer and Milton;
perhaps above Shakespeare too.

1443
Survival
Present Concerns: Essays
by C. S. Lewis, "On
Living in an Atomic Age"
(1948), para. 13–14,
pp. 79–80.

It is part of our spiritual law never to put survival
first: not even the survival of our species. We must
resolutely train ourselves to feel that the survival
of Man on this Earth, much more of our own
nation or culture or class, is not worth having
unless it can be had by honourable and merciful
means.

The sacrifice is not so great as it seems.
Nothing is more likely to destroy a species or a
nation than a determination to survive at all costs.
Those who care for something else more than
civilization are the only people by whom
civilization is at all likely to be preserved. Those
who want Heaven most have served Earth best.
Those who love Man less than God do most for
Man.

1444
Suspicion
The Screwtape Letters,
"Screwtape Proposes a
Toast" (1959), para. 28,
p. 164.

Suspicion often creates what it suspects.

1445
**Swift,
Jonathan**
Selected Literary Essays,
"Addison" (1945),
para. 2, p. 154.

Swift and Pope were by no means always serious and they knew very well what it was to be melancholy. One would have found more mirth in their conversation than in Addison's: not only epigram and repartee, but frolic and extravaganza—even buffoonery. It is true that they regarded satire as a "sacred weapon," but we must not so concentrate on that idea as to forget the sheer *vis comica* which brightens so much of their work. Swift's "favourite maxim was *vive la bagatelle.*" *Gulliver* and the *Dunciad* and the whole myth of Scriblerus have missed their point if they do not sometimes make us "laugh and shake in Rabelais' easy chair." Even their love of filth is, in my opinion, much better understood by schoolboys than by psychoanalysts: if there is something sinister in it, there is also an element of high-spirited rowdiness. Addison has a sense of humour; the Tories have, in addition, a sense of fun. But they have no "habit" of cheerfulness. Rage, exasperation, and something like despair are never far away.

1446
**Swift,
Jonathan**
Selected Literary Essays,
"Addison" (1945),
para. 6, p. 158.

Swift is hard . . . to classify. There is, to be sure, no doubt of his churchmanship, only of his Christianity, and this, of itself, is significant.

1447
**Swift,
Jonathan:**
*Gulliver's
Travels*
Selected Literary Essays,
"Addison" (1945),
para. 6, pp. 158–159.

Some parts of *Gulliver* seem inconsistent with any religion—except perhaps Buddhism. . . . And yet there is much to set on the other side. His priestly duties were discharged with a fidelity rare in that age. The ferocity of the later *Gulliver* all works up to that devastating attack on Pride which is more specifically Christian than any other piece of ethical writing in the century, if we except William Law.

1448
Symbol
The Personal Heresy:
A Controversy, chap. 5,
para. 2, p. 97.

Two kinds of symbol must surely be distinguished. The algebraical symbol comes naked into the world of mathematics and is clothed with value by its masters. A poetic symbol—like the Rose, for Love, in Guillaume de Lorris—comes trailing clouds of glory from the real world, clouds whose shape and colour largely determine and explain its poetic use. In an equation, x and y will do as well as a and b; but the *Romance of the Rose* could not, without loss, be re-written as the *Romance of the Onion,* and if a man did not see why, we could only send him back to the real world to study roses, onions, and love, all of them still untouched by poetry, still raw.

1449
Symbol
Taliessin Through Logres,
. . . Arthurian Torso,
"Williams and the
Arthuriad" (1948), chap.
IV, para. 7, p. 317.

A symbol has a life of its own. An *escaped* metaphor—escaped from the control of the total poem or philosophy in which it belongs—may be a poisonous thing.

1450
Symbolism
Studies in Medieval and
Renaissance Literature,
"Edmund Spenser,
1552-99" (1954),
para. 26, p. 137.

Symbols are the natural speech of the soul, a language older and more universal than words.

1451
Tasso:
Gerusalemme
Studies in Medieval and
Renaissance Literature,
"Tasso" (1940s?),
para. 12, p. 120.

No poem is more completely, and in a sense
severely, the poem it set out to be and no other.
. . . In this perfect keeping, which enables us to
accept Tasso's world as real while we are reading,
lies the great charm of the poem; in that and in
something better. I mean that quite unforced and
quite sincere elevation of sentiment which makes
us feel that Tasso is, in a very serious and even
reverent sense of the word, the most *boyish* of
the poets.

1452
Taste
Christian Reflections,
"Christianity and
Culture" (1940), section
III, para. 8, pp. 30–31.

Being fallen creatures we tend to resent offences
against our taste, at least as much as, or even
more than, offences against our conscience or
reason; . . . The tendency is easily observed among
children; friendship wavers when you discover that
a hitherto trusted playmate actually *likes* prunes.
But even for adults it is "sweet, sweet, sweet
poison" to feel able to imply "thus saith the Lord"
at the end of every expression of our pet aversions.
To avoid this horrible danger we must perpetually
try to distinguish, however closely they get
entwined both by the subtle nature of the facts
and by the secret importunity of our passions,
those attitudes in a writer which we can honestly
and confidently condemn as real evils, and those

qualities in his writing which simply annoy and
offend us as men of taste. This is difficult, because
the latter are often so much more obvious and
provoke such a very violent response.

1453
Technology
Selected Literary Essays,
"De Descriptione
Temporum" (1955),
para. 17, pp. 10–11.

[The birth of the machines] is on a level with the
change from stone to bronze, or from a pastoral
to an agricultural economy. It alters Man's place in
nature. . . . What concerns us . . . is its psychological effect. How has it come about that we use
the highly emotive word "stagnation," with all its
malodorous and malarial overtones, for what
other ages would have called "permanence"? Why
does the word "primitive" at once suggest to us
clumsiness, inefficiency, barbarity? When our
ancestors talked of the primitive church or the
primitive purity of our constitution they meant
nothing of that sort. . . . Why does "latest" in
advertisements mean "best"? Well, let us admit
that these semantic developments owe something
to the nineteenth-century belief in spontaneous
progress which itself owes something either to
Darwin's theorem of biological evolution or to that
myth of universal evolutionism which is really so
different from it, and earlier. . . . But I submit that
what has imposed this climate of opinion so firmly
on the human mind is a new archetypal image. It
is the image of old machines being superseded by
new and better ones. For in the world of
machines the new most often really is better and
the primitive really is the clumsy. And this image,
potent in all our minds, reigns almost without
rival in the minds of the uneducated. For to them,
after their marriage and the births of their
children, the very milestones of life are technical
advances. From the old push-bike to the motor-
bike and thence to the little car; from

gramophone to radio and from radio to television; from the range to the stove; these are the very stages of their pilgrimage. But whether from this cause or some other, assuredly that approach to life which has left these footprints on our language is the thing that separates us most sharply from our ancestors and whose absence would strike us as most alien if we could return to their world. Conversely, our assumption that everything is provisional and soon to be superseded, that the attainment of goods we have never yet had, rather than the defence and conservation of those we have already, is the cardinal business of life, would most shock and bewilder them if they could visit ours.

1454
Technology and Christianity

God in the Dock,
"Answers to Questions on Christianity" (1944), para. 1, p. 48.

Christianity does *not* replace the technical. When it tells you to feed the hungry it doesn't give you lessons in cookery. If you want to learn *that*, you must go to a cook rather than a Christian.

1455
Teetotalism

Letters of C. S. Lewis (16 March 1955), para. 1, p. 262.

I do however strongly object to the tyrannic and unscriptural insolence of anything that calls itself a Church and makes teetotalism a condition of membership. Apart from the more serious objection (that Our Lord Himself turned water into wine and made wine the medium of the only rite He imposed on all His followers), it is so provincial (what I believe you people call "small town"). Don't they realize that Christianity arose in the Mediterranean world where, then as now, wine was as much part of the normal diet as bread? It was the 17th Century Puritans who first made the universal into a rich man's luxury.

1456
Temperance
The Lion, the Witch and the Wardrobe, chap. 4, p. 32.

At first Edmund tried to remember that it is rude to speak with one's mouth full, but soon he forgot about this and thought only of trying to shovel down as much Turkish Delight as he could, and the more he ate the more he wanted to eat, and he never asked himself why the Queen should be so inquisitive.

1457
Temptation
God in the Dock, "The Pains of Animals" (The Reply [to Dr. Joad] by C. S. Lewis—1950), para. 11, p. 169.

If Dr Joad thinks I pictured Satan "tempting monkeys," I am myself to blame for using the word "encouraged." I apologize for the ambiguity. In fact, I had not supposed that "temptation" (that is, solicitation of the will) was the only mode in which the Devil could corrupt or impair. It is probably not the only mode in which he can impair even human beings; when Our Lord spoke of the deformed woman as one "bound by Satan" [Footnote: Luke xiii, 16], I presume He did not mean that she had been tempted into deformity. Moral corruption is not the only kind of corruption. But the word *corruption* was perhaps ill-chosen and invited misunderstanding. *Distortion* would have been safer.

1458
Temptation
Mere Christianity, bk. III, chap. 11, para. 7, pp. 124–125.

A silly idea is current that good people do not know what temptation means. This is an obvious lie. Only those who try to resist temptation know how strong it is. . . . A man who gives in to temptation after five minutes simply does not know what it would have been like an hour later. That is why bad people, in one sense, know very little about badness. They have lived a sheltered life by always giving in. We never find out the strength of the evil impulse inside us until we try to fight it: and Christ, because He was the only man who never yielded to temptation, is also the only man who knows to the full what temptation means—the only complete realist.

1459
Thanksgiving
Letters: C. S. Lewis/
Don Giovanni Calabria
(10 August 1948),
para. 7, pp. 49, 51.

We ought to give thanks for all fortune: if it is "good," because it is good, if "bad" because it works in us patience, humility and the contempt of this world and the hope of our eternal country.

1460
Theology and Politics
God in the Dock,
"Christian Apologetics"
(1945), para. 11, p. 94.

Theology teaches us what ends are desirable and what means are lawful, while Politics teaches what means are effective.

1461
Theology in Daily Life
God in the Dock,
"Christian Apologetics"
(1945), para. 14, p. 98.

To conclude—you must translate every bit of your Theology into the vernacular. This is very troublesome and it means you can say very little in half an hour, but it is essential. It is also of the greatest service to your own thought. I have come to the conviction that if you cannot translate your thoughts into uneducated language, then your thoughts were confused.

1462
Theology, Liberal
Christian Reflections,
"Modern Theology and
Biblical Criticism" (1959),
para. 10, pp. 157–158.

All theology of the liberal type involves at some point—and often involves throughout—the claim that the real behaviour and purpose and teaching of Christ came very rapidly to be misunderstood and misrepresented by His followers, and has been recovered or exhumed only by modern scholars. . . . This daily confirms my suspicion of the same approach to Plato or the New Testament. The idea that any man or writer should be opaque to those who lived in the same culture, spoke the same language, shared the same habitual imagery and unconscious assumptions, and yet be transparent to those who have none of these advantages, is in my opinion preposterous. There is an *a priori* improbability in it which almost no argument and no evidence could counterbalance.

1463

Theory

The Discarded Image, chap. 2, para. 5, 18, p. 14.

The great masters do not take any Model quite so seriously as the rest of us. They know that it is, after all, only a model, possibly replaceable.

1464

Thomas à Kempis

The Letters of C. S. Lewis to Arthur Greeves (25 May 1941), para. 6, p. 490.

I read the *Imitation [of Christ]* pretty nearly every day, but it's rather like creatures without wings reading about the stratosphere.

1465

Time

Out of the Silent Planet, chap. 16, p. 100.

"A world is not made to last for ever, much less a race; that is not Maleldil's [God's] way."

1466

Time

The Screwtape Letters, Letter XV, pp. 67–68.

Humans live in time . . . therefore . . . attend chiefly to two things, to eternity itself and to . . . the Present. For the Present is the point at which time touches eternity . . . in it alone freedom and actuality are offered.

1467

Time

The Screwtape Letters, Letter XV, para. 3, 5, pp. 68–70.

The Future is, of all things, the thing least like eternity. It is the most completely temporal part of time—for the Past is frozen and no longer flows, and the Present is all lit up with eternal rays. . . .

Hence nearly all vices are rooted the Future. Gratitude looks to the Past and love to the Present; fear, avarice, lust and ambition look ahead.

. . . With the present . . . there, and there alone, all duty, all grace, all knowledge, and all pleasure dwell.

1468
Time
Miracles, Appendix B, para. 10, pp. 176–177.

It is probable that Nature is not really in Time and almost certain that God is not. Time is probably (like perspective) the mode of our perception. There is therefore in reality no question of God's at one point in time (the moment of creation) adapting the material history of this universe in advance to free acts which you or I are to perform at a later point in Time. To Him all the physical events and all the human acts are present in an eternal Now. The liberation of finite wills and the creation of the whole material history of the universe (related to the acts of those wills in all the necessary complexity) is to Him a single operation. In this sense God did not create the universe long ago but creates it at this minute—at every minute.

1469
Time
Christian Reflections, "Historicism" (1950), chap. 9, para. 26, p. 113.

Where, except in the present, can the Eternal be met?

1470
Tolerance
Letters of C. S. Lewis (13 March 1956), para. 2, p. 268.

Well, let's go on disagreeing but don't let us *judge.* What doesn't suit us may suit possible converts of a different type. My model here is the behaviour of the congregation at a "Russian Orthodox" service, where some sit, some lie on their faces, some stand, some kneel, some walk about, and *no* one takes the slightest notice of what anyone else is doing. That is good sense, good manners, and good Christianity. "Mind one's own business" is a good rule in religion as in other things.

1471
Tolkien, J.R.R.
Letters of C. S. Lewis
(15 May 1959), p. 287.

No one ever influenced Tolkien—you might as well try to influence a bander-snatch. We listened to his work, but could affect it only by encouragement. He has only two reactions to criticism; either he begins the whole work over again from the beginning or else takes no notice at all.

1472
Tolkien, J.R.R.:
The Lord of the Rings
On Stories, "Tolkien's *The Lord of the Rings*" (1954), para. 3, p. 84.

Here are beauties which pierce like swords or burn like cold iron; here is a book that will break your heart.

1473
Tolstoy, Leo
The Letters of C. S. Lewis to Arthur Greeves (29 March 1931), para. 3–5, pp. 409–410.

The most interesting thing that has happened to me since I last wrote is reading *War and Peace*—at least I am now in the middle of the 4th and last volume so I think, bar accidents, I am pretty sure to finish it. It has completely changed my view of novels.

Hitherto I had always looked on them as rather a *dangerous* form—I mean dangerous to the health of literature as a whole. I thought that the strong "narrative lust"—the passionate itch to "see what happened in the end"—which novels aroused, necessarily injured the taste for other, better, but less irresistible, forms of literary pleasure: and that the growth of novel reading largely explained the deplorable division of readers

into low-brow and high-brow—the low being
simply those who had learned to expect from
books this "narrative lust," from the time they
began to read, and who had thus destroyed in
advance their possible taste for better things. I
also thought that the intense desire which novels
rouse in us for the "happiness" of the chief
characters (no one feels that way about Hamlet or
Othello) and the selfishness with which this
happiness is concerned, were thoroughly bad. . . .

Tolstoy, in this book, has changed all that. I
have felt everywhere—in a sense—you will know
what I mean—that sublime *indifference* to the life
or death, success or failure, of the chief
characters, which is not a *blank* indifference at all,
but almost like submission to the will of God.
Then the variety of it. The war parts are just the
best descriptions of war ever written: all the
modern war books are milk and water to this:
then the rural parts—lovely pictures of village life
and of religious festivals in wh. the relations
between the peasants and the nobles almost make
you forgive feudalism: the society parts, in which I
was astonished to find so much humour—there is
a great hostess who always separates two guests
when she sees them getting really interested in
conversation, who is almost a Jane Austen
character. There are love-passages that have the
same sort of intoxicating quality you get in
Meredith: and passages about soldiers chatting
over fires which remind one of Patsy Macan: and
a drive in a sledge by moonlight which is better
than Hans Andersen. And behind all these, and
uniting them, is the profound, religious conception
of life and history wh. is beyond J. Stephens and
Andersen, and beside which Meredith's worldly
wisdom—well just *stinks,* there's no other word.

1474 **Translation** *Selected Literary Essays,* "The Literary Impact of the Authorised Version" (1950), para. 1, p. 126.	No translation can preserve the qualities of its original unchanged. On the other hand, except where lyrical poetry is in question, the literary effect of any good translation must be more indebted to the original than to anything else.
1475 **Translation** *English Literature in the* *Sixteenth Century,* bk. II.II, para. 41, p. 250.	Most of us, I suspect, would advise a mediocre poet, if he must translate, to avoid the greater originals and choose the less, as if these would be easier. But this is probably a mistake. The great poets have so much wealth that even if you lose two-thirds of it on the voyage home you can still be rich on the remainder: slighter art, when it loses the perfection of its original form, loses all power of pleasing.
1476 **Translation** *English Literature in the* *Sixteenth Century,* bk. III.III.III, para. 19, p. 492.	A poetic translation is always to some extent a new work of art.
1477 **Transposition** *The Weight of Glory,* "Transposition" (1949), para. 9, 12, 14–15, 30, pp. 60–64, 71.	If the richer system is to be represented in the poorer at all, this can only be by giving each element in the poorer system more than one meaning. The transposition of the richer into the poorer must, so to speak, be algebraical, not arithmetical. If you are to translate from a language which has a large vocabulary into a language that has a small vocabulary, then you must be allowed to use several words in more than one sense. If you are to write a language with twenty-two vowel sounds in an alphabet with only five vowel characters than you must be allowed to give each of those five characters more than one value. If you are making a piano version

of a piece originally scored for an orchestra, then the same piano notes which represent flutes in one passage must also represent violins in another.

. . . We understand pictures only because we know and inhabit the three-dimensional world. If we can imagine a creature who perceived only two dimensions and yet could somehow be aware of the lines as he crawled over them on the paper, we shall easily see how impossible it would be for him to understand. At first he might be prepared to accept on authority our assurance that there was a world in three dimensions. But when we pointed to the lines on the paper and tried to explain, say, that "This is a road," would he not reply that the shape which we were asking him to accept as a revelation of our mysterious other world was the very same shape which, on our own showing, elsewhere meant nothing but a triangle? And soon, I think, he would say, "You keep on telling me of this other world and its unimaginable shapes which you call solid. But isn't it very suspicious that all the shapes which you offer me as images or reflections of the solid ones turn out on inspection to be simply the old two-dimensional shapes of my own world as I have always known it? Is it not obvious that your vaunted other world, so far from being the archetype, is a dream which borrows all its elements from this one?"

. . . Transposition occurs whenever the higher reproduces itself in the lower. Thus, to digress for a moment, it seems to me very likely that the real relation between mind and body is one of Transposition. We are certain that, in this life at any rate, thought is intimately connected with the brain. The theory that thought therefore is merely a movement in the brain is, in my opinion, nonsense; for if so, that theory itself would be merely a movement, an event among atoms, which may have speed and direction but of which it would be meaningless to use the words "true" or "false."

. . . We now see that if the spiritual is richer than the natural (as no one who believes in its existence would deny) then this is exactly what we should expect. And the sceptic's conclusion that the so-called spiritual is really derived from the natural, that it is a mirage or projection or imaginary extension of the natural, is also exactly what we should expect; for, as we have seen, this is the mistake which an observer who knew only the lower medium would be bound to make in every case of Transposition. The brutal man never can by analysis find anything but lust in love; the Flatlander never can find anything but flat shapes in a picture; physiology never can find anything in thought except twitchings of the grey matter. It is no good browbeating the critic who approaches a Transposition from below. On the evidence available to him his conclusion is the only one possible. . . .

I have tried to stress throughout the inevitableness of the error made about every transposition by one who approaches it from the lower medium only. The strength of such a critic lies in the words "merely" or "nothing but." He sees all the facts but not the meaning. Quite truly, therefore, he claims to have seen all the facts. There *is* nothing else there; except the meaning. He is therefore, as regards the matter in hand, in the position of an animal. You will have noticed that most dogs cannot understand *pointing*. You point to a bit of food on the floor: the dog, instead of looking at the floor, sniffs at your finger. A finger is a finger to him, and that is all. His world is all fact and no meaning. And in a period when factual realism is dominant we shall find people deliberately inducing upon themselves this doglike mind.

1478
Tribulation
Letters of C. S. Lewis
(2 September 1949),
para. 2, p. 219.

God, who foresaw your tribulation, has specially armed you to go through it, not without pain but without stain.

1479
Trilemma
The Lion, the Witch and the Wardrobe, chap. 5, p. 45.

"Logic!" said the Professor half to himself. "Why don't they teach logic at these schools? There are only three possibilities. Either your sister is telling lies, or she is mad, or she is telling the truth. You know she doesn't tell lies and it is obvious that she is not mad. For the moment then and unless any further evidence turns up, we must assume that she is telling the truth."

1480
Trinity
Christian Reflections,
"The Poison of
Subjectivism" (1943),
chap. 6, para. 21,
pp. 79–80.

We must remind ourselves that Christian theology does not believe God to be a person. It believes Him to be such that in Him a trinity of persons is consistent with a unity of Deity. In that sense it believes Him to be something very different from a person, just as a cube, in which six squares are consistent with unity of the body, is different from a square. (Flatlanders, attempting to imagine a cube, would either imagine the six squares coinciding, and thus destroy their distinctness, or else imagine them set out side by side, and thus destroy the unity. Our difficulties about the Trinity are of much the same kind.)

1481
Trust
The World's Last Night,
"On Obstinacy in Belief"
(1955), para. 13, p. 26.

To love involves trusting the beloved beyond the evidence, even against much evidence. No man is our friend who believes in our good intentions only when they are proved. No man is our friend

who will not be very slow to accept evidence
against them. Such confidence, between one man
and another, is in fact almost universally praised
as a moral beauty, not blamed as a logical error.
And the suspicious man is blamed for a meanness
of character, not admired for the excellence of his
logic.

1482 **Truth** *God in the Dock,* "Myth Became Fact" (1944), para. 10, p. 66.	Truth is always *about* something, but reality is that *about which* truth is.

1483 **Truth,** **Discovery of** *Letters of C. S. Lewis* (8 May 1939), p. 166.	The process of living seems to consist in coming to realize truths so ancient and simple that, if stated, they sound like barren platitudes. They cannot sound otherwise to those who have not had the relevant experience: that is why there is no real teaching of such truths possible and every generation starts from scratch.

1484 **Tyndale,** **William** *Selected Literary Essays,* "The Literary Impact of the Authorised Version" (1950), para. 12, p. 131.	There is something new about Tyndale; for good or ill a great simplification of approach. . . . The novelty is the rejection of the allegorical senses. That rejection he shares with most of the Reformers and even, as regards parts of the Bible, with a Humanistic Papist like Colet. . . . What is interesting is not Tyndale's negation of the allegories but his positive attitude towards the literal sense. He loves it for its "grossness." "God is a Spirit," he writes, "and all his words are spiritual. His literal sense is spiritual." That is very characteristic of Tyndale's outlook. For him, just as God's literal sense is spiritual, so all life is religion: cleaning shoes, washing dishes, our humblest natural functions, are all "good works."

1485
Tyndale, William
English Literature in the Sixteenth Century, bk. II.I.I, para. 33, p. 182.

"If God spare my life, ere many years I will cause a boy that driveth the plough to know more of the scriptures than thou dost," and the fulfilment of that vaunt is the history of his life. The constancy of his purpose triumphed not only over perpetual danger, exile, poverty, and persecution, but even (which may be rarer) over all that was personal in the vaunt itself. In May 1531, speaking to one of the numerous spies whom Henry sent to entrap him, he offered that "if it would stand with the king's most gracious pleasure to grant only a bare text of the scripture to be put forth among his people," he would in return write no more and would put himself in England at the king's mercy—thus throwing life and life-work together to the wolf. Every line he wrote was directly or indirectly devoted to the same purpose: to circulate the "gospel"—not, on his view, to be identified with the Gospels—either by comment or translation.

1486
Tyndale, William
English Literature in the Sixteenth Century, bk. II.I.I, para. 44–47, pp. 187–188.

Tyndale is trying to express an obstinate fact which meets us long before we venture into the realm of theology; the fact that morality or duty (what he calls "the Law") never yet made a man happy in himself or dear to others. It is shocking, but it is undeniable. We do not wish either to be, or to live among, people who are clean or honest or kind as a matter of duty: we want to be, and to associate with, people who like being clean and honest and kind. The mere suspicion that what seemed an act of spontaneous friendliness or generosity was really done as a duty subtly poisons it. In philosophical language, the ethical category is self-destructive; morality is healthy only when it is trying to abolish itself. In theological language, no man can be saved by works. The whole purpose of the "gospel," for Tyndale, is to deliver us from morality. Thus, paradoxically, the "puritan" of modern imagination—the cold, gloomy heart, doing as duty what happier and richer souls do without thinking of it—is precisely the enemy which historical Protestantism arose and smote. What really matters is not to obey moral rules but to be a creature of a certain kind. The wrong kind of creature is damned (here, as we know; hereafter, as Tyndale believes) not for what it does but for what it is. "An adder is hated not for the euill it hath done but for the poyson that is in it." "We must first be euill ere we do euill, and good before we do good." And we cannot change our own nature by any moral efforts.

. . . Of freedom in the true sense—of spontaneity or disinterestedness—Nature knows nothing. And yet, by a terrible paradox, such disinterestedness is precisely what the moral law demands. The law requires not only that we should do thus and thus but that we should do it with "a free, a willing, a lusty, and a louing hart." Its beginning and end is that we should love God and our neighbours. It demands of us not only acts but new motives. This is what merely moral men—those who are now called "puritans" though Tyndale, I am afraid, identified them with the Papists—never understand. The first step is to see the law as it really is, and despair. Real life does not begin till "the cockatrice of thy poysoned nature hath beheld herselfe in the glasse of the righteous law of God" (*Brief Declaration*). For, when God "buildeth he casteth all downe first. He is no patcher" (*Obedience*).

After the "thunder" of the law comes the "rain" of the gospel. Though Nature knows nothing of freedom, Supernature does. There is one will in existence which is really free and that will can join us to itself so that we share its freedom: "as a woman though she be neuer so poore, yet when she is maried, is as rich as her husband."

The transition comes by the gift of faith which immediately and almost by definition passes into love. We are confronted with the redemption which God performed "to winne his enemye, to ouercomme him with loue, that he might see Loue and loue againe."

1487

Tyndale, William: Bible Translation

English Literature in the Sixteenth Century, bk. II.I.II, para. 6, p. 207.

As a scholar, Tyndale, while always retaining his independence, is deeply indebted to Erasmus's Latin version of the New Testament, to Luther, and to the Vulgate. He is also in full sympathy with Luther's conception of what Biblical translation should be—a homely, racy affair that can reach the heart and mind of a plough-boy. . . . He is a free translator and does not scruple to omit a noun where he thinks a pronoun will serve better or to interpolate a clause when he thinks the meaning would be difficult without it.

1488

Tyndale, William: Bible Translation

English Literature in the Sixteenth Century, bk. II.I.II, para. 13, p. 214.

Tyndale and Coverdale remain the base: but after Tyndale nearly all that is of real value was done by Geneva, Rheims, and Authorized. Our Bible is substantially Tyndale corrected and improved by that triad—almost in collaboration.

1489
**Tyndale,
William:
Compared
with
Thomas More**
Selected Literary Essays,
"The Literary Impact of
the Authorised Version"
(1950), para. 13, p. 132.

Tyndale's fame as an English writer has been most unjustly overshadowed both by the greater fame of More and by his own reputation as a translator. He seems to me the best prose writer of his age. He is inferior to More in what may be called the elbow-room of the mind and (of course) in humour. In every other respect he surpasses him; in economy, in lucidity, and above all in rhythmical vitality. He reaches at times a piercing quality which is quite outside More's range.

1490
**Tyndale,
William:
Compared
with
Thomas More**
*English Literature in the
Sixteenth Century,* bk.
II.I.I, para. 10,
pp. 164–165.

The opposed martyrs Thomas More and William Tyndale . . . though they were deeply divided by temper as well as by doctrine, . . . also had a great deal in common. They must not, except in theology, be contrasted as the representatives respectively of an old and a new order. Intellectually they both belonged to the new: both were Grecians (Tyndale a Hebraist as well) and both were arrogantly, perhaps ignorantly, contemptuous of the Middle Ages. . . . Both disapproved of the annulment of the king's marriage. To the men themselves what they had in common doubtless seemed a mere "highest common factor": but it was enough, had the world followed that only, to have altered the whole course of our history. Nor is it, perhaps, irrelevant to add that they were alike in their fate; even curiously alike, since both risked death by torture and both were mercifully disappointed, for More was only beheaded (not disembowelled alive) and they strangled Tyndale at the stake before they lit the fire.

1491
Tyndale, William: Compared with Thomas More
English Literature in the Sixteenth Century, bk. II.I.I, para. 50–51, pp. 190–192.

[What strikes us] is the beautiful, cheerful integration of Tyndale's world. He utterly denies the medieval distinction between *religion* and secular life. . . .

As a writer, Tyndale is almost inevitably compared with More. In one quality he is obviously inferior to his great antagonist: that is, in humour. . . . Digressions are a fault in both, not always from the same causes. Tyndale's is the digressiveness of a stretched mind, full of its theme and overflowing all bounds in its impetuous and happy prodigality: More's, sometimes, the rambling of a brooding, leisurely mind—a man talking, with the whole evening before him and the world full of interesting things. Where Tyndale is most continuously and obviously superior to More is in style. He is, beyond comparison, lighter, swifter, more economical. . . . The rhythm is excellent, the sort of rhythm which is always underlining the argument. In its sharpness of edge, its lucidity, its power of driving the reader on. . . . What we miss in Tyndale is the many-sidedness, the elbow-room of More's mind; what we miss in More is the joyous, lyric quality of Tyndale. . . . In More we feel all the "smoke and stir" of London; the very plodding of his sentences is like horse traffic in the streets. In Tyndale we breathe mountain air. Amid all More's jokes I feel a melancholy in the background; amid all Tyndale's severities there is something like laughter, that laughter which he speaks of as coming "from the low bottom of the heart." But they should not be set up as rivals, their wars are over. Any sensible man will want both.

1492
Tyranny
God in the Dock, "On
Punishment: A Reply to
Criticism" in "The
Humanitarian Theory
of Punishment" (1954),
para. 10, p. 300.

"Useful," and "necessity" was always "the tyrant's plea."

1493
Under-standing
God in the Dock, "Myth Became Fact" (1944), para. 8, pp. 65–66.

Human intellect is incurably abstract. Pure mathematics is the type of successful thought. Yet the only realities we experience are concrete—this pain, this pleasure, this dog, this man. While we are loving the man, bearing the pain, enjoying the pleasure, we are not intellectually apprehending Pleasure, Pain or Personality. When we begin to do so, on the other hand, the concrete realities sink to the level of mere instances or examples: we are no longer dealing with them, but with that which they exemplify. This is our dilemma—either to taste and not to know or to know and not to taste—or, more strictly, to lack one kind of knowledge because we are in an experience or to lack another kind because we are outside it. As thinkers we are cut off from what we think about; as tasting, touching, willing, loving, hating, we do not clearly understand. The more lucidly we think, the more we are cut off: the more deeply we enter into reality, the less we can think. You cannot *study* Pleasure in the moment of the nuptial embrace, nor repentance while repenting, nor analyse the nature of humour while roaring with laughter. But when else can you really know these things? "If only my toothache would stop, I could write another chapter about Pain." But once it stops, what do I know about pain?

1494
Unselfishness
The Screwtape Letters,
Letter XXVI, para. 2,
p. 121.

A woman means by Unselfishness chiefly taking trouble for others; a man means not giving trouble to others. . . . Thus while the woman thinks of doing good offices and the man of respecting other people's rights, each sex, without any obvious unreason, can and does regard the other as radically selfish.

1495
Utilitarianism
The Magician's Nephew,
chap. 6, p. 72.

Now that she was left alone with the children, she took no notice of either of them. And that was like her too. In Charn she had taken no notice of Polly (till the very end) because Digory was the one she wanted to make use of. Now that she had Uncle Andrew, she took no notice of Digory. I expect most witches are like that. They are not interested in things or people unless they can use them; they are terribly practical.

1496 **Value Judgments** *A Preface to "Paradise Lost,"* chap. II, para. 4, p. 11.	As regards a *skill,* . . . only the skilled can judge the skilfulness, but that is not the same as judging the value of the result. It is for cooks to say whether a given dish proves skill in the cook; but whether the product on which this skill has been lavished is worth eating or no is a question on which a cook's opinion is of no particular value. We may therefore allow poets to tell us (at least if they are experienced in the same *kind* of composition) whether it is easy or difficult to write like Milton, but not whether the reading of Milton is a valuable experience. For who can endure a doctrine which would allow only dentists to say whether our teeth were aching, only cobblers to say whether our shoes hurt us, and only governments to tell us whether we were being well governed?
1497 **Vicariousness** *God in the Dock,* "The Grand Miracle" (1945), para. 8, pp. 85–86.	In the Incarnation we get, of course, this idea of vicariousness of one person profiting by the earning of another person. In its highest form that is the very centre of Christianity. And we also find this same vicariousness to be a characteristic, or, as the musician would put it, a *leit-motif* of nature. It is a law of the natural universe that no being can exist on its own resources. Everyone,

everything, is hopelessly indebted to everyone and everything else. In the universe, as we now see it, this is the source of many of the greatest horrors: all the horrors of carnivorousness, and the worse horrors of the parasites, those horrible animals that live under the skin of other animals, and so on. And yet, suddenly seeing it in the light of the Christian story, one realizes that vicariousness is not in itself bad; that all these animals, and insects, and horrors are merely that principle of vicariousness twisted in one way. For when you think it out nearly everything good in nature also comes from vicariousness. After all, the child, both before and after birth, lives on its mother, just as the parasite lives on its host, the one being a horror, the other being the source of almost every natural goodness in the world. It all depends upon what you do with this principle.

1498

Virgil: Similes

Studies in Medieval and Renaissance Literature, "Dante's Similes" (1940), para. 3, p. 66.

[In Virgil] the real purpose of simile is to turn epic poetry from a solo to an orchestra in which any theme the poet chooses may be brought to bear on the reader at any moment and for any number of purposes.

1499

Virgin Birth

Miracles, chap. 15, para. 12, p. 138.

No woman ever conceived a child, no mare a foal, without Him. But once, and for a special purpose, He dispensed with that long line which is His instrument: once His life-giving finger touched a woman without passing through the ages of interlocked events. Once the great glove of Nature was taken off His hand. His naked hand touched her. There was of course a unique reason for it. That time He was creating not simply a man but the Man who was to be Himself: was creating Man anew: was beginning, at this divine and human point, the New Creation of all things. The whole soiled and weary universe quivered at this direct injection of essential life—direct, uncontaminated, not drained through all the crowded history of Nature.

1500
Virtue
Mere Christianity, bk. III, chap. 2, para. 10, p. 77.

Right actions done for the wrong reason do not help to build the internal quality or character called a "virtue," and it is this quality or character that really matters.

1501
Virtue
Mere Christianity, bk. III, chap. 2, para. 11, p. 77.

We might think that God wanted simply obedience to a set of rules: whereas He really wants people of a particular sort.

1502
Virtue
Mere Christianity, bk. III, chap. 5, para. 13, p. 94.

Virtue—even attempted virtue—brings light; indulgence brings fog.

1503
Virtue
English Literature in the Sixteenth Century, bk. III.I, para. 8, p. 322.

Virtue is lovely, not merely obligatory; a celestial mistress, not a categorical imperative.

1504
Vivisection
God in the Dock, "Vivisection" (1947), para. 7–8, 10, pp. 226–228.

The vast majority of vivisectors have no such [Christian] theological background. They are most of them naturalistic and Darwinian. Now here, surely, we come up against a very alarming fact. The very same people who will most contemptuously brush aside any consideration of animal suffering if it stands in the way of "research" will also, on another context, most vehemently deny that there is any radical difference between man and the other animals. On the naturalistic view the beasts are at bottom

---

just the same *sort* of thing as ourselves. Man is simply the cleverest of the anthropoids. . . . We sacrifice other species to our own not because our own has any objective metaphysical privilege over others, but simply because it is ours. It may be very natural to have this loyalty to our own species, but let us hear no more from the naturalists about the sentimentality of anti-vivisectionists. If loyalty to our own species, preference for man simply because we are men, is not a sentiment, then what is? It may be a good sentiment or a bad one. But a sentiment it certainly is. Try to base it on logic and see what happens!

But the most sinister thing about modern vivisection is this. If a mere sentiment justifies cruelty, why stop at a sentiment for the whole human race? There is also a sentiment for the white man against the black, for a *Herrenvolk* against the non-Aryans, for "civilized" or "progressive" peoples against "savage" or "backward" peoples. Finally, for our own country, party, or class against others. Once the old Christian idea of a total difference in kind between man and beast has been abandoned, then no argument for experiments on animals can be found which is not also an argument for experiments on inferior men.

. . . The victory of vivisection marks a great advance in the triumph of ruthless, non-moral utilitarianism over the old world of ethical law; a triumph in which we, as well as animals, are already the victims, and of which Dachau and Hiroshima mark the more recent achievements. In justifying cruelty to animals we put ourselves also on the animal level. We choose the jungle and must abide by our choice.

1505 **Vivisection** *God in the Dock,* "Vivisection" (1947), para. 8, p. 227.	Once the old Christian idea of a total difference in kind between man and beast has been abandoned, then no argument for experiments on animals can be found which is not also an argument for experiments on inferior men. If we cut up beasts simply because they cannot prevent us and because we are backing our own side in the struggle for existence, it is only logical to cut up imbeciles, criminals, enemies, or capitalists for the same reasons.
1506 **Vocation** *Perelandra,* chap. 2, p. 24.	One never can see, or not till long afterwards, why *any* one was selected for *any* job. And when one does, it is usually some reason that leaves no room for vanity.
1507 **Vocation** *A Severe Mercy,* Letter to Sheldon Vanauken (5 & 8 January 1951), pp. 105–106.	I think there is a great deal to be said for having one's deepest spiritual interest distinct from one's ordinary duty as a student or professional man. St Paul's *job* was tent-making. When the two coincide I shd. have thought there was a danger lest the natural interest in one's job and the pleasures of gratified ambition might be mistaken for spiritual progress and spiritual consolation; and I think clergymen sometimes fall into this trap. . . . In fact, the change [to a Christian ministry] might do good or harm. I've always been glad myself that Theology is not the thing I earn my living by. On the whole, I'd advise you to get on with your tent-making. The performance of a *duty* will probably teach you quite as much about God as academic Theology wd. do. Mind, I'm not certain: but that is the view I incline to. [Second letter] Look: the question is not whether we should bring God into our work or not. We certainly should and must: as MacDonald

says "All that is not God is death." The question is whether we should simply (a.) Bring Him in in the dedication of our work to Him, in the integrity, diligence, and humility with which we do it or also (b.) Make His professed and explicit service our job. The A vocation rests on all men whether they know it or not; the B vocation only on those who are specially called to it. Each vocation has its peculiar dangers and peculiar rewards.

1508
Vulgarity
Selected Literary Essays,
"High and Low Brows"
(1939), para. 18, p. 275.

It is low hearts and not low brows that are vulgar.

1509

War

God in the Dock, "The Conditions for a Just War" (1939), para. 1, p. 326.

If War is ever lawful, then peace is sometimes sinful.

1510

War

Letters of C. S. Lewis (8 May 1939), para. 3, p. 166.

My memories of the last war haunted my dreams for years. Military service, to be plain, includes the threat of every *temporal* evil; pain and death which is what we fear from sickness; isolation from those we love which is what we fear from exile: toil under arbitrary masters, injustice, humiliation, which is what we fear from slavery: hunger, thirst and exposure wh. is what we fear from poverty. I'm not a pacifist. If it's got to be it's got to be. But the flesh is weak and selfish and I think death would be much better than to live through another war. Thank God he has not allowed my *faith* to be greatly tempted by the present horrors. I do not doubt that whatever misery He permits will be for our ultimate good unless by rebellious will we convert it to evil. But I get no further than Gethsemane: and am daily thankful that that scene of all others in Our Lord's life did not go unrecorded. But what state

---

of affairs in this world can we view with
satisfaction? If we are unhappy, then we are
unhappy. If we are happy, then we remember that
the crown is not promised without the Cross and
tremble.

1511
War
The Weight of Glory,
"Learning in War-Time"
(1939), para. 4,
pp. 21–22.

War creates no absolutely new situation: it simply
aggravates the permanent human situation so that
we can no longer ignore it. Human life has always
been lived on the edge of a precipice. Human
culture has always had to exist under the shadow
of something infinitely more important than itself.
If men had postponed the search for knowledge
and beauty until they were secure, the search
would never have begun. We are mistaken when
we compare war with "normal life." Life has never
been normal.

1512
War
The Weight of Glory,
"Learning in War-Time"
(1939), para. 14, p. 31.

What does war do to death? It certainly does not
make it more frequent: 100 per cent of us die,
and the percentage cannot be increased. . . . Does
it increase our chances of painful death? I doubt
it. . . . Does it decrease our chances of dying at
peace with God? I cannot believe it. If active
service does not persuade a man to prepare for
death, what conceivable concatenation of
circumstances would?

1513
War
The Screwtape Letters,
Letter V, para. 2, p. 27.

[Senior devil Screwtape to junior devil
Wormwood:] How disastrous for us is the
continual remembrance of death which war
enforces. One of our best weapons, contented
worldliness, is rendered useless. In war-time not
even a human can believe that he is going to live
forever.

1514

War

Mere Christianity, bk. III, chap. 7, para. 8, 10, pp. 106–107.

Does loving your enemy mean not punishing him? No, for loving myself does not mean that I ought not to subject myself to punishment—even to death. If one had committed a murder, the right Christian thing to do would be to give yourself up to the police and be hanged. It is, therefore, in my opinion, perfectly right for a Christian judge to sentence a man to death or a Christian soldier to kill an enemy. I always have thought so, ever since I became a Christian, and long before the war, and I still think so now that we are at peace. It is no good quoting "Thou shalt not kill." There are two Greek words: the ordinary word to *kill* and the word to *murder.* And when Christ quotes that commandment He uses the *murder* one in all three accounts, Matthew, Mark, and Luke. And I am told there is the same distinction in Hebrew. All killing is not murder any more than all sexual intercourse is adultery. When soldiers came to St John the Baptist asking what to do, he never remotely suggested that they ought to leave the army: nor did Christ when He met a Roman sergeant-major—what they called a centurion.
. . . We may kill if necessary, but we must not hate and enjoy it.

1515

War

English Literature in the Sixteenth Century, bk. I.II.II, para. 10, p. 153.

We have discovered that the scheme of "outlawing war" has made war more like an outlaw without making it less frequent and that to banish the knight does not alleviate the suffering of the peasant.

1516

War

Studies in Medieval and Renaissance Literature, "Edmund Spenser, 1552–99" (1954), para. 5, p. 123.

Conquest is an evil productive of almost every other evil both to those who commit and to those who suffer it.

1517
War:
Atomic Bomb
Present Concerns: Essays by C. S. Lewis, "On Living in an Atomic Age" (1948), para. 1–2, p. 73.

In one way we think a great deal too much of the atomic bomb. "How are we to live in an atomic age?" I am tempted to reply: "Why, as you would have lived in the sixteenth century when the plague visited London almost every year, or as you would have lived in a Viking age when raiders from Scandinavia might land and cut your throat any night; or indeed, as you are already living in an age of cancer, an age of syphilis, an age of paralysis, an age of air raids, an age of railway accidents, an age of motor accidents."

In other words, do not let us begin by exaggerating the novelty of our situation. Believe me, dear sir or madam, you and all whom you love were already sentenced to death before the atomic bomb was invented: and quite a high percentage of us were going to die in unpleasant ways. We had, indeed, one very great advantage over our ancestors—anaesthetics; but we have that still. It is perfectly ridiculous to go about whimpering and drawing long faces because the scientists have added one more chance of painful and premature death to a world which already bristled with such chances and in which death itself was not a chance at all, but a certainty.

1518
War:
Atomic Bomb
Present Concerns: Essays by C. S. Lewis, "On Living in an Atomic Age," para. 3, pp. 73–74.

If we are all going to be destroyed by an atomic bomb, let that bomb when it comes find us doing sensible and human things—praying, working, teaching, reading, listening to music, bathing the children, playing tennis, chatting to our friends over a pint and a game of darts—not huddled together like frightened sheep and thinking about bombs. They may break our bodies (any microbe can do that) but they need not dominate our minds.

1519
War:
Atomic Bomb
Present Concerns: Essays by C. S. Lewis, "On Living in an Atomic Age," para. 6–7, p. 75.

What the wars and the weather (are we in for another of those periodic ice ages?) and the atomic bomb have really done is to remind us forcibly of the sort of world we are living in. . . . And this reminder is, so far as it goes, a good thing. We have been waked from a pretty dream, and now we can begin to talk about realities.

We see at once (when we have been waked) that the important question is not whether an atomic bomb is going to obliterate "civilization." The important question is whether "Nature"—the thing studied by the sciences—is the only thing in existence.

1520
War, Nuclear
God in the Dock, "Is Progress Possible?" (1958), para. 2–3, p. 312.

As a Christian I take it for granted that human history will some day end; and I am offering Omniscience no advice as to the best date for that consummation. I am more concerned by what the Bomb is doing already.

One meets young people who make the threat of it a reason for poisoning every pleasure and evading every duty in the present. Didn't they know that, Bomb or no Bomb, all men die (many in horrible ways)? There's no good moping and sulking about it.

1521
War, Nuclear
God in the Dock, "Is Progress Possible?" (1958), para. 7, p. 312.

[By] the advance, and increasing application, of science . . . we shall grow able to cure, and to produce, more diseases—bacterial war, not bombs, might ring down the curtain—to alleviate, and to inflict, more pains, to husband, or to waste, the resources of the planet more extensively. We can become either more beneficent or more mischievous. My guess is we shall do both; mending one thing and marring another, removing old miseries and producing new ones, safeguarding ourselves here and endangering ourselves there.

1522
Weather

The Letters of C. S. Lewis to Arthur Greeves (6 December 1931), para. 2, pp. 431–432.

That is a thing you and I have to be thankful for—the fact that we do not only don't dislike but positively enjoy almost every kind of weather. We had about three days of dense fog here lately. That was enough to tax even my powers of doing without the sun, but though it became oppressive in the end I felt that it was a cheap price to pay [for] its beauties. There was one evening of mist about three feet deep lying on the fields under the moon—like the mist in the first chapter of Phantastes. There was a morning (up in the top wood) of mist pouring *along the ground* through the fir trees, so thick and visible that it looked tangible as treacle. Then there were afternoons of fairly thin, but universal fog, blotting out colour but leaving shapes distinct enough to become generalised—silhouettes revealing (owing to the suppression of detail) all sorts of beauties of grouping that one does not notice on a coloured day. Finally there were days of *real* fog: days of chaos come again: specially fine at the pond, when the water was only a darker tinge in the fog and the wood on the far side only the ghostliest suggestion: and to *hear* the skurry of the waterfowl but not to see them. Not only was it an exciting time in itself but by the contrast has made to day even more beautiful than it would have been—a clear, stinging, winter sunshine.

1523
Williams, Charles

Letters of C. S. Lewis (21 December 1941), para. 2–3, pp. 196–197.

He is an ugly man with rather a cockney voice. But no one ever thinks of this for 5 minutes after he has begun speaking. His face becomes almost angelic. Both in public and in private he is of nearly all the men I have met, the one whose address most overflows with *love*. It is simply irresistible. These young men and women were lapping up what he said about Chastity before the end of the hour.

. . . He is largely a self-educated man, labouring under an almost oriental richness of imagination ("Clotted glory from Charles" as Dyson called it) which could be saved from turning silly or even vulgar in print only by a severe early discipline which he never had. But he is a lovely creature. I'm proud of being among his friends.

1524
Williams, Charles
The Letters of C. S. Lewis to Arthur Greeves (30 January 1944), para. 5, pp. 500–501.

As for the man: he is about 52, of humble origin (there are still traces of cockney in his voice), ugly as a chimpanzee but so radiant (he emanates more *love* than any man I have ever known) that as soon as he begins talking whether in private or in a lecture he is transfigured and looks like an angel. He sweeps some people quite off their feet and has many disciples. Women find him so attractive that if he were a bad man he cd. do what he liked either as a Don Juan or a charlatan. He works in the Oxford University Press. In spite of his "angelic" quality he is also quite an earthy person and when Warnie, Tolkien, he and I meet for our pint in a pub in Broad Street, the fun is often so fast and furious that the company probably thinks we're talking bawdy when in fact we're v. likely talking Theology. He is married and, I think, youthfully in love with his wife still.

1525
Williams, Charles
Poems, "To Charles Williams" (1945), p. 105.

Your death blows a strange bugle call, friend, and
   all is hard
To see plainly or record truly. . . .
Is it the first sting of the great winter, the world-
   waning? Or the cold of spring?

A hard question and worth talking a whole night
   on. But with whom?

Of whom now can I ask guidance? With what
    friend concerning your death
Is it worth while to exchange thoughts unless—oh
    unless it were you?

1526
**Williams,
Charles**
*Essays Presented to
Charles Williams,*
Preface, para. 3, p. vi.

[Williams] was a novelist, a poet, a dramatist, a
biographer, a critic, and a theologian: a "romantic
theologian" in the technical sense which he
himself invented for those words. A romantic
theologian does not mean one who is romantic
about theology but one who is theological about
romance, one who considers the theological
implications of those experiences which are called
romantic. The belief that the most serious and
ecstatic experiences either of human love or of
imaginative literature have such theological
implications, and that they can be healthy and
fruitful only if the implications are diligently
thought out and severely lived, is the root
principle of all his work.

1527
**Williams,
Charles**
*Taliessin Through Logres,
. . . Arthurian Torso,*
"Williams and the
Arthuriad" (1948),
chap. II, para. 23, p. 291.

Williams . . . starts from the very depth of the
romantic tradition and, without ceasing to be
romantic, advances to the acceptance of all that is
at first sight furthest from romanticism. In him
the poetic tradition which had begun in
Pantheism, antinomianism, and revolt, ends in
Nicene theology, moral severity, and the
celebration of restraint. His ideal poetry is that
which can "grow mature with pure fact."

1528
**Williams,
Charles**

*Taliessin Through Logres,
. . . Arthurian Torso,*
"Williams and the
Arthuriad" (1948),
chap. IV, para. 25,
p. 335.

Two spiritual maxims were constantly present to
the mind of Charles Williams: "This also is Thou"
and "Neither is this Thou." Holding the first we
see that every created thing is, in its degree, an
image of God, and the ordinate and faithful
appreciation of that thing a clue which, truly
followed, will lead back to Him. Holding the
second we see that every created thing, the highest
devotion to moral duty, the purest conjugal love,
the saint and the seraph, is no more than an
image, that every one of them, followed for its
own sake and isolated from its source, becomes
an idol whose service is damnation. The first
maxim is the formula of the Romantic Way, the
"affirmation of images": the second is that of the
Ascetic Way, the "rejection of images." Every soul
must in some sense follow both. The Ascetic must
honour marriage and poetry and wine and the
face of nature even while he rejects them; the
Romantic must remember even in his Beatrician
moment "Neither is this Thou."

1529
**Williams,
Charles:** *He
Came Down
from Heaven*

*The Letters of C. S.
Lewis to Arthur Greeves*
(30 January 1944),
para. 3, p. 500.

The starting point for interpreting Chas. Williams
is *He Came Down from Heaven* (Methuen) where
Florence will find some of his main ideas
explained directly—i.e. not in imaginative form.

1530
**Williams,
Charles:**
*The Place
of the Lion*
The Letters of C. S.
Lewis to Arthur Greeves
(26 February 1936),
para. 5–6, p. 479.

I have just read what I think a really great book, "The Place of the Lion" by Charles Williams. . . .

It is not only a most exciting fantasy, but a deeply religious and (unobtrusively) a profoundly learned book. The reading of it has been a good preparation for Lent as far as I am concerned: for it shows me (through the heroine) the special sin of abuse of intellect to which all my profession are liable, more clearly than I ever saw it before. I have learned more than I ever knew yet about humility. In fact it has been a big experience. Do get it, and don't mind if you don't understand everything the first time. It deserves reading over and over again. It isn't often now-a-days you get a *Christian* fantasy.

1531
Wisdom
The Pilgrim's Regress, bk.
7, chap. 8, p. 125.

"And what is this valley called?"

"We call it now simply Wisdom's Valley: but the oldest maps mark it as the Valley of Humiliation."

1532
**Women:
Emancipation**
Present Concerns: Essays
by C. S. Lewis, "Modern
Man and His Categories
of Thought" (1946),
para. 5, pp. 62–63.

The Emancipation of Women. (I am not of course saying that this is a bad thing in itself; I am only considering one effect it has had in fact.) One of the determining factors in social life is that in general (there are numerous individual exceptions) men like men better than women like women. Hence, the freer women become, the fewer exclusively male assemblies there are. Most men, if free, retire frequently into the society of their own sex: women, if free, do this less often. In modern social life the sexes are more continuously mixed than they were in earlier periods. This probably has many good results: but it has one bad result. Among young people, obviously, it reduces the amount of serious argument about ideas. When the young male bird is in the presence of the young female it must (Nature insists) display its plumage. Any mixed society thus becomes the scene of wit, banter, persiflage, anecdote—of everything in the world rather than prolonged and rigorous discussion on ultimate issues, or of those serious masculine friendships in which such discussion arises. Hence, in our student population, a lowering of metaphysical energy. The only serious questions now discussed are those which seem to have a "practical" importance (i.e. the psychological and sociological problems), for these satisfy the intense practicality and concreteness of the female. That is, no doubt, her glory and her proper contribution to the common wisdom of the race. But the proper glory of the masculine mind, its disinterested concern with truth for truth's own sake, with the cosmic and the metaphysical, is being impaired. Thus again, as the previous change cuts us off from the past, this cuts us off from the eternal. We are being further isolated; forced down to the immediate and the quotidian.

1533
Women in the Church

God in the Dock,
"Priestesses in the
Church?" (1948), para. 3,
8–9, 11–13, pp. 235–239.

I have every respect for those who wish women to be priestesses. I think they are sincere and pious and sensible people. Indeed, in a way they are too sensible. This is where my dissent from them resembles Bingleys' dissent from his sister. I am tempted to say that the proposed arrangement would make us much more rational "but not near so much like a Church."

. . . Common sense, disregarding the discomfort, or even the horror, which the idea of turning all our theological language into the feminine gender arouses in most Christians, will ask "Why not?" Since God is in fact not a biological being and has no sex, what can it

matter whether we say *He* or *She, Father* or
Mother, Son or *Daughter?"*

But Christians think that God Himself has
taught us how to speak of Him. To say that it
does not matter is to say either that all the
masculine imagery is not inspired, is merely
human in origin, or else that, though inspired, it is
quite arbitrary and unessential. And this is surely
intolerable: or, if tolerable, it is an argument not
in favour of Christian priestesses but against
Christianity.

. . . The Church claims to be the bearer of a
revelation. If that claim is false then we want not
to make priestesses but to abolish priests. If it is
true, then we should expect to find in the Church
an element which unbelievers will call irrational
and which believers will call supra-rational. There
ought to be something in it opaque to our reason
though not contrary to it.

. . . We men may often make very bad priests.
That is because we are insufficiently masculine. It
is no cure to call in those who are not masculine
at all. A given man may make a very bad
husband; you cannot mend matters by trying to
reverse the roles. He may make a bad male
partner in a dance. The cure for that is that men
should more diligently attend dancing classes; not
that the ballroom should henceforward ignore
distinctions of sex and treat all dancers as neuter.
That would, of course, be eminently sensible,
civilized, and enlightened, but, once more, "not
near so much like a Ball.". . .

With the Church, we are farther in: for there
we are dealing with male and female not merely
as facts of nature but as the live and awful
shadows of realities utterly beyond our control
and largely beyond our direct knowledge. Or
rather, we are not dealing with them but (as we

shall soon learn if we meddle) they are dealing
with us.

1534
**Women:
Sexuality and
Justice**
God in the Dock, "We
Have No 'Right to
Happiness' " (1963),
para. 27, pp. 321–322.

A society in which conjugal infidelity is tolerated
must always be in the long run a society adverse
to women. Women, whatever a few male songs
and satires may say to the contrary, are more
naturally monogamous than men; it is a biological
necessity. Where promiscuity prevails, they will
therefore always be more often the victims than
the culprits. Also, domestic happiness is more
necessary to them than to us. And the quality by
which they most easily hold a man, their beauty,
decreases every year after they have come to
maturity, but this does not happen to those
qualities of personality—women don't really care
twopence about our *looks*—by which we hold
women. Thus in the ruthless war of promiscuity
women are at a double disadvantage. They play
for higher stakes and are also more likely to lose.
I have no sympathy with moralists who frown at
the increasing crudity of female provocativeness.
These signs of desperate competition fill me with
pity.

1535
Words
*The Letters of C. S.
Lewis to Arthur Greeves*
(21 March 1916),
para. 3, p. 96.

Isn't it funny the way some combinations of
words can give you—almost apart from their
meaning—a thrill like music?

1536
Words
Studies in Words, chap.
1, para. 3, p. 3.

I am sometimes told that there are people who
want a study of literature wholly free from
philology; that is, from the love and knowledge of
words. Perhaps no such people exist. If they do,
they are either crying for the moon or else

---

resolving on a lifetime of persistent and carefully guarded delusion. If we read an old poem with insufficient regard for change in the overtones, and even the dictionary meanings, of words since its date—if, in fact, we are content with whatever effect the words accidentally produce in our modern minds—then of course we do not read the poem the old writer intended. What we get may still be, in our opinion, a poem; but it will be our poem, not his. If we call this *tout court* "reading" the old poet, we are deceiving ourselves. If we reject as "mere philology" every attempt to restore for us his real poem, we are safeguarding the deceit. Of course any man is entitled to say he prefers the poems he makes for himself out of his mistranslations to the poems the writers intended. I have no quarrel with him. He need have none with me. Each to his taste.

1537
Words
Studies in Words (1960), chap. 1, para. 10, p. 7–8.

Verbicide, the murder of a word, happens in many ways. Inflation is one of the commonest; those who taught us to say *awfully* for "very," *tremendous* for "great," *sadism* for "cruelty," and *unthinkable* for "undesirable" were verbicides. Another way is verbiage, by which I here mean the use of a word as a promise to pay which is never going to be kept. The use of *significant* as if it were an absolute, and with no intention of ever telling us what the thing is significant of, is an example. So is *diametrically* when it is used merely to put *opposite* into the superlative. Men often commit verbicide because they want to snatch a word as a party banner, to appropriate its "selling quality." Verbicide was committed when we exchanged *Whig* and *Tory* for *Liberal* and *Conservative*. But the greatest cause of verbicide is the fact that most people are obviously far more anxious to express their approval and disapproval of things than to describe them. Hence the tendency of words to become less descriptive and more evaluative; then to become evaluative, while still retaining some hint of the sort of goodness or badness implied; and to end up by being purely evaluative—useless synonyms for *good* and for *bad.* . . . *Rotten,* paradoxically has become so completely a synonym for "bad" that we now have to say *bad* when we mean "rotten."

1538
Words
Studies in Words,
chap. 1, para. 31, p. 17.

Most of us who are interested in such things soon learn that if you want to discover how a man pronounces a word it is no use asking him. Many people will produce in reply the pronunciation which their snobbery or anti-snobbery makes them think the most desirable. Honest and self-critical people will often be reduced to saying, "Well, now you ask me, I don't really know." Anyway, with the best will in the world, it is extraordinarily difficult to sound a word—thus produced cold and without context for inspection—exactly as one would sound it in real conversation. The proper method is quite different. You must stealthily guide the talk into subjects which will force him to use the word you are chasing. You will then hear his real pronunciation; the one he uses when he is off his guard, the one he doesn't know he uses.

1539
Work
The Weight of Glory,
"The Inner Ring" (1944),
para. 18, p. 104.

The quest of the Inner Ring will break your hearts unless you break it. But if you break it, a surprising result will follow. If in your working hours you make the work your end, you will presently find yourself all unawares inside the only

---

circle in your profession that really matters. You will be one of the sound craftsmen, and other sound craftsmen will know it.

1540
Work
Letters to an American Lady, (19 March 1956), para. 1, p. 53.

There can be intemperance in work just as in drink.

1541
Work
The Four Loves, chap. 6, para. 2, pp. 163–164.

A garden . . . teems with life. It glows with colour and smells like heaven and puts forward at every hour of a summer day beauties which man could never have created and could not even, on his own resources, have imagined . . . when the garden is in its full glory the gardener's contributions to that glory will still have been in a sense paltry compared with those of nature. Without life springing from the earth, without rain, light and heat descending from the sky, he could do nothing. When he has done all, he has merely encouraged here and discouraged there, powers and beauties that have a different source. But his share, though small, is indispensable and laborious. When God planted a garden He set a man over it and set the man under Himself. When He planted the garden of our nature and caused the flowering, fruiting loves to grow there, He set our will to "dress" them. Compared with them it is dry and cold. And unless His grace comes down, like the rain and the sunshine, we shall use this tool to little purpose. But its laborious—and largely negative—services are indispensable.

1542
**Work,
Compulsive**
The Four Loves, chap. 3,
para. 36–37, p. 75.

Mrs Fidget, as she so often said, would "work her fingers to the bone" for her family. They couldn't stop her. Nor could they—being decent people— quite sit still and watch her do it. They had to help. Indeed they were always having to help. That is, they did things for her to help her to do things for them which they didn't want done.

The Vicar says Mrs Fidget is now at rest. Let us hope she is. What's quite certain is that her family are.

1543
**World
Religions and
Christianity**
Miracles, chap. 10, para.
1, p. 68.

All the essentials of Hinduism would, I think, remain unimpaired if you subtracted the miraculous, and the same is almost true of Mohammedanism. But you cannot do that with Christianity. It is precisely the story of a great Miracle. A naturalistic Christianity leaves out all that is specifically Christian.

1544
**World
Religions and
Christianity**
God in the Dock, "Some
Thoughts" (1948),
para. 6, p. 149.

Some hazy adumbrations of a doctrine of the Fall can be found in Paganism; but it is quite astonishing how rarely outside Christianity we find—I am not sure that we ever find—a real doctrine of Creation. In Polytheism the gods are usually the product of a universe already in existence—Keats' *Hyperion,* in spirit, if not in detail, is true enough as a picture of pagan theogony. In Pantheism, the universe is never something that God made. It is an emanation, something that oozes out of Him, or an appearance, something He looks like to us but really is not, or even an attack of incurable schizophrenia from which He is unaccountably suffering. Polytheism is always, in the long run, nature-worship; Pantheism always, in the long run, hostility to nature. None of these beliefs really leaves you free *both* to enjoy your breakfast *and* to mortify your inordinate appetites—much less to mortify appetites recognised as innocent at present lest they should become inordinate.

1545
World Religions and Christianity
Mere Christianity, bk. II, chap. 1, para. 1, p. 43.

If you are Christian you do not have to believe that all the other religions are simply wrong all through. If you are an atheist you do have to believe that the main point in all the religions of the whole world is simply one huge mistake. If you are a Christian, you are free to think that all these religions, even the queerest ones, contain at least some hint of the truth.

1546
World Religions and Christianity
Surprised by Joy, chap. 15, para. 7, pp. 235–236.

There were really only two answers possible: either in Hinduism or in Christianity. Everything else was either a preparation for, or else (in the French sense) a *vulgarization* of, these. Whatever you could find elsewhere you could find better in one of these. But Hinduism seemed to have two disqualifications. For one thing, it appeared to be not so much a moralized and philosophical maturity of Paganism as a mere oil-and-water coexistence of philosophy side by side with Paganism unpurged; the Brahmin meditating in the forest, and, in the village a few miles away, temple prostitution, *sati,* cruelty, monstrosity. And secondly, there was no such historical claim as in Christianity.

1547
World Religions: Hinduism
Letters of C. S. Lewis (8 February 1956), para. 4, p. 267.

Your Hindus certainly sound delightful. But what do they *deny?* That has always been my trouble with Indians—to find any proposition they wd. pronounce false. But truth must surely involve exclusions?

1548 **World** **Religions:** **Hinduism** *Letters of C. S. Lewis* (30 April 1959), para. 1, p. 285.	Thanks for *Christ and India*. It confirms what I had, less clearly, thought already—that the difficulty in preaching Christ in India is that there is no difficulty. One is up against true Paganism— the best sort of it as well as the worst—hospitable to all gods, naturally religious, ready to take any shape but able to retain none.
1549 **World** **Religions:** **Islam** *Taliessin Through Logres,* *. . . Arthurian Torso,* "Williams and the Arthuriad" (1948), chap. III, para. 18, pp. 308–309.	Islam denies the Incarnation. It will not allow that God has descended into flesh or that Manhood has been exalted into Deity. . . . It stands for all religions that are afraid of matter and afraid of mystery. . . . Mere Monotheism blinds and stifles the mind like noonday sun in the Arabian deserts till we may well "call on the hills to hide us."
1550 **World** **Religions:** **Monotheism** *The Allegory of Love,* chap. II.III, para. 2, p. 57.	Monotheism should not be regarded as the rival of polytheism, but rather as its maturity. Where you find polytheism, combined with any speculative power and any leisure for speculation, monotheism will sooner or later arise as a natural development. The principle, I understand, is well illustrated in the history of Indian religion. Behind the gods arises the One, and the gods as well as the men are only his dreams. . . . The best minds embrace monotheism.
1551 **Worldview** *The Discarded Image,* Epilogue, para. 15, pp. 222–223.	It is not impossible that our own Model [worldview] will die a violent death, ruthlessly smashed by an unprovoked assault of new facts— unprovoked as the *nova* of 1572. But I think it is more likely to change when, and because, far-reaching changes in the mental temper of our descendants demand that it should. The new

Model will not be set up without evidence, but the evidence will turn up when the inner need for it becomes sufficiently great. It will be true evidence. But nature gives most of her evidence in answer to the questions we ask her. Here, as in the courts, the character of the evidence depends on the shape of the examination, and a good cross-examiner can do wonders. He will not indeed elicit falsehoods from an honest witness. But, in relation to the total truth in the witness's mind, the structure of the examination is like a stencil. It determines how much of that total truth will appear and what pattern it will suggest.

1552
Worship: Mary Magdalene
Letters to an American Lady (1 November 54), pp. 35–36.

The allegorical sense of her great action dawned on me the other day. The precious alabaster box which one must *break* over the Holy Feet is one's *heart*. Easier said than done. And the contents become perfume only when it is broken. While they are safe inside they are more like sewage. All very alarming.

1553
Writing
The Letters of C. S. Lewis to Arthur Greeves (30 May 1916), para. 7, p. 104.

Whenever you are fed up with life, start writing: ink is the great cure for all human ills, as I have found out long ago.

1554
Writing
The Letters of C. S. Lewis to Arthur Greeves (14 June 1916), para. 8, pp. 109–110.

What you want is practice, practice, practice. It doesn't matter what we write (at least this is my view) at our age, so long as we write continually as well as we can. I feel that every time I write a page either of prose or of verse, with real effort, even if it's thrown into the fire next minute, I am so much further on.

1555
Writing
The Letters of C. S. Lewis to Arthur Greeves (20 June 1916), para. 1, p. 110.

It is impossible to write one's best if nobody else ever has a look at the result.

1556
Writing
The Letters of C. S. Lewis to Arthur Greeves (28 August 1930), para. 4, pp. 385–386.

I am sure that some are born to write as trees are born to bear leaves: for these, writing is a necessary mode of their own development. If the impulse to write survives the hope of success, then one is among these. If not, then the impulse was at best only pardonable vanity, and it will certainly disappear when the hope is withdrawn.

1557
Writing
English Literature in the Sixteenth Century, bk. I.II.II, para. 7, p. 151.

To the present day one meets men, great readers, who write admirably until the fatal moment when they remember that they are writing.

1558
Writing
Letters to Children (26 June 1956), para. 3–7, p. 64.

1. Always try to use the language so as to make quite clear what you mean and make sure yr. sentence couldn't mean anything else.
2. Always prefer the plain direct word to the long, vague one. Don't *implement* promises, but *keep* them.
3. Never use abstract nouns when concrete ones will do. If you mean "More people died" don't say "Mortality rose."
4. In writing. Don't use adjectives which merely tell us how you want us to *feel* about the thing you are describing. I mean, instead of telling us a thing was "terrible," describe it so that we'll be terrified. Don't say it was "delightful"; make *us* say "delightful" when we've read the description. You see, all those words (horrifying, wonderful,

hideous, exquisite) are only like saying to your readers "Please will you do my job for me."
5. Don't use words too big for the subject. Don't say "infinitely" when you mean "very"; otherwise you'll have no word left when you want to talk about something *really* infinite.

1559
Writing
Letters to Children (31 August 1958), para. 1, p. 80.

[After explaining some weaknesses in a child's stories:] I hope you don't mind me telling you all this? One can learn only by seeing one's mistakes.

1560
Writing
God in the Dock, "Cross-Examination" (1963), para. 37, p. 263.

The way for a person to develop a style is (a) to know exactly what he wants to say, and (b) to be sure he is saying exactly that. The reader, we must remember, does not start by knowing what we mean. If our words are ambiguous, our meaning will escape him. I sometimes think that writing is like driving sheep down a road. If there is any gate open to the left or the right the readers will most certainly go into it.

1561
Writing, Autobiographical
English Literature in the Sixteenth Century, Introduction, para. 87, p. 58.

It is never safe to attribute a man's imaginations too directly to his experience.

1562
Writing, Christian
God in the Dock, "Christian Apologetics" (written 1945, published 1970), para. 9, p. 93.

Our Faith is not very likely to be shaken by any book on Hinduism. But if whenever we read an elementary book on Geology, Botany, Politics, or Astronomy, we found that its implications were Hindu, that would shake us. It is not the books written in direct defence of Materialism that make the modern man a materialist; it is the materialistic assumptions in all the other books. In the same way, it is not books on Christianity that will really trouble him [the anti-Christian]. But he would be troubled if, whenever he wanted a cheap popular introduction to some science, the best work on the market was always by a Christian.

1563
Writing, Christian
Christian Reflections, "Christianity and Literature," para. 14, p. 9.

The Christian writer: . . . if his talents are such that he can produce good work by writing in an established form and dealing with experiences common to all his race, he will do so. . . . It is to him an argument not of strength but of weakness that he should respond fully to the vision only "in his own way." And of every idea and of every method he will ask not "Is it mine?" but "Is it good?"

1564
Writing, Creative
English Literature in the Sixteenth Century, bk. III.I, para. 97, p. 379.

Returning to work on an interrupted story is not like returning to work on a scholarly article. Facts, however long the scholar has left them untouched in his notebook, will still prove the same conclusions; he has only to start the engine running again. But the story is an organism: it goes on surreptitiously growing or decaying while your back is turned. If it decays, the resumption of work is like trying to coax back to life an almost extinguished fire, or to recapture the confidence of a shy animal which you had only partially tamed at your last visit.

1565
Zeal

God in the Dock,
"Meditation on the Third
Commandment" (1941),
para. 5, p. 198.

The danger of mistaking our merely natural, though perhaps legitimate, enthusiasms for holy zeal, is always great.

BIBLIOGRAPHIES

ALPHABETICAL LISTING OF WORKS CITED

The Abolition of Man. New York: Macmillan, 1947.

The Allegory of Love. London: Oxford University Press, 1938.

Boxen: The Imaginary World of the Young C. S. Lewis. Edited by Walter Hooper. New York: Harcourt Brace Jovanovich, 1985. (These stories were written between 1905 and 1913.)

Christian Reflections. Edited by Walter Hooper. Grand Rapids, Mich.: Eerdmans, 1967.

The Dark Tower: And Other Stories. Edited by Walter Hooper. New York: Harcourt Brace Jovanovich, 1977.

The Discarded Image. Cambridge: Cambridge University Press, 1964.

English Literature in the Sixteenth Century, Excluding Drama. London: Oxford University Press, 1973.

An Experiment in Criticism. Cambridge: Cambridge University Press, 1961.

Fern-Seed and Elephants and Other Essays on Christianity. Edited by Walter Hooper. London: Collins-Fontana Books, 1975.

The Four Loves. New York: Harcourt Brace Jovanovich, 1960.

God in the Dock: Essays on Theology and Ethics. Edited by Walter Hooper. Grand Rapids, Mich.: Eerdmans, 1970.

The Great Divorce. New York: Macmillan, 1946.

A Grief Observed. New York: Bantam, 1976.

The Horse and His Boy. New York: Collier/Macmillan, 1970.

The Last Battle. New York: Collier/Macmillan, 1970.

Letters of C. S. Lewis. Edited by W. H. Lewis. New York: Harcourt Brace Jovanovich, 1966.

The Letters of C. S. Lewis to Arthur Greeves (1914–1963). Edited by Walter Hooper. New York: Collier/Macmillan, 1986.

Letters to an American Lady. Edited by Clyde Kilby. Grand Rapids, Mich.: Eerdmans, 1967.

Letters to Children. Edited by Lyle W. Dorsett and Marjorie Lamp Mead. New York: Macmillan, 1985.

Letters: C. S. Lewis/Don Giovanni Calabria. Translated and edited by Martin Moynihan. Ann Arbor, Mich.: Servant Books, 1988.

Letters to Malcolm: Chiefly on Prayer. New York: Harcourt Brace Jovanovich, 1964.

The Lion, the Witch and the Wardrobe. New York: Collier/Macmillan, 1970.

The Magician's Nephew. New York: Collier/Macmillan, 1970.

Mere Christianity. New York: Macmillan, 1952.

Miracles. New York: Macmillan, 1960.

Narrative Poems. Edited by Walter Hooper. New York: Harcourt Brace Jovanovich, 1979.

Of Other Worlds: Essays and Stories. Edited by Walter Hooper. New York: Harcourt Brace Jovanovich, 1966.

On Stories and Other Essays on Literature. Edited by Walter Hooper. New York: Harcourt Brace Jovanovich, 1982.

Out of the Silent Planet. New York: Macmillan, 1965.

Perelandra. New York: Macmillan, 1965.

The Personal Heresy: A Controversy. New York: Oxford, 1939.

The Pilgrim's Regress. Grand Rapids, Mich.: Eerdmans, 1958.

Poems. Edited by Walter Hooper. New York: Harcourt Brace Jovanovich, 1964.

A Preface to Paradise Lost. New York: Oxford University Press, 1961.

Present Concerns. Edited by Walter Hooper. New York: Harcourt Brace Jovanovich, 1986.

Prince Caspian. New York: Collier/Macmillan, 1970.

The Problem of Pain. New York: Macmillan, 1962.

Reflections on the Psalms. New York: Harcourt, Brace & World [now Harcourt Brace Jovanovich], 1958.

Rehabilitations and Other Essays. London: Oxford University Press, 1939.

The Screwtape Letters. New York: Macmillan, 1982.

Screwtape Proposes a Toast and Other Pieces. London: Collins, 1977.

Selected Literary Essays. Edited by Walter Hooper. Cambridge: Cambridge University Press, 1979.

The Silver Chair. New York: Collier/Macmillan, 1970.

Spenser's Images of Life. Edited by Alastair Fowler. Cambridge: Cambridge University Press, 1967.

Spirits in Bondage. London: William Heinemann, 1919.

Studies in Medieval and Renaissance Literature. Edited by Walter Hooper. Cambridge: Cambridge University Press, 1966.

Studies in Words. 2d ed. Cambridge: Cambridge University Press, 1967.

Surprised by Joy: The Shape of My Early Life. New York: Harcourt Brace Jovanovich, 1955.

Till We Have Faces. Grand Rapids, Mich.: Eerdmans, 1966.

That Hideous Strength. New York: Macmillan, 1965.

They Asked for a Paper: Papers and Addresses. London: Geoffrey Bles, 1962.

The Voyage of the Dawn Treader. New York: Collier/Macmillan, 1970.

The Weight of Glory and Other Addresses. Revised and expanded edition. New York: Macmillan, 1980.

The World's Last Night and Other Essays. New York: Harcourt Brace Jovanovich, 1960.

BOOKS EDITED OR WITH CONTRIBUTIONS BY LEWIS

Lewis, C. S., et. al. *Essays Presented to Charles Williams.* Grand Rapids, Mich.:
Eerdmans, 1966. Preface and essay by C. S. Lewis.

Macdonald, George. *George MacDonald: An Anthology.* London: Geoffrey Bles, 1946.
Edited and with introduction by C. S. Lewis.

Vanauken, Sheldon. *A Severe Mercy.* San Francisco: Harper & Row, 1977. Includes letters
by C. S. Lewis.

Williams, Charles. *Taliessin Through Logres, The Region of the Summer Stars, Arthurian
Torso.* Grand Rapids, Mich.: Eerdmans, 1974. Introduction and commentary by C. S.
Lewis.

CHRONOLOGICAL LISTING OF WORKS CITED

The date assigned to a book, collection, or excerpt in the text is the date of first
publication in final revised form. Exceptions are the stories in *Boxen* and individual
letters, papers, articles, and sermons, which are ordered by date of composition,
presentation, first publication, and preaching, respectively. Note also that excerpts are
taken from the most commonly available text—which accounts for dates differing in
the Bibliography of Works Cited.

1905–1913—*Boxen: The Imaginary World of the Young C. S. Lewis* (not published
   until 1985)
1919—*Spirits in Bondage*
1926—*Dymer* (see *Narrative Poems*)
1933—*The Pilgrim's Regress*
1936—*The Allegory of Love*
1938—*Out of the Silent Planet*
1939—*Rehabilitations and Other Essays*
1939—*The Personal Heresy*
1940—*The Problem of Pain*
1942—*The Screwtape Letters*
1942—*A Preface to "Paradise Lost"*
1943—*Perelandra*
1943—*The Abolition of Man*
1945—*That Hideous Strength*
1945—*The Great Divorce*
1946—*George MacDonald: An Anthology* (edited and with introduction by C. S. Lewis)
1947—*Miracles*
1947—*Essays Presented to Charles Williams* (preface and essay by Lewis)
1948—*Arthurian Torso* (in *Taliessin Through Logres*, 1974)
1949—*The Weight of Glory and Other Addresses* (first published as *Transpositions and
   Other Addresses*)
1950—*The Lion, the Witch and the Wardrobe*

1951—*Prince Caspian*
1952—*Mere Christianity* (first published separately as *Broadcast Talks*, 1942; *Christian Behavior*, 1943; *Beyond Personality*, 1944—revised when collected)
1952—*The Voyage of the Dawn Treader*
1953—*The Silver Chair*
1954—*The Horse and His Boy*
1954—*English Literature in the Sixteenth Century, Excluding Drama*
1954—Joy Davidman, *Smoke on the Mountain* (foreword by C. S. Lewis)
1955—*The Magician's Nephew*
1955—*Surprised by Joy*
1956—*The Last Battle*
1956—*Till We Have Faces*
1958—*Reflections on the Psalms*
1960—*The Four Loves*
1960—*Studies in Words*
1960—*The World's Last Night and Other Essays*
1961—*A Grief Observed*
1961—*An Experiment in Criticism*
1962—*They Asked for a Paper: Papers and Addresses* (All of the essays in this volume are documented in other more accessible collections.)
1964—*Letters to Malcolm: Chiefly on Prayer* (a portion published in 1963 as *Beyond the Bright Blur*)
1964—*The Discarded Image: An Introduction to Medieval and Renaissance Literature*
1964—*Poems*, Walter Hooper, ed.
1965—*Screwtape Proposes a Toast and Other Pieces*
1966—*Studies in Medieval and Renaissance Literature*, Walter Hooper, ed.
1966—*Letters of C. S. Lewis*, W. H. Lewis, ed.
1966—*Of Other Worlds: Essays and Stories*, Walter Hooper, ed.
1967—*Christian Reflections*, Walter Hooper, ed.
1967—*Spenser's Images of Life*, Alastair Fowler, ed.
1967—*Letters to an American Lady*, Clyde Kilby, ed.
1969—*Narrative Poems*, Walter Hooper, ed.
1969—*Selected Literary Essays*, Walter Hooper, ed.
1970—*God in the Dock*, Walter Hooper, ed.
1975—*Fern-Seed and Elephants and Other Essays on Christianity*, Walter Hooper, ed.
1977—*The Dark Tower and Other Stories*, Walter Hooper, ed.
1977—Sheldon Vanauken, *A Severe Mercy* (includes letters by C. S. Lewis)
1979—*The Letters of C. S. Lewis to Arthur Greeves (1914–1963)*, Walter Hooper, ed. (first published as *They Stand Together: The Letters of C. S. Lewis to Arthur Greeves (1914–1963)*)
1985—*Letters to Children*, Lyle W. Dorsett and Marjorie Lamp Mead, eds.
1986—*Present Concerns*
1988—*Letters: C. S. Lewis/Don Giovanni Calabria*, Martin Moynihan, ed. and trans. (Portions were published in article form in 1985 and in book form in 1987 as *The Latin Letters of C. S. Lewis*.)

INDEX